Misogyny as Hate Crime

Misogyny as Hate Crime explores the background, nature and consequences of misogyny as well as the legal framework and UK policy responses associated with misogyny as a form of hate crime. Taking an intersectional approach, the book looks at how experiences of misogyny may intersect with other forms of hate crime such as disablism, Islamophobia, antisemitism and transphobia.

From the sexist and derogatory comments about women by former US President Donald Trump, to legislative changes in Chile and Peru making street harassment illegal, misogyny presents a challenge to scholars, practitioners, policy makers, and women globally. The increasing importance of the internet has seen misogyny move into these digital spaces but has also provided a platform for movements such as #MeToo and #TimesUp, highlighting the scale of sexual harassment and abuse. In 2016, Nottinghamshire Police in partnership with Nottingham Women's Centre became the first force in England and Wales to record misogyny as a hate crime. Since then other police forces have introduced similar schemes to tackle misogyny. More recently, the Law Commission of England and Wales has undertaken a review of the legislation on hate crime and in their consultation paper of proposals for reform has suggested 'adding sex or gender to the protected characteristics'. In March 2021, the Government announced that police forces in England and Wales will be required to record crimes motivated by hostility based on sex or gender from this autumn. The murder of Sarah Everard has been a 'watershed moment' in the Government's response to violence against women. Sarah Everard's kidnap and murder who went missing while walking home from a friend's flat in South London on 3 March 2021, ignited a national conversation about violence against women.

Against this background, the book speaks both to the proposed reforms of the hate crime legislation around misogyny, and the broader issues around experiences of and legal responses to misogyny. It showcases the work of leading scholars in this area alongside that of activists and practitioners, whose work has been invaluable in opening up public discussion on misogynistic hate crime and encouraging wider social change. In recognising the intersections of different forms of prejudice, the book provides an innovative contribution to these 'hate debates', highlighting the complexities of creating separate strands of hate crime.

Providing a comprehensive understanding of the debates around inclusion of misogyny as a form of hate crime, this ground-breaking book will be of great interest to students, scholars and activists interested in gender, hate crime, feminism, criminology, law, policing and sociology.

Irene Zempi is a Senior Lecturer in Criminology, Department of Criminology & Criminal Justice, Nottingham Trent University.

Jo Smith is a Senior Lecturer in Law, Brighton Business School, University of Brighton.

Victims, Culture and Society
Edited by: Sandra Walklate, University of Liverpool, UK and Monash University, Australia
Kerry Carrington, Queensland University of Technology, Australia

Concerns about victimisation have multiplied over the last fifty years. *Victims, Culture and Society* explores the major concepts, debates and controversies that these concerns have generated across a range of disciplines, but particularly within criminology and victimology. As the impacts of globalisation, the movement of peoples and the divergences between the global North and global South have become ever more apparent, this series provides an authoritative space for original contributions in making sense of these far-reaching changes on individuals, localities and nationalities. These issues by their very nature demand an interdisciplinary approach and an interdisciplinary voice outside conventional conceptual boundaries. *Victims, Culture and Society* offers the space for that voice.

Each author adopts a strong personal view and offers a lively and agenda-setting treatment of their subject matter. The monographs encompass a transnational, global or comparative approach to the issues they address. Examining new areas of both empirical and theoretical enquiry, the series offers the opportunity for innovative and progressing thinking about the relationship between victims, culture and society. The books will be useful and thought-provoking resources for the international community of undergraduates, postgraduates, researchers and policymakers working within the broad field of victimisation.

Genocide and Victimology
Edited by Yarin Eski

Family Activism in the Aftermath of Fatal Violence
Elizabeth A. Cook

Misogyny as Hate Crime
Edited by Irene Zempi and Jo Smith

For more information about this series, please visit: www.routledge.com/Victims-Culture-and-Society/book-series/VICS

Misogyny as Hate Crime

Edited by
Irene Zempi and Jo Smith

LONDON AND NEW YORK

First published 2022
by Routledge
2 Park Square, Milton Park, Abingdon, Oxon OX14 4RN

and by Routledge
605 Third Avenue, New York, NY 10158

Routledge is an imprint of the Taylor & Francis Group, an informa business

© 2022 selection and editorial matter, Irene Zempi and Jo Smith; individual chapters, the contributors

The right of Irene Zempi and Jo Smith to be identified as the authors of the editorial material, and of the authors for their individual chapters, has been asserted in accordance with sections 77 and 78 of the Copyright, Designs and Patents Act 1988.

All rights reserved. No part of this book may be reprinted or reproduced or utilised in any form or by any electronic, mechanical, or other means, now known or hereafter invented, including photocopying and recording, or in any information storage or retrieval system, without permission in writing from the publishers.

Trademark notice: Product or corporate names may be trademarks or registered trademarks, and are used only for identification and explanation without intent to infringe.

British Library Cataloguing-in-Publication Data
A catalogue record for this book is available from the British Library

Library of Congress Cataloging-in-Publication Data
A catalog record has been requested for this book

ISBN: 978-0-367-90317-6 (hbk)
ISBN: 978-0-367-52129-5 (pbk)
ISBN: 978-1-003-02372-2 (ebk)

DOI: 10.4324/9781003023722

Typeset in Times New Roman
by codeMantra

Contents

List of contributors ix
Acknowledgements xi

Introduction 1
IRENE ZEMPI AND JO SMITH

PART 1
Theorising misogyny, gender and 'hate crime' 17

1 A feminist theoretical exploration of misogyny and hate crime 19
   MARIAN DUGGAN AND HANNAH MASON-BISH

2 Extending the concept, or extending the characteristics?
   Misogyny or gender? 40
   KIM McGUIRE

PART 2
Online and offline spaces 63

3 Gender as a protected characteristic: a legal perspective 65
   CHARA BAKALIS

4 Online misogyny as a hate crime: #TimesUp 79
   KIM BARKER AND OLGA JURASZ

5 From sexism to misogyny: can online echo chambers
   stay quarantined? 99
   ALEXANDRA KRENDEL

PART 3
Identities and lived experiences 119

6 Adolescent girls' experiences of street harassment: emotions, comments, impact, actions and the law 121
RACHEL HARDING, LUCY BETTS, DAVID WRIGHT, SHEINE PEART AND CATARINA SJOLIN

7 Misogyny, hate crimes and gendered Islamophobia: muslim women's experiences and responses 140
AMINA EASAT-DAAS

8 The intersection of antisemitism and misogyny 155
LESLEY KLAFF

9 An exposition of sexual violence as a method of disablist hate crime 178
JANE HEALY

10 Trans identities, cisgenderism and hate crime 195
MICHAELA ROGERS

11 "Not the right kind of woman": transgender women's experiences of transphobic hate crime and trans-misogyny 213
BEN COLLIVER

PART 4
Practice and activism 229

12 A call to feminist praxis: the story of Nottinghamshire's misogyny hate crime policy 231
ZAIMAL AZAD AND SOPHIE MASKELL

13 Policing misogyny as a hate crime – the Nottinghamshire Police experience 249
SUE FISH

14 Informing legal change: the language of misogyny hate crime, gender and enhancing protection through criminal law 269
LOUISE MULLANY, LORETTA TRICKETT AND VICTORIA HOWARD

15 **Our Streets Now: demanding an end to public
   sexual harassment**   288
   MAYA TUTTON

   Conclusion   308
   IRENE ZEMPI AND JO SMITH

   Index   311

Contributors

Zaimal Azad is a Hate Crime Officer Projects at Nottingham City Council.

Chara Bakalis is a Principal Lecturer in Law at Oxford Brookes University.

Dr Kim Barker is a Senior Lecturer in Law at Open University.

Dr Lucy Betts is a Professor in Social Developmental Psychology at Nottingham Trent University.

Dr Ben Colliver is a Lecturer in Criminology at Birmingham City University.

Dr Marian Duggan is a Senior Lecturer in Criminology at University of Kent.

Dr Amina Easat-Daas is a Lecturer in Politics at De Montfort University.

Sue Fish is a former Chief Constable of Nottinghamshire Police.

Rachel Harding is a Research Fellow at Nottingham Trent University.

Dr Jane Healy is Deputy Head of the Department of Social Science and Social Work at Bournemouth University.

Dr Victoria Howard is a Research Fellow at the Centre for Children, Young People and Families at University of Nottingham.

Dr Olga Jurasz is a Senior Lecturer in Law at Open University.

Lesley Klaff is a Senior Lecturer in Law at Sheffield Hallam University.

Alexandra Krendel is an Associate Lecturer in Linguistics and English Language at University of Lancaster.

Dr Hannah Mason-Bish is a Senior Lecturer in Sociology and Criminology at Sussex University.

Sophie Maskell was the Safer for Women Project Coordinator at Nottingham Women's Centre and is now a Policy Advisor to the Domestic Abuse Commissioner for England and Wales.

Dr Kim McGuire is a Senior Lecturer in Law at University of Central Lancashire.

Professor Louise Mullany is a Professor in Sociolinguistics at University of Nottingham.

Dr Sheine Peart is a Lecturer on the Professional Studies Team at Bishop Grosseteste University.

Dr Michaela Rogers is a Senior Lecturer in Social Work at University of Sheffield.

Catarina Sjolin is a Judge at Lincoln Crown Court.

Dr Loretta Trickett is an Associate Professor in Law at Nottingham Trent University.

Maya Tutton is the co-founder (with Gemma Tutton) of 'Our Streets Now'.

Dr David Wright is a Senior Lecturer in Linguistics at Nottingham Trent University.

Acknowledgements

We would like to thank all of the authors who contributed to this edited collection. We appreciate all the hard work that you have put into your chapters, particularly given the challenges that 2020 has presented, both personally and professionally. Your expertise, experience and enthusiasm have brought so much to this collection, and it has been a privilege to work with you all.

In addition, we would like to thank all of those who attended and participated in the British Society of Criminology Hate Crime Network Conference 'Misogyny as Hate Crime' at Nottingham Trent University in May 2019 that inspired this edited collection.

Also, we are grateful for the support that has been provided by the staff at Routledge in the production of this text.

Last but not least, we would like to say thank you to all of those people in our lives who encourage us to think about and challenge the misogyny that we see affecting the lives of women and girls around the world. For our families, friends, colleagues and students who support us in all that we do.

Introduction

Irene Zempi and Jo Smith

The purpose of this edited collection is to showcase the work of leading scholars, policy makers and practitioners researching/working in and around misogyny in the UK. It covers the background, nature and consequences of misogyny as well as the legal framework and national policy responses.

In May 2016, Nottinghamshire Police in partnership with Nottingham Women's Centre became the first force in England and Wales to record misogyny as a hate crime (BBC 2016). The overall recommendations from that project called for the policy to be rolled out nationally, along with publicity to increase reporting and education to help change behaviours (Mullany and Trickett 2018). Since then other police forces have introduced similar schemes to tackle misogyny (Andersson 2020; Sparrow 2020; North Yorkshire Police 2021). Citizens UK, along with the Fawcett Society and senior Jewish and Muslim faith leaders, have co-signed a letter urging the National Police Chiefs' Council to act on a national roll-out (Fawcett 2018). More recently, the Law Commission has undertaken a review of the legislation on hate crime and in their consultation paper of proposals for reform has suggested 'adding sex or gender to the protected characteristics' (Law Commission 2020). In March 2021, the Government announced that police forces in England and Wales will be required to record crimes motivated by hostility based on sex or gender from this autumn. The murder of Sarah Everard has been a 'watershed moment' in the Government's response to violence against women. Sarah Everard's kidnap and murder who went missing while walking home from a friend's flat in South London on 3 March 2021, ignited a national conversation about violence against women.

This is a contemporary and important area of public and academic discussion in the UK and globally. From the sexist and derogatory comments about women by former US President Donald Trump (Filipovic 2017), to legislative changes in Chile and Peru making street harassment illegal (DLA Piper 2014; Quiroz 2017), from the targeting of #MeToo protesters in Japan (Inagaki and Lewis 2018; Mora and Oda 2018; McCurry 2020), to the sexist abuse reported by women during the 2018 football world cup in Russia (Masters 2018), misogyny in its many shapes and forms presents a challenge to scholars, practitioners, policy makers and women around the world. The increasing importance of the internet in our lives has seen misogyny

DOI: 10.4324/9781003023722

move into these digital spaces, but has also provided a platform for global activist movements such as #MeToo and #TimesUp, which have driven an awareness campaign highlighting the scale of sexual harassment and abuse experienced by women (Khomami 2017).

This book was conceived following a conference in May 2019 at Nottingham Trent University (BSC 2021) organised by Dr Irene Zempi on behalf of the British Society of Criminology Hate Crime Network. Inspired by the ongoing Law Commission review of the legislation criminalising hate crime in England and Wales (Law Commission 2020), the conference focused on misogyny, gender and hate crime. The event was held in Nottingham – the city in which misogyny had first been formally recognised as hate crime – which was an acknowledgement of the important work undertaken by Nottingham Women's Centre, Citizens UK and the Nottinghamshire Police in creating this recognition (BBC 2016; Citizens UK 2020).

Participation in the conference, along with the wider public discussion on the appropriateness of including misogyny or gender as hate crime, made it clear that there was a wide range of academic, activist and policy work being undertaken under the umbrella of 'misogyny as hate crime'. Assembling some of this work into an edited collection was an obvious complement to the conference, allowing the work being undertaken in this area to have the wider reach that a book provides. This text therefore brings together, in one volume, a range of academic, activist and practitioner works that provide an understanding of the debates around the inclusion of misogyny as a form of hate crime. The book draws from an intersectional approach, looking at how experiences of misogyny may intersect with (for example) experiences of disablism, Islamophobia, antisemitism and prejudice against gender identity. In recognising the intersections of different forms of prejudice, this book provides an innovative contribution to these 'hate debates', highlighting the complexities of creating separate strands of hate crime. It also requires us to think about how women experience misogyny in different ways.

With the importance of intersectionality in mind, we sought contributions from a wide range of authors, both those who had presented their work at the conference, and others working in the field. Whilst many of those who we approached were able to provide these, unfortunately a few were not. As a result, there are voices absent from this edited collection, and there are some groups whose experiences are not represented in full. We encourage the readers to continue to explore the debates around misogyny/gender and hate crime by reading further about experiences of misogyny, including from those groups that we were unable to include. One valuable resource is the International Network of Hate Studies (INHS 2021a), whose website provides a regularly updated bibliography of publications across all areas of hate crime, including gender-based hate (INHS 2021b).

The introduction now seeks to provide a brief understanding of some of the key concepts and legislation in England and Wales. These ideas will be explored in more depth throughout subsequent chapters. The following sections will look at, in turn: what the term 'hate crime' means; the most recent official statistics for hate crime in England and Wales; and the legislation which criminalises (some) acts of hate. A summary of the aforementioned Law Commission consultation paper (Law Commission 2020) will follow.

What is hate crime

The term hate crime, whilst commonly used, is not necessarily clearly applied, with different and sometimes conflicting definitions and understandings being offered by academia, policy and practice (Chakraborti and Garland 2015). Broadly speaking, the term 'hate crime' refers to the targeting and victimisation of an individual because of their identity.

For some, such as Perry (2001, p. 10), this targeting represents:

> a mechanism of power and oppression, intended to reaffirm the precarious hierarchies that characterise a given social order. It attempts to re-create simultaneously the threatened (real or imagined) hegemony of the perpetrator's group and the 'appropriate' subordinary identity of the victim's group. It is a means of marking both the Self and the Other in such a way as to re-establish their 'proper' relative positions, as given and reproduced by broader ideologies and patterns of social and political inequality.

Thus, for Perry (2001), hate crime is about the power that exists between those at the top of societal hierarchies, and the Others below them: it about the power to construct the inferiority of the Other, and the power to construct the 'appropriate way to be Other: of how Others should perform their difference' (Smith 2019, p. 22). This approach identifies hate crime as an experience which goes on beyond the individual event, and situates this within social contents and structures of power (Chakraborti and Garland 2015).

Another notable approach to understanding hate crime is provided by Chakraborti and Garland, for whom hate crime involves 'acts of violence, hostility and intimidation directed towards people because of their identity or perceived "difference"' (Chakraborti and Garland 2015; see also Chakraborti et al. 2014). Not only does this simplify the definition of hate crime, but it recognises the role of the vulnerability of the target, and their difference.

Beyond academic understandings of what hate crime is and what it might mean, official definitions have developed. Although 'hate crime' is sometimes used as shorthand to refer to any acts motivated by prejudice, hostility or hate, the official definitions take a stricter approach in requiring the behaviour to amount to a criminal offence. The Crown Prosecution Service ("CPS") and police use a definition (CPS 2018) which interprets hate crime as:

> Any criminal offence which is perceived by the victim or any other person, to be motivated by hostility or prejudice, based on a person's disability or perceived disability; race or perceived race; or religion or perceived religion; or sexual orientation or perceived sexual orientation or transgender identity or perceived transgender identity.

A further term used by the police is 'hate incident'. This describes behaviours which meet the official definition of hate crime save for not amounting to criminal acts (College of Policing 2014, p. 3): 'it must be clearly understood that evidence of an offence is not a requirement for a hate incident to be recorded'. As this quote makes clear, even though a criminal offence may not have occurred, the police are required to record hate incidents as such. This acknowledges that such acts may precede criminal acts of hate, and can still be distressing and harmful.

When it comes to the official definition of hate crime (CPS 2018) there are five 'monitored strands', also referred to as 'protected characteristics': race or ethnicity, religion or belief, sexual orientation, disability and transgender identity. For an offence to be treated as a 'hate crime'[1] it must be targeted towards one (or more) of these identities. Nationally, the five strands of monitored hate crime are the minimum categories that police forces are expected to record. Locally, police forces can extend their own policy response to include other categories that they believe should also be protected groups of hate crime. This is the basis upon which Nottinghamshire Police Force began recording misogyny as hate crime (BBC 2016).[2]

Current legislation

Whilst there is no one single piece of legislation which criminalises or punishes hate, there are four main legal provisions that comprise hate crime and hate speech laws in England and Wales. These include:

- Aggravated offences (Crime and Disorder Act 1998, ss. 28–32)

These are separate, aggravated versions of 11 existing criminal offences (including assault, public order offences, harassment and criminal damage) which carry higher maximum penalties than the "base" offence to which they relate. Aggravated offences only apply in respect of racial and religious hostility (and not the other three monitored strands).

- Enhanced sentencing (Criminal Justice Act 2003, ss. 145 and 146)

Enhanced sentencing is available for all five of the monitored strands of hate, is applicable to any criminal offence[3] and requires the sentence to be increased, but within the existing maximum sentence available.

The legal test for both aggravated offences and enhanced sentencing is proof that either the offence was "motivated by hostility" towards the protected characteristic; or the defendant "demonstrated hostility" towards the protected characteristic at the time of committing the offence.

There are also a number of "hate speech" offences. These include:

- Offences of "stirring up" hatred (Public Order Act 1986, ss. 18–21 and 29B–29F)

Introduction 5

The law here prohibits individuals from using threats, abuse or insults, where doing so is intended to or is likely to stir up hatred in respect of race, religion and sexual orientation (there is no equivalent offence for disability or transgender status). These offences do not criminalise conduct expressing or inciting hostility or hatred towards specific individuals; rather, they address acts (such as use of words, material or behaviour) intended or likely to cause others to hate entire groups.

- Offence of "racialist chanting" at a football match (Football (Offences) Act 1991, s 3(1))

It is also an offence to "engage or take part in chanting of an indecent or racialist nature at a designated football match".

What is apparent from the legislation is that there are inconsistencies in terms of how the law applies to the different monitored strands. Whilst all of the strands can benefit from the sentencing uplifts provided for in the Criminal Justice Act 2003, the aggravated offences only relate to religiously and racially motivated hate. There is no legislation prohibiting 'stirring up' hatred in respect of disability or transgender identity. This creates a hierarchy within the legislation in terms of the different strands, as well as reaffirming the 'silo approach to identity' (Mason-Bish 2015, p. 24). The legal framework for hate crime, as it current stands, favours seeing victims of hate crime as falling into discrete groups, and fails to acknowledge how this might limit recognition of how the intersections of hate might affect one's experiences of victimisation.

Hate crime statistics

The Home Office has been gathering data on the prevalence of recorded hate crime in England and Wales since 2011 (and for racist incidents since 2009) (Home Office 2020a).[4] Noting only hate crimes in relation to the five recognised 'protected characteristics',[5] the most recent figures show that there were 105,090 hate crimes recorded by the police in England and Wales in year ending March 2020 (Home Office 2020b). This represents an increase of 8% compared with year ending March 2019 (97,446 offences). As in previous years, the majority of hate crimes were race hate crimes, accounting for around three-quarters of offences (72%; 76,070 offences). Race hate crimes increased by 6% between year ending March 2019 and year ending March 2020. Religious hate crimes fell by 5% (to 6,822 offences), sexual orientation hate crimes increased by 19% (to 15,835), disability hate crimes increased by 9% (to 8,469) and transgender identity hate crimes increased by 16% (to 2,540) (Home Office 2020b).

With misogyny/gender not being formally recognised as a protected characteristic on a national basis, the data on misogynistic or gendered hate crime remains more limited. Data from the Office of National Statistics as part of the CSEW for 2016–2018 (ONS 2018) estimate that there were 67,000 gender hate crimes targeting individuals, 57,000 of these directed towards women. This made gender hate crime the second most self-reported form of hate in relation to the identity characteristics (after age). Nearly a quarter of all gender-based hate incidents reported in this survey by women and girls occurred to those aged 16–24, and a quarter to those aged 25–44 (ONS 2018). A study by Citizens UK (Samanani and Pope 2020) found that 22.4% of hate crime and incidents reported to them were motivated by gender and 33.5% involved gender as an additional factor to another identity characteristic; 84.4% of those who experienced gender hate crime were women. Just over 30% of all the women sampled had experienced hate crime based on gender (Samanani and Pope 2020, p. 21). Whilst overall (across all categories of hate crime) men were more likely to report the targeting involved the use of threats or physical violence – 29.4% of women reported experiencing physical violence as compared to 61.4% of men – women were more likely to report being threatened with sexual violence compared to men (45.2% compared to 16.2%) or being subject to sexual violence (42.7% compared to 12.5%) (Samanani and Pope 2020, p. 20). Further evidence of violence against women is provided through the chapters in this edited collection.

Law Commission consultation on hate crime

The Law Commission of England and Wales is an independent body established by statute to make recommendations to the government on reform of the law in England and Wales. In September 2020, the Law Commission published their consultation regarding the reform of hate crime and hate speech laws (Law Commission 2020). Their remit includes considering the legislative provisions set out earlier in this introduction, around aggravated offences, the enhanced sentencing regime, 'stirring up' offences and the offence of racialist chanting (Law Commission 2020).

The consultation focuses on two main questions:

1 Who should these laws protect?
2 How should these laws work?

The consultation applies to the law of England and Wales. The Law Commission invited responses to the consultation paper from 23 September 2020 to 24 December 2020. After analysing all the responses to the consultation, the Law Commission will make final recommendations for reform to the Government, with the Government to decide whether to implement the recommendations.

Key provisional proposals for reform

In summary, the key provisional proposals the Law Commission (2020) make are to:

- Equalise protection across all existing hate crime strands

  The Law Commission propose that this be done by extending the protections of aggravated offences and stirring up hatred offences so that all of the five currently protected characteristics, and any additional characteristics that are added (for example, sex/gender), are treated equally in law.
- Add a new characteristic of "sex or gender" (but consider implications further for sexual offences and domestic abuse)

  In particular, the Law Commission propose adding the characteristic of "women" to hate crime laws (if sex or gender-based hate crime protection were to be limited to the female sex or gender) but note that further thought is needed in relation to the implications of this in the context of sexual offences and domestic abuse (discussed below in more detail).
- Create aggravated versions of "communications offences" – to recognise the harm caused by online hate

  The Law Commission propose adding certain other specified aggravated offences – notably the "communications offences" in section 127 of the Communications Act 2003 and section 1 of the Malicious Communications Act 1988.
- Reform the "stirring up hatred" offences so that they are easier to prosecute in cases of intentionally stirring up hatred, and more stringent where such intention cannot be proven
- Extend racist "football chanting" offences to cover homophobia and potentially other characteristics

In addition, the Law Commission also discuss other possible reforms on which they seek views. Key here is the proposal to consolidate the specific hate crime offences and related reforms into a single "Hate Crime Act". This would simplify the currently complex legislative framework. A further proposal looks at revising the test for the application of hate crime laws so that it is better adapted to recognise certain forms of crime that are targeted towards disabled people. The Law Commission also suggest the establishment of a Hate Crime Commissioner to drive forward best practice in preventing hate crime and supporting its victims.

Characteristics

In the case of the current five protected characteristics, the Law Commission (2020) state that there is a strong case for their continued inclusion in hate crime laws. The Law Commission (2020) also consider some further refinements of the definitions currently used: including "asexuality" within the definition of sexual orientation; revising the transgender definition to make explicit reference to people who are transgender, non-binary, cross-dressing or intersex; considering whether the disability definition should include a mistaken presumption that a person is not disabled (so allowing the law to respond to abuse and violence experienced by disabled people who are challenged when using disability accessible services). Moreover, the consultation asked for stakeholder views in respect of the characteristics of "age", "sex workers", "homelessness", "alternative subcultures" and "philosophical beliefs".

Women, sex or gender

The Law Commission consider the case for adding a characteristic of "women", "sex" or "gender" to the list of protected characteristics, applying three criteria for deciding whether any additional characteristics should be recognised in hate crime laws – need, additional harm, suitability. The main point of contention is whether protection should be limited to "women" or apply to "sex" or "gender" more widely. Three questions become relevant:

1   Should protection be limited to women only or should it be gender-neutral?
2   If protection is limited to women, how should it be framed?
3   If protection is gender-neutral, how should it be framed?

In relation to these questions, it is concluded that there is a strong in-principle case that can be made for inclusion of 'women', based on the evidence of the prevalence and harm caused by crimes that are motivated by or demonstrate hostility towards women. However, it is argued that the use of the term misogyny in hate crime laws would create a key problem. Hate crime laws in England and Wales protect identity characteristics (race, religion or sexual orientation) or groups (transgender or disabled people). Misogyny is neither an identity characteristic nor a group; it is an example of prejudice, like homophobia. Recognising specific prejudice rather than groups or characteristics would constitute a significant shift in legal approach and create (further) inconsistency within hate crime laws. If the protection were limited to women only, framing the law around the term "women" rather than "misogyny" avoids these problems, because it relates to a group, not a form of prejudice. If a gender-neutral approach to terminology is preferred, the Law Commission's 'provisional view is that the more inclusive term of gender, as opposed to sex, would better capture a wider range of victim experience' (Law Commission 2020, p. 277).

However, the Law Commission also note that there are practical concerns that need to be considered in respect of the suitability criterion; most notably the risk that hate crime laws could prove unhelpful in the context of crimes that already recognised as highly gendered: namely, sexual offences, domestic abuse and other VAWG crimes such as FGM and forced marriage. Their concern is that the legal requirement to prove *additional* sex or gender-based hostility in these contexts may prove more harmful than helpful. The Law Commission propose that this concern might be mitigated in the form of a carve out for specific offences, e.g. sexual offences, forced marriage, FGM and crimes committed in the domestic abuse context. It is argued that even if these highly gendered crimes were to be excluded from gender-based aggravation, a gender-based hate crime category might still carry wider benefits particularly in relation to the gendered harassment that women face on the street, as well as the considerable amount of online abuse that is disproportionately targeted against women (Law Commission 2020).

This book speaks both to the proposed reforms of the hate crime legislation around misogyny, and the broader issues around experiences of and legal responses to misogyny. It showcases the work of leading scholars in this area alongside that of activists and practitioners, whose work has been invaluable in opening up public discussion on misogynistic hate crime and encouraging wider social change.

Summary of chapters

In Chapter 1, Marian Duggan and Hannah Mason-Bish offer a critical feminist perspective on the issue of gender hostility and its potential inclusion in hate crime protections. To provide context to this discussion, the authors revisit core feminist theorising on men's violence towards women thus demonstrating how feminist theorising informed subsequent hate crime theorising and policy implementation. The authors' examination of women's experiences of hate crime highlights the importance of recognising misogyny within already recognised hate crime strands (intersectional focus) and also the need to have a separate gender category. It is concluded that a gender-specific focus on misogyny is important in order to understand and address the true nature and impact of hate crimes towards women.

In Chapter 2, Kim McGuire engages with the arguments for and against including misogyny as one of the hate crime protected characteristics, and the difficulty of proving gender bias. The author argues that in order to ensure that offences against women could be recognised as including bias, 'gender' as a protected characteristic would suffice, and would also cover prejudice towards men, non-binary individuals, and those who are gender free. Drawing upon international comparisons, the author proposes that new and specific legislation may be needed to address certain offences, particularly those predominantly experienced by women and girls. The chapter also discusses the potential limitations of legislation, and the need for accompanying awareness raising initiatives.

In Chapter 3, Chara Bakalis notes that there are three different forms of hate crime laws in England and Wales, Scotland and Northern Ireland. All three of these systems have been subject to major law reform proposals in recent years. In England and Wales, this was carried out by the Law Commission (2020); in Scotland, by Lord Bracadale (Scottish Government 2018) and in Northern Ireland, by Judge Marrinan (Department of Justice 2020).

The author discusses the reasoning used in these reviews especially in relation to the inclusion of gender in hate crime legislation, as well as with regard to the process of adding protected characteristics to hate crime legislation. It is argued that although all three reviews reached the same conclusion on gender, there were some differences in their approach and reasoning. To this end, the chapter highlights four key themes that emerged from the three reviews, namely: (a) the link between the symbolic and practical aspects of hate crime legislation, (b) the issue of hierarchies of hate and whether states should adopt an open or closed category of hate crime characteristics, (c) what role should be played by existing evidence of targeted violence against certain groups in the decision about which characteristics should be included in hate crime legislation and (d) issues relating specifically to the addition of gender to hate crime legislation. The chapter concludes that whilst gender seems to fit the hate crime paradigm well, there are certain difficulties associated with the practical implementation of adding gender to hate crime legislation.

In Chapter 4, Kim Barker and Olga Jurasz argue for the reform of hate crime laws to incorporate gender as one of the protected characteristics. The authors take a critical view of the misogyny campaigns as well as the current legal status quo with respect to gender and hate crime. They highlight gaps and inconsistencies in the key campaigns as well as deficiencies in the current legal system in England and Wales in addressing online (and offline) misogyny. For example, they argue that whilst current protected categories include sexual orientation and transgender identity, the current hate crime legislation does not provide legal avenues for addressing misogyny as a hate crime. The authors propose that capturing the misogynistic aspect of certain hate crimes – especially online – is possible through reform: firstly, by adding gender to the list of protected characteristics under hate crime legislation in England and Wales, and secondly, by creating new offences committed on or using social media, which can adequately capture misogynistic forms of abuse. Addressing the phenomenon of online misogyny from this dual perspective will give recognition to the existence of misogynistic hostility (by recording these as specific hate crimes in the criminal statistics) but also allow to prosecute and use sentencing uplifts, where evidence of gendered aggravation is present in the underlying criminal act.

In Chapter 5, Alexandra Krendel considers how sexist language is a prevalent issue online and how sexist beliefs shared by men online are being applied to women offline. Drawing on Manne's (2018) distinction between sexism and misogyny, the author discusses the sexist beliefs that are prevalent in the loose network of anti-feminist websites and communities known as the 'manosphere', and the extent to which these beliefs can be considered a solely online phenomenon. The author notes the differences between the five sub-groups of the 'manosphere' (Men's Rights Activists, Pick-up Artists; Men-Going-Their-Own-Way (MGTOW); Incels; TRP) and suggests that although these five sub-groups of the 'manosphere' are distinct from one another in their prescribed approach towards women, 'manosphere' forums are characterised by essentialised statements about gender relations between men and women. Having demonstrated the sexist beliefs which underpin the 'manosphere', this chapter considers whether the speech of the 'manosphere' constitutes hate speech, and how this speech should be considered in comparisons to the other harms described in this edited collection.

In Chapter 6, Rachel Harding, Lucy Betts, David Wright, Sheine Peart and Catarina Sjolin, a team of academics from sociology, psychology, linguistics, law and education, present a multidisciplinary perspective on a study undertaken with three secondary schools in the UK on adolescents' experiences of street harassment. Specifically, the study explored adolescents' emotional responses following sexual harassment, their descriptions and reflections of sexual harassment, as well as the implications of these experiences for adolescents' education and legal rights. The findings show that the negative emotions experienced by adolescent girls following sexual harassment incidents were more severe than those of boys, and that the sexual harassment incidents experienced by girls also appear to be different to those of boys. The chapter concludes by discussing the impact of sexual harassment on adolescents' learning such as disruption and distraction, and the implications for how far sexual harassment is covered by UK law.

In Chapter 7, Amina Easat-Daas examines Muslim women's experiences of gendered Islamophobia, misogyny and hate crime. The author draws on statistical evidence to show that Muslim women are disproportionately impacted by gendered Islamophobia in the UK, France and Belgium (as well as globally), but cautions that reported incidents are just the 'tip of the iceberg'. The author outlines the two key theoretical frameworks employed in this chapter, namely, Orientalism and Intersectionality. The author demonstrates how contemporary gendered Islamophobia is rooted in Orientalism on the basis that stereotypes surrounding Muslim women in today's society reflect orientalist discourses. These stereotypes actually mark Muslim women, especially those who are visibly Muslim, as 'ideal' targets to attack. The chapter concludes with a discussion of Muslim women-led initiatives responding to gendered Islamophobia, misogyny and hate crime.

In Chapter 8, Lesley Klaff discusses the intersection of antisemitism and misogyny. The chapter first describes the nature of antisemitism drawing on the blood libel, the conspiracy libel, and the economic libel. The chapter then considers the history of misogyny in antisemitism, especially in relation to the Holocaust. The author also discusses contemporary misogyny in antisemitism. The chapter offers examples of far right and far left antisemitism directed at high profile Jewish women, including Members of Parliament, actresses, and other UK celebrities. It also refers to antisemitic incidents towards girls and women who are visibly Jewish in public spaces in the UK. The chapter concludes with emphasising the importance of developing a policy argument for recognising gendered antisemitism as a unique subcategory of misogynistic hate crime.

In Chapter 9, Jane Healy draws from a wider piece of research into disability hate crime, to look at disabled women's experiences of hate crime and misogyny. Using an intersectional approach to analysis highlights an issue noted in other chapters across this edited collection; namely that dividing hate crime into distinct and separate strands fails to properly represent experiences of hate. The chapter draws particular attention to how disabled women's experiences of hate crime often involves sexual assault and sexual violence; this leads the author to argue that using understandings of both hate crime and gendered violence are necessary to properly conceptualise these experiences. The chapter concludes by revisiting the importance of intersectionality in understanding the interplay of disability, gender and misogyny.

Chapter 10 engages with theoretical and conceptual discussions around gender identity. In this chapter, Michaela Rogers examines the everyday experiences of hate crime, violence and victimisation in trans and non-binary people's lives. The chapter provides an overview of the theoretical and conceptual frameworks that can be employed in order to explore the problem of transphobic hate crime. Specifically, the concepts of cisgenderism, transphobia and trans-misogyny are employed in order to explore the ways in which trans and non-binary people experience inclusion/exclusion and belonging/non-belonging, as well as experiences of hate, violence and victimisation. The chapter also discusses the ongoing conflict between some feminists, and queer activists and scholars as well as feminists who identify as trans allies. The chapter concludes by providing a snapshot of transphobic hate crime in the UK.

In Chapter 11, Ben Colliver sheds light on the ways in which transgender women experience transphobic hate crime, racism and trans-misogyny simultaneously, and the impact this can have upon victims. The chapter draws on qualitative data conducted with trans people living in the UK. As such, the chapter frames some of the conceptual and theoretical debates outlined in the previous chapter within empirical research. The empirical results are contextualised within the often-complex relationships between cisgender, gay male culture, masculinity and femininity. Indeed, the author provides empirical evidence to demonstrate that trans-misogyny is not exclusive to heteronormative, cis-normative spaces; rather, transgender women experience trans-misogyny within two dominant spaces: LGBTQ+ spaces and sex-segregated spaces. The chapter notes that trans-misogyny is often perpetrated by other women who seek to 'police' the authenticity of transgender women.

In Chapter 12, Zaimal Azad and Sophie Maskell reflect upon how the women-led, grassroots campaign from Nottingham Women's Centre (and Nottingham Citizens) contributed to Nottinghamshire Police's decision to record misogyny as a hate crime. The authors argue for the women's voices to be heard, and call upon policy makers, researchers and community-based practitioners to continuously re-centre the voices of women and girls across all of their praxis. The chapter concludes that this policy should be seen as a call to action for 'feminist praxis', and to this end, continue to work together (policy makers, academia, organisations, communities) in order to understand and respond to women's experiences of violence.

In Chapter 13, Sue Fish, as the former Chief Constable of Nottinghamshire, explores the decision-making process undertaken by Nottinghamshire Police as the first police force in the UK to adopt misogyny as a hate crime, and its subsequent implementation. The author reflects on the considerations which affected the policy development as well as the reactions to this policy. The author also outlines the constitutional and legal position of the tripartite structure between the Chief Constable, Police and Crime Commissioner, and the Home Secretary at local and national levels, as well as considering the legitimacy of such decision making, and the impact of the policy on other police forces.

In Chapter 14, Louise Mullany, Loretta Trickett and Victoria Howard discuss the benefits and challenges of including misogyny as a hate crime category, both locally at the level of individual police force policy changes, and nationally in terms of changes in the law. Taking an interdisciplinary approach, integrating criminology, language and linguistics, the authors analyse the impact of misogyny hate crime on everyday lives of women and girls, from multiple stakeholder perspectives. The authors also examine how the language choice of the term 'misogyny' hate crime is received and interpreted and also consider alternative terms, specifically those proposed by the Law Commission's (2020) Hate Crime Consultation. The chapter makes the case for a national roll-out of the policy, and highlights the importance of education as a tool for tackling gender-based hate crime.

In Chapter 15, Maya Tutton introduces us to the campaign 'Our Streets Now', which is a nationwide campaign calling to make public sexual harassment illegal in the UK. Maya, who is also the co-founder of this campaign with her sister Gemma, discusses the reasons behind starting the campaign, including their own personal experiences of sexual harassment. The chapter examines the nature, extent and impact of public sexual harassment upon young women, and explores how 'Our Streets Now' is working to empower them to speak out about the misogyny they face, and the changes that should be made in order to tackle this problem. Indeed, there are two key aspects to this campaign: awareness and education, and legislative solutions. The chapter highlights the importance of digital feminist campaigning, and the involvement of young women in social justice movements.

Notes

1 As noted in the next section, there is no single 'Hate Crime Act', although some argue that reform of the legislation to simplify the complexity, inconsistencies and fragmented nature of the law in this area could be beneficial (Walters et al. 2017, p. 25).
2 Other forces have chosen to record incidents which target alternative subcultures (Garland and Hodkinson 2014; BBC 2015) and sex workers (Campbell 2014) as motivated by hostility or prejudice.

3 The enhanced sentencing provisions will not be used to 'double count' the hostility or prejudice in the aggravated offences, as this has already been taken into account by the offence being aggravated by the 'hate'.
4 The hate crime statistics collected by the Home Office relate only to hate crimes recorded by the police as such, are only for England and Wales (excluding the Greater Manchester police), and only show those strands of hate which are nationally monitored. The Crime Survey for England and Wales ("CSEW") provides an alternative source of data on the prevalence of hate crime, through a self-report study. The CSEW suggests a higher rate of hate crime than the Home Office data, as it captures those acts which were not reported to and subsequently recorded by the police (see, for example, the 2018 Hate Crime Report by the Home Office (2018) which incorporates the findings of the CSEW).
5 Race or ethnicity, religion or belief, sexual orientation, disability and transgender identity.

References

Andersson, J., 2020. What is Misogyny? The meaning and legal definition amid calls to make it a hate crime [online]. Available at: https://inews.co.uk/inews-lifestyle/women/misogyny-meaning-what-definition-legal-hate-crime-explained-657136 [Accessed 25 January 2021].

BBC, 2015. Subculture abuse classed as hate crime. BBC News. Available at: https://www.bbc.com/news/uk-england-leicestershire-34919722 [Accessed 2 September 2018].

BBC, 2016. Nottinghamshire Police records misogyny as a hate crime [online]. Available at: https://www.bbc.co.uk/news/uk-england-nottinghamshire-36775398 [Accessed 1 December 2019].

BSC, 2021. British Society of Criminology hate crime network. Available at: https://www.britsoccrim.org/networks/hate-crime-network/#Previous%20Events [Accessed 25 January 2021].

Campbell, R., 2014. Not getting away with it: linking sex work and hate crime in Merseyside. In: Chakraborti, N. and Garland, J., eds. *Responding to Hate Crime: The Case for Connecting Policy and Research*. Bristol: Policy Press, 2014, pp. 55–70.

Chakraborti, N. and Garland, J. 2015. *Hate Crime: Impact, Causes and Responses*. 2nd ed. London: Sage.

Chakraborti, N., Garland, J. and Hardy, S.-J., 2014. *The Leicester Hate Crime Project: Findings and Conclusions* [online]. University of Leicester. Available at: https://www2.le.ac.uk/departments/criminology/hate/documents/fc-full-report [Accessed 25 January 2021].

Citizens UK, 2020. Make misogyny a hate crime [online]. Available at: https://www.citizensuk.org/hate_misogyny [Accessed 25 January 2021].

College of Policing, 2014. *Hate Crime Operational Guidance*. Coventry: College of Policing. Available at: http://www.college.police.uk/What-we-do/Support/Equality/Documents/Hate-Crime-Operational-Guidance.pdf [Accessed 25 January 2021].

Communications Act 2003, c. 21.

CPS, 2018. Hate crime [online]. Available at: https://www.cps.gov.uk/hate-crime [Accessed 26 January 2021].

Crime and Disorder Act 1988, c. 37.

Criminal Justice Act 2003, c. 44.

Department of Justice, 2020. Hate crime legislation in Northern Ireland [online]. Available at: https://www.justice-ni.gov.uk/sites/default/files/publications/justice/hate-crime-review.pdf [Accessed 25 January 2021].

DLA Piper, 2014. Street harassment: know your rights. Available: https://www.trust.org/contentAsset/raw-data/7ea3c510-0595-40c4-ab35-f3208f28b0b0/file [Accessed 25 January 2021].

Fawcett, 2018. Campaigners call for police chiefs to make misogyny a hate crime nationwide ahead of key vote [online]. Available at: https://www.fawcettsociety.org.uk/news/campaigners-call-for-police-chiefs-to-make-misogyny-a-hate-crime-nationwide-ahead-of-key-vote [Accessed 1 December 2019].

Filipovic, J., 2017. Our president has always degraded women – and we've always let him. *Time* [online]. 5 December. Available at: https://time.com/5047771/donald-trump-comments-billy-bush/ [Accessed 25 January 2021].

Football (Offences) Act 1991, c. 19.

Garland, J. and Hodkinson, P., 2014. '"F**king freak! What the hell do you think you look like?": experiences of targeted victimization among goths and developing notions of hate crime'. *British Journal of Criminology*, 54(4), pp. 613–631. DOI: 10.1093/bjc/azu018.

Home Office, 2018. Hate crime, England and Wales, 2017 to 2019 [online]. Available at: https://assets.publishing.service.gov.uk/government/uploads/system/uploads/attachment_data/file/748598/hate-crime-1718-hosb2018.pdf [Accessed 25 January 2021].

Home Office, 2020a. Hate crime statistics [online]. Available at: https://www.gov.uk/government/collections/hate-crime-statistics [Accessed 25 January 2021].

Home Office 2020b. Hate crime, England and Wales, 2019 to 2020 [online]. Available at: https://www.gov.uk/government/statistics/hate-crime-england-and-wales-2019-to-2020 [Accessed 25 January 2021].

Inagaki, K. and Lewis, L. 2018. Japan pushes back against #MeToo movement. *Financial Times* [online]. 3 May. Available at: https://www.ft.com/content/d64bd404-4a08-11e8-8ee8-cae73aab7ccb [Accessed 25 January 2021].

INHS, 2021a. Home page [online]. International Network of Hate Studies. Available at: https://internationalhatestudies.com/ [Accessed 25 January 2021].

INHS, 2021b. Publications: gender-based hate [online]. International Network of Hate Studies. Available at: https://internationalhatestudies.com/topic/gender-based-hate-crime/ [Accessed 25 January 2021].

Khomami, N., 2017. #MeToo: how a hashtag became a rallying cry against sexual harassment. *The Guardian* [online]. 20 October. Available at https://www.theguardian.com/world/2017/oct/20/womenworldwide-use-hashtag-metoo-against-sexual-harassment [Accessed 25 January 2021].

Law Commission, 2020. *Hate Crime Laws: A Consultation Paper*. London: Law Commission. Available at: https://s3-eu-west-2.amazonaws.com/lawcom-prod-storage-11jsxou24uy7q/uploads/2020/10/Hate-crime-final-report.pdf [Accessed 25 January 2021].

Malicious Communications Act 1988, c. 27.

Manne, K., 2018. *Down Girl: The Logic of Misogyny*. Oxford: Oxford University Press.

Mason-Bish, H., 2015. Beyond the silo: rethinking hate crime and intersectionality. In: Hall, N., Corb, A., Giannasi, P. and Grieve, J.G.D., eds. *The Routledge International Handbook on Hate Crime*. Oxon: Routledge, 2015, pp. 24–33.

Masters, J., 2018. The World Cup sexism that won't go away – female reports on the front line [online]. 5 July. Available at: https://edition.cnn.com/2018/07/04/football/world-cup-female-journalist-harassment-spt-intl/index.html [Accessed 25 January 2021].

McCurry, J., 2020. Japan town's sole female councillor ousted after accusing mayor of sexual assault. *The Guardian* [online]. 8 December. Available at: https://www.theguardian.com/world/2020/dec/08/japan-towns-sole-female-councillor-ousted-after-accusing-mayor-of-sexual-assault [Accessed 18 January 2021].

Mora, K. and Oda, S., 2018. Me Too becomes We Too in victim-blaming Japan. *Japan Times* [online]. 15 May. Available at: https://www.japantimes.co.jp/news/2018/05/15/national/social-issues/becomes-victim-blaming-japan/ [Accessed 19 January 2021].

Mullany, L. and Trickett, L., 2018. Misogyny hate crime evaluation report [Online]. Available at: https://www.nottingham.ac.uk/lipp/documents/misogyny-evaluation-report.pdf. [Accessed 1 January 2021].

North Yorkshire Police, 2021. North Yorkshire Police announce misogyny now recognised as hate crime [online]. Available at: https://northyorkshire.police.uk/staying-safe/hate-crime/north-yorkshire-police-announce-misogyny-now-recognised-hate-crime/ [Accessed 26 January 2021].

ONS, 2018. Number of CSEW incidents of hate crimes per 12 months, England and Wales: years ending March 2016 and March 2018 [online]. Available at: https://www.ons.gov.uk/peoplepopulationandcommunity/crimeandjustice/adhocs/009335numberofcsewincidentsofhatecrimesper12monthsenglandandwales2015to2018 [Accessed 25 January 2021].

Perry, B., 2001. *In the Name of Hate: Understanding Hate Crimes*. London: Routledge.

Public Order Act 1986, c. 64.

Quiroz, N., 2017. Catcalling and whistling: street harassment illegal in Chile [online]. 4 April. Available at: https://chiletoday.cl/catcalling-and-whistling-street-harassment-illegal-in-chile/ [Accessed 20 January 2021].

Samanani, F. and Pope, S., 2020. *Overcoming Everyday Hate in the UK: Hate Crime, Oppression and the Law*. London: Citizens UK. Available at: https://d3n8a8pro7vhmx.cloudfront.net/newcitizens/pages/3760/attachments/original/1599728331/Academic_Report_V.6_-_web_compress_3.pdf?1599728331 [Accessed 25 January 2021].

Scottish Government, 2018. Independent review of hate crime legislation in Scotland. Final report [Online]. Available at: https://www.gov.scot/binaries/content/documents/govscot/publications/progress-report/2018/05/independent-review-hate-crime-legislation-scotland-final-report/documents/00535892-pdf/00535892-pdf/govscot%3Adocument/00535892.pdf [Accessed 20 January 2021].

Smith, J., 2019. *Feminist women's experiences of online gendered hate*. PhD thesis, University of Surrey.

Sparrow, A., 2020. Labour mayors back plan to make police record misogyny as hate crime. *The Guardian* [online]. 5 July. Available at: https://www.theguardian.com/uk-news/2020/jul/05/labour-mayors-back-plan-to-make-police-record-misogyny-as-hate [Accessed 25 January 2021].

Walters, M. et al., 2017. *Hate Crime and the Legal Process*. Brighton: University of Sussex.

Part 1
Theorising misogyny, gender and 'hate crime'

1 A feminist theoretical exploration of misogyny and hate crime

Marian Duggan and Hannah Mason-Bish

Introduction

Misogyny – the dislike of, contempt for or ingrained prejudice against, women – is the most pervasive and historic form of hatred that transcends time, space and place. 'Hate crime' as a standalone concept is understood as the targeted victimisation of a person on the basis of their identity, although currently in England and Wales it is only legally recognised if aligned to the victim's race, religion, disability, sexual orientation or transgender identity. Many women who fear or have experienced male violence recognise that gender, both theirs and that of their assailant, often informs related actions and responses (Vera-Gray 2018). The obscuring of this fact by the demarcation of, and focus upon, legally 'recognised' facets of her identity is disingenuous to women's individual and shared experiences of male violence as women. The degree to which misogyny informs hate crimes committed by men against women is difficult to discern as a gendered analysis is often omitted from examining rationales.

Few jurisdictions recognise gender as constituting a discreet category for legally recognised hostility. In England and Wales, the Law Commission have proposed a public consultation to discern the level of support for implementing a gender-specific focus to domestic hate crime legislation. This demonstrates that, like critical studies on race relations and religious persecution, feminist theorising on misogyny and sexism has finally resonated with policy makers. As with recognised hate crime strands, the emergent knowledge which critiqued structural and institutional discrimination and persecution has informed and sustained analyses of interpersonal victimisation. In other words, individual acts of hate crime do not occur in a vacuum thus must be understood in their wider cultural context. This underpins the strong argument for disaggregated data collection whereby gender hostility is foregrounded in order to expose the varied manifestations of misogyny. However, as we will argue in this chapter, the 'hate crime paradigm' is already inherently gendered as masculine, therefore adding identity categories to the list of strands is not enough. Instead, we propose a radical overhaul that recognises and addresses the silencing effect of current

DOI: 10.4324/9781003023722-1

hate crime frameworks of analysis on women's experiences of targeted victimisation. As feminist researchers working in the (largely separated) arenas of male violence against women and hate crime, we have long questioned the curious divisions between these two fields. In this chapter, we aim to present an insight into why they are, and will remain, uneasy bedfellows if gender or misogyny becomes recognised a distinct category of hate crime.

We begin by revisiting core feminist theorists on male violence against women to demonstrate how they (along with other civil rights advocates) informed subsequent hate crime theorising and policy implementation. Understanding feminist theorising requires an acknowledgement of historical perspectives in feminism. Until the latter part of the twentieth century, feminism focused on highlighting women's oppression and inequality in a way which measured it against the rights and freedoms afforded to men. The original aim of feminist theorising was to prioritise women's experience over – and in relation to – that of men. In doing so, approaches sought to espouse sameness (among women), demarcate difference (from men) and expose (patriarchal) dominance. Situating women's social, political, structural, legal and economic positionality in relation to men helped to depict inequalities in citizenship, as well as how power informed and sustained gender hierarchies. This was often at the expense of recognising other important facets of identity, such as race, sexuality or class. Feminist terminology referring to 'sex' or 'gender' was often used interchangeably; more recently, greater understandings of diversity have emerged along with explorations of sex and gender as separate entities. Feminism's focus on how gender stereotypes, roles and expectations contribute to and exacerbate women's social and structural oppression has benefitted greatly from intersectional approaches. Therefore, our exploration of the hate crime paradigm employs an intersectional approach to highlight how the gendered nature of victimisation is obscured in this discourse. We conclude by suggesting that a gender-specific focus on misogyny is vital if society is to understand and address the true nature and impact of hate crimes towards women.

Analysing feminist theories on misogyny

A plethora of feminist research into men's violence against women (such as intimate partner violence, sexual harassment/violence, female genital mutilation, trafficking, forced marriage, femicide, female infanticide and 'honour' killings) has exposed the inherently gendered nature of this harm. Importantly, research has shown that there are very few places women can consider as safe from male violence, especially when in the home, and that men's fatal violence rarely comes 'out of the blue' (Dobash et al. 2009). Central to this work has been highlighting the ubiquity of misogyny, primarily through exposing the patriarchal infrastructures which inform and sustain the commission of gendered harms (Walby 1989). This section explores misogyny using a range of feminist literature on men's interpersonal

A feminist theoretical exploration 21

and institutional violence against women. The primacy of gender advanced understandings around gendered relations but negated to address other relevant aspects of identity (such as race, religion or sexuality). The emergence of greater intersectional analyses of gendered violence because of these critiques added both nuance and depth of insight, and are explored more fully in the subsequent section.

Situating misogyny: fear, safety and space

Feminist theorising on women's safety in public and private spaces highlighted the primacy of (gendered) expectations around individual responsibility. Crime control, personal safety and avoiding violence had always been conceptualised as women's responsibility (as the potential victim) on both a formal and informal basis. This was often rendered evident in so-called 'safety' campaigns and literature, aimed at women, which informed them how to act, dress and behave to lessen their vulnerability to male violence (Stanko 1992). These messages inferred that some degree of such violence was inevitable and that the targets would be (lone, inebriated) women. Furthermore, this state of affairs was not considered unusual or uncharacteristic; rather, it was carefully constructed to fit the culturally familiar 'stranger danger' narrative (Stanko 1995).

These patriarchal discourses successfully individualised and pathologised particular aberrant male assailants in a way that allowed masculinity as a potential cause of violence against women to remain unproblematised. Contrastingly, all women are expected to assume the role and responsibility of potential victims and protect themselves accordingly; failure to do so can result in victim-blaming and accusations of culpability (Burt 1980). How women are supposed to protect themselves from male sexual predators is also heavily influenced by patriarchal ideas. So pervasive are societal expectations of femininity that recourse to masculinisation was as likely to incur male wrath, albeit of a different, less sexualised, nature (Corteen 2002). Male violence towards lesbian, bisexual and queer women – particularly those who present in a way that has been socially coded as 'butch' or androgynous – is often more physical than sexual in nature (homophobia is explored further in the following section). Instead, women are expected to perform femininity for the male gaze but remain alert and ready to police this when necessary. Such efforts reinforced the focus on 'stranger danger' despite overwhelming evidence indicating that the most dangerous place for most women is in the home (Aldridge and Browne 2003).

Feminists had to fight long and hard to have women's vulnerability to male victimisation in the private (domestic) sphere taken seriously. Patriarchal conceptualisations of gender hierarchies in the home situated the male in a position of authority and with control over his wife and children. The majority of domestic violence cases involve women as victims and men as perpetrators (UN Women 2013). In cases where the violence proves fatal, the overwhelming majority of victims are women and perpetrators are men. The growth and diversity in domestic violence research has led to greater awareness and understanding of how experiences may differ for victims who are in same-sex relationships (Donovan and Hester 2014), from minority cultures (Day and Gill 2020), or are male (Gadd et al. 2002). However, attempts to neutralise the gendered aspect of domestic violence perpetration are dangerous: compared to men, women engage in domestic violence less frequently, less severely and with far fewer fatal consequences. Women are much more likely to be harmed or killed by their current or former male partner than vice versa (Long et al. 2018). With a death toll averaging two women a week, domestic violence remains one of the most pervasive and sustained forms of misogyny in the UK (Long et al. 2018).

Similarly, the failure to consider rape within marriage a crime in England and Wales until 1991 demonstrated the patriarchal notion of women (wives) as male property. Upon saying "I do", wives were considered to have consented to all future sexual intercourse with their husbands. Russell's (1982) study with married women demonstrated the impact of this on rape victims. Despite finding that 14% of her sample had experiences that were commensurate with legal definitions of rape (at the time), fewer than 1% of these women described it as 'rape' (1982, p. 67). For many, the repeated nature of their victimisation (along with the identity of their assailant) may also have disabused them of the idea that it was rape due to the pervasiveness of 'rape myths' (Burt 1980). Cultural stereotypes of isolated incidents, occurring at night, involving young women being violently attacked by a male stranger came to popularise the imagery surrounding rape. A vital breakthrough in challenging this came from Liz Kelly's (1988) seminal work which showcased that many women experience sexual violence on a 'continuum'. She proved that sexual victimisation was a constant feature in most women's lives, committed by men who were strangers or acquaintances (including partners), and evolved as they moved through the life course.

Importantly, Kelly's research also showed how ongoing exposure to this violence led to the development of internalised (often unconscious) coping mechanisms. Women minimised, overlooked, excused, rationalised and justified male violence in ways that suggested either that 'nothing really happened' (Kelly and Radford 1990) or that the woman was in some way responsible for what had happened to her. Feelings of responsibility coupled with rape myths were powerful social regulators, ensuring that women conformed to patriarchal gender roles that demarcated between 'good' (i.e. chaste, married and compliant) and 'bad' (i.e. promiscuous, provocative or prostituted) women. They also worked in men's favour, allowing them to commit sexual violence against certain women with relative impunity (Brownmiller 1975). In her detailed book on rape across time, space and place, Brownmiller (1975) documents the pervasiveness of men's sexual violence towards women in a range of settings: conflict, peace, the street, the home, the family, committed by state agents and civilians, as individuals, in pairs and in groups. She powerfully states the following:

> From prehistoric times to the present, I believe, rape has played a critical function. It is nothing more or less.
>
> (Brownmiller 1975, p. 15)

Likewise, MacKinnon's (1991, p. 1301) assertion that 'women are sexually assaulted because they are women; not individually or at random, but on the basis of sex, because of their membership in a group defined by gender' also shows the functioning of systemic oppression through misogyny. These ideas continue to hold relevance, with research demonstrating the impact of 'rape culture' on all (not just raped) women, particularly in situationally specific contexts such as university campuses where engagement in the sexual victimisation of women becomes part of male group bonding and identity (Sanday 1996; Phipps et al. 2017). Therefore, focusing on how misogyny informs male violence against women is crucial to understanding a range of factors: how it manifests; how it shapes social and legal responses; how it impacts victims; how it ensures perpetrator impunity and/or rationalisations; and how it can escalate to fatal levels. As Stanko clearly stated: 'To lose sight and insight by ignoring how gender matters impoverishes any analyses of violence' (2006, p. 551).

Misogyny as systemic oppression

Gendered oppression is accompanied by systematic violence which specifically targets the female 'Other' in ways which range from harassment and intimidation through to serious harm and death (Young 1990). This systematic violence is marked out by the social context surrounding it, which not only facilitates such harm but may also go some way to justifying its commission. Systemic violence demarcates probable targets on the basis of their group membership and may act on a continuum where everyday gendered (micro)oppressions operate in addition to (and inform) more overt, harmful misogynistic acts. The knowledge that they are vulnerable to male victimisation on account of their gender impacts on women's sense of self, dignity and freedom, while random, periodic and irregular attacks on women ensure a constant baseline of fear (Young 1990).

Feminist challenges to the normalisation of male violence towards women highlighted the discursive invisibility afforded to perpetrators. In doing so, they addressed the power of language and importance of agency and naming. Sheffield's (1992) description of male violence against women as 'sexual terrorism' was intended to powerfully indicate the sexual dynamics shaping women's fears and experiences of victimisation. Pain's (2014) conceptualisation of domestic violence as 'everyday terrorism' highlighted the repeated and cyclical nature of some women's fear and trepidation.

Terrorism was also the descriptor used by hooks (1981) in her examination of Black women's treatment in American history. Notions of terrorism call to mind randomness and unpredictability within a framework of purposeful, targeted attacks; for many women, this accurately captures the volatility of misogyny in their lives. However, somewhat unlike traditional notions of 'terrorists', the breadth of feminist research into women's victimisation has repeatedly evidenced the interpersonal nature of this from men with whom they have close relationships (Britton 2000).

Men who harm the women they are closest to – partners, family, friends, colleagues – hold views or endorse behaviours that can easily be translated to women who are strangers. A man who lacks respect for a woman (on the basis of her gender and/or any other factor) may make sexualised, vulgar, threatening or abusive comments towards her while passing on the street, or in a vehicle, or when out with friends just because he feels like doing so. A significant characteristic of most crime is that it is opportunistic and done 'in the moment' (Cohen and Felson 1979). Currently, he can do this while knowing that there will be little recourse for his actions, either socially or legally, so long as the remarks he makes are misogynistic. If he can express these sentiments anonymously, then there is even less incentive to refrain from acting in ways that purposefully hurt women. Feminist theorising has recently evidenced the rapid growth in expressions of virtual victimisation through cybersexism (Poland 2016), revenge porn (Citron 2014), broader acts of image-based sexual abuse (DeKeseredy and Schwartz 2016; McGlynn et al. 2017) online misogyny (Lewis et al. 2018) and technology-facilitated sexual violence (Henry and Powell 2018). Online activities may also incentivise offline violence (Williams 2006). The online domain evidences the difference between being vulnerable and being vulnerable to victimisation; women do not need to be classed as vulnerable (although some are) to be recognised as vulnerable to misogyny, they just need to be accessible.

Misogyny detrimentally impacts women. As well as physically and sexually (Tjaden and Thoennes 1998), the abuse and effects can be psychological (Briere and Jordan 2004; Bates 2017) and thus harmful to women's mental health (Westbrook 2008; Silvestri and Crowther-Dowey 2016). These impacts can be felt from indirect misogyny, as demonstrated in Perry and Alvi's (2011) research on the 'in terrorem' effect of hate crimes, where knowledge of individual acts affects the wider community. Yet despite the raft of changes made to awareness campaigns, policing practices, prosecution policies and wider criminal justice mechanisms, most women still choose not to report their experiences of male violence to authorities. Reasons for this range from feeling that there is little (or nothing) the authorities can do through to victims feeling responsible for what has happened to them. There are inherent risks in calling for, or accessing, justice processes as women, especially when these are characterised as vengeful attempts to criminalise 'ordinary' men. As a result, 'the dangerousness of violent men is rarely challenged by criminal justice. Women largely still choose to keep victimization away from state intervention' (Stanko 2007, p. 218).

Hate crime studies have been strongly influenced by critical feminist theorising. However, the theoretical schism between identity politics and violence against women has resulted in segregated policies and laws. The evolution of hate crime and feminist studies along intersectional lines allows a greater recognition of how misogyny informs and sustains systemic violence, oppressively functioning to maintain group privilege or domination while also marking out targeted groups as vulnerable to persecution based on identity alone. Violence is often a social and symbolic practice, where bonds are strengthened as a result of shared identity formation and persecution of the 'other' (Young 1990). Furthermore, individuals who commit acts of violent (misogynistic) persecution may find this tolerated and legitimised as a result of the patriarchal status quo:

> [W]hite, middle-class men are rarely held accountable for their violence as their identities are not criminalized, there is a huge latitude for their behaviour, and they are seen as always/already redeemable.
> (Russo 2018, p. 97)

However, as Carol Smart (1976) has stated, laws alone do not protect women from men's violence, so advocating for more law may not always be the right response. Instead, Britton (2000) suggests that a more appropriate focus might be on justice, rather than law, to offer a better framework for redress and/or harm reduction. Enfranchisement is also highlighted by Barbaret (2014) who, in her global analysis of gendered citizenship, advocates for women to be afforded greater agency in contributing to aspects of public and private life in which they are directly affected. This is especially important when read alongside McPhail (2002, p. 135), who noted some time ago that '[w]hat may be "new" arguments for many actors within the hate crime police domain are actually old arguments within the feminist movement'. The following section demonstrates this by applying feminist theorising to explore the manifestations of misogyny in hate crimes, demonstrating how crucial gender dynamics are routinely overlooked.

Theorising misogyny within the existing hate crime paradigm

The previous section demonstrated the extent to which research and theory on men's violence against women has formed a distinct and separate body of knowledge that has influenced law, policy and practice. Born from feminist campaigning and linked to often carceral and criminal justice initiatives, gendered violence as distinct category has been separated from the hate crime policy domain. This is also demonstrated by women's organisations often being reticent to campaign for the inclusion of gender in hate crime provisions for fear that it might dilute the focus on women's experiences and subsume them within a larger policy umbrella which incorporates a variety of biases (Gill and Mason-Bish 2013). In this section, we explore why it is important to highlight misogyny within already recognised hate crime strands and the consequences of not having a separate gender category. We suggest that although women clearly experience hate crime, they are routinely overlooked in policy efforts which foreground the experience of minoritised men. In short, for most women, hate crime will always have a gendered dimension whether this is officially acknowledged or not.

The intersectional experiences of women

Coined by Kimberlé Crenshaw (1991), intersectionality is the principle of understanding how categories such as race and gender intersect to create multiple layers of oppression. They are produced and sustained by systems of patriarchy, white supremacy and capitalism. Hate crime can be understood as a way of maintaining the dominant position of whiteness, heteropatriarchy and ableism. Offenders are drawing on common cultural narratives to act out this dominance. What Crenshaw (1991) was critical of was that too often, the experiences of Black women were missing in any understanding of racial (and gendered) discrimination. They faced a double, multi-layered form of injustice which was complex. Similarly, feminist work on violence against women came from a white perspective and failed to include women of colour in campaigning or policy developments. Collins (2017) took this further to note that the move towards private, intimate violence that came to dominate western feminist campaigning efforts elides the public harassment that women of colour experience. The emergence of feminist disability studies has also pushed for further focus on the nuances of how disabled women experience hostility and violence (Mays 2006; Shah et al. 2016). Put simply, policy campaigning and criminal justice initiatives have not been successful at recognising how women might be victimised.

Critics of hate crime policy have argued that one of its failings has been the lack of recognition of intersectional experiences of hate crime. Nancy Fraser's (2005) work would suggest that we should be unsurprised by this because recognition struggles often force a focus on simplistic identities that do not really challenge underlying structures. Moran and Sharpe (2004) describe this as the 'either/or' logic, pointing out that violence is either seen as hate crime or something else. They challenge that it is very difficult to find research or indeed prosecutions of transgender experiences of racist violence for example (2004). Although police forces have the ability to tick multiple boxes in police reports for hate crime, there is little evidence to suggest that this then leads to demonstrably different victim support mechanisms. This is indicative of the limited capacity of current justice processes to address intersecting experiences of harm. We argue here that this failure to recognise intersectionality is especially the case for women and that even in the established victim categories of hate crime policy, the focus is often on men. As Sloan notes:

> Crimes against gay women, female Muslims, disabled women, trans women and women from other racial backgrounds ... all share the fact

that they are women; however, the femaleness goes under-examined compared with examining the 'otherness' of such victims relative to the general population.

(2017, p. 73)

It's about men

In her critique of hate crime legislation, Amber Ault asserts that the development of policy in this area has been 'marred by sexism' (1997, p. 50). The seemingly gender-neutral categories enshrined in law mainly apply to violence against men. The male experience is seen as the referential form of hate crime and this has been evidenced by particular figurehead crimes which have garnered media attention and policy focus. Most people would be hard pushed to name a high profile hate crime case involving a woman as the victim. Yet many could cite the racist murder of Stephen Lawrence (UK), or James Byrd Jr (US). The homophobic murder of Jody Dobrowski (UK) or Mathew Shepard (US). The simplicity of motivation in these cases, seemingly unmarred by the complex interaction of gender, meant that they were used as examples of hate crime which then went on to shape policy and campaigning efforts.

Also of relevance though, has been the direction of feminist campaigning that ran in parallel to hate crime activism. As the former was shifting focus onto the home as the place of male violence against women, local activists highlighting racism and homophobia were gathering empirical evidence about victimisation on the streets. Until the last five years, there has been very little discussion about how women experience hate crime. Research by Gill and Mason-Bish (2013) showed a lack of support for hate crime initiatives meaning that stakeholders were not in a position to ensure that the experiences of women were understood or explicitly discussed in relation to hate crime. Simply put, without a clear understanding of the role of misogyny in hate crime and with the male experience as the key normative category, women's experiences of hate – and particularly their intersectional dimensions – have been obscured.

As a case in point, Ault (1997) draws particularly on violence against lesbians and how this has been muted in both research and policy. Specifically, she says:

> The presentation of lesbians and gay men as a seamless collective in the literature, policies, and grassroots practices focused on homophobic violence inscribes lesbians as more like gay men than heterosexual women, frequently makes invisible what may be real and important differences between the experiences of gay men and lesbians, avoids situating both anti-gay and anti-lesbian violence in a larger context of violence against women, and constructs anti-lesbian violence as a "hate crime", while excluding anti-woman violence from this category.
>
> (Ault 1997, p. 50)

This means that differences in the gendered victimisation of lesbians are lost. This can be noted in data collection efforts, whereby very few reports by either the public sector or criminal justice agencies separate the experiences of lesbians and gay men. Scholars such as Karen Corteen (2002) have found that, as they were seen to transgress both gender and sexuality norms, lesbians were at increased risk from violent attacks. Women were more likely to be targeted when they were not performing gender appropriately – such as when wearing trousers, no make-up or flat shoes (Corteen 2002). The gendered nature of violence against lesbians was demonstrated in 2019, during which a lesbian couple were viciously attacked while on a London bus. Melania Geymonat and Chris Hannigan were targeted by four male teenagers who asked them to kiss each other, made sexual gestures and demanded to know how they had sex. Media reports subsequently lost the nuance of gender by subsuming this lesbian experience under the broader umbrella of homophobia (i.e. 'sexual orientation'). The lack of attention paid to addressing misogyny in hate crimes against lesbians means women are less likely to report victimisation (Bartle 2000). This in turn affects deficits in understanding around lesbians' specific needs as victims of crime, or in terms of recovery strategies.

The tendency of policy and practice to overlook the experiences of women does not only apply to lesbians and bisexuals within the LGBT umbrella. For transgender and non-binary people, legal redress took many years to catch up. Sentence enhancement for sexual orientation hate crimes was added to legislation in 2003, but transgender identity was not added until 2012. Police and Crown Prosecution Services have traditionally merged homophobic and transphobic policy, arguably creating an even less nuanced picture about the experiences of victims. For transgender and non-binary people, hate crimes often focus on their masculine or feminine gender presentation (particularly associated physical traits). They are significantly more likely to be victims of all forms of hate crime than non-transgender LGB people are, and to have experienced it on more than one occasion (Antjoule 2016). Walters et al. (2017) describe this as a form of systemic genderism which means that not only are trans people more likely to suffer hate crime, but the lack of societal support afforded to them, combined with a poor police response means that they suffer from compounded harms. Trans women in particular share the gendered experiences of their cis-ters by being subject to higher rates of sexual assault and abuse. The Human Rights Campaign points out that the majority of trans and non-binary people murdered each year are trans women of colour (HRC 2020). They share other high-risk characteristics with cisgender women including prevalence of sex work, homelessness and poverty. It is this combination of womanhood, transphobia and structural misogyny that makes them vulnerable to hate crime. In her personal account of being transgender, Rebecca Dittman (2003) talks about how she spent many years completely invisible because she was a white man. To live as a transwoman is to become hypervisible and have her gender and behaviour assessed as fair game. She is living as a visible woman, with all of the scrutiny that this entails (Dittman 2003).

One domain of academic scholarship and research which has been attuned to gendered dimensions of motivation and public visibility is in the area of religiously motivated hate crimes. Chakraborti and Zempi (2012) contend that the concept of Islamophobia is often portrayed as gender neutral in its application but for Muslim women, their experiences suggest that anti-Muslim sentiment and misogyny are intertwined. It is reinforced by a popular portrayal of veiled Muslim women in particular as culturally dangerous, 'doing gender' in a way that is at odds with Western values. Research has demonstrated the prevalence of Islamophobic hate Muslim women face and that it is more commonplace in their daily lives than for Muslim men (Mason-Bish and Zempi 2018). Furthermore, the victimisation demonstrates the way that misogyny and Islamophobia work together. In their research on veiled Muslim women, Mason-Bish and Zempi (2018) found many examples of women being seen as 'agents of terror' because of their wearing of the veil in public spaces. When being subject to abuse, attackers would reference their clothing, demanding to see their faces and bodies. Threats of sexual harassment and rape were not uncommon. They often described this as a form of sexual terrorism and took restrictive measures in their everyday lives such as staying home or only leaving the house with a male friend or relative. Muslim women and in particular those wearing a face veil represent a popular cultural image of the dangerous other – assumed to be an oppressed woman with little agency and yet also under suspicion of being a terrorist.

Women as weapons

The development of hate crime policy in the global north has been significantly shaped to redress the historic persecution of minoritised groups (Jenness and Grattet 2001). All of the victim groups within hate crime provisions share a long history of violence, subjugation and discrimination both in public life and at the hands of the criminal justice system. Yet within this has been relatively little connection made with the experiences of women in conflict zones and the way that hate crimes against them have operated as a form of ethnic cleansing. During the Balkan conflict it is estimated that up to 50,000 women and girls were raped as part of a strategy of ethnic cleansing. They were brutalised, raped with objects, burned, forced to have abortions and watch female family members be violated. The extreme misogyny towards women during the Srebrenica massacre demonstrates how gender is a central feature in the genocides experienced by women across the world (Remembering Srebrenica 2017). Hateful atrocities against women during the Rwandan genocide, in Vietnam, during WW2 and currently towards the Yazidi women in ISIS areas have often been described as "weapons" of war and subsumed within the broader remit of "crimes against humanity".

Some feminist scholars argue that this is problematic because it takes the focus away from women as individual victims and an understanding of the intersectional interplay between them as ethnic minorities and as women (Henry 2014). Henry points out that to overly focus on rape in conflict is to overlook other forms of victimisation that impacted men and women as minorities. In this sense, it is problematic to assume that the experience of women in war is only about their gender as in reality it is often much more complicated than that (Grewal 2010).

As with the targeting of ethnic minority women during wartime, Chapter 8 indicates that the historic prejudice experienced by Jewish women has long roots yet it is still very much alive. She highlights how high profile celebrities and Members of Parliament have been subject to harassment and persecution that displays both antisemitic and misogynistic tones. Luciana Berger MP left the Labour party in 2019 after voicing concerns about the amount of anti-Jewish sentiment she was experiencing. This included serious threats to her life and typically misogynistic abuse including "images of her head being Photoshopped onto rats and pornographic photos, letters signed by self-declared supporters of her former party leader and delivered to her office by hand, warning that she would be raped, stabbed and covered in acid" (Kentish 2019). Researcher Seth Stephens-Davidowitz found that Jewish women MPs were 15% more likely to receive abuse online than their male peers with far-right websites profiling them and singling them out for abuse. This is misogynistic in nature, commenting on their appearance, body and professional status (Harpin 2018).

Racism is inherently gendered and can be further noted in the experiences of Black politician Diane Abbott. Amnesty International found that in the run-up to the 2017 general election, Abbott received 45% of all hateful tweets targeting female MPs. She commented:

> It's highly racialised and it's also gendered because people talk about rape and they talk about my physical appearance in a way they wouldn't talk about a man. I'm abused as a female politician and I'm abused as a black politician.
>
> (Elgot 2017)

Feminist scholars have urged caution around the tendency to see particular individuals as exceptional cases, or offenders as far-right extremists. Palmer (2020) outlines how, in order to understand misogynoir, one must challenge the "distinctive brand of hatred directed at Black women" which is often used by white women to maintain hierarchical structures of domination. Additionally problematic is the way that hate crime narratives around race are dominated by the experiences of Black men and how white women claim control of stories around misogyny. This combination ensures that the intersectional experiences of black women are silenced or seen as exceptional.

Intersectional margins

Hateful violence and abuse experienced by disabled women is often seen as a 'niche issue' in policy and practice (Morris 1996; Thiara et al. 2011). Specifically within hate crime research there has been little attempt to interrogate the way that misogyny and disablism interplay in offending behaviour. Yet disabled women are twice as likely to experience sexual assault and have high rates of domestic abuse; institutional violence and street harassment (Chenoweth 1996; Thiara et al. 2011; ONS 2018). Nixon (2009) describes the complexity of their experiences as 'compound oppression' and speaks to the way that misogyny and disablism operate together. For example, women with visual impairments have spoken about the hostility shown towards them including comments about their appearance and their sex appeal (Kavanagh 2019). Wheelchair users talk about how they have been forcibly pushed without their consent and subjected to a barrage of verbal hostility when they raise an objection (Low 2019). As Sherry (2016) has shown, hate crimes against disabled women are often hyperviolent and hypersexualised in an ableist world that views the disabled body as an object of pity or disgust.

Despite evidence to suggest the prevalence of disability hate crimes against women, it is questionable as to whether including misogyny in hate crime provisions would make a difference. Critics have noted that for disability hate crime there has been confusion over motivation and a difficulty in police and justice agencies taking adequate records of hostility (Mason-Bish 2012). Rates for prosecution and conviction of disability hate crimes remain stubbornly low in the UK (CPS 2019). Scholars have suggested that this is partly down to a struggle to move beyond the assumption that disabled people are victimised because of their perceived vulnerability (Mason-Bish 2012; Roulestone and Sadique 2012). Given that there is already debate about whether domestic violence or rape are hate crimes, it is possible that the inclusion of misogyny in hate crime policy would do little to improve the poor services currently afforded to disabled women. In her life narrative research, Simplican points out that "ableism and sexism intersect to construct disabled women as asexual, miserable and powerless" (2017, p. 115) and that feminist disability studies aim to retrieve the dismissed voice and those who have been misrepresented. As such, consultations around hate crime and misogyny have the power to open these conversations and to develop an understanding about the experiences of disabled women outside of assumed frameworks. Yet it is doubtful whether this can actually achieve wider structural change.

The opportunity for discussion amongst stakeholders, victims and criminal justice practitioners has been one of the benefits of hate crime policy development. For some marginalised groups of women these opportunities have been utilised to develop 'bespoke' approaches to hate. As Campbell (2018) has noted, sex workers are stigmatised due to a combination of 'whorephobia' and misogyny. They experience prejudice and 'othering' and are targeted for being 'fallen women'. In response to the murders of several sex workers, including Anne Marie Foy in 2005, Merseyside Police amended their hate crime policy to include sex workers as a protected group. This involved working with local community partnerships; speaking with sex workers about their needs and looking for trends and patterns of violence and abuse towards them. Since then, a handful of other forces have adopted a similar approach, with mixed evaluations. While applauding such initiatives to encourage reporting, there was caution around the fact that most cases resulted in no further action (N8 2019). Furthermore, focus on the 'vulnerability' of particular groups of women arguably does little to dismantle the structures of patriarchy, heteronormativity and capitalism which fundamentally reinforce their oppression.

In this section we have examined the way that women as victims of hate crime experience complex, nuanced and compound harms when victimised. Yet this is the problem. As Ault (1997) attests, when male experiences of hate crime are seen as the reference point, then adding or addressing misogyny is either too messy or too complicated. This in part explains the exclusion of gender as a discreet category of hate crime, and of wider understanding about women's experiences. Yet without an intersectional understanding of hate crime we are not forced to confront challenging questions. The carceral framework that has dominated hate crime initiatives favours the experiences of cisgender heterosexual ('cishet') white women to the detriment of minoritised men and women. While the Nottinghamshire initiative around street harassment has focused attention on the everyday misogyny that women experience, there is much to suggest that it will be mainly white women who report (Stavri 2016). As feminist Zoe Stavri critiqued, it is likely to be that reports increase when 'a Nice White Lady™ is victimised by a Nasty Black Or Brown Man™'. How do we develop a hate crime framework that is inclusive of women but that is also intersectional? Many would argue that while we are committed to a carceral solution to hate crime, this is not a possibility.

Conclusion

Moran (2001) considered how the legal recognition of offences motivated by identity hostility had the potential to offer several possible outcomes to those affected by targeted victimisation, ranging from redress through to the potential for a reduction in such harm. In addition, the shift in focus towards the perpetrator's motivations or intentions when undertaking the act provided new ways of thinking about and understanding the social and structural factors informing hostility and how it manifested in instances of interpersonal victimisation. However, Moran also cautioned against allowing such a focus to shift attention too far from wider contributory factors:

A focus upon the perpetrator threatens to occlude an important theme that has been central to the politics of violence in general and the victim survey movement in particular; the failure of State institutions and, in particular, those of criminal justice to take certain types of violence seriously and the violence of those same institutions.

(2001, p. 334)

Continuing to render invisible this ever-present hostility could be considered a form of institutional misogyny in itself. Stanko (2006) states that to challenge violence we must tackle its legitimation; to do this requires listening carefully to the discourses used by victims, perpetrators and others to examine who, or what, is condoned and/or condemned. Recognising the ways in which patriarchy operates – through covert mechanisms which function to sustain women's oppression through to overt acts of male violence – is essential to effectively challenge misogyny on individual and societal levels. Taking a three-tiered approach, feminist activism therefore needs to continue highlighting and challenging how misogyny operates on the micro level (for individuals), the meso level (for cultural/societal change), and the macro level (for legislative/policy change). Social harms which manifest on a macro scale may be experienced very differently on a micro level, therefore, examining structural violence allows for greater inclusion by focusing on experience as well as identity while ensuring that men's violence against women is not placed in a cultural or socio-political vacuum (Barbaret 2014). Furthermore, without wider social change there will be little positive effect from criminalising behaviours which perpetrators do not consider to be problematic:

> Societal structures that devalue women and reinforce male power, social norms which dictate rigid gender stereotypes, myths that justify violence, and peer approval of violence in our day-to-day environments – these are all common factors underlying difference forms of VAWG [violence against women and girls].
>
> (Cerise and Dustin 2011, p. 14)

As this chapter has argued, women are being short-changed in hate crime policy despite feminist efforts heavily informing the adoption of its victim-focused framework. Feminist theory and praxis endeavour to improve women's social, economic, legal and political situations by challenging patriarchy. The plethora of different feminist approaches are aligned in their focus on women, but have demonstrated the potential for greater dialogue and interconnectivity. A primacy of gender can include consideration of other characteristics, identities and factors, but to do so must allow room for multiple voices and experiences. The advances made through identity politics offered greater insight into theorising the experiences of black and ethnic minority women, lesbian/bisexual/queer women, trans women, disabled women, women from different class backgrounds, and so forth. Reinforcing a gender focus grounded in women's lived experiences enhances our understanding of misogyny's cultural specificities. Similarly, a focus on misogyny within these bodies of knowledge, such as queer theory, critical feminist race theory and masculinities theories will benefit feminist endeavours to fully expose, challenge and tackle misogyny on a broader scale. Capturing multiple sites of discrimination in police recorded hate crimes is crucial to ensure that the addition of a misogyny or gender-focused category does not become merely a repository for the experiences of specific women (namely those who are white, able bodied, cisgender, heterosexual). By capturing the range of misogynistic experiences (including sub-criminal hostilities or hate incidents) that all women are subjected to, particularly women with minority statuses, will shed light on the parameters of misogyny while expanding our understandings of and beyond misogynoir and transmisogyny.

On a final note, we recognise that to speak of misogyny is to risk (invite?) counter-discussions about misandry. As feminist theorists, we welcome these discussions: first, because they help highlight the nuanced gender differences between the two concepts which make them impossible to compare without doing a disservice to either, and second, because they both highlight the damaging effects of patriarchy on individuals and society. Misappropriations of feminism as misandrist ('man-hating') are misguided; feminism is, and always has been, focused on patriarchy, not individual men (unless those men are actively supporting or embodying the patriarchal forces to which we are opposed). Furthermore, it is not just feminists who recognise that misogyny and misandry are incomparable. As the famous saying goes: "Men are afraid women will laugh at them; women are afraid men will kill them". Misogyny matters.

References

Aldridge, M.L. and Browne, K.D., 2003. Perpetrators of spousal homicide: a review. *Trauma, Violence and Abuse*, 4(3), pp. 265–276. DOI: 10.1177/1524838003004003005.

Antjoule, N., 2016. *The Hate Crime Report: Homophobia, Biphobia and Transphobia in London*. London: Galop.

Ault, A., 1997. When it happens to men, it's 'hate' and 'a crime': hate crime policies in the contexts of gay politics, movement organizations, and feminist concerns. *Journal of Poverty*, 1(1), pp. 49–63. DOI: 10.1300/J134v01n01_04.

Barbaret, R., 2014. *Women, Crime and Criminal Justice: A Global Enquiry*. London: Routledge.

Bartle, E., 2000. Lesbians and hate crime. *Journal of Poverty*, 4(4), pp. 23–43. DOI: 10.1300/J134v04n04_02.

Bates, S., 2017. Revenge porn and mental health: A qualitative analysis of the mental health effects of revenge porn on female survivors. *Feminist Criminology*, 12(1), pp. 22–42. DOI: 10.1177/1557085116654565.

Briere, J. and Jordan, J., 2004. Violence against women: Outcome complexity and implications for assessment and treatment. *Journal of Interpersonal Violence*, 19(11), pp. 1252–1276. DOI: 10.1177/0886260504269682.

Britton, D., 2000. Feminism in criminology: engendering the outlaw. *The ANNALS of the American Academy of Political and Social Science*, 571(1), pp. 57–76. DOI: 10.1177/000271620057100105.

Brownmiller, S., 1975. *Against Our Will: Men, Women and Rape*. New York: Simon and Schuster.

Burt, M., 1980. Cultural myths and support for rape. *Journal of Personality and Social Psychology*, 38(2), pp. 217–230. DOI: 10.1037/0022-3514.38.2.217.

Campbell, R., 2018. Beyond hate: policing sex work, protection and hate crime. In: Sanders, T. and Laing, M., eds. *Policing the Sex Industry: Protection, Paternalism and Politics*. Abingdon: Routledge, 2018, pp. 53–72.

Cerise, S. and Dustin, H., 2011. We need an integrated approach to ending violence. *Criminal Justice Matters*, 85(1), pp. 14–15. DOI: 10.1080/09627251.2011.599622.

Chakraborti, N. and Zempi, I., 2012. The veil under attack: gendered dimensions of Islamophobic victimisation. *International Review of Victimology*, 18(3), pp. 269–284. DOI: 10.1177/0269758012446983.

Chenoweth, L., 1996. Violence against women with disabilities: silence and paradox. *Violence Against Women*, 2(4), pp. 391–411. DOI: 10.1177/1077801296002004004.

Citron, D., 2014. *Hate Crimes in Cyberspace*. London: Harvard University Press.

Cohen, L. and Felson, M., 1979. Social change and crime rate trends: a routine activity approach. *American Sociological Review*, 44(4), pp. 588–608. DOI: 10.2307/2094589.

Collins, P.H., 2017. On violence, intersectionality and transversal politics. *Ethnic and Racial Studies*, 40(9), pp. 1460–1473. DOI: 10.1080/01419870.2017.1317827.

Corteen, K., 2002. Lesbian safety talk: problematising definitions and experiences of violence, sexuality and space. *Sexualities*, 5(3), pp. 259–280. DOI: 10.1177/1363460702005003001.

CPS, 2019. Hate crime report 2018–19 [online]. Available at: https://www.cps.gov.uk/sites/default/files/documents/publications/CPS-Hate-Crime-Annual-Report-2018-2019.PDF [Accessed 6 September 2020].

Crenshaw, K., 1991. Mapping the margins: intersectionality, identity politics, and violence against women of colour. *Stanford Law Review*, 43(6), pp. 375–395. DOI: 10.2307/1229039.

Day, A.S. and Gill, A.K., 2020. Applying intersectionality to partnerships between women's organizations and the criminal justice system in relation to domestic violence. *The British Journal of Criminology*, 60(4), pp. 830–850. DOI: 10.1093/bjc/azaa003.

DeKeseredy, W.S. and Schwartz, M.D., 2016. Thinking sociologically about image-based sexual abuse: The contribution of male peer support theory. *Sexualization, Media, & Society*, 2(4), pp. 1–8. DOI: 10.1177/2374623816684692.

Dittman, R.J., 2003. Policing hate crime. from victim to challenger: a transgendered perspective. *Probation Journal*, 50(3), pp. 282–288. DOI: 10.1177/0264550503503007.

Dobash, R., Dobash, R. and Cavanagh, K., 2009. 'Out of the blue': men who murder an intimate partner. *Feminist Criminology*, 4(3), pp. 194–225. DOI:10.1177/1557085109332668.

Donovan, C. and Hester, M., 2014. *Domestic Violence and Sexuality: What's Love Got to Do with It?* Bristol: Bristol University Press.

Elgot, J., 2017. Diane Abbott more abused than any other female MP during election. *The Guardian* [online]. 5 September 2017. Available at: https://www.theguardian.com/politics/2017/sep/05/diane-abbott-more-abused-than-any-other-mps-during-election [Accessed 6 September 2020].

Fraser, N., 2005. Reframing justice in a globalizing world. *New Left Review*, 36(77), pp. 1–19. DOI: 10.1590/S0102-64452009000200001.

Gadd, D., Farrall, S., Lombard, N. and Dallimore, D., 2002. *Domestic Abuse against Men in Scotland*. Edinburgh: Scottish Executive.

Gill, A. and Mason-Bish, H., 2013. Addressing violence against women as a form of hate crime. *Feminist Review*, 105(1), pp. 1–20. DOI: 10.1057/fr.2013.17.

Grewal, K., 2010. Rape in conflict, rape in peace: questioning the revolutionary potential of international criminal justice for women's human rights. *Australian Feminist Law Journal*, 33(1), pp. 57–79. DOI: 10.1080/13200968.2010.10854444.

Harpin, L., 2018. Misogyny and antisemitism are 'attempt to silence' people trying to bring about change, conference hears. *The Jewish Chronicle* [online]. 26 November 2018. Available at: https://www.thejc.com/news/uk/misogyny-and-antisemitism-are-attempt-to-silence-people-trying-to-bring-out-people-1.473095 [Accessed 6 September 2020].

Henry, N., 2014. The fixation on wartime rape: feminist critique and international criminal law. *Social and Legal Studies*, 23(1), pp. 93–111. DOI: 10.1177/0964663913499061.

Henry, N. and Powell, A., 2018. Technology-facilitated sexual violence: a literature review of empirical research. *Trauma, Violence and Abuse*, 19(2), pp. 195–208. DOI: 10.1177/1524838016650189.

hooks, b., 1981. *Ain't I a Woman: Black Women and Feminism*. Boston, MA: South End Press.

HRC, 2020. Violence against the transgender and gender non-conforming community in 2020 [online]. Available at: https://www.hrc.org/resources/violence-against-the-trans-and-gender-non-conforming-community-in-2020 [Accessed 6 September 2020].

Jenness, V. and Grattet, R., 2001. *Making Hate a Crime: From Social Movement to Law Enforcement*. New York: Russell Sage Foundation.

Kavanagh, A., 2019. Just ask don't grab campaign [online]. Available at: https://caneadventures.blog/just-ask-dont-grab-campaign/ [Accessed 6 September 2020].

Kelly, L., 1988. *Surviving Sexual Violence*. Minneapolis: University of Minnesota Press.

Kelly, L. and Radford, J., 1990. 'Nothing really happened': the invalidation of women's experiences of sexual violence. *Critical Social Policy*, 10(30), pp. 39–53. DOI: 10.1177/026101839001003003.

Kentish, B., 2019. 'The abuse made me physically ill': Luciana Berger reveals toll of fighting antisemitism while Labour MPs refused to stand by her. *The Independent* [online]. 9 November 2019. Available at: https://www.independent.co.uk/news/uk/politics/luciana-berger-labour-antisemitism-jeremy-corbyn-election-latest-liberal-democrats-finchley-a9196696.html [Accessed 6 September 2020].

Lewis, R., Rowe, M. and Wiper, C., 2018. Misogyny online: extending the boundaries of hate crime. *Journal of Gender-Based Violence*, 2(3), pp. 519–536. DOI: 10.1332/239868018X15375304472635.

Long, J. et al., 2018. *Annual Report on UK Femicides 2018*. London: Femicide Census.

Low, H., 2019. Spikes – and other ways disabled people combat unwanted touching [online]. Available at: https://www.bbc.co.uk/news/disability-49584591 [Accessed 6 September 2020].

MacKinnon, C., 1991. Reflections on sex equality under law. *Yale Law Journal*, 100(5), pp. 1281–1328. DOI: 10.2307/796693.

Mason-Bish, H., 2012. Conceptual issues in the construction of disability hate crime. In: Roulstone, A. and Mason-Bish, H. eds. *Disability, Hate Crime and Violence.* London: Routledge, 2012, pp. 11–24.

Mason-Bish, H. and Zempi, I., 2018. Misogyny, racism, and Islamophobia: street harassment at the intersections. *Feminist Criminology*, 14(5), pp. 540–559. DOI: 10.1177/1557085118772088.

Mays, J., 2006. Feminist disability theory: domestic violence against women with a disability. *Disability and Society*, 21(2), pp. 147–158. DOI: 10.1080/09687590500498077.

McGlynn, C., Rackley, E. and Houghton, R., 2017. Beyond 'revenge porn': The continuum of image-based sexual abuse. *Feminist Legal Studies*, 25(1), pp. 25–46. DOI: 10.1007/s10691-017-9343-2.

McPhail, B., 2002. Gender-bias hate crimes: a review. *Trauma, Violence and Abuse*, 3(2), pp. 125–133. DOI: 10.1177/15248380020032003.

Moran, L., 2001. Affairs of the heart: hate crime and the politics of crime control. *Law and Critique*, 12(3), pp. 331–344. DOI: 10.1023/A:1013758417185.

Moran, L. and Sharpe, A.N., 2004. Violence, identity and policing: the case of violence against transgender people. *Criminal Justice*, 4(4), pp. 395–417. DOI: 10.1177/1466802504048656.

Morris, J., 1996. *Encounters with Strangers: Feminism and Disability.* London: The Women's Press.

N8, 2019. Policing vulnerability: learning from the sex work liaison officer role in West Yorkshire Police [online]. Available at: https://n8prp.org.uk/policing-vulnerability-learning-from-sex-work-liaison-officer-role-in-west-yorkshire-police/ [Accessed 6 September 2020].

Nixon, J., 2009. Domestic violence and women with disabilities: locating the issue on the periphery of social movements. *Disability and Society*, 24(1), pp. 77–89. DOI: 10.1080/09687590802535709.

ONS, 2018. Sexual offences in England and Wales: year ending March 2017 [online]. Available at: https://www.ons.gov.uk/peoplepopulationandcommunity/crimeandjustice/articles/sexualoffencesinenglandandwales/yearendingmarch2017 [Accessed 6 September 2020].

Pain, R., 2014. Everyday terrorism. *Progress in Human Geography*, 38(4), pp. 531–550. DOI: 10.1177/0309132513512231.

Palmer, L., 2020. Diane Abbott, misogynoir and the politics of Black British feminism's anticolonial imperatives: 'in Britain too, it's as if we don't exist'. *The Sociological Review*, 63(8), pp. 508–523. DOI: 10.1177/0038026119892404.

Perry, B. and Alvi, S., 2011. 'We are all vulnerable': the in terrorem effects of hate crimes. *International Review of Victimology*, 18(1), pp. 57–71. DOI: 10.1177/0269758011422475.

Phipps, A., Ringrose, J., Renold, E. and Jackson, C., 2017. Rape culture, lad culture and everyday sexism: Researching, conceptualizing and politicizing new mediations of gender and sexual violence. *Journal of Gender Studies,* 27(1), pp. 1–8. DOI: 10.1080/09589236.2016.1266792.

Poland, B., 2016. *Haters: Harassment, Abuse, and Violence Online.* Lincoln: University of Nebraska Press.

Remembering Srebrenica, 2017. Gender and genocide: remembering Srebrenicas's women's delegation [online]. Available at: https://www.srebrenica.org.uk/news/gender-and-genocide-remembering-srebrenicas-womens-delegation/ [Accessed 6 September 2020].

Roulestone, A. and Sadique, K., 2012. Vulnerable to misinterpretation: disabled people, 'vulnerability' and the fight for legal recognition. In: Roulestone, A. and Mason-Bish, H. eds. *Disability, Hate Crime and Violence*. London: Routledge, 2012, pp. 25–39.

Russell, D., 1982. *Rape in Marriage*. New York: Macmillan.

Russo, A., 2018. *Feminist Accountability: Disrupting Violence and Transforming Power*. 1st ed. New York: New York University Press.

Sanday, P. R., 1996. Rape-prone versus rape-free campus cultures. *Violence against Women*, 2(2), pp. 191–208. DOI: 10.1177/1077801296002002006.

Shah, S., Tsitsou, L. and Woodin, S., 2016. Hidden voices: disabled women's experiences of violence and support over the life course. *Violence against Women*, 22(10), pp. 1189–1210. DOI: 10.1177/1077801215622577.

Sheffield, C., 1992. Hate violence. In: Rothenberg, P., ed. *Race, Class and Gender in the United States*. New York: St Martin's, pp. 432–441.

Sherry, M., 2016. *Disability Hate Crimes: Does Anyone Really Hate Disabled People?* London: Routledge.

Silvestri, M. and Crowther-Dowey, C., 2016. *Gender and Crime*. 2nd Ed. London: Sage.

Simplican, S.C., 2017. Feminist disability studies as methodology: life-writing and the abled/disabled binary. *Feminist Review*, 115(1), pp. 46–60. DOI: 10.1057/s41305-017-0039-x.

Sloan, J., 2017. Sex doesn't matter? The problematic status of sex, misogyny, and hate. *Journal of Language and Discrimination*, 1(1), pp. 61–82. DOI: 10.1558/jld.33114.

Smart, C., 1976. *Women, Crime and Criminology: A Feminist Critique*. Boston, MA: Routledge and Kegan Paul.

Stanko, E., 1992. The case of fearful women: gender, personal safety and the fear of crime. *Women and Criminal Justice*, 4(1), pp. 117–135. DOI: 10.1300/J012v04n01_06.

Stanko, E., 1995. Women, crime and fear. *The ANNALS of the American Academy of Political and Social Science*, 539(1), pp. 46–58. DOI: 10.1177/0002716295539001004.

Stanko, E., 2006. Theorising about violence: observations from the Economic and Social Research Council's Violence Research Program. *Violence against Women*, 12(6), pp. 543–555. DOI: 10.1177/1077801206289137.

Stanko, E., 2007. From academia to policy making: changing police responses to violence against women. *Theoretical Criminology*, 11(2), pp. 209–219. DOI: 10.1177/1362480607075848.

Stavri, Z., 2016. I have revised my opinion of Wikileaks: it's trash [online]. Available at: https://anotherangrywoman.com/2016/07/ [Accessed 6 September 2020].

Thiara, R., Hague, G. and Mullender, A., 2011. Losing out on both counts: disabled women and domestic violence. *Disability and Society*, 26(6), pp. 757–771. DOI: 10.1080/09687599.2011.602867.

Tjaden, P. and Thoennes, N., 1998. *Prevalence, Incidence, and Consequences of Violence Against Women: Findings from the National Violence Against Women Survey*. Washington, DC: National Institute of Justice and Centers for Disease Control and Prevention Research in Brief.

UN Women, 2013. *Violence against Women Prevalence Data: Surveys by Country*, s. l. UN Women.

Vera-Gray, F., 2018. *The Right Amount of Panic: How Women Trade Freedom for Safety*. Bristol: Policy Press.

Walby, S., 1989. Theorising patriarchy. *Sociology*, 23(2), pp. 213–234. DOI: 10.1177/0038038589023002004.

Walters, M., Wiedlitzke, S., Owusu-Bempah, A. and Goodall, K., 2017. *Hate Crime and the Legal Process: Options for Law Reform*. Sussex: University of Sussex.

Westbrook, L., 2008. Vulnerable subjecthood: The risks and benefits of the struggle for hate crime legislation. *Berkeley Journal of Sociology*, 52, pp. 3–23.

Williams, M., 2006. *Virtually Criminal: Crime, Deviance and Regulation Online*. London: Routledge.

Young, I., 1990. *Justice and the Politics of Difference*. Princeton, NJ: Princeton University Press.

2 Extending the concept, or extending the characteristics? Misogyny or gender?

Kim McGuire

To ensure that 'women' as a category would be covered by any new legislation, 'gender' would suffice, and would also cover prejudice towards males. However, this chapter will discuss fears by some groups that utilising 'gender' would downplay in-built prejudice towards women as a factor in violence against females. Arguably, proving a bias motivation, or a demonstration of 'hostility' could prove problematic – potentially requiring a 'pattern of behaviour' similar to gender legislation in the US. Current UK reporting shows 90% of domestic violence victims are female, although this may underestimate actual figures (SafeLives 2020). Proving domestic violence as a female-gendered bias issue would require evidence of hostility towards females (in general), or the violence being motivated by this. However, domestic or 'partner violence', is often perceived as a dispute between two persons. Currently gay, lesbian and transgender persons are covered by existing UK 'hate crime' categories: including gender would potentially provide a more nuanced understanding of certain types of violence, and would include both males and females. However, proving a potential gender bias may be difficult.

Introduction

Since March 2019 the Law Commission has been reviewing hate crime legislation, and in particular whether a sufficient range of characteristics are protected by the hate crime legislation. The review is considering, amongst other issues, whether the criminal law responds adequately to hostility based on sex or gender characteristics (with misogyny being a particular concern). It will also consider the current range of specific offences and aggravating factors in sentencing, and the most appropriate models to ensure that the criminal law provides consistent and effective protection from conduct motivated by hatred of protected groups or characteristics. The report is expected in 2021 (Law Commission n.d.).

This chapter will engage with several crucial issues regarding hate crime: its misconception, the arguments for potential extension to include misogyny, or alternatively gender, and the difficulty of proving bias. 'Hate

Crime' is a term overused by many groups, not least politicians, the public, the police, victims and victim advocates. The term hate crime does not exist in the legislation. 'Hate' itself is not a factor in law. The various hate crime provisions, specifically including the Crime and Disorder Act 1998 and the Criminal Justice Act 2003, do not require proof that the accused 'hates' the recipient; rather that they are motivated by hostility or demonstrate hostility *towards certain protected characteristics.* Currently the UK identifies the following such characteristics, for prosecution as: race, religion, sexual orientation or transgender identity and disability. This chapter is considering the above legislation requirements. Whilst police forces can extend the protected characteristics for the purposes of recording, these cannot legal be prosecuted within the legislation as it exists at the time of writing this chapter. Moreover, this chapter does not engage with legislation regarding online abuse, or the 'stirring up' offences.

Perceptions from not just the lay public, but also politicians (as discussed below), reveal misunderstanding regarding the 'hate element', what constitutes a 'hate crime', and the criteria for successful prosecution. Hate is not an element in the legislation, which depends upon 'hostility'. Currently, successful prosecution for a 'hate crime', as per the Crime and Disorder Act 1998 s28, or the Criminal Justice Act s146, depends upon proving firstly a criminal act, and that at the time of committing the offence, or immediately before or after doing so, the offender:

a   demonstrates towards the victim of the offence hostility based on the victim's membership (or presumed membership) of a [protected group]; or
b   the offence is motivated (wholly or partly) by hostility towards members of a [protected group] based on their membership of that group.

The ability to convict based upon *demonstration of hostility* to a protected characteristic is crucial. This section of the legislation was included because prosecution was found to be problematic in the United States, where proof rests upon proving motivation. This is one reason, discussed below, why 'misogyny' will prove difficult to prosecute, and why the author prefers gender as a protected characteristic. This chapter argues that however offensive beliefs may be, and these include misogyny, without any accompanying act the perpetrator cannot be convicted. In common with Jenness and Grattet (2001) it also argues that 'gender' as a protected characteristic, would be an acceptable route for prosecution, based upon an actual crime. However, drawing upon international comparisons, this chapter also proposes that new and specific legislation may be needed to address certain offences, particularly those predominantly experienced by women and girls for example, sexual harassment. Finally, it will briefly discuss the difficulty of perceiving gender bias, and hence the potential limitations of legislation, and the need for accompanying awareness raising initiatives.

Misogyny

Recent discussions regarding extensions to existing hate crime legislation have conflated misogyny with hate crime. On 9 March 2020, for example, Wera Hobhouse, the MP for Bath in south-west England, presented her Hate Crime (Misogyny) Bill (2020) addressing misogyny – which is defined therein as 'the dislike of, contempt for, or ingrained prejudice against women'. The Bill is intended to make motivation by misogyny an aggravating factor in criminal sentencing; to require police forces to record hate crimes motivated by misogyny; and for connected purposes.

In January 2019 a coalition of campaign groups and MPs, including MPs Jo Swinson, Stella Creasy and Peter Bottomley, the former home secretary Jacqui Smith, the Nottinghamshire Police and Crime Commissioner, Paddy Tipping, Citizens UK, Women's Aid and the Fawcett Society, called on the Metropolitan Police Commissioner, Cressida Dick, to make misogyny a hate crime. Their demands, however, conflated gender[1] and misogyny, stating that:

> gender hate incidents were at least as common as any hate crime recorded by police. There were 67,000 such incidents last year, with 57,000 of them targeted at women, according to figures from the Crime Survey of England and Wales. People aged between 16 and 44 were most commonly targeted.
>
> (Topping 2019)

The Guardian quoted the letter as saying:

> Women are targeted with harassment on the street and online on an everyday basis...Accepting this as normal creates an environment in which one in five women have experienced sexual assault, and each week two women are murdered by a partner or ex-partner.
>
> (Topping 2019)

Since 2016, Nottinghamshire police have introduced misogyny hate crime recording, although it cannot be prosecuted as such. An online survey of Nottinghamshire residents found that 87% supported the move (Topping 2019). Many people do not consider the legality of such initiatives and are thus disappointed when prosecution does not follow. A Misogyny Hate Crime Review by Mullany and Trickett (2018), noted that:

> Much of this behaviour on this spectrum is criminal behaviour, there's no doubt about that. People could have gone to the police about it before. But because of the culture we have it's just acceptable to intimidate women on the street, to go up to a woman and touch her backside, or to comment on her body and put her in fear of an assault.
>
> (BBC News, 2018)

More recently, work by Loretta Trickett and Louise Mullany continues to highlight misogyny or gender bias (see Chapter 14 of this book).

There have been fears by some groups that utilising 'gender' rather than misogyny would downplay the in-built prejudice argued to be a factor in violence against women. In 2018, for example, the Fawcett Society's Westminster Hall Debate briefing paper stated that: 'It is important that the hate crime in question is misogyny hate crime, not gender hate crime, recognising the direction of the power imbalance within society and the reality of the endemic scale of violence against women and girls' (Fawcett Society 2018). However, in 2019 the language changed, with their website stating: 'New Fawcett data reveals gender is the most common cause of hate crime for women' (Fawcett Society 2019).

Misogyny would require a reconceptualisation of the current 'hate crime' concept

Many believe that 'misogyny' *per se* could constitute a hate crime, or would initially have preferred this concept, but this would be a significant change to the current operation of hate crime legislation. This is because for current 'hate crimes' a demonstration of hostility *towards a protected characteristic* is an aggravating feature of an actual crime, it is not a crime in itself. For prosecution, there is no need to prove motivation, since demonstrating hostility suffices. In practice proving motivation is more difficult than demonstrating hostility. Furthermore, as noted above, 'hatred' is not a requirement of 'hate crime' legislation. Whilst misogyny is specifically female focussed, gender includes all genders, and those with no gender. However, it is important to note that the most prevalent offences against women are domestic violence and sexual harassment, discussed further below. Not all these offences will include a gender bias, nor a 'misogynist' mindset, nor be a demonstration of these, but many may. This chapter will argue that to ensure that offences against women could be recognised as including bias, 'gender' as a protected characteristic would suffice, and would also cover prejudice towards men, the non-binary, and the gender free.

Whilst not denying that misogyny exists, the author argues that to include misogyny as a hate crime characteristic would be to completely reconceptualise the current concept of 'hate crime'. This is because it would criminalise the perpetrator's attitude towards a group, rather than seeing this attitude as an aggravating factor in base crimes committed against a particular protected characteristic. Indeed, misogyny is defined in the Oxford English Dictionary (2021b),[2] – and in the Hate Crime (Misogyny) Bill 2020 as: 'dislike of, contempt for, or ingrained prejudice against women'. Hence, this refers to an internal belief, attitude or position.

As noted above, current 'hate crime' legislation requires there to be a designated 'protected characteristic' associated with a 'base crime' to be committed against that group, being either motivated by hostility, or demonstrating hostility, to that identity. Hence misogyny does not fit within current conceptions of a hate crime: it may be a motivation of the perpetrator, but it is not a protected characteristic of the victim. However, if 'gender' became a protected characteristic, hostility towards this characteristic may suggest an internal misogynistic bias, and hence 'misogyny' would be addressed. This is analogous to combatting homophobia, not by making homophobia illegal, but by making sexual orientation a protected characteristic. However, as with all 'hate crimes' gender hostility would still need to be proven or demonstrated at the time a perpetrator commits a *base offence*.

Scotland

Whilst this chapter is focussing upon England and Wales it is useful to draw comparison with Scotland. This is because they have already completed their review of Hate Crime, considered extending the characteristics, and reported in 2018 (Scottish Government 2018). Whilst the legal jurisdiction varies, there are political, social and cultural links, and a shared issue with gender-based violence. In the Scottish report, Lord Bracadale chose gender over misogyny, not least because, as he commented, there are multiple interpretations of the term misogyny. Lord Bracadale thus urged '… caution in considering exactly what is meant in the particular context' (Scottish Government 2018, 4.12). He noted that:

> Engender define it as "systems or actions that deliberately subordinate women and reflect the actor's understanding that women are not their equals." Some use the terms 'misogyny' and 'sexism' as synonymous, while others would argue that misogyny is often more targeted or negative and used to assert male dominance over women.
> (Scottish Government 2018, 4.12)

Lord Bracadale noted how many conflate 'misogyny' with 'sexism' and, if used as a basis for a criminal offence, it could lead to prosecutions for 'unacceptable beliefs': for example, those that express contempt based on gender (Scottish Government 2018, 4.12). Literature and examples from history have long emphasised the inherent dangers in prohibiting thought or belief, or internal motivation, *per se*, not least under totalitarian regimes: Assessing 'genuine' conversion has proven problematic (Corner 2009).

As noted above, hatred or contempt are not currently crimes in the UK, provided one does not act upon these sentiments to the detriment of others. Lord Bracadale thus chose gender over misogyny, with recommendation nine adhering to current interpretations of 'hate crime', including those of England and Wales, i.e., that there was an offence, and that it was *motivated by hostility* based on (gender), *or demonstrated hostility* based on (gender) (Scottish Government 2018, 4.50). If legislation included misogyny, the argument could be made that any thought, any hint of sexism, could potentially be prosecuted. That the law could be so widened has arguably weakened legitimate calls for gender violence to be recognised, as individuals disseminate examples of overzealous policing of 'hate incidents' against currently protected characteristics. Indeed, much publicity has been given to ridiculing the prosecution of 'wolf whistling' in the street. Popular TV programmes, for example '*Loose Women*' debated 'Does a wolf whistle put a spring in your step?' (Loose Women 2019). The conclusion of the panel was that context was important. For some, this act is seen as an innocuous method of showing attraction, or is amusing, but to others it is demeaning, offensive, intimidating and potentially threatening, not least because no one knows what else the perpetrator may do, particularly if they felt their act had not had the desired effect (whatever that might be).

In UK legislation offensive thoughts are not eligible for prosecution. Even offensive acts must meet strict criteria. Indeed, no current UK legislation prosecutes thought without accompanying criminal acts, although the ability to report perception of hate incidents exists, as recording of 'misogyny' illustrates. However, perception of incidents does not automatically translate into 'offences'. As noted above, successful prosecution will depend upon proof of a criminal offence, with the accompanying motivation or demonstration of hostility to the protected characteristic.

Gender as a protected characteristic

Currently sexual orientation is an existing UK 'Hate Crime' characteristic, as is transgender. This chapter argues that although sexuality and transgender differ from gender identity, the causes for victimisation are often similar. Perpetrator behaviour may be motivated by or demonstrating hostility to the victim because they perceive the latter is in some way 'transgressing' imagined gender boundaries, or indeed, is representative of these. I argue that including gender as a protected characteristic years earlier could have avoided introducing separate groups for sexual orientation and transgender. This is not to dispute that these groups have specific issues, merely that much hostility may actually be based upon 'gender' rather than 'sexual orientation', for example. Moreover, current laws do not *explicitly* protect those who are non-binary, or gender free: including gender would cover a wide variety of gender identities, including those who feel themselves to be non-gendered, analogous to the fact that religious hate crime covers those who do not identify with a religion.

Including gender would potentially provide a more nuanced understanding of certain types of violence and would not be exclusive to violence against women. However, this chapter is not now arguing for the removal of sexual orientation or transgender, since these characteristics have been recognised as protected for some time.

Conceptualising gender

The Oxford English Dictionary (2021a) defines gender as:

> either of the two sexes (male and female), especially when considered with reference to social and cultural differences rather than biological ones. The term is also used more broadly to denote a range of identities that do not correspond to established ideas of male and female.

Whilst 'gender' and 'sex' are often confused, or used interchangeably, this chapter utilises the idea of gender as a social construct, referring to societal interpretations and perceptions of humans, based upon presumed biological sex (Kessler and McKenna 1978). This includes 'Femmephobia' – denigration and negation of assumed sex-attributed aspects (Hoskin 2019). Clearly these are binary definitions. As such, it could be argued femmephobia is representative of misogyny. However, this chapter argues that femmephobia can be more fully defined as a subset of sexism that suggests that femininity and things regarded as feminine are inherently inferior, bad, weak, stupid, non-preferable, valueless, disempowering: those deemed representative of 'masculinity' are seen as inherently good, strong. Hence, all persons exhibiting such 'feminine' qualities would be perceived in this way, not solely women and female-presenting people; this has implications for some gay men (Levitt et al. 2003). Given that femininity is only an associative, relational term, referring to things that are culturally associated with women, denigration of that which is feminine is to denigrate that which is female-ish (Levitt et al. 2003). As Hoskin (2019, p. 686) notes:

> Since the 1970s social science researchers have documented the cultural devaluation of femininity and its impact on experiences of discrimination among sexual and gender minorities. Yet, despite the continued and accumulating evidence demonstrating the role of anti-femininity (or femmephobia) in these experiences, little research has specifically examined femininity as an intersecting component of discrimination.

Whilst academic study has debated interpretations of 'gender' (Perry 2001; Chakraborti and Garland 2009), this chapter considers criminal acts that may be perpetrated because of perceptions of such characteristics and relating to women only. Regarding which acts specifically, it is useful to note that as early as 1993 the United Nations defined violence against women as:

> any act of gender-based violence that results in, or is likely to result in, physical, sexual or psychological harm or suffering to women, including threats of such acts, coercion or arbitrary deprivations of liberty, whether occurring in public or in private life.
>
> (United Nations 1993)

Specific arguments for inclusion/exclusion of gender as a characteristic

Arguments for perceiving all gender-related crimes as capable of being bias crimes are evinced in the idea that '... at least some degree of hatred, hostility, or disrespect for all women... (is present)' (Copeland and Wolfe 1991; Gaffney 1997). Whilst this may sound redolent of misogyny, it is argued here that potential misogyny motivated offences can be covered by gender as a protected characteristic, and thus within 'hate crime' legislation. Assuming a bias may exist is similar to calls for the recording of incidents involving disability to be initially so considered: often these are unrecognised as such, and assumed to be related to the 'vulnerability' of the victim (CPS 2020). However, as Jenness (2003) notes, such a position does not automatically assume that a bias is necessarily present. Hence, I argue that, as with all 'hate crimes', the requirement to demonstrate hostility towards the characteristic, at the time of the offence, or proof of bias motivation would still exist.

From a social change perspective, many academics, for example Bornstein (2006), see gender as 'central to the perpetration of homophobic and transphobic violence', although, as stated above, these have been recognised separately as bias categories. Some academics place particular emphasis upon patriarchy, with Bornstein (2006) defining such violence as a 'gender defender' concept, perpetuating 'the violence of male privilege and all its social extensions'. Many, for example Jenness and Grattet (2001), argue that bias crimes are 'message crimes' and the legislation is therefore equally a message – the social denigration of unacceptable attitudes and beliefs. Conversely, failing to recognise potential bias may be seen as acceptance of these prejudices. Hodge argues that gender bias can be defined 'if the motive for the crime is to reinforce supremacy and intimidate women, [or men], as a group' (Mason-Bish, 2010).

However, as my own research (McGuire 2013) argues, there is a perception that those excluded from bias legislation are given a lower priority in the eyes of policing, and the criminal justice system, than those included (Mason-Bish 2010). Including gender would therefore emphasise that victims were worthy of redress (McPhail 2002). Moreover, including gender could *emphasise* a positive obligation on the state to maintain the confidence of victims, to offer protection, and to properly investigate offences. This would be synonymous with recent human rights cases involving racism and ethnic hatred. Indeed, according to Karen Reid in The Practitioner's Guide to The European Convention on Human Rights (Reid 2020 as cited in UK Human Rights blog n.d.):

> there has been a recent emphasis on the condemnation of racism and ethnic hatred with corresponding positive obligations on the state to maintain the confidence of minorities in the ability of the authorities to

protect them from racist violence, and to investigate properly incidents of racial hatred.

(Menson v United Kingdom, App No 47916/99 – ECHR 2003)

Furthermore, as McCollum (2010) argues, 'without a full consideration and integration of power relations hate crimes can be depoliticised as motivated by irrational prejudice, rather than domination, exclusion and control'. Such recognition is crucial in intimate partner violence contexts as a plethora of academic texts, over decades, evidences (Heise 1998; Jewkes et al. 2015; McCarthy et al. 2018).

US comparison

Perhaps tellingly, no jurisdictions worldwide include misogyny as an offence. As noted, the UK does not include gender as a bias crime, and despite an increasing awareness of and concern about violence towards women worldwide, few jurisdictions do so include. Even fewer convictions have occurred. In 2018 32 US states, plus the District of Columbia, include gender, with a further 18 including 'gender identity' (Anti-Defamation League 2020). Jenness (2003, p. 73) described the 2002 televised press conference in which the US Justice Department announced they had invoked the federal hate crimes statute for the first time to charge (an) alleged murderer (Rice) with hate crime because 'Criminal acts of hate run counter to what is best in America, our belief in equality and freedom... we will pursue, prosecute, and punish those who attack law-abiding Americans out of hatred for who they are'. Jenness describes this as the 'first federal prosecution of hate crime based on gender' but also that 'evidence suggests the 'source of hatred' is twofold: sexuality and gender' (2003, p. 74). The victims were lesbians, and in the UK this may have been defined as a case of 'sexual orientation' bias crime, although the perpetrator evinced hatred for all women, and especially 'lesbians and gays'. Chakraborti and Garland (2015) have argued for hate crime to be attuned to the intersectional nature of identity; thus, the harassment of lesbian women may be caused by homophobia and misogyny.

However, I argue that gender would encompass homophobia and misogyny, because such crimes are often perpetrated due to the perpetrator's belief that the victim had in some way transgressed 'acceptable' socially constructed boundaries of male or female behaviour. Whilst multiple reasons may exist, prosecution is more likely to be successful if it focuses upon one identifiable protected characteristic to enable sentence enhancement. This has similarities with early feminist work on the primary locus of oppression – such work did not deny intersectionality but highlighted a dominant factor in oppression (Evans et al. 2005; Goodman et al 2009). This is not to dispute, as Schiek (2018) argues, there has been critique of anti-discrimination legislation that fails to appreciate intersectionality. Arguably, single focus is promoted to enable prosecution. In the US case above, multiple interpretations of motive were voiced. The defendant, Rice, told law enforcement officials that he intentionally selected women to assault "because they are more vulnerable than men", that he "hates gays", and that the victims in this case "deserved to die because they were lesbian whores" (as cited in Jenness 2003, p. 74). The defendant made '… numerous physical and verbal assaults upon randomly selected women, including acts of road rage, physical assaults, demeaning sexual comments, and threats of injury or death…'. (Jenness 2003, p. 74). Not all the latter fit neatly within interpretations of 'vulnerability', or sexual orientation.

Whilst intersectionality may exist, *gender bias* can be missed if legislation does not include this, as is evident in the UK case of Levi Bellfield. According to UK police and media reports Bellfield:

> … spoke of 'hatred' and 'intense loathing' of women; a former girlfriend described how he had confessed that he would wait in alleyways wanting to: "hurt, kill, stab or rape women" (Long 2010). Bellfield had a reputation for sexually harassing under-age girls, pestering them from a van with blacked-out windows in which he kept a mattress, blankets and a baseball bat.

As Long (2010) argues "if Bellfield's hate-motivated violence had been directed at victims on the basis of their perceived race, religion or belief, sexual orientation, disability or transgender identity, his crimes would clearly have been recognised as hate crimes". Notably, Long (2010) is focusing upon the violent act, the characteristics of the victim, the motivation of the perpetrator, within the context of existing 'hate crime' legislation.

The fact remains, however, that perceptions of hate crime, whether by the victim or another, are areas of current confusion, partly due to a lack of awareness and also confusion over the meaning, the legal definitions, the protected characteristics. Extending protected characteristics to include gender will not automatically resolve these issues, without accompanying education, unfortunately beyond the remit of this chapter.

Examples of violence against women: should gender bias be considered?

In 2017, the Crown Prosecution Service published a Violence Against Women and Girls (VAWG) Strategy for 2017–2020 providing a framework outlining an overarching framework to address crimes:

> …that have been identified as being committed primarily but not exclusively by men against women. These crimes include domestic abuse, rape, sexual offences, stalking, harassment, so-called 'honour-based' violence including forced marriage, female genital mutilation, child abuse, human trafficking focusing on sexual exploitation, prostitution, pornography and obscenity.
>
> (CPS 2017)

The Crown Prosecution Service recognises VAWG as a form of discrimination against women and a fundamental issue of human rights arising from gender inequality (CPS 2017). The framework is in line with the CPS's Public Sector Equality Duty (EHRC 2020) and draws upon the UK's ratification of relevant United Nations Conventions on Violence Against Women (UN Women n.d.), and the Government's strategy on ending VAWG 2016–2020 (Home Office 2019). Article 40 of the Istanbul Convention – which the UK Government signed in 2012 and is committed to ratifying (although as of 2020 it has not) sets out obligations on sexual harassment:

> Parties [to the Convention] shall take the necessary legislative or other measures to ensure that any form of unwanted verbal, non-verbal or physical conduct of a sexual nature with the purpose or effect of violating the dignity of a person, in particular when creating an intimidating, hostile, degrading, humiliating or offensive environment, is subject to criminal or other legal sanction.
>
> (Council of Europe 2011)

Many, including the White Ribbon Organisation (2020), argue that ratification 'would commit the UK government to following a strong set of minimum standards to protect and support women, prosecute perpetrators and prevent violence against women'.

Below the chapter will consider domestic violence and sexual harassment, and will argue that a gender bias potential should be considered in the former, via gender as a protected characteristic. However, it will argue that specific legislation may be required for sexual harassment cases, as created by other jurisdictions. Whilst not all domestic abuse will be gendered, clearly some will. Indeed, domestic abuse is a prevalent form of abuse for women, often accompanied by verbal demonstrations of hostility based upon gender. The Office for National Statistics (ONS 2019) states that in the year ending March 2019, 7.5% women and 3.8% men declared themselves victims of domestic violence. 75% of domestic related crimes recorded by the police to March 2019 were female, and 74% of domestic homicides were female in the two years to March 2018 (ONS 2019). Estimates from the Crime Survey for England and Wales could not be obtained for the year ended June 2020 due to the Covid 19 lockdown and collection concerns about confidentiality and respondent safeguarding, since information was taken via the telephone. However, there was a 9% increase overall in domestic abuse reported to the police (774,491 offences, excluding Greater Manchester police) – some of this reflects improved recording, although there was a rise in demand for domestic abuse-related services, for example by Refuge (ONS 2020).

Numerically, the statistics show that in the year ending March 2018, an estimated 2.0 million adults aged 16–59 years experienced domestic abuse in the last year (1.3 million women, 695,000 men) (ONS 2018). The police recorded 599,549 domestic abuse-related crimes in the year ending March

2018 (ONS 2018). This was an increase of 23% recorded from the previous year, although less than self-reported incidents. Many do not report to the police, and many reports are not recorded by the police: it is argued here that recognition of gender bias may serve to raise awareness of the unacceptability of such practices – both the abuse, and its under-recognition (ONS 2018). The police made 225,714 arrests for domestic abuse-related offences (in the 39 police forces that could supply adequate data). This equates to 38 arrests per 100 domestic abuse-related crimes recorded (ONS 2018). The percentage of convictions secured for domestic abuse-related prosecutions is at its highest level since the year ending March 2010. In the year ending March 2018, 76% of prosecutions resulted in a conviction (ONS 2018). However, reported figures may well underestimate actual offences, the widely accepted 'dark figure of crime' (Biderman et al. 1967).

Violence against women is a major social problem, but often 'normalised' within domestic relationships, or media representations. However, including domestic violence within hate crime is contentious amongst hate crime scholars and those working or researching in the field of gender-based violence, for the points discussed below.

Since such violence is widespread there have been fears that inclusion of gender would swamp hate crime statistics. Moreover, that including gender would detract from, and diminish other bias categories (McPhail 2003). This is, however, in complete contrast to rights-based arguments, for example those of the EU, with the emphases on fundamental rights, the promotion of human dignity, freedom and human rights. Others argue that inclusion into the realm of hate crime might distract from violence against women as a specific area of criminality needing extra resources and policing training. Proving gendered bias within domestic violence would require evidence of demonstrating hostility towards women (in general), or the violence being motivated by this. However, domestic or 'partner violence', has historically often been perceived as a dispute between two persons, and thus proof of repeated behaviour of an offender, over several relationships may be required for conviction of a gender bias crime, as has been the case in the US. These issues will be discussed further below.

Consideration of 'gender bias' in domestic abuse cases

Whilst this chapter argues for gender to be the protected characteristic, it is focussing specifically upon women and girls, due to the larger numbers reported, recorded, prosecuted and in historical context. However, as noted above, this gender focus is also driven by rejection of 'misogyny' within legislation – seen as a concentration on the internal belief of the perpetrator, and by recognition that gender has wider considerations. The latest figures from the Crime Survey for England and Wales, published October 2020, and covering to June 2020 (ONS 2020), show the continued prevalence of abuse against women including domestic abuse.

In July 2020 the first reading in the House of Lords of the Domestic Abuse Bill (2019–2021) took place. As noted above, in 2019 Stella Creasy MP had called for Amendment 84, requiring recording of misogyny in domestic abuse cases. However, the Bill read in 2020 did not specifically refer to gender, sex or misogyny, nor any requirement to so record. I argue that rather than include within the Bill, making gender a protected characteristic would enable this potential bias element to be considered within all offences, including domestic violence.

With no specific mention of gendered violence, the Domestic Abuse Bill (2019–2021) as a standalone piece of legislation fails to highlight such offences as potentially containing a 'hate crime' element. However, utilising 'hate crime' legislation would be in keeping with the piecemeal approach to protecting women, but also an extension of this, and a useful 'supplement' to a Domestic Abuse Bill. If successful, the criminal act would be the domestic abuse, the aggravating factor would be the demonstration of hostility, or motivation, based upon the protected characteristic of gender. This could equally apply to same-sex relationships, as these are not immune to violence, nor to hostility towards the gender identity of the victim (Ristock 2002). Historically, the protection of women has tended to come via anti-discriminatory legislation, or various pieces of protective measures and legislation, not 'hate crime'.[3] In 2009, the UK Government launched 'Together we can End Violence Against Women and Girls: a strategy'. The aims of this were to enable women to 'live their lives free from harassment or violence' and 'to live a life without fear of violence and to live in a culture where violence against women is unacceptable' (Home Office 2009).

Legal redress for women did not include tackling gender-based offences, or indeed, misogyny, by making gender a protected bias characteristic, but by several distinct pieces of legislation, as mentioned above. How this is perceived varies, with many arguing that this approach is preferable to creating a 'hate crime' characteristic: it is seen as wider ranging in dealing with the particularities of gender crimes, and therefore the victimisation against women receives greater quality of service by such means (Mason-Bish 2011). Indeed, inclusion of gender as a bias crime in the US was resisted by the Anti-Defamation League who argued that 'although gender-related crime represents a serious threat to society… it is a distinct type of victimisation… (and should not be addressed as a bias crime)' (Chen 1997). Others argue that gender fits the hate crime paradigm because women are indiscriminately selected due to gender, the assault is often unprovoked, there is no other motive and gender-based epithets often accompany the act (McPhail 2002).

However, as Mason-Bish argues, historically the UK has fixated upon domestic violence, underplaying the other forms of violence against women (Kelly and Lovett 2005; Mason-Bish 2011). Moreover, as Goodey (2005) notes, victims of domestic violence include both men and women, as a focus upon 'gender' would acknowledge. Crucially, a distinction must be made between 'an *approach* that is sensitive to complex gendered dynamics and

Misogyny or gender? 53

a *definition* of domestic abuse that focuses on only one particular gendered dynamic' (Dempsey 2011, p. 15). The latter, may, for example, focus only upon an assumption of male-on-female violence which would, as Dempsey argues, make 'abuse in same-sex relationships ... marginalised at best and more often simply invisible' (Dempsey 2011, p. 390).

The Domestic Abuse Bill (2019–2021) aims to create a statutory definition of domestic abuse, based on the existing cross-party definition:

1 This section defines 'domestic abuse' for the purposes of this Act.
2 Behaviour of a person ('A') towards another person ('B') is 'domestic abuse' if –

   a A and B are each aged 16 or over and are personally connected to each other, and
   b the behaviour is abusive.

3 Behaviour is 'abusive' if it consists of any of the following –

   a physical or sexual abuse;
   b violent or threatening behaviour;
   c controlling or coercive behaviour;
   d economic abuse (see subsection (4));
   e psychological, emotional or other abuse;

and it does not matter whether the behaviour consists of a single incident or a course of conduct.

I would argue that a focus upon 'gender' bias *per se*, rather than related specifically to domestic violence (although it would include such violence) would illuminate bias, and contribute to the tackling of this abuse. It is recognised, as discussed above, for example, that 'Femmephobia' exists within lesbian, gay, bisexual and transgender communities (Levitt et al. 2003). Moreover, domestic violence is often portrayed by the police and criminal justice services as 'a problem of individual men and their relationships... (rendering) the gendered aspect invisible and (obscuring) any focus on wider issues of misogyny' (Stanko 2001). Arguably the very use of the term 'domestic' suggests little link with wider *public order* issues – a driving force for previous bias legislation as discussed above. However, as long ago as the 1990s, academics were arguing for a reinterpretation of domestic abuse as a shared concern '...wrongs not just against their individual victims, but against all of us insofar as we identify with those victims as our fellow citizens – they are wrongs in which we collectively share, and which we make 'ours'" (Marshall and Duff 1998). Such comments support the argument for inclusion within 'hate crime legislation' – acknowledging a public interest in such protection.

From a numerical standpoint, as Hodge (2011) argues, not being a stigmatised *minority* group hinders acceptance into the 'bias category'. However, her study of New Jersey also revealed the resistance to include rape, sexual assault and domestic violence as bias crimes, partly due to perceived differences in the offences, but also the difficulty of *proof* (Hodge 2011). Clearly gender hate crime covers a wide range of offences, not solely domestic abuse. Making gender a protected characteristic would not require a reinterpretation of all domestic abuse cases as containing a gender bias element, but it might lead to a recognition of this element of many such cases. Whilst 'proving gender animus' in domestic abuse cases may be problematic, this is not sufficient reason for exclusion, although existing attempts have their own difficulties. In Massachusetts, for example, 'the Attorney General instituted a policy whereby gender-based hate crime requires at least two previous restraining orders issued to protect two different domestic partners' (Jenness 2003).

Sexual harassment

It is important to note other common experiences of violence against women. A recent House of Commons report on sexual harassment highlighted that '... the prevalence and impact of sexual harassment is not recognised or understood in the same way by many men' (House of Commons 2017, p. 5). Moreover, that law and policy send conflicting messages on the issue (House of Commons 2017). A survey published by Ipsos Mori on International Women's Day in March 2018 showed '...that respondents in Britain thought that, from more than 20 options, sexual harassment and sexual violence were respectively the second and fourth most important issues facing women and girls in Britain today' (Mori 2018).

There is no specific criminal offence of sexual harassment in the UK, unlike in some other countries, for example Portugal, New Zealand and France. Portugal was the first signatory to the Istanbul Convention, and street harassment and catcalling are already illegal in Portugal (Portuguese Penal Code, Article 170):

> Whoever harasses another person, practising before her acts exhibitionist in character, formulating proposals of a sexual tenor or embarrassing her with contact of a sexual nature, is punished with a penalty of imprisonment of a year, or a penalty fine of up to 120 euros if a more serious penalty is not applicable under any other legal provision.

Section 4 of New Zealand's Summary Offences Act 1981 states that anyone who 'uses any threatening or insulting words and is reckless whether any person is alarmed or insulted by those words; or addresses any indecent or obscene words to any person' can be fined up to $1,000. France introduced a 'sexist outrage' law allowing for on-the-spot fines of between €90 and €750 for behaviour such as obscene gestures and noises, degrading comments or following someone insistently in the street (Tidley 2019). The Law amends the Penal code, and covers, amongst other things, sexist insults, degrading or humiliating comments or hostile and offensive 'sexual or sexist' behaviour towards a person in public areas, schools or workplaces. Its introduction came weeks after the widely publicised sexual harassment and physical violence against Marie Laguerre in Paris in 2018. The legislation had been mooted for some time, and was passed in a climate of change, and amidst widespread protest against such behaviour, not least by the #MeToo movement and its French equivalent #BalanceTonPorc ('rat on your pig'). Ms Schiappa, France's gender equality minister, had argued for a French bill in 2017, saying that it was 'completely necessary because at the moment street harassment is not defined in the law…We can't currently make a complaint' (BBC News 2017).

The need for awareness raising

Whether the UK would benefit from such specific sexual harassment legislation is debatable, not least because it already has a plethora of legislation that could potentially be used, as noted above. These do not, however, specifically address gendered violence. I therefore argue that introducing such legislation could be an extra measure alongside making gender a hate crime characteristic, highlighting the gendered nature of much female victimisation. Moreover, despite existing legislation, albeit not specifically gendered, few seem aware, or willing to report such behaviour in the UK, or elsewhere (McGuire 2013).

Indeed, in Portugal:

> the necessity for a measure to combat verbal abuse toward women was first proposed by the non-profit organisation UMAR (Union of Women for Alternatives and Answers), which received funding in 2010 from the Dutch government to travel around the country and raise awareness of the issue.
>
> (Peláez 2016)

UMAR head, Maria Jose Magalhaes stated that:

> …most women had been verbally assaulted on the street and also that both men and women confused sexual assault with seduction or praise. They didn't know what assault was. There was an idea that it wasn't serious because sexism is so ingrained in our culture.
>
> (Peláez 2016)

As the discussion on the popular TV programme 'Loose Women' above, demonstrated, and academics such as Hilary McCollum (2010) have argued, victims do not necessarily recognise themselves as such. McCollum (2010) relates this to knowledge of the perpetrator in some cases, but I also relate this to perceptions of the act, partly due to cultural norms and expectations.

McCollum links under-recognition of 'hate crimes' to the use of the word 'hate' which she argues 'can feel too big a word, especially for crimes committed by people known to the victim' (McCollum 2010). The Ministry of Justice Report of 2014 similarly highlighted the difficulty police officers had in recognising disability bias crimes, including those by persons known to the victim, because of the evocative nature of the term 'hate' (Ministry of Justice 2014). I argue that social norms can make identification of bias difficult in some cases, not least the gendered. Hence awareness raising, not least by legislation, is necessary.

Historically and/or culturally, offences involving female victims have not been identified as demonstrating hostility or motivated by hostility, based upon gender. Indeed, religious and legal traditions often justify and legalise the right of men to control and chastise their intimate partner. Men's violence against women (domestic, sexual and in public) is still reinforced in many contexts and media representations, despite significant social and legal changes. Other academics have considered gender bias and awareness of this. Reiser, for example, considers the socio-cultural norms, socialisation, class and age differences as factors that may help to explain why both men and women may fail to acknowledge the potential of bias within the act committed (Reiser 2001; Dunbar 2006). Recent research by Promundo (2018) found '...that young men who sexually harass come from all income levels, all educational backgrounds and all ages, but that the strongest factor in the perpetration of sexual harassment was attitudes about what it means to be a man'. Hegemonic masculinity may be a useful concept here, premised upon the existence of a dominant form of masculinity, and one that emphasises strength, toughness, hereosexuality. Early criticism of the concept came from the gay liberation movement, which emphasised the oppression of men, as well as by men, linked to such gender stereotypes (Connell et al. 2005, p. 831).

McCollum (2010), focusing upon women, doubts that defining violence against women and girls as hate crime would help its victims access services and redress. Partly this is due to the difficulty of the term 'hate'. I argue that utilising 'misogyny' would further exacerbate any self-recognition as a victim, because it is associated with 'hatred of women' in the eyes of many. There is no doubt that there is a need to raise awareness if gender is included as a potential bias characteristic, not least because information widely disseminated to the public often includes 'gender' as though it were already a protected characteristic, drawing upon equality legislation.

Conclusion

The existence of protected characteristics, and the extension to include gender, may help to change socio-cultural norms by acknowledging the unacceptability of such bias, although the work of Conaghan and McGuire argues for the minor role of legal discourse in achieving societal change

(Conaghan 2009; McGuire 2013). Hence I would also argue for wider publicity and greater education on these issues, although beyond the remit of this chapter to discuss.

As a representative of the criminal justice service stated:

> … building a case based on evidence of hostility is not just about semantics. Parliament did not pass this law (Criminal Justice Act 2003) in some misguided bout of political correctness….The way that we prosecute sends a message. The messages we send have real consequences. The wrong message damages the confidence of… people. The wrong approach also undermines that fundamental principle of equality before the law that all prosecutors should be spending their working lives trying to uphold.
>
> (Respondent in McGuire 2013)

The hate crime legislation is argued by academics and legislators to contain a critical symbolic message, saying that '… this behaviour is deeply criminal and has to be punished severely' (Respondent in McGuire 2013). Moreover, by failing to recognise such crimes, the opportunity '… to condemn the prejudice and hostility of the offender is missed' (McGuire 2013). If sufficiently well promoted, legislation can send a particular message, and may encourage a change in society. Sentence enhancement is but one issue to consider, and may not be the most effective method of dealing with all such crimes. As noted, there may be a need for specific crimes for example of 'sexual harassment' in public, similar to France or Portugal. However, including gender as a protected characteristic for any crime would widen the protection and raise awareness more. It may encourage victims to report, and perpetrators to desist. Whilst the law does not necessarily promote a change in attitudes it would at least provide an avenue of redress. However, if a potential bias element is under-recognised, being lost in and to perception, so too will the potential to effect change.

Notes

1. Gender differs from misogyny, being defined by the Oxford English Dictionary (2021a) as:

    either of the two sexes (male and female), especially when considered with reference to social and cultural differences rather than biological ones. The term is also used more broadly to denote a range of identities that do not correspond to established ideas of male and female.

2. Definition from Oxford English Dictionary (2021b) – the origin is 'Mid-17th century from Greek misos 'hatred' + gunē 'woman'', extended in 2002 to include 'dislike of, contempt for, or ingrained prejudice against women'.
3. There are a range of different criminal offences. These include sexual assault and voyeurism under the Sexual Offences Act 2003, harassment and stalking under the Protection from Harassment Act 1997, and 'revenge porn', where the

distribution of a private sexual image of someone without their consent and with the intention of causing them distress is an offence under the Criminal Justice and Courts Act 2015. The Public Order Act 1986 is also relevant legislation if a victim felt harassment, alarm or distress as a consequence of sexual harassment in public.

References

Anti-Defamation League, 2020. Hate crime map [online]. Anti-Defamation League. Available at: https://www.adl.org/adl-hate-crime-map [Accessed 1 December 2020].

BBC News, 2017. France minister Schiappa plans anti-street harassment law [online]. 16 October. Available at: https://www.bbc.co.uk/news/world-europe-41637723 [Accessed 1 December 2020].

BBC News, 2018. Misogyny hate crime in Nottinghamshire gives 'shocking' results [online]. 9 July. Available at: https://www.bbc.co.uk/news/uk-england-nottinghamshire-44740362 [Accessed 1 December 2020].

Biderman, A.D. and Reiss, A.J. (1967) On exploring the 'dark figure' of crime. *The ANNALS of the American Academy of Political and Social Science*, 374(1), pp. 1–15. DOI: 10.1177/000271626737400102.

Bornstein, K., 2006. Gender terror, gender rage. In: Stryker, S. and Whittle, S., eds. *The Transgender Studies Reader*. London: Routledge, pp. 236–255.

Chakraborti, N. and Garland, J., 2009. *Hate Crime: Impact, Causes and Responses*. 1st ed. London: Sage.

Chakraborti, N. and Garland, J., 2015. *Hate Crime: Impact, Causes and Responses*. 2nd ed. London: Sage.

Chen, K., 1997. Including gender in bias crime statutes: feminist and evolutionary perspectives. *William and Mary Journal of Women and the Law*, 3(1), pp. 277–328. Available at: http://scholarship.law.wm.edu/wmjowl/vol3/iss1/13,278.

Conaghan, J., 2009. Intersectionality and the feminist project in law. In: Grabham, E., Cooper, D., Krishnadas, J. and Herman, D., eds. *Intersectionality and Beyond. Law Power and the Politics of Location*. London: Routledge, 2009, pp. 21–48.

Connell, R.W. and Messerschmidt, J.W., 2005. Hegemonic masculinity: rethinking the concept. *Gender and Society*, 19(6), pp. 829–859. DOI: 10.1177/0891243205278639.

Copeland, L. and Wolfe, L., 1991. *Violence against Women as Bias-Motivated Hate Crime: Defining the Issues*. New York: Centre for Women Policy Studies.

Corner, P., ed., 2009. *Popular Opinion in Totalitarian Regimes: Fascism, Nazism, Communism*. Oxford: Oxford University Press.

Council of Europe, 2011. Council of Europe Convention on preventing and combating violence against women and domestic violence [online]. Available at: https://www.coe.int/en/web/conventions/full-list/-/conventions/rms/090000168008482e [Accessed 1 December 2020].

CPS, 2017. Violence against women strategy 2017–2020 [online]. Available at: https://www.cps.gov.uk/sites/default/files/documents/publications/VAWG-Strategy-2017-2020.pdf [Accessed 1 December 2020].

CPS, 2020. Disability hate crime and other crimes against disabled people – prosecution guidance [online]. Available at: https://www.cps.gov.uk/legal-guidance/disability-hate-crime-and-other-crimes-against-disabled-people-prosecution-guidance [Accessed 1 December 2020].

Crime and Disorder Act 1998 (c. 37).
Criminal Justice Act 2003 (c. 44).
Criminal Justice and Courts Act 2015 (c. 2).
Dempsey, B., 2011. Gender neutral laws and heterocentric policies: 'domestic abuse as gender-based abuse' and same-sex couples. *Edinburgh Law Review*, 15(3), pp. 381–405. DOI: 10.3366/elr.2011.0058.
Domestic Abuse Bill (2019–2021) HL Bill 124. *Parliament: House of Commons*. London: UK Parliament.
Dunbar, E., 2006. Race, gender and sexual orientation in hate crime victimization: identity politics or identity risk? *Violence and Victims*, 21(3), pp. 323–337. DOI: 10.1891/vivi.21.3.323.
EHRC, 2020. Public sector equality duty [online]. Available at: https://www.equalityhumanrights.com/en/advice-and-guidance/public-sector-equality-duty [Accessed 17 January 2021].
Evans, K.M., Kincade, E.A., Marbley, A.F. and Seem, S.R., 2005. Feminism and feminist therapy: lessons from the past and hopes for the future. *Journal of Counselling and Development*, 83(3), 269–277. DOI: 10.1002/j.1556-6678.2005.tb00342.x.
Fawcett Society, 2018. *Misogyny as a Hate Crime Westminster Hall Debate, 7th March 2018 9.30-11.00am*. Briefing paper [online]. Available at: https://www.fawcettsociety.org.uk/misogyny-hate-crime-westminster-hall-debate-briefing [Accessed 1 December 2020].
Fawcett Society, 2019. New Fawcett data reveals gender is the most common cause of hate crime for women. Fawcett Society [online]. 14 January 2019. Available at: https://www.fawcettsociety.org.uk/news/new-fawcett-data-reveals-gender-is-most-common-cause-of-hate-crime-for-women [Accessed 1 December 2020].
Gaffney, P., 1997. Amending the Violence against Women Act: creating a rebuttable presumption of gender animus in rape cases. *Journal of Law and Policy*, 6(1), pp. 247–289.
Goodey, J., 2005. *Victims and Victimology: Research, Policy and Practice*. London: Pearson.
Goodman, L.A., Smyth, K.F., Borges, A.M. and Singer, R., 2009. When crises collide: how intimate partner violence and poverty intersect to shape women's mental health and coping? *Trauma, Violence, and Abuse*, 10(4), 306–329. DOI: 10.1177/1524838009339754.
Hate Crime (Misogyny) Bill (2019–2021).
Heise, L.L., 1998. Violence against women: an integrated, ecological framework. *Violence against Women*, 4(3), pp. 262–290. DOI: 10.1177/1077801298004003002.
Hodge, J.P., 2011. *Gendered Hate: Exploring Gender in Hate crime Law*. Lebanon, NH: North Eastern University Press.
Home Office, 2009. Together we can end violence against women and girls: a strategy [online]. Available at: https://webarchive.nationalarchives.gov.uk/20100408130405/http://www.homeoffice.gov.uk/documents/vawg-strategy-2009/end-violence-against-women2835.pdf?view=Binary [Accessed 02 January 2021].
Home Office, 2019. Strategy to end violence against women and girls: 2016–2020 [online]. Available at: https://www.gov.uk/government/publications/strategy-to-end-violence-against-women-and-girls-2016-to-2020 [Accessed 02 January 2021].
Hoskin, R.A., 2019. Femmephobia: the role of anti-femininity and gender policing in LGBTQ+ people's experiences of discrimination. *Sex Roles*, 81(11–12), pp. 686–703. DOI: 10.1007/s11199-019-01021-3.

House of Commons, 2017. Women's and equalities committee report: sexual harassment of women and girls in public places [online]. Sixth Report of Session 2017–19. Available at: https://publications.parliament.uk/pa/cm201719/cmselect/cmwomeq/2148/2148.pdf [Accessed 02 January 2021].

Ipsos Mori, 2018. International Women's Day: global misperceptions of equality and the need to press for progress [online]. Available at: https://www.ipsos.com/ipsos-mori/en-uk/international-womens-day-global-misperceptions-equality-and-need-press-progress [Accessed 02 January 2021].

Jenness, V., 2003. Engendering hate crime policy: gender, the 'dilemma of difference', and the creation of legal subjects. *Journal of Hate Studies*, 2(1), pp. 73–97. DOI: 10.33972/jhs.12.

Jenness, V. and Grattet, R., 2001. *Making Hate a Crime: From Social Movement to Law Enforcement*. New York: Russell Sage Foundation.

Jewkes, R., Flood, M., and Lang, J., 2015. From work with men and boys to changes of social norms and reduction of inequities in gender relations: a conceptual shift in prevention of violence against women and girls. *Lancet*, 385(9977), pp. 1580–1589. DOI: 10.1016/S0140-6736(14)61683-4.

Kelly, L. and Lovett, J., 2005. *What a Waste. The Case for an Integrated Violence against Women Strategy*. London: Women's National Commission.

Kessler, S.J. and McKenna, W., 1978. *Gender: An Ethnomethodological Approach*. New York: John Wiley.

Law Commission, n.d. Hate crime [online]. Available at: https://www.lawcom.gov.uk/project/hate-crime/ [Accessed 1 December 2020].

Levitt, H., Gerrish, E.A. and Hiestand, K.R., 2003. The misunderstood gender: a model of modern femme identity. *Sex Roles*, 48(3/4), pp. 99–113. DOI: 10.1023/A:1022453304384.

Long. J., 2010. Should violence against women in the UK be seen as hate crime? [online]. Open Democracy. Available at: https://www.opendemocracy.net/en/5050/should-violence-against-women-in-uk-be-seen-as-hate-crime/ [Accessed 18 February 2013].

Loose Women, 2019. [TV] ITV. 11 April 2019.

Marshall, S.E. and Duff, R.A., 1998. Criminalization and sharing wrongs. *Canadian Journal of Law and Jurisprudence*, 11(1), pp. 7–22. DOI:10.1017/S0841820900001661.

Mason-Bish, H., 2010. Future challenges for hate crime policy: lessons from the past. In: Chakraborti, N., ed. *Hate Crime: Concepts, Policy, Future Directions*. London: Routledge, pp. 58–77.

Mason-Bish, H., 2011. Examining the boundaries of hate crime policy: considering age and gender. *Criminal Justice Policy Review*, 24(3), pp. 297–316. DOI: 10.1177/0887403411431495.

McCarthy, K.J., Mehta, R. and Haberland, N.A., 2018. Gender, power, and violence: a systematic review of measures and their association with male perpetration of IPV. *PLoS ONE*, 13(11). DOI: 10.1371/journal.pone.0207091.

McCollum, H., 2010. Violence against women as hate crime? Panel discussion. *Feminism in London Conference*. Available at: http://www.feminisminlondon.org.uk/feminism-in-london-2010/speeches/hilary-mccollums-speech/ [Accessed 23 March 2013].

McGuire, K., 2013. Perception of hate crime: the enduring difficulty of the law as agent of social change. *Contemporary Issues in Law: Hate Crime*, 13(1), pp. 19–33.

McPhail, B.A., 2002. Gender-bias hate crimes: a review. *Trauma, Violence and Abuse*, 3(2), pp. 125–143.

McPhail, B.A., 2003. A feminist policy analysis framework. Through a gendered lens. *The Social Policy Journal*, 2(2–3), pp. 39–61. DOI: 10.1300/J185v02n02_04.

Menson v United Kingdom [2003] App No. 47916/99 ECHR.

Ministry of Justice, 2014. Statistics on women and the criminal justice system 2013 [online]. Available at: https://assets.publishing.service.gov.uk/government/uploads/system/uploads/attachment_data/file/380090/women-cjs-2013.pdf [Accessed 1 December 2020].

Mullany, L. and Trickett, L., 2018. Misogyny hate crime evaluation report [online]. Nottingham Woman's Centre. Available at: http://www.nottinghamwomenscentre.com/wp-content/uploads/2018/07/Misogyny-HateCrime-Evaluation-Report-June-2018.pdf [Accessed 1 December 2020].

ONS, 2018. Domestic abuse in England and Wales: year ending March 2018 [online]. Available at: https://www.ons.gov.uk/peoplepopulationandcommunity/crimeandjustice/bulletins/domesticabuseinenglandandwales/yearendingmarch2018 [Accessed 1 December 2020].

ONS, 2019. Domestic abuse victim characteristics, England and Wales: year ending March 2019 [online]. Available at: https://www.ons.gov.uk/peoplepopulationandcommunity/crimeandjustice/articles/domesticabusevictimcharacteristicsenglandandwales/yearendingmarch2019 [Accessed 2 January 2021].

ONS, 2020. Crime in England and Wales: year ending June 2020 [online]. Available at: https://www.ons.gov.uk/peoplepopulationandcommunity/crimeandjustice/bulletins/crimeinenglandandwales/yearendingjune2020 [Accessed 2 January 2021].

Oxford English Dictionary, 2021a. Gender [online]. Available at: https://www.lexico.com/definition/gender [Accessed 17 January 2021].

Oxford English Dictionary, 2021b. Misogyny [online]. Available at: https://www.lexico.com/definition/misogyny [Accessed 17 January 2021].

Peláez, M.W., 2016. Portugal bans the verbal harassment of women [online]. 19 February. Available at: https://www.equaltimes.org/portugal-bans-the-verbal?lang=en#.X38BSu17nD4 [Accessed 2 January 2021].

Perry, B., 2001. *In the Name of Hate: Understanding Hate Crimes*. London: Routledge.

Portuguese Penal Code, Article 170.

Promundo, 2018. Unmasking sexual harassment: how toxic masculinities drive men's abuse in the US, UK and Mexico and what we can do to end it [online]. Available at: https://promundoglobal.org/resources/unmasking-sexual-harassment/ [Accessed 2 January 2021].

Public Order Act 1986 (c. 64).

Protection from Harassment Act 1997 (c. 40).

Reid, K., 2020. *A Practitioner's Guide to the European Convention on Human Rights*. 6th ed. London: Sweet and Maxwell.

Reiser, C., 2001. *Reflections on Anger: Women and Men in a Changing Society*. Westport, CT: Praeger.

Ristock, J., 2002. *No More Secrets: Violence in Lesbian Relationships*. London: Routledge.

SafeLives, 2020. Who are the victims of domestic abuse? [online]. Available at: https://safelives.org.uk/policy-evidence/about-domestic-abuse/who-are-victims-domestic-abuse [Accessed 1 December 2020].

Schiek, D., 2018. On uses, mis-uses and non-uses of intersectionality before the Court of Justice (EU). *International Journal of Discrimination and the Law*, 18(2–3), pp. 82–103. DOI: 10.1177/1358229118799232.

Scottish Government, 2018. Independent review of hate crime legislation in Scotland. Final report [Online]. Available at: https://www.gov.scot/binaries/content/documents/govscot/publications/progress-report/2018/05/independent-review-hate-crime-legislation-scotland-final-report/documents/00535892-pdf/00535892-pdf/govscot%3Adocument/00535892.pdf [Accessed 2 January 2021].

Sexual Offences Act 2003 (c. 42).

Stanko, E., 2001. Re-conceptualising the policing of hatred: confessions and worrying dilemmas of a consultant. *Law and Critique*, 12(3), pp. 309–329. DOI: 10.1023/A:1013784203982.

Summary Offences Act 1981, no. 113 (New Zealand).

Tidley, A., 2019. France issues 447 fines under new 'sexist outrage' street harassment law. *Euronews*. 30 April. Available at: https://www.euronews.com/2019/04/30/france-fines-447-people-under-new-street-harassment-law [Accessed 2 January 2021].

Topping, A., 2019. Campaigners and MPs call for misogyny to be made a hate crime: letter sent to Met police commissioner says women are being left unprotected. *The Guardian* [online]. 14 January 2019. Available at: https://www.theguardian.com/society/2019/jan/14/campaigners-and-mps-call-for-misogyny-to-be-made-a-hate [Accessed 2 January 2021].

UK Human Rights blog, n.d. Article 14 anti-discrimination. [online]. Available at: https://ukhumanrightsblog.com/incorporated-rights/articles-index/article-14/ [Accessed 2 January 2021].

United Nations, 1993. Resolution 48/104. Declaration on the elimination of violence against women [online]. Available at: http://www.un-documents.net/a48r104.htm [Accessed 2 January 2021].

UN Women, n.d. How we work [online]. Available at: https://www.unwomen.org/en/how-we-work [Accessed 17 January 2021].

White Ribbon Organisation, 2020. Call out for the UK to ratify the Istanbul Convention [online]. 8 June 2020. Available at: https://www.whiteribbon.org.uk/news/2020/6/8/call-out-for-the-uk-to-ratify-the-istanbul-convention [Accessed 2 January 2021].

Part 2
Online and offline spaces

3 Gender as a protected characteristic

A legal perspective

Chara Bakalis

Introduction

The question of whether gender should be included in hate crime legislation as a protected characteristic has been of central concern to three separate law reform projects in the UK in the last three years. By way of background, there are three separate and distinct legal systems in the UK: Scotland, Northern Ireland, England and Wales. Whilst some legislation is shared by two or even all three legal systems, other legislation is devolved to each separate country to develop and create under their own charge. Hate crime laws fall under the latter category, and as such, three different forms of hate crime law exist in each of the separate UK jurisdictions. All three of these systems have been subject to major law reform proposals in recent years. In Scotland, this was led by Lord Bracadale who published his findings in 2018 (Lord Bracadale 2018). In Northern Ireland, the independent review was conducted by Judge Marrinan whose final recommendations were published in November 2020 (Judge Marrinan 2020b). The English and Welsh review is being carried out by the Law Commission for England and Wales (hereafter 'Law Commission') which published its consultation paper in September 2020 with a final report due the following year (Law Commission 2020).

Currently, gender is not a protected characteristic under any of the hate crime frameworks in the UK. Scholars have engaged with this topic at an academic level and from a range of different perspectives for a number of years (see, for example, McPhail 2002; Gill and Mason-Bish 2013; Walters and Tumath 2014; Mason-Bish and Duggan 2019; Haynes and Schweppe 2020b), and the general trend has been in favour of including gender as a protected characteristic in hate crime legislation. All three law reform proposals arrived at the same conclusion, and have recommended that the law be amended to reflect this. Whilst the result in each review was the same, the different ways in which this conclusion was reached reveals a number of insights about the process of deciding which characteristics to include in hate crime legislation. It should be noted that although Lord Bracadale's review of Scottish hate crime legislation proposed the inclusion of gender into hate crime legislation, this has been delayed by the Scottish Parliament in

DOI: 10.4324/9781003023722-3

their Hate Crime and Public Order Bill 2020 whereby sex can be added at a later date should it be deemed necessary, but is not to be included in legislation for the moment. This caution is indicative of the particular complexities relating to the inclusion of gender in hate crime legislation which means that even though the principled reasons for doing so are compelling, the practical difficulties make this change far from straightforward. This chapter will focus on analysing the reasoning used in these reviews in order to gain an understanding specifically into the problems relating to the inclusion of gender in hate crime legislation, as well as forming general insights into the process of adding protected characteristics to hate crime legislation. It will highlight issues of general importance for any legal system wishing to consider adding gender to its legislation.

This chapter adopts a legal analysis of the process by which decisions about protected characteristics are made. By its nature, hate crime law, whichever form it takes, is about increasing the punishment of behaviour that is already criminal. Thus, whilst practical considerations are important, as are criminological insights into the harm caused by hate crime, it is also crucial that we recognise that hate crime exists within the framework of a legal system which itself is subject to certain values and principles which hate crime law must adhere to (Horder 2019). The Criminal Law in particular is a tool by which the state can exert extraordinary power over its citizens, and through which it can ultimately impose the greatest punishment of all – the removal of our liberty. Thus, for legal scholars, hate crime law, like all criminal law, must strike a balance between giving the state the necessary powers to protect victims on the one hand, but on the other must give sufficient safeguards to citizens from unwarranted state control. The criminal law has over time developed a number of principles and values which maintain this balance, and hate crime law must be subject to these.

This chapter will begin by summarising the reasoning adopted in the reviews and will pick out a number of important themes. It will then go on to discuss these themes in more detail and evaluate their relevance to some of the important areas of debate within hate crime scholarship.

Summary of the review and emerging overarching themes

Whilst all three reviews have recommended the addition of gender to hate crime legislation, each review finds itself at a different stage of the law reform process. Lord Bracadale's independent review published its final recommendations in 2018. However, although a number of his reform proposals have been incorporated by the Scottish Hate Crime Bill, his view that gender should be included as a protected characteristic has not been fully implemented. An enabling clause has been added to the Hate Crime and Public Order (Scotland) Bill 2020 which would allow ministers to add sex to hate crime legislation in future. In the meantime, there is a recommendation that a Working Group be set up to consider whether there is a need to create a separate stand-alone misogynistic harassment offence. Thus, for the moment at least, gender will not be given protection in hate crime legislation in Scotland. Judge Marrinan's review of hate crime legislation in Northern Ireland published its final recommendations in November 2020, so it is still too soon to know whether his proposal to include gender as a protected characteristic will be adopted by the Northern Irish Assembly. Finally, the Law Commission's review of hate crime legislation in England and Wales is currently in its consultation phase, and the final report has yet to be published. Therefore, we are still some time away from this particular reform being enacted into law, and the Scottish government's decision to delay the inclusion of gender suggests that this is still a live issue that is far from concluded. As will be seen in the discussion below, this is mainly because whilst on the face of it there are compelling arguments in favour of adding gender to hate crime legislation, doing so raises fairly complex issues that can make this addition fraught with difficulties.

This section will summarise how the three different reviews approached the issue and will discuss the rationales put forward for including gender in hate crime legislation. This section will also highlight some general themes that emerge from the three reviews, and these themes will be further developed and analysed in the following section.

Broadly speaking, all three reviews adopt a similar approach to answer the question about adding gender to hate crime legislation. Two key stages can be identified. Firstly, they consider whether there is a justification, as a matter of principle to add gender to hate crime legislation. Secondly, having established a case in principle, the reviews then look at the more specific issues which arise when adding gender to hate crime legislation, such as how this would fit within a system that already recognises certain offences relating to violence against women and girls.

Stage 1: principled case for including gender

The starting point for all three reviews is whether there is a principled case for including gender as a protected characteristic. However, this question itself is made up of two parts: firstly, it requires an articulation of the purpose of hate crime law generally; and secondly, a discussion of how this underlying purpose can help us decide which characteristics ought to be protected.

Purpose of hate crime law

Lord Bracadale identifies three main aims of hate crime law (Lord Bracadale 2018, p. 11):

1   Firstly, hate crime causes additional harm to victims, victim groups and to society more generally than other crimes. This is the hate crime 'hurts more' argument;

2 Secondly, hate crimes send an important symbolic message;
3 Thirdly, hate crime has a practical benefit as there is a clear set of rules and procedures within the criminal justice system to deal with hate crime.

Lord Bracadale (2018) makes it clear that hate crime is not about giving certain victims greater protection as hate crimes are about additional punishment for already existing offences. Therefore, he states that even if a group does not come within hate crime legislation, they are still given protection within the criminal justice system through ordinary offences. However, this point does not sit easily alongside his recognition that inclusion in hate crime legislation brings with it certain practical benefits. This contradiction between on the one hand not wishing to be seen to be privileging certain groups, whilst at the same time accepting that including a group within hate crime legislation brings with it certain advantages is an interesting paradox. It touches on the problem of whether limiting hate crime to certain groups creates a 'hierarchy' of hate (Chakraborti and Garland 2012) which runs counter to the inclusive nature of hate crime policy. This issue is also touched upon by the other reviews and is one of the themes that emerges from this analysis and will be considered in more detail in the section below. The Law Commission (2020) agrees with these broad aims but is more specific about what the symbolic function of hate crime law is, which is to posit hate crime legislation within the broader equality (or non-discrimination) movement. The inclusion of equality to the explanation of hate crime law has an additional benefit. It is often said that hate crime law sends a message to society that hatred of certain groups is 'wrong' and not to be tolerated. Linking this to the need to ensure equality, particularly amongst groups that suffer discrimination, ensures that there is a justification for why only certain groups are included.

Judge Marrinan's discussion on the justification for hate crime is laid out in the consultation paper that preceded his final report (Judge Marrinan 2020a). The first two rationales that he identifies for justifying the existence of hate crime include the argument that 'hate crimes hurt more' and the symbolic purpose of hate crimes (Judge Marrinan 2020a). Along with the Law Commission, he too links the symbolic purpose directly to the concept of equality. Judge Marrinan (2020a) cites the Organisation for Security and Co-operation in Europe (OSCE) which states this point and argues that '…hate crime laws both express the social value of equality and foster the development of those values' (OSCE 2009, p. 7). The third rationale that he identifies for justifying the existence of hate crime laws is the greater culpability of the offender (Judge Marrinan 2020a). What is interesting to note here is the fact that Marrinan has not included the practical benefits of being included in hate crime legislation as a rationale for the existence of hate crimes. He does recognise those practical benefits and cites Lord Bracadale in this regard (Judge Marrinan 2020b), but he does not see those as part of the *principled* rationale for the existence of hate crime law (as laid out in Judge Marrinan 2020a). This is in contrast to the Bracadale and Law Commission reviews, that see an intrinsic link between the rationale for the existence of hate crime legislation and the practical benefits that accrue. Whilst at first sight this may not seem to be a particularly noteworthy distinction, in the next section it will be argued that this difference in approach is another important theme that emerges from the reviews that is worthy of further consideration.

How do we decide the protected characteristics

Having articulated the underlying purpose of hate crime law, the next stage in deciding whether there is a principled justification for extending protection to gender is to identify the rules by which we decide which groups should be given protection. All three reviews either implicitly or explicitly disagree with keeping the category of characteristics open, and all three express a preference for the characteristics to be defined in statute. This links back to the point made above about the issues which arise in relation to the hierarchies of hate. Although there was unanimity within the reviews on this issue, other jurisdictions such as in some states of Australia (Victoria and the Northern Territory) and Canada, have opted for more open definitions of characteristics and so this is an issue worth exploring further as it will be of interest to lawmakers.

In spite of this unanimity about open/closed categories, some differences do emerge when considering the different criteria used for deciding which characteristics to include. The Scottish review adopted three criteria (Lord Bracadale, 2018):

a   whether there is evidence that hostility towards a particular characteristic is manifested;
b   whether the characteristic and the form of hostility is such that society would like to make special provision for it;
c   what the practical consequence of inclusion would be.

The Law Commission (2020) adopted a similar approach. It focused first on whether there is evidence of targeting violence against a group which they referred to as there being a 'demonstrable need'. It then looked at whether this targeted violence causes 'additional harm' to society. This is similar to the second element in the Scottish approach, but is much more specific about how we decide whether there is a good reason for society to make special provision for this particular characteristic. Finally, the Law Commission looked at the suitability of including the new characteristic. This is broadly similar to the third Scottish element which is concerned with any practical consequences of adding a particular characteristic. Thus both the Bracadale and Law Commission reviews adopt a mixture of practical (elements 1 and 3) and theoretical (element 2) criteria for making this decision.

The Northern Irish approach, however, more clearly distinguishes between the theoretical reasons for including a characteristic and any practical concerns there may be with adding a particular characteristic (Judge Marrinan 2020b). Thus, for Judge Marrinan, in determining whether a characteristic should be added, his primary concern is whether there is an argument in principle to do so. He considers a number of different ways in which this principled argument could be structured, and ultimately decides that the principle of equality should be the defining element here (Judge Marrinan 2020b). This fits in with his earlier endorsement of the OSCE view that the underlying harm caused by hate crime is linked to the social value of equality. Thus, he uses the characteristics protected under equality legislation as a preliminary guide to which groups to include in hate crime legislation.

This is not to say that Judge Marrinan is not interested in the practical considerations raised in the Bracadale report and that of the Law Commission. In fact, he is mindful of the principle of minimal criminalisation which means that we should not be creating additional criminal liability where there is no need to do so (Judge Marrinan 2020b). However, he argues that over-reliance on police data for evidence of targeted violence is misplaced as police data on its own is not always a reliable or accurate tool for understanding patterns of offending (Judge Marrinan 2020b). This question over the role that evidence of targeted violence should play in determining which characteristics should be included is the third theme that emerges from these reports and will be discussed in more detail below.

Stage 2: specific issues relating to adding gender as a protected characteristic

Whilst the case in principle for adding gender appears to be compelling and clear, all three reviews raised some particular issues relating to gender that make this a far less straightforward characteristic to include in hate crime legislation than appears at first. These concerns centre on whether including gender into hate crime legislation will indeed benefit women (who are seen as the most likely group to be victims of gendered violence) or whether the sheer amount of crime against women will overwhelm the system and have a detrimental effect on the protection offered to other victims of hate crime. The particular problems relating to the inclusion of gender is the fourth theme that emerges from the reviews and will be discussed below.

Analysis of general themes

The previous section outlined the general approach used in all three reviews when deciding whether to include gender in hate crime legislation. All three reviews reached the same conclusion on gender but there were some differences in their approach and reasoning which has highlighted some important issues which relate more generally to hate crime law and to the process of adding characteristics to hate crime legislation. This section will consider these in more depth. The four themes are: (a) the link between the symbolic and practical aspects of hate crime legislation, (b) the issue of hierarchies of hate and whether states should adopt an open or closed category of hate crime characteristics, (c) what role should be played by existing evidence of targeted violence against certain groups in the decision about which characteristics should be included in hate crime legislation and (d) issues relating specifically to the addition of gender to hate crime legislation. These themes are discussed in detail below:

The symbolic and practical aspects of hate crime legislation

The first issue to consider is the interplay between the symbolic and practical aspects of hate crime legislation. The reviews placed varying levels of weight on these factors, and this reveals some core insights into the process of deciding which protected characteristics to include in legislation as well as some more general insights about hate crime more generally.

The symbolic aspects of hate crime articulated in the reports include the following: the additional harm caused to victims, their communities and society more generally; the harm to broader equality values of society; and the recognition of the additional wrongfulness of the defendant's conduct in hate crimes. All three reviews also highlighted the practical benefits which ensue as a result of a group being included in hate crime legislation from a policing and social policy point of view. However, both Lord Bracadale's review and that of the Law Commission saw these practical benefits as part of the rationale for hate crime legislation, whereas for Judge Marrinan, they were a side-effect of hate crime legislation but they did not form part of the justification for hate crime legislation.

What may seem on the face of it to be a fairly small divergence in the weight placed on the importance of the practical benefits can in fact be very revealing about an important aspect of hate crime legislation. Undoubtedly, being included in hate crime legislation brings with it practical benefits. However, the importance placed on this when determining whether to include a protected characteristic in hate crime legislation needs further reflection. If the practical benefits are seen as part of the justification we have for hate crime legislation rather than a by-product, then this can cause problems. This is because inclusion in hate crime legislation becomes a proxy for vulnerable groups to be given the attention and protection they deserve by the police. This should not be the case. If a group is particularly vulnerable and requires special attention by the police, this should be a question of police resourcing, and it should not require inclusion in hate crime legislation for them to be given this protection. It is important to remember that hate crimes are about punishing a perpetrator more for existing criminal offences, and *all* victims of those offences are deserving of protection, and not just victims of hate crime.

Interestingly, Lord Bracadale picked up on this point when he said that he does not "think that hate crime legislation is about giving some individuals greater or lesser 'protection' than others in comparable situations, simply because of an identity characteristic" (Lord Bracadale 2018, p. 33). However, this statement does not sit well with his later decision to include the practical benefits as one of the rationales for the existence of hate crime law and highlights the problem of conflating the two. This points to an essential paradox in hate crime legislation. On the one hand we do not want to draw too much attention to the additional practical benefits of inclusion as a protected characteristic, but on the other hand if there are *no* practical benefits to inclusion, then this might raise the question of whether there is any point in having hate crime legislation.

In order to reconcile these two points, a distinction needs to be drawn between on the one hand, the problem of targeted violence and the needs of a group that may be particularly vulnerable, and which is essentially a policing issue; and on the other hand, the additional harm caused to society by hate crimes which is essentially how we justify the existence of hate crime laws. For this reason, it is important to decouple the symbolic and practical benefits of hate crime legislation. This is not to say that no practical benefits should ensue as a result of inclusion. The point is that these practical benefits should not form part of the rationale or justification for the existence of hate crime legislation. This links back to the point made in the introduction to this piece which is that we must at all times remember that hate crime legislation punishes perpetrators more for existing criminal offences, and so our justification for the existence of hate crime needs to be linked to this. The practical benefits which ensue from inclusion in hate crime legislation cannot explain why we punish offenders more and thus should not form part of the justification for hate crime legislation.

Opened or closed protected characteristics/hierarchies of hate

It is a central concern of some hate crime scholars that the process of naming particular protected characteristics in hate crime legislation sends a signal that some victims are more worthy of protection than others, thus creating a 'hierarchy of hate' (Chakraborti and Garland 2012). Given that hate crime as a discipline is by its very nature concerned with protecting those who are sidelined in society, it is clearly of grave concern if the form which hate crime legislation takes becomes itself the perpetrator of exclusion and marginalisation. There are ways around this problem such as to leave more open categories of characteristics either by reference to a broad principle such as 'vulnerability' or 'difference' (Chakraborti and Garland 2012). Alternatively, the state could enact legislation such as that in the Northern Territory of Australia (Sentencing Act 1995 (NT), s. 6A) which states that hate crime is committed when 'hate against a group of people' is manifested during the commission of an offence. Alternatively, a non-exhaustive list of characteristics can be created such as in Canada (Canadian Criminal Code, section 718(2)(a)(i)) or New South Wales in Australia (Crimes (Sentencing Procedure) Act 1999 (NSW), s. 21A(2)(h)). All three reviews considered this issue, but ultimately all three opted for a closed category of protected characteristics. It is worth reflecting on this notion of 'hierarchies of hate' further and consider to what extent it is something that should be of concern to lawmakers when deciding which characteristics to include in hate crime legislation.

Having an open category of hate crime characteristics does bring with it certain problems. For example, the experience in Australia has not been wholly positive where the open category has resulted in paedophiles being included in legislation which has been very controversial (Mason 2014). In Canada, whilst the category is open, judges have not necessarily used this to extend the categories of hate crime (Schweppe 2012). Furthermore, an open category which allows judges to decide which characteristics to include on a case by case basis is open to criticism from a rule of law point of view (Bakalis 2017). These concerns were a key driver in the reviews for not opting to go down the open category route.

However, even beyond these arguments, it is not clear that creating hierarchies of hate is necessarily inconsistent with the broader aims of hate crime legislation. In fact, arguably, creating hierarchies of hate within the legislation is both necessary and desirable. To begin with, even those who advocate an open category of victims, such as the one currently used in Australia or Canada, are still inadvertently perpetuating a 'hierarchy of hate' as not all victims of 'hate' are included in these open categories – it is only those victims of *characteristic-based* hate that are included. Similarly, if you were to base legislation on an open category such as 'vulnerability' or 'difference', then again, not *all* victims of hate are included – only those who fit the definition of 'vulnerable' or 'different'. The only way to truly remove the 'hierarchies of hate' in hate crime legislation would be to include *all* victims of *hate* – with no reference either to group, characteristic or any other limitation. However, doing so would in fact undermine the very basis of hate crime legislation. By definition, hate crime laws punish some perpetrators more for the same behaviour because of who their victim is and/or their motivation/demonstration of hostility. This additional punishment needs to be justified in some way as the underlying behaviour is already a criminal offence, and so we need to explain why punishment should be increased in the case of hate crime victims. Over time, various justifications for this have been put forward such as historical disadvantage, bolstering of the broader equality agenda or because hate crimes cause additional harm to society. Whilst scholars might disagree about the rationale for hate crime law, the point is that a rationale of sorts does have to be set forth to explain why the behaviour is worthy of *greater* punishment. If we were to remove the hierarchies of hate by saying that all victims of *hate* should be included in legislation, then essentially, we would be arguing that hate crime is about criminalising 'hate'. Yet this would be an unsatisfactory basis for explaining why we have hate crime legislation.

We need to be circumspect about using the Criminal Law to punish an emotion (Duff and Marshall 2018), and doing so would diminish the very real harm caused to society by hate crimes. Therefore, whilst we refer to this area of the law as 'hate crime', the term 'hate' is really a proxy or shorthand for all the different reasons we may have for wishing to give additional protection to certain groups, and so ultimately 'hate crime' law does not have much to do with criminalising 'hate' at all. As a result, there have long been discussions about whether hate crime law should instead be called something else entirely such as 'bias crimes' (Lawrence 1999, p. 9).

Ultimately, the term hate crime has stuck, but clearly hate crime law is not in fact about criminalising the pure emotion of 'hate'. Once it is acknowledged that hate crime is in fact about protecting broader societal values, then it becomes clear that some groups need more protection than others, and that hate crime characteristics should correlate with those groups. Viewed through this lens, the concept of hierarchies of hate is not something that should concern lawmakers. In fact, creating hierarchies recognises the reality that crimes motivated by hostility against certain groups are more damaging to society. Without this, the justification for the existence of hate crimes falls away.

Use of evidence for deciding protected characteristics

Another interesting issue that came up during the reviews and which has wider implications for the inclusion of other characteristics is to do with the extent to which evidence of targeted violence is needed before including a particular characteristic in hate crime legislation.

Both the Law Commission and Lord Bracadale placed a great deal of emphasis on the need for evidence, and indeed in their three-part test for deciding whether a characteristic should be included, existing evidence of targeted violence was top of their list. Judge Marrinan's report also took evidence into account and viewed the need for evidence as a way to ensure compliance with the principle of minimal criminalisation. However, proof of evidence was not itself part of the test put forward for deciding protected characteristics. In fact, Judge Marrinan was more circumspect about the role more generally that evidence should play in this decision, and he cautioned against the over-reliance on data, particularly in cases where data may be hard to come by. The report was mindful of the point made by Haynes and Schweppe (2020a) that evidence of targeted violence could be scant because the police are not recording it, and not because targeted violence is not occurring. This is an important point and presents a dilemma for lawmakers. The principle of minimal criminalisation requires us to ensure that criminal offences are only created where there is a clear need to do so (Horder 2019). But, particularly in the case of hate crimes where we are dealing with existing criminal behaviour, the only way we can know whether targeted violence is occurring is if the police record it as such. The police tend to only record targeted violence if required to do so by law.

The obvious way of getting around this problem is to find ways of creating that evidence base. This could be done either by requiring the police to record existing criminal behaviour when targeted against a group in order to determine the scale of the problem, or by conducting other research that can help understand how prolific the violence is. For example, Nottinghamshire police force in England began recording misogynistic hate crime in 2016, which meant that some data already exists about the scale of the problem even before gender has been recognised as a protected characteristic under hate crime legislation (Mullany and Trickett 2018, see also Chapter 14 in this book). Data can also be found from a number of other sources including official criminal statistics as well as those compiled by non-governmental bodies and charities with an interest in a particular area. For example, the Law Commission relied on a number of different surveys to reach their conclusion on gender (Law Commission 2020).

However, this approach still gives a central role to evidence of targeted violence as part of the decision about which characteristics to include in hate crime legislation. As was mentioned above, given that hate crime is about punishing existing criminal behaviour *more* harshly, this needs to be justified, and evidence of targeted violence is not sufficient justification for this. It is the harm caused to the broader values of society that justify the existence of hate crimes. When viewed in this way, this suggests that evidence should only ever be tangential to any decision about whether a protected characteristic should be included, and what should come first is an examination of whether inclusion of the protected characteristic is necessary from the point of view of principle. As a consequence of this, we need to ensure that evidence of targeted violence is used in the correct way when making a decision about which characteristics to include in hate crime legislation. From the point of view of the principle of minimal criminalisation, evidence of targeted violence is required to demonstrate that a threshold of 'need' has been passed. However, this must not be confused with using evidence of targeted violence itself as providing the justification for inclusion in hate crime legislation. This is a nuanced point, but it is important to make this distinction, otherwise we run the risk of hate crime being viewed as being about targeted violence rather than about broader values of society. This links in with the point made earlier about hierarchies and about the symbolic aspects of the law. Hate crime is not really about hate or targeted violence. It is about something deeper than this, and we have to ensure that this is reflected in how we decide which characteristics to include in hate crime legislation.

Issues specifically relating to gender

The previous section highlighted some general issues relating to the legal process of adding protected characteristics to hate crime legislation. This section will focus on issues which arise specifically in relation to gender which means that whilst the evidence in favour of including gender appeared to be overwhelming in all three reviews, the practical reality of operationalising this is not straightforward. The issues centre around whether hate crime law is the most appropriate vehicle for protecting women from gender-based violence or whether including gender will overwhelm the system and will have a negative impact on other victims of hate crime. These problems can be illustrated by considering the impact that adding gender will have on sexual offences on the one hand, and non-sexual offences on the other.

In relation to the sexual offences, the issue is as follows. If gender is added to hate crime legislation, and sexual offences are subject to hate crime legislation (either as aggravated offences or as part of the sentencing process) does this mean that *all* sexual offences become by definition hate crimes? If the answer is yes, there is a concern that the sheer number of hate crimes will rise dramatically and this will threaten to overwhelm the efficient running of the hate crime regime. The fear is that this will have an impact on resourcing and might side-line the other protected characteristics. Alternatively, a distinction could be made between sexual offences which are hate crimes and those which are not (Walters and Tumath 2014) so that not all sexual offences are categorised as hate crimes. However, the concern is that this might create a hierarchy amongst sexual offences suggesting that those which are not also hate crimes are somehow not quite as serious. Ultimately this would cause a disservice to women and would defeat the purpose of adding gender to hate crime in the first place.

There are also problems in relation to non-sexual offences such as harassment or assault as the worry is that the label 'hate crime' mis-characterises the real motivation behind these offences which is often sexual in nature, rather than 'hostility' which underlies hate crimes. This causes two issues. Firstly, it may mean that few cases of gender-based harassment ever reach the evidential threshold for hate crime as there is no evidence of 'hostility'. Secondly, even if a gender-based case is characterised as a hate crime, this does not capture appropriately the harm that is caused to women. Thus again, adding gender to hate crime may not in fact help women at all.

It is these issues that led the Scottish government to delay the inclusion of gender into hate crime legislation. There is an enabling clause in the Hate Crime and Public Order (Scotland) Bill currently before the Scottish Parliament which will allow gender to be added at a later date, but in the meantime, a Working Group will be set up to determine whether there is a case for creating a stand-alone gender-based harassment offence. It is beyond the scope of this chapter to determine the pros and cons of such an offence, particularly as we do not yet have any details on how this might operate. However, it is important to point out that even if such an offence were to be created, it would be targeted at sexual harassment, and thus would be dealing with a different type of harm than hate crime offences which are interested in hostility towards a particular characteristic. It would also be much more restricted in scope as it would be a single offence covering a limited set of behaviour, unlike adding gender to hate crime legislation which would cover all offences. Thus, a gender-based sexual harassment offence is not a replacement for a gender-based hate crime offence, but is tackling a different type of wrong altogether. From this point of view, the delay in adding gender in order to await the outcome of the Working Group does not appear to be warranted. This view was shared by Judge Marrinan who advised against a delay which could take years (Judge Marrinan 2020b).

This still leaves the issue in relation to the sexual offences. This was something that particularly concerned the Law Commission, and they have considered the possibility of removing sexual offences and domestic violence cases entirely from the hate crime regime in order to avoid this problem altogether (Law Commission 2020). Some groups might feel let down by this as it appears to give gender less protection than the other protected characteristics, and it undoubtedly adds an additional layer of complexity to an already complicated area of the law. However, at least this solution does address some of the concerns outlined above in relation to the overlap between sexual offences and hate crime law. It is not ideal and comes with a cost, but it is inevitable that as hate crime law matures, some compromises will need to be made along the way. This does appear to be a solution, even though it will result in fairly complex hate crime laws which apply differently to different characteristics. It remains to be seen whether this solution is ultimately adopted by the legislator in England and Wales, but this discussion clearly indicates that whilst the argument in favour of adding gender is compelling, there are practical concerns about what inclusion will mean that it does require a way around this.

Conclusion

This discussion has highlighted the central importance of adopting a carefully thought through process for deciding which characteristics to include in hate crime legislation. Choosing which protected characteristics to include goes beyond a simple policy or practical decision; rather, it goes to the heart of what hate crime law is *about*. It strikes to the heart of our understanding not just about the scope of hate crime law, but about the very reason why we have hate crimes laws in the first place and how we justify their existence and the elevation of certain victims above others. At the same time, the discussion has shed light on the difficulties associated with the practical implementation of adding gender to hate crime legislation. Whilst gender seems to fit the hate crime paradigm well, these additional concerns raise particular difficulties which can create a stumbling block for some lawmakers. However, these are not insurmountable, and gender can be included in hate crime legislation but most likely at the expense of a simple and streamlined hate crime framework which treats all characteristics the same.

References

Bakalis, C., 2017. The victims of hate crime and the principles of the criminal law. *Legal* Studies, 37(4), pp. 718–738. DOI:10.1111/lest.12171.

Canadian Criminal Code Section 718(2)(a)(i).

Chakraborti, N. and Garland, J., 2012. Reconceptualising hate crime victimization through the lens of vulnerability and difference. *Theoretical Criminology*, 16(4), pp. 499–514.

Crimes (Sentencing Procedure) Act 1999 (NSW) S 21A(2)(h).

Duff, R.A. and Marshall, S.E., 2018. Criminalizing hate. In: Brudholm, T. and Schepelern Johansen, B., eds. *Hate, Politics, Law: Critical Perspectives on Combating Hate*. New York: Oxford University Press, pp. 115–149.

Gill, A.K. and Mason-Bish, H., 2013. Addressing violence against women as a form of hate crime: limitations and possibilities. *Feminist Review*, 105(1), pp. 1–20. DOI: 10.1057/fr.2013.17.

Haynes, A. and Schweppe, J., 2020a. *Frameworks for Determining Protected Characteristics in Hate Crime Legislation*. Limerick: University of Limerick.

Haynes, A. and Schweppe, J., 2020b. You can't have one without the other one: "gender" in hate crime legislation. *Criminal Law Review*, 2, pp. 148–166.

Horder, J., 2019. *Ashworth's Principles of Criminal Law*. 9th ed. Oxford: Oxford University Press.

Law Commission, 2020. *Hate Crime Laws A Consultation Paper*. London: Law Commission.

Lawrence, F.M., 1999. *Punishing Hate: Bias Crimes under American Law*. Cambridge, MA: Harvard University Press.

Lord Bracadale, 2018. *Independent Review of Hate Crime Legislation in Scotland: Final Report*. Edinburgh: Justice Directorate, Scottish Government.

Judge Marrinan, 2020a. *Hate Crime Legislation in Northern Ireland, an Independent Review, Consultation Paper January 2020*. Belfast: Department of Justice, Northern Ireland.

Judge Marrinan, 2020b. *Hate Crime Legislation in Northern Ireland, An Independent Review, Consultation Paper November 2020*. Belfast: Department of Justice, Northern Ireland.

Mason, G., 2014. Victim attributes in hate crime law: difference and the politics of justice. *British Journal of Criminology*, 54(2), pp. 161–179.

Mason-Bish, H. and Duggan, M., 2019. Some men deeply hate women, and express that hatred freely": examining victims' experiences and perceptions of gendered hate crime. *International Review of Victimology*, 26(1), pp. 112–134. DOI: 10.1177/0269758019872903.

McPhail, B.A., 2002. Gender-bias hate crimes: a review. *Trauma, Violence and Abuse*, 3, pp. 125–143. DOI: 10.1177/15248380020032003.

Mullany, L. and Trickett, L., 2018. *Misogyny Hate Crime Evaluation Report*. Nottingham: Nottingham Women's Centre.

Office for Democratic Institutions and Human Rights, 2009. *Hate Crime Laws: A Practical Guide*. Warsaw: OSCE ODIHR.

Schweppe, J., 2012. Defining characteristics and politicising victims: a legal perspective. *Journal of Hate Studies*, 10(1), pp. 173–178. DOI: 10.33972/jhs.118.

Sentencing Act 1995 (NT) S 6A.

Walters, M. and Tumath, J., 2014. Gender hostility, rape and the hate crime paradigm. *Modern Law Review*, 77, pp. 563–596. DOI: 10.1111/1468-2230.12079.

4 Online misogyny as a hate crime
#TimesUp

Kim Barker and Olga Jurasz

Introduction: the legacy of the patriarchy – a 'gender' problem

> The social construction of online violence is flawed, as is the absence of appropriate regulation and enforcement. This is largely due to the social construction we adopt for the regulation of digital spaces. There is a conception that our "online" is very different from our "offline," yet, even if this is the situation, the standard concepts that have been adopted are now in need of some pressing reconstruction.
>
> (Barker and Jurasz 2014, p. 87)

Misogyny – be it online or offline – is not a new phenomenon. As a social issue deeply rooted in the gendered structures and hierarchies of power, it transcends millennia and geographical boundaries (Stein 2008). However, in the past few years, campaigns for the criminalisation of misogyny have become a prominent topic in the UK media, especially in light of calls by activists (Nottingham Citizens 2014; CitizensUK 2018) and some politicians (Creasy 2020; Hobhouse 2020) to 'make misogyny a hate crime'. This sits within the wider context of ongoing law reform consultations on the subject of amending hate crime legislation in England and Wales (Law Commission 2019), Scotland (Hate Crime and Public Order (Scotland) Bill 2020), and in Northern Ireland (Department of Justice 2019). All of these glossy campaigns, and high-profile political posturing have undoubtedly drawn attention to the issues of misogynistic behaviours, whilst implying that it is normal, and to be expected. What is becoming increasingly clear from these concerted efforts at awareness raising, is that misogynistic behaviours, particularly those spilling from the offline environment into the online environment now receive increased levels of scrutiny, yet this has not – to date – translated into effective protection for women online. Fundamentally while the law has developed in other areas to offer some limited protections for women, there remains a lack of protection from the law, from social media platforms, from policing practice, and from the scattered and piecemeal legal provisions that might be considered applicable to online misogyny. The fragmented responses to online misogyny highlight above all else that

DOI: 10.4324/9781003023722-4

there is a need for 'joined-up thinking' (Barker and Jurasz 2020c, p. 58) to tackle this phenomenon.

Online misogyny: old wine, new bottles?

The hostility that misogyny generates is directed towards women because they are women (Barker and Jurasz 2019a). Despite the long-standing existence of misogyny, online outlets are providing new spaces for communicating this 'new' form of established hostility (Jane 2017, p. 4). Our definition recognises the foundations of misogyny, so that, "Put simply, online misogyny is a form of gender-based cyberhate, directed against women because they are women" (Barker and Jurasz 2019a, p. 25). In the online sphere, the rise of feminist activism and the increase in women's everyday participation in online spaces have been met with a severe backlash in the form of online abuse – especially text-based (Lewis et al. 2017; Barker and Jurasz 2019b; Barker and Jurasz 2021a) – as well as a rise in online misogynistic behaviours. Textual and image-based violence directed at women highlight the Internet's rapid evolution into a space that is increasingly hostile and damaging to women. This overshadows the ideals of the Internet, such as openness, parity, and freedom to equally participate and express oneself, not to mention the immense benefits in terms of social connectivity, professional and social networking (Berners-Lee and Berners-Lee 2020). This is particularly noticeable in relation to women who are outspoken online – typically, albeit not limited to, women who identify as feminist or who express feminist views. This includes women politicians (Amnesty International 2017; Barker and Jurasz 2019c; Morgan 2020), activists (e.g. Gina Miller, Greta Thunberg) and frequently also academics who share their (feminist) work online (Phipps 2014; Barlow and Awan 2016). The backlash that women receive for participating online has severe consequences – not least on the individual level for the person involved but also broader, societal and participatory harms which are not currently captured within the legal system (Barker and Jurasz 2021a). Online abuse of women – especially in its misogynistic forms and also through gendered misinformation (malicious information which is intended to spread falsehoods and cause harm to women) (Barker and Jurasz 2020a) – has severe silencing effects, designed to drive women away from online public spaces, discredit them, and constrain the topics discussed by women publicly (Sobieraj 2018). As such, these behaviours create a range of broader harms – including participatory, social, and also democratic ones (Barker and Jurasz 2021a) – which reinforce the existing inequalities, patriarchy, and discrimination against women.

Online misogyny has been linked to the prevalence of violence against women (Barker and Jurasz 2019d, 2020a), and violent extremism (Duriesmith et al. 2018), as well as identified in literature as an obstacle to feminism (Barker and Jurasz 2019b), women's participation in public and political life (Barker and Jurasz 2019b, 2021a), a major factor in anti-feminism and anti-gender movements (Ging and Siapera 2019), and in fuelling the alt right and white supremacy (Anti-Defamation League 2018; Koulouris 2018). The upsurge in online misogyny is stark, with Amnesty International stating in 2018 that abuse against women online has become an incredibly common experience (Amnesty International 2018), whereas other research highlights that women who do not suffer some form of online abuse now fall into the minority, with the EU Fundamental Rights Agency Reporting that:

> the risk of young women aged between 18 and 29 years becoming a target of threatening and offensive advances on the internet is twice as high as the risk for women between 40 and 49 years, and more than three times as high as the risk for women aged between 50 and 50 years.
> (FRA 2014)

Whilst online misogyny may appear to be a phenomenon attributable to the significant rise in social media and Internet use – and therefore a problem specific to the online environment – it is not. The scale of online abuse of women and online misogyny confirms the deficiencies in the existing socio-legal structures and systems which continuously fail to deal with these issues and instead perpetuate the abuse and discrimination that occur online. Online misogyny, although perpetrated using tools specific to online platforms, and taking forms specific to online environments (e.g. text-based abuse in the forms of abusive and misogynistic tweets), merely mirrors the social attitudes towards women which have long been observed and criticised offline (Barker and Jurasz 2014) as well as gender relations (Wajcman 2010), the structural and systemic discrimination of women, and the emanations of the patriarchy long existing (and thriving) every day in offline environments across the globe.

As such, there exists a level of interconnectedness between online and offline misogyny and therefore, the two need to be addressed together as socio-cultural phenomena, both causing serious societal harms and perpetuating unequal and discriminatory gender relations. That said, a comprehensive response to these phenomena requires an appreciation and understanding of the specific environments in which misogyny is taking place. For instance, misogyny is no longer a purely offline occurrence, nor is it purely online. The distinction between online and offline is blurred, but in addressing the harms of online misogyny, specific considerations must be made, including recognition of the remoteness of the perpetrators, and also the associated 'stranger danger' harms that arise with offensive online communications sent at a physical distance (Barker and Jurasz 2021a). Legally defining misogyny is far from straightforward (Barker and Jurasz 2020b, 2021b) – we should not be expecting legal regulations to neatly address behaviours in all forms – a one size fits all approach to misogyny is not likely to improve protections for women, either online or off. Where law is concerned, attention needs to be given to the subtle differences between online and offline environments, and their respective regulatory regimes – especially the need to reform the laws concerning online communications, particularly those using social media.[1] However, these differences should under no circumstances detract from the need to tackle online misogyny and the online abuse of women, maintaining the overarching aim of preventing, curtailing and punishing Online Violence Against Women (OVAW) and misogynistic behaviours, including where such abusive behaviours amount to crimes motivated by hostility and/or prejudice and/or bias based on a person's gender. Drawing on this, in the next two sections, we take a critical view of the misogyny campaigns as well as the current legal status quo in relation to gender and hate crime. We particularly highlight the gaps and inconsistencies in the key campaigns as well as deficiencies of the current legal system in England and Wales in relation to including gender-based hate, before proposing avenues for reform.

Misogyny campaigns: how did we get here?

Proposals to make misogyny a hate crime are a relatively recent development in the UK. Whilst it is difficult to identify the precise time when the rhetoric of 'misogyny hate crime' entered the public sphere, it has certainly gained public attention – and attracted further campaigning on this issue – following the decision of the Nottinghamshire Police in 2016 to recognise misogyny as hate crime in their recording practices (Nottingham Citizens 2014). The decision was preceded by the campaign by Nottingham Citizens and the release of the *No Place for Hate* report in 2014 which suggested that 38% of women reporting a hate crime explicitly linked it to their gender (Nottingham Citizens 2014, p. 14).[2] Following the reported success of the policy by Nottinghamshire Police (Mullany and Trickett 2018), a limited number of other police forces in England have followed suit – e.g. North Yorkshire Police (North Yorkshire Police 2016) and Northamptonshire Police (Cohen and Hymas 2020). However, not all police forces have decided to record *misogyny* as hate crime – for instance, Avon and Somerset Police record instances of *gender* hate crimes instead (Ashcroft 2017).

The resulting lack of consistency in flagging incidents (rather than crimes, given the legal impossibility here currently) motivated by misogyny vs. those motivated by gender creates a skewed picture of the prevalence and scale of such behaviours and the motivations behind them. Focusing on misogyny looks at much more narrow and specific motivations as opposed to gender which, although is most commonly suggested as including women, could just as well include crimes committed against persons who do not identify as cisgender. The latter highlights just one of the many problems which arise – legally and otherwise – with calls for recording misogyny as a hate crime and the proposal to make misogyny (as opposed to sex and/or gender) an aggravating factor in criminal sentencing, as suggested by the Hate Crime (Misogyny) Bill 2019–2021.

Recording misogyny as a hate crime

As we previously argued (Barker and Jurasz 2019a), the decision to record or flag misogyny as a hate crime does not have a grounding in the existing hate crime framework in England and Wales (nor in the UK generally). Rather, the discretion of whether to flag certain offences as being motivated by misogyny lies with the given police force. Importantly, it is crucial to note that the decision to identify a specific crime as a 'misogynistic hate crime' does not (and, *legally*, cannot) result in prosecution of the offence as a hate crime due to the lack of legislative basis for it. Consequently, it brings no further avenue of redress for the victim of a crime motivated by misogyny – in the absence of a *relevant* protected characteristic within the legal hate crime framework, the perpetrator cannot be held accountable for committing a hate crime nor have a sentence increased in light of an aggravating factor being judicially recognised where there is no protected characteristic. This is an important distinction, yet one that has been continuously ignored in the public campaigns calling for police forces to 'make misogyny a hate crime'. At most, police recording instances of misogyny could be helpful in gathering data on women's perceptions of factors that motivate crimes committed against them, which could then inform broader hate crime reform (Barker and Jurasz 2020b), although it should be noted that gender disaggregated data does not currently form part of the crime statistics here. However, the substantive legal point arising in this context is that a specific protected characteristic must exist within the existing legal framework on hate crime in order to make a difference – legally speaking – to the victims of criminal incidences where there may be hostility or prejudice present (as discussed below). Where there is no protected characteristic, there is no legal consideration to be made of prejudice.

Misogyny, campaigns, and the law: a definitional conundrum?

The absence of a legal definition of misogyny (Barker and Jurasz 2019d, 2021b), as well as an absence of provisions in the existing criminal law of England and Wales suggesting that misogyny is a crime, make it difficult to accurately capture the nature of the conduct that campaigns propose be criminalised. For instance, there appears to be a lack of consensus or uniform understanding of what exactly constitutes misogynistic 'conduct', misogynistic 'criminal' conduct or misogynistic 'motivation' to commit a crime. More specifically, the notion of a crime being motivated by 'misogyny' is being conflated with 'gender motivated'/'gender-based crime' – the latter being a much wider term than misogyny. Also, it is important to note that not every crime committed against a woman will be automatically misogynistic, unless a specific legal threshold (which remains to be proposed by the campaigners and/or further determined by the law makers) is met. The situation is made worse by the fact that in order to record an incident, someone must perceive the act as a hate crime so there is no statutory threshold to satisfy as such, making the *recording* of hate incidents entirely subjective. Thus far, the widespread calls for 'making misogyny a hate crime' do not seem to suggest a broader understanding of the legal dimension of such proposals either, especially what is required, and at what threshold, in order to capture misogyny within the hate crime framework. Furthermore, as highlighted by Mullany and Trickett (2018), Nottinghamshire Police's recent evaluation of the pilot found that many of the participants were not familiar with the policy and did not fully understand the concept of misogyny hate crime. Unsurprisingly then, that these well-intentioned campaigns face mixed results and different levels of support amongst both the general public, public figures (Creasy 2020; The Scotsman 2020), academics (Barker and Jurasz 2020b), law makers,[3] and police forces (Quinn 2018).

The absence of online misogyny

Finally, the notion of *online* misogyny has been largely left outside the realm of campaigns as well as calls by the politicians to make misogyny a hate crime. For instance, according to the *No Place for Hate* report (Nottingham Citizens 2014), online abuse was the second least experienced type of hate crime (amongst those reported and recorded), but no conclusions were drawn in the report indicating the extent of online misogyny experienced by women in Nottinghamshire. This is problematic, especially given the prevalence of online abuse of women and girls (e.g. EIGE 2017) as well as the wide-ranging impact it has on their public participation, and the multiple harms associated with such forms of abuse (Barker and Jurasz 2021a).

More generally, what can be observed is relatively little engagement by campaigners and law makers with reforming the law to facilitate a more adequate regulatory framework for social media related offences dealing with abuse motivated by gender hostility. *If* such engagement were forthcoming, to reform online communications regulation, it is possible that this could form the basis for prosecuting misogyny and gender related social media crimes as hate crimes (should the relevant thresholds be met). This is a key shortcoming, especially in the context of the overwhelming amount of initiatives and calls for making misogyny a hate crime. It appears that online misogyny, whilst not unheard of or unknown to the campaigners (indeed, on many occasions, even suffered by them personally) and law makers, is an afterthought. Even where initiatives are targeted at addressing online hate crime, the prosecution rate is recorded as lower than 1% of all reported cases (Vaughan 2019) – a damning statistic.

Online misogyny and hate crime: the legal status quo[4]

Evaluating the scope of the current legal provisions to address online misogyny requires an assessment of both the hate crime provisions, but also the online regulatory elements of domestic law. Above all else, there are two key points worthy of note at the outset here: first, the hate crime framework in England and Wales requires that there be a characteristic which be protected in law in order for prejudice to arise in respect of that characteristic. Therefore, to suggest that misogyny can be a hate crime sends a mixed message and indicates that misogyny ought to be protected. Second, the communications provisions in the UK framework were all enacted before the social media age and were designed to address non-digital means of communication. Consequently, situating online misogyny in the legal framework poses a number of potential considerations. The next section therefore explores the legal status quo in England and Wales with respect to hate crime and demonstrates some of the key deficiencies of the current legislative framework in addressing online misogyny.

Misogyny within the hate crime framework

Misogyny – be it online or offline – is currently not captured within the hate crime framework in England and Wales. Given that misogyny is not listed as a protected characteristic in the hate crime legislation, it means that a crime committed against a woman with prejudice and/or hatred due to misogyny cannot be prosecuted as a hate crime (as it currently cannot be captured for enhanced sentencing purposes) by the courts in England and Wales. However, we argue that *capturing* the misogynistic aspect of certain hate crimes – especially when they happen online – is possible through meaningful reform: first, by adding gender to the list of protected characteristics under hate crime legislation in England and Wales, and second, by creating new offences committed on or using social media, which can adequately capture the plethora of forms of violence (both textual and image-based) experienced online, including but not limited to, misogynistic forms of abuse (Barker and Jurasz 2019a).

The current legal framework in England and Wales represents a three-fold approach to punishing hate crime: first, through aggravated offences (ss. 28–32 of the Crime and Disorder Act 1998); second, through offences of 'stirring up hatred' (Part 3 and 3A of the Public Order Act 1986), and third, through provisions allowing for enhanced sentencing (ss. 145 and 146 of the Criminal Justice Act 2003). In order for a crime to be prosecuted as hate crime, two elements must be satisfied: (i) there must be an incidence of underlying criminal conduct (provided for in the criminal law of England and Wales) and (ii) it must be shown that it was motivated by hostility or involved a demonstration of hostility on the basis of any of the five current protected characteristics: race, religion, sexual orientation, transgender identity, or disability.

However, although hate crimes in England and Wales are recorded for all five of the currently protected characteristics, there exists a distinct level of disparity between the legislative provisions relating to individual characteristics. For instance, race and religion appear to have been afforded much greater protection within the current framework by the mere virtue of being covered in all provisions dealing with hate crime (i.e. aggravated offences, stirring up offences, and enhanced sentencing). This approach has been heavily criticised (Schweppe 2012; Law Commission 2014; Mason 2014; Barker and Jurasz 2017a) for leading to arguably discriminatory and unequal outcomes under the current framework. In addition, the current provisions create a 'hierarchy of harms' (Barker and Jurasz 2019a) where victimisation due to some characteristics (notably race and religion) is effectively perceived to be more harmful than victimisation of and harms sustained by the victims of crimes motivated by hostility or bias based on sexual orientation and/or disability and/or transgender identity.

This largely unresolved issue of the hierarchy of characteristics (and by extension, harms) also prompts questions about the status of characteristics which may be added in the future – for example, gender (as suggested by the authors: Barker and Jurasz 2019a) or misogyny (as suggested by various campaigners). In addition, with regard to the latter, there arises an issue about the suitability of such a characteristic vis-à-vis the characteristics listed in the current statutory framework. Currently protected characteristics use terminology that refers to examples of specific demographics rather than terms phrased to capture discrimination, prejudice, or hatred due to these demographics (e.g. race rather than racism; sexual orientation rather than homophobia). Accordingly, it is difficult to see how protecting 'misogyny' rather than 'gender' and or 'sex' would fit – not least linguistically but also conceptually – within the current provisions.

The conceptual challenges posed by suggestions of capturing misogyny as a hate crime characteristic, are not the only barriers to clear reform in this area. Online manifestations of misogyny are increasingly problematic, but the law addressing abusive communications also requires reform in order to adequately capture the harms caused by online misogynistic abuses.

Online misogyny as a communications challenge

Where the hate crime framework fails to capture gender, there are other aspects of the criminal law that also fail to offer adequate protections for online abuses of women, particularly misogynistic text-based abuses perpetrated through social media (Barker and Jurasz 2019a). Much like the hate crime framework, and its many tranches of reform, consultation, and policy discussions, the regulation of platforms – especially communication platforms[5] – has witnessed a similar level of attention albeit at an increased velocity. Again, much like the hate crime framework, the legal regime that – supposedly – addresses offensive and abusive communications operates to create a hierarchy of harms, across a disparate collection of potential offences that capture criminal behaviours perpetrated through communication channels.

The communications regulatory framework under the law in England and Wales operates on a multidimensional basis, with different modes of communication – for example, post, electronic communications, and public electronic communications networks – all falling within this broad regime (Smith 2015). The second dimension to this paradigm is that of the nature of the communication, which is categorised according to (i) its content and (ii) the type of communications service used to communicate it.

The fragmented approach (of the hate crime provisions) is replicated with the online communication provisions, none of which – irrespective of medium or mode – capture gender perspectives (Barker and Jurasz 2019a). There is an – albeit limited – argument that it is unfair to critique communications provisions that were legislated on prior to the social media age.[6] That said, the current approach that the law of England and Wales adopts focuses on three distinct yet overlapping aspects: first, offences of threats and threats to kill (s. 4, s. 4A, s. 5 Public Order Act 1986, and s. 16 Offences Against the Person Act 1861); second, offences of stalking and harassment (s. 2A and s. 4A Protection from Harassment Act 1997, introduced in s. 111 Protection of Freedoms Act 2012, and s. 2 and s. 4 Protection from Harassment Act 1997); and third, pure communications offences relating to gross and indecent communications (s. 1 Malicious Communications Act 1988, and s. 127 Communications Act 2003). The latter, communications offences, are both offences of 'sending' and are therefore also concerned with the means by which the communication has been conveyed, as well as with the content of the purported message. This double focus of the offences really means that there is no specific focus falling purely on the content, nor on the means of the communication.

Above all else, what this fragmentation shows is that the divergent legal areas which relate to capturing misogyny as a hate crime – the hate framework, and communications provisions – are not easily altered to capture online misogyny. This fact is something that is seemingly neither understood nor appreciated by campaigners and lay activists – and is something that campaigns for capturing online misogyny as a hate crime conveniently skim over. What is more concerning is that, put simply, changing one provision to capture misogyny – as has been suggested by multiple campaign groups, and politicians alike (Creasy 2020) – will have untold foreseeable, and unpredictable consequences – with implications that only a holistic approach to law reform can mitigate. Unfortunately to date, campaigners and the criminal justice system alike have overlooked the need to address the fragmentation of law and policy in areas such as that encompassing misogyny. It is not a failing purely of English law (Barker and Jurasz 2019a) nor is it a challenge uniquely faced by the UK Government and legal bodies – the fragmentation of legal responses poses significant barriers for the European Commission, and for European gender equality law alike (Barker and Jurasz 2020c, 2021a).

Consequently, what the disparate legal aspects – when considered in parallel – show is that there has historically, and contemporarily, been a lack of joined-up thinking (Barker and Jurasz 2017b) when addressing issues of misogyny, and more latterly, online misogyny. Even now, with concurrent packages of law reform promised to address online regulation, platform dominance, and digital duties of care, there remains a distinct gulf between different levels of responsibility and thinking. More than this though, the absence of considerations of gender is stark – particularly astonishing in platform regulation discussions (Barker and Jurasz 2020c) as well as within hate crime legislation.

These omissions and oversight are also particularly notable where case law is concerned. The absence of gender considerations is not an omission which is solely the fault of statutory provisions (i.e. hate crime legislation and communications offences). Similarly, it is not solely the fault of policymaking, law reform, or platform regulation, but is something which has been consistently ostracised when it comes to case law which evidences the impact of online misogyny – albeit where such limited case law exists. For instance, while the statistics regarding reported cases involving communications network offences seem to have risen – recorded offences of malicious communications in England and Wales in 2019 show a 14% increase on those from the previous year – from 184,986 in 2018, to 211,421 in 2019 (ONS 2019) – the number of incidences involving a prosecution where there is a gendered element to the offensive communication are unknown. That said, there have been several high-profile prosecutions where extreme online abuse has been the source of criminal investigation in England and Wales.

For instance, *R v Nimmo and Sorley* (2014)[7] saw custodial sentences issued to 'online trolls' for their Twitter harassment campaigns targeted at campaigner, Caroline Criado-Perez, and Stella Creasy MP, for their involvement in the movement to include women on bank notes. The prosecutions here were pursued on the basis of a s. 127 Communications Act 2003 offence, which focuses on the improper use of a public communications network as the basis for criminality, rather than the sole content of the threatening messages. The prosecution here paid little *substantive* attention to the content of the messages sent by Nimmo and Sorley to their respective victims, focussing instead on the manner of the messaging (Barker 2018). Not only does this ignore the gendered motivations within the threatening communications, it also excludes notions of gender-based abuses that could form the basis of a criminally prosecutable offence in respect of online misogyny (should one exist). The judicial sentencing remarks, whilst recognising the incredibly damaging effects of online communications threatening physical harm, failed to acknowledge or engage with the explicitly sexualised nature of the communications sent to both victims by both perpetrators (Barker and Jurasz 2021a). Digital, online communications conveying rape and death threats are by their very nature gendered forms of abuse amounting – in this instance – to online misogynistic abuse, and yet, there has been no real consideration given to this aspect of online violence.

This situation is replicated in the other high-profile case addressing extreme online sexualised abuse suffered by the anti-Brexit campaigner, Gina Miller. In *R v Viscount St Davids* (2017),[8] the prosecution was also pursued in response to messages posted on social media platforms as another s. 127 Communications Act 2003 infraction. The distinction in this case compared to *R v Nimmo & Sorley* is that the messages here were posted on Facebook and included racialised harassment, alongside threats to assassinate. That said, the posts were also incredibly gendered in their content, and also included threats of physical harm. The sentencing remarks highlighted again, the damage of online abuse to victims who suffer it, but also once again overlooked any elements of gender, or of the sexualised abuse contained within the posts. As such, the case also failed to fully demonstrate the intersectional nature of the online abuse suffered by Gina Miller – and, more broadly, many other victims of online hate.

Whilst criticism cannot be levied unjustly at the individual judges sitting in *R v Nimmo Sorley* and in *R v Viscount St Davids*, there is a much broader perspective to be considered here. First, there is no scope within the current legal framework addressing hate, nor that addressing online communications for gender-based analysis to be considered. Second, the messages in both cases were dealt with as communications misuse offences rather than instances of threatening behaviour, or racial harassment, meaning that neither court could consider imposing higher sentences because more serious prosecutions were not pursued under other criminal provisions. Not only is there an absence of considerations of gender in cases where the substantive abuse is overwhelmingly gendered in its content, but the prosecutorial decision making is also gender-blind, in that in these two high-profile case examples featuring sexualised online communications, more serious offences were not pursued. If more serious offences – beyond the communications network misuse provisions – had been considered, this would not per se have factored in a gendered perspective, but it would – at the very least – have sent clear signals that messages of this kind will not be tolerated given their level of harm (Barker and Jurasz 2021a) and their impact on women.

Ultimately, given the fragmentation of hate crime, and of the communications misuse provisions in England and Wales, repeated failings are the only consistent variable. The state of the various criminal law provisions does little to inspire confidence about capturing instances of online misogyny, particularly where it is incredibly harmful. While there are no specific provisions – yet – addressing the sexualised nature of abusive communications such as those seen in *R v Nimmo & Sorley*, and in *R v Viscount St Davids*, the law in this area is crying out for reform, but it is reform which must be considered, and careful (Barker and Jurasz 2017b, 2019a, 2020b) so as to not do more harm than good to the rights of women.

Avenues for reform

The legal status quo does little to inspire confidence that a gendered perspective will be forthcoming in this area. That said, there are potential avenues of law reform that could – and should – be pursued to ensure that there are alterations to substantive legal provisions – rather than confusing and glossy campaigns, or well-intentioned but misleading initiatives – that would allow for the capturing of misogynistic behaviours, both online and offline. In order to ensure that there is meaningful change, reform is required in two distinct but connected areas: first, in adding a gender aggravator, and second, in reforming communications offences to focus on the substance rather than the means of sending. By addressing the phenomenon of online misogyny from this dual perspective, there will be a noticeable reduction in the fragmentation of responses to violence against women and girls, especially when manifested in its online forms.

A gender aggravator[9]

Traditionally, and historically, law enforcement and law reform bodies have been one-dimensional, focussing almost exclusively on aspects that exclude women from the legal framework. Not only does this approach no longer have a place in contemporary society, but allowing it to continue to go unchecked means that gender-based harms – such as online misogyny – will consistently be omitted (despite their growing prevalence), allowing the legal system to reflect and replicate the patriarchal tendencies that are entrenched in society more broadly. This ultimately manifests itself to mean that women who are recipients – and then victims – of online abusive communications which evince hostility on the basis of gender – such as those sent in *R* v *Nimmo & Sorley* – are not currently covered in the legal system as it stands, even if the state sees a benefit in addressing the lesser problems of misusing a communications network.

Given the endemic patriarchal tendencies, and the repeated failings to include gender within the hate crime framework, it is now time to add gender as one of the protected characteristics. In doing so, this would not only give recognition to the prevalence of everyday misogyny. In making this change, and recognising the existence of misogynistic hostility, the legal system would be catering for situations where criminal acts – which are aggravated by a manifestation of gendered hostility to not only be prosecuted as hate crimes, but also to be recorded as specific hate crimes in the criminal statistics. Moreover, such reform would then allow sentencing uplifts to be considered where evidence of gendered aggravation is present in the underlying criminal act. To put this slightly differently, if gender existed within the hate crime framework as a protected characteristic, it could have been considered in the sentencing of the convicted twitter trolls Nimmo & Sorley, where the underlying criminal offence would still have been a s. 127 Communications Act 2003 misuse offence. In considering the gender hostility in the content of the offences, the courts could – had gender existed as a protected characteristic – have increased the sentencing on the basis of this hostility. In this respect, the custodial sentences could have been increased as a result – much like the racial aggravation was a factor in the sentencing in *R* v *Viscount St Davids*. This approach would not only bring gender within the hate crime framework, but it would offer a mechanism by which to capture harms which are currently excluded or belittled as being attached to sensitivities around gender.

Social media content offences

The second aspect which requires law reform in the area of online misogyny is the law relating to social media more broadly. Whilst much has been written elsewhere about the need for, and scope of online regulation,[10] particularly relating to online hatred (Citron 2014; Poland 2016; Alkiviadou 2018) and online abuses (Donath 1999; Lewis et al. 2017), the recommendation here is one for specific legislation addressing the contents of social media communications. This recommendation is one which is now more pressing than previously, and despite previous opposition to such a suggestion (House of Lords 2014) the online environment and social norms have changed and become much more polarised. Such shifts now suggest that there is not only increased use of online communication, but also greater levels of online abusive communications in correlation to the usage rises, which stand in stark contrast to the lack of legislative attention given to reform in this area of law. The law relating to communications (which also captures social media communications) has not been updated since before the rise of the Internet Giants (Facebook, YouTube, Twitter).[11] The incredibly dated nature of the law in this area, together with the emergence of smartphones has created a situation which leaves much to be desired. Abusive communications, can no longer be addressed purely through notions of criminalising misuses of communications networks as the various fragmented pieces of legislation indicate, not least because of the difficulties in satisfying the public interest test for prosecution, and the threshold of 'grossly offensive' which resides in s. 127 Communications Act 2003 (Maij 2016, para. 32; Barker and Jurasz 2019a). These communications misuse offences, which undoubtedly still have a place, are no longer the ones which online abusive communications should be addressed through. The focus must change so that the content of the offences is the predominant consideration, rather than the medium and means of communicating. This is an especially pressing point given that the offences relate to the *sending* of grossly offensive communications (Barker and Jurasz 2019a). The emphasis therefore falls on the *sending* rather than the content of the communications alone. Similarly, no significant attention has yet fallen on the harms that arise through such sending.

While there are long-awaited, and much promised reform agendas at play within the UK – and the EU – in the form of the Online Safety Bill,[12] and the Digital Services Act,[13] there are other aspects of domestic law reform in England and Wales that must pay greater attention to the gendered elements of online abusive communications. Reform work is ongoing in respect of offensive and abusive communications, alongside the Online Harms programme of work, and both of these must work in combination, and with the hate crime framework to ensure that online misogyny is appropriately captured. The unusual concurrent timing of these programmes of law reform offers a unique opportunity to address – holistically – this issue in statutory form, offering not only a chance at progressive legal reform, but also sending a clear signal that embedded patriarchal tendencies will be forced to change, not least because the legal system is one of the most patriarchal elements of modern society. That said, the Online Harms White Paper is – sadly – not particularly encouraging in this respect though, notably because out of the 23 harms listed within it (UK Government 2019), there is no specific mention of any with a gender connotation. This remains a significant omission, and it is to be hoped that this is addressed either in the draft Online Safety Bill, or in the relevant parliamentary debates as the Bill progresses. Failing to adequately address the content of social media communications within these overlapping areas of law reform will continue to disregard notions of gender-based hostility resulting in online misogyny, despite its prevalence, and despite its repeated emergence in all manner of online contexts including social media, online fora, and online games (Lorenz and Browning 2020).

Conclusions: fixing the 'gender' problem?

The rise in the discourse surrounding misogyny, but especially online misogyny is not entirely unexpected. The patriarchal tendencies which are deeply rooted in society have proven incredibly difficult to overcome. The challenges that offline misogyny have posed, are spreading – unsurprisingly – across the online sphere too. Not only are abusive communications a legal challenge, they are increasingly also a challenge for gender, and for equality.

In addressing the harmful, and widespread phenomenon of online misogyny, there is a growing need to introduce law reform – not for the sake of creating more law, but more effective, better law. In its pure legal form, statutory amendment is just one step that needs to be taken. Much, much more is required in order to tackle the broader issues of misogyny in society, and this requires attention from a range of sectors, not just the legal one. The unexpected, and associated challenge with a multisectoral drive for change is that it brings with it campaigns, initiatives, and social pressure which whilst well-intended, and usually more high-profile with greater support than protracted legal debate, often causes more problems in the interim than it proposes to solve. Interest, awareness raising, and support for reform are vital elements in any effective and sustained change, but they must take place within a framework where there is a workable *legal* appreciation – if not understanding – of what it is that is being campaigned for. Frequently there are campaigns for making misogyny a hate crime – this in itself, whilst headline-grabbing is misleading (Barker and Jurasz 2020b). To make misogyny a hate crime requires steps to misogyny a characteristic – this is not aligned with anything in the hate crime framework and would have the opposite effect to that intended by campaigns. As such, it is something of a misnomer to campaign for such a thing to happen. Not only is it evidence of a misunderstanding of the legal technicalities, but is damaging to public will, especially when such campaigns may lead to – as is possible – bad laws, and contradictory messages.

Similarly, what is also concerning, is that some of the campaigns focus on a singular issue – to make misogyny a hate crime – and beyond that, do not situate the campaign in the broader area of violence against women. Not only does this invariably lead to issue-dominated law reform, but it also causes damage to more holistic considerations of frameworks to prevent and combat violence against women, and gender stereotypes. Above all else, what this shows is the need for the fostering of a clearer understanding in campaigning – and advocacy – of the legal aspects of hate crime, and the role of gender within it, rather than claiming that misogyny is a hate crime.

What is ultimately required to address the challenges posed by misogyny in its online forms, and effectively call #TimesUp, is specific 'joined-up thinking' that goes beyond the criminal law. By operating on this basis, it would be possible to enact reform in two specific legal ways (as outlined above), and in so doing, these proposals would enhance the protections embedded within the legal framework for the abuse of women for being women – on and offline. Moreover, it would also allow the legal framework to move forward and reduce the influence of the patriarchy. Beyond that, this proposal puts violence against women and girls – even online violence – at the heart of legal mechanisms, as well as in compliance with other legal instruments, including the Convention on the Elimination of All Forms of Discrimination against Women (CEDAW) (Barker and Jurasz 2019b). It also sends a very clear #TimesUp signal to online misogyny.

Notes

1 The need to reform the law dealing with social media was considered by the House of Lords Communications Committee (2014), where the conclusion was reached that there was no need to introduce additional or revised legal provisions addressing the communications provisions in the UK. This position – which the authors disagreed with in 2014 – is even more unsustainable now.
2 It is worth noting that the category of 'gender' rather than 'sex' or 'misogyny' was used by the respondents.
3 For example, the Law Commission in England and Wales is currently reviewing the adequacy of protection offered by hate crime legislation. As of June 2020, the Consultation Paper has not yet been published. However, the information paper published by the Law Commission suggests that the Law Commission will not be consulting on whether or not to add 'misogyny' to the list of protected characteristics. Instead, the extension of protected characteristics to potentially include 'sex' and/or 'gender' is proposed (Law Commission 2019, p. 11).
4 For an in-depth legal analysis of online misogyny and hate crime, see in particular Chapters 3 and 4 in: Barker, K., Jurasz, O., 2019a. *Online Misogyny as a Hate Crime: A Challenge for Legal Regulation?* Routledge.

5 Taken here to be defined as online interactive platforms designed to encourage sharing of personal messaging, and to non-exhaustively include Facebook, Twitter, WhatsApp, and Instagram. The legal definition of a communications platform under the various communications provisions in England and Wales categorises a communications platform as a public communications network.
6 Almost all of the legal provisions in England and Wales addressing communications, and the misuses of communications networks were introduced pre-smartphones, pre-social media, and pre-internet platform. As such, the provisions are being stretched to accommodate behaviours they were never intended to deal with, and which were, unforeseeable at the time of legislative drafting.
7 *R* v *Nimmo* and *Sorley* (2014) unreported. The sentencing remarks are available online given the significance of the issues being addressed in the case, even in the absence of an official law report given the lack of seniority of the court holding the hearing.
8 *R* v *Viscount St Davids* (2017) unreported. The judgment and the sentencing remarks are available online – again, like *R* v *Nimmo and Sorley* because of the significance of the issue under consideration – but there is no official law report of the judgment given the lack of seniority of the court.
9 For a fuller discussion of 'gender aggravator', also in the context of other jurisdictions, see: Barker and Jurasz (2017a, 2019e, 2020d).
10 This piece does not engage in a detailed discussion of internet regulation broadly understood.
11 For instance, the Malicious Communications Act 1988 was last updated in 2001, whereas the 'newer' Communications Act 2003 was introduced in 2000.
12 The much-awaited Online Safety Bill has been promised by mid 2021 given that the promised reform in this area in the UK at least, has been rumbling since the Internet Safety Consultation in late 2017.
13 The ongoing Digital Services Act Consultation by the European Commission (which runs until September 2020) is expected to update – at the very least – Directive 2000/31/EC of the European Parliament and of the Council of 8 June 2000 on Certain Legal Aspects of Information Society Services, in Particular Electronic Commerce, in the Internal Market ('Directive on Electronic Commerce') [2000] OJ L178/1, (e-Commerce Directive 2000).

References

Alkiviadou, N., 2018. Hate speech on social media networks: towards a regulatory framework. *Information and Communications Technology Law*, 28(1), pp. 19–35. DOI: 10.1080/13600834.2018.1494417.

Amnesty International, 2017. Unsocial media: tracking Twitter abuse against women MPs [online]. 3 September. Available at: https://medium.com/@AmnestyInsights/unsocial-media-tracking-twitter-abuse-against-women-mps-fc28aeca498a [Accessed 26 March 2020].

Amnesty International, 2018. Toxic Twitter – a toxic place for women [online]. 18 March. Available at: https://www.amnesty.org/en/latest/research/2018/03/online-violence-against-women-chapter-3/#topanchor [Accessed 04 August 2020].

Anti-Defamation League, 2018. When women are the enemy: the intersection of misogyny and white supremacy. Available at: https://www.adl.org/resources/reports/when-women-are-the-enemy-the-intersection-of-misogyny-and-white-supremacy [Accessed 24 March 2020].

Ashcroft, E., 2017. Cat-calling and wolf-whistling now classed as gender-hate crimes by Avon and Somerset Police. *Bristol Post* [online]. 16 October 2017. Available at:

www.bristolpost.co.uk/news/bristol-news/gender-hate-now-recognised-crime-635194?utm_content=bufferf8757&utm_medium=social&utm_source=twitter.com&utm_campaign=buffer [Accessed 29 March 2020].

Barker, K., 2018. *R v Nimmo and Sorley* (2014). In: Rackley, E. and Auchmuty, R., eds. *Women's Legal Landmarks: Celebrating 100 Years of Women and Law in the UK and Ireland.* Oxford: Hart, pp. 608–610.

Barker, K. and Jurasz, O., 2014. Gender, human rights and cybercrime: are virtual worlds really that different? In: Asimow, M., Brown, K. and Papke, D., eds. *Law and Popular Culture: International Perspectives.* Cambridge: Cambridge Scholars Publishing, pp. 79–100.

Barker, K. and Jurasz, O., 2017a. Submission of evidence to Scottish government independent review of hate crime legislation (Bracadale review) [online]. Open University. December 2017. Available at: http://oro.open.ac.uk/52612/ [Accessed 10 June 2020].

Barker, K. and Jurasz, O., 2017b. Submission of evidence to the UN special rapporteur on violence against women, its causes and consequences, Dr Dubravka Šimonović [online]. Open University. November 2017. Available at: http://oro.open.ac.uk/52611/ [Accessed 1 July 2020].

Barker, K. and Jurasz, O., 2019a. *Online Misogyny as a Hate Crime: A Challenge for Legal Regulation?* London: Routledge.

Barker, K. and Jurasz, O., 2019b. Online misogyny: a challenge for digital feminism? *Journal of International Affairs*, 72(2), pp. 95–113.

Barker, K. and Jurasz, O., 2019c. Violence against women in politics (#vawp) – the antithesis of (online) equality [online]. Scottish Policy and Research Exchange Blog. 10 May. Available at: https://spre.scot/violence-against-women-in-politics-online/ [Accessed 24 March 2020].

Barker, K. and Jurasz, O., 2019d. Expert response to One Scotland consultation on amending Scottish hate crime legislation [online]. Scottish Parliament. Available at: http://oro.open.ac.uk/66207/.

Barker, K. and Jurasz, O., 2020a. Gendered misinformation and online violence against women in politics: capturing legal responsibility? [online]. Co-Inform. 18 March. Available at: https://coinform.eu/gendered-misinformation-online-violence-against-women-in-politics-capturing-legal-responsibility/ [Accessed 24 March 2020].

Barker, K. and Jurasz, O., 2020b. Why misogyny and hate crime reforms need more than slick campaigns [online]. *The Conversation.* 26 March. Available at: https://theconversation.com/why-misogyny-and-hate-crime-reforms-need-more-than-slick-campaigns-134265 [Accessed 10 June 2020].

Barker, K. and Jurasz, O., 2020c. Online violence against women as an obstacle to gender equality: a critical view from Europe. *European Equality Law Review* [online], 2020(1), pp. 47–60. Available at: https://www.equalitylaw.eu/downloads/5182-european-equality-law-review-1-2020-pdf-1-057-kb [Accessed 4 August 2020].

Barker, K. and Jurasz, O., 2020d. Consultation response: hate crime legislation in Northern Ireland – an independent review [online]. Available at: http://oro.open.ac.uk/71520/1/Barker%20%26%20Jurasz%20-%20NI%20Hate%20Crime%20Review%20Consultation%20Response%20%282020%29.pdf [Accessed 4 August 2020].

Barker, K. and Jurasz, O., 2021a. Text-based (sexual) abuse and violence against women: towards law reform? In: Bailey, J., Flynn, A. and Henry, N., eds.

Handbook of Technology-Facilitated Violence and Abuse: International Perspectives and Experiences. Bingley: Emerald Publishing Limited.

Barker, K. and Jurasz, O., 2021b. Misogynistic harassment: A stumbling block for scots hate crime reform? *Juridical Review*, 2021(1), pp. 1–17.

Barlow, C. and Awan, I., 2016. 'You need to be sorted out with a knife': the attempted silencing of women and people of Muslim faith within academia. *Social Media + Society*, 2(4), pp. 1–11. DOI: 10.1177/2056305116678896.

Berners-Lee, T. and Berners-Lee, R., 2020. Why the web needs to work for women and girls. The Web Foundation [online]. 12 March. Available at: https://webfoundation.org/2020/03/web-birthday-31/ [Accessed 30 June 2020].

CitizensUK, 2018. #MisogynyIShate: a summer of campaigning across Greater Manchester. 5 September. Available at: https://www.citizensuk.org/misogyny_gmc [Accessed 30 June 2020].

Citron, D.K., 2014. *Hate Crimes in Cyberspace*. Cambridge, MA: Harvard University Press.

Cohen, C. and Hymas, C., 2020. Treat misogyny as a hate crime, say MPs, as they lay amendment to change law. *The Telegraph* [online]. 10 June 2020. Available at: https://www.telegraph.co.uk/politics/2020/06/10/treat-misogyny-hate-crime-say-mps-lay-amendment-change-law/ [Accessed 30 June 2020].

Communications Act 2003 (c. 21).

Creasy, S., 2020. Why we're campaigning to change the law and make misogyny a hate crime. *The Telegraph* [online]. 11 June 2020. Available at: https://www.telegraph.co.uk/women/politics/fighting-change-law-make-misogyny-hate-crime/ [Accessed 30 June 2020].

Crime and Disorder Act 1998 (c. 37).

Criminal Justice Act 2003 (c. 44).

Department of Justice, 2019. Review of hate crime legislation launched [online]. 6 June. Available at: https://www.justice-ni.gov.uk/news/review-hate-crime-legislation-launched [Accessed 30 June 2020].

Directive 2000/31/EC of the European Parliament and of the Council of 8 June 2000 on Certain Legal Aspects of Information Society Services, in Particular Electronic Commerce, in the Internal Market ('Directive on Electronic Commerce') [2000] OJ L178/1, (e-Commerce Directive 2000).

Donath, J., 1999. Identity and deception in the virtual community. In: Smith, M.A. and Kollock, P., eds. *Communities in Cyberspace*. London: Routledge, pp. 29–59.

Duriesmith, D., Ryan, L. and Zimmerman, S., 2018. Misogyny as violent extremism [online]. Available at: http://www.internationalaffairs.org.au/australianoutlook/misogyny-as-violent-extremism/ [accessed 29 March 2020].

EIGE, 2017. Cyberviolence against women and girls [online]. 23 June. Available at: https://eige.europa.eu/publications/cyber-violence-against-women-and-girls [Accessed 30 June 2020].

FRA, 2014. Violence against women: an EU-wide survey. Main results report [online]. Publications Office of the European Union. Available at: https://fra.europa.eu/en/publication/2014/violence-against-women-eu-wide-survey-main-results-report [Accessed 1 December 2020].

Ging, D. and Siapera, E., 2019. *Gender Hate Online. Understanding the New Anti-feminism*. Cham: Palgrave Macmillan.

Hate Crime (Misogyny) Bill 2019–2021 (2019). *Parliament: House of Commons*. London: UK Parliament. Available at: https://services.parliament.uk/Bills/2019-21/hatecrimemisogyny.html.

Hate Crime and Public Order (Scotland) Bill 2020. Available at: https://beta.parliament.scot/bills-and-laws/bills/hate-crime-and-public-order-scotland-bill.

Hobhouse, W., 2020. IWD 2020: recognise misogyny as a hate crime [online]. 9 March. Available at: https://www.libdems.org.uk/iwd-2020-misogyny-hate-crime [Accessed 30 June 2020].

House of Lords, 2014. Social media and criminal offences. House of Lords Select Committee on Communications. 29 July. The Stationery Office Limited (HL 37).

Jane, E., 2017. *Misogyny Online: A Short (and Brutish) History*. London: SAGE.

Koulouris, T., 2018. Online misogyny and the alternative right: debating the undebatable. *Feminist Media Studies*, 18(4), pp. 750–761. DOI: 10.1080/14680777.2018.1447428.

Law Commission, 2014. Hate crime: should the current offences be extended? (Law Com No. 348). Available at: http://www.lawcom.gov.uk/app/uploads/2015/03/lc348_hate_crime.pdf [Accessed 9 May 2021].

Law Commission, 2019. Hate crime: background to our review [online]. Available at: https://s3-eu-west-2.amazonaws.com/lawcom-prod-storage-11jsxou24uy7q/uploads/2019/07/6.5286-LC_Hate-Crime_Information-Paper_A4_FINAL_030719_WEB.pdf [Accessed 14 June 2020].

Lewis, R., Rowe, M. and Wiper, C., 2017. Online abuse of feminists as an emerging form of violence against women and girls. *The British Journal of Criminology*, 57(6), pp. 1462–1481. DOI: 10.1093/bjc/azw073.

Lorenz, T. and Browning, K., 2020. Dozens of women in gaming speak out about sexism and harassment. *The New York Times* [online]. 23 June. Available at: https://www.nytimes.com/2020/06/23/style/women-gaming-streaming-harassment-sexism-twitch.html?smtyp=cur&smid=tw-nytimes [Accessed 30 June 2020].

Malicious Communications Act 1988 (c. 27).

Maij, M., 2016. Ending cyberdiscrimination and online hate, report by rapporteur Marit Maij. Council of Europe Parliamentary Assembly Committee on Equality and Non-discrimination, (Doc 14217). 13 December. Available at: https://pace.coe.int/en/files/23234/html [Accessed 9 May 2021].

Mason, G., 2014. Victim attributes in hate crime law: difference and politics of justice. *The British Journal of Criminology*, 54(2), pp. 161–179. DOI: 10.1093/bjc/azt073.

Morgan, D., 2020. Women in politics face 'daily' abuse on social media [online]. *BBC Politics Wales*. 24 May. Available at: https://www.bbc.co.uk/news/uk-wales-politics-52785157 [Accessed 1 December 2020].

Mullany, L. and Trickett, L., 2018. Misogyny hate crime evaluation report. Nottingham Woman's Centre [online]. Available at: http://www.nottinghamwomenscentre.com/wp-content/uploads/2018/07/Misogyny-HateCrime-Evaluation-Report-June-2018.pdf [Accessed 29 March 2020].

North Yorkshire Police, 2016. North Yorkshire Police announce misogyny now recognised as hate crime [online]. Available at: https://northyorkshire.police.uk/staying-safe/hate-crime/north-yorkshire-police-announce-misogyny-now-recognised-hate-crime/ [Accessed 1 April 2020].

Nottingham Citizens, 2014. No place for hate [online]. Available at: https://www.citizensuk.org/notts_commission [Accessed 29 March 2020].

Offences against the Person Act 1861 (c. 100).

ONS, 2019. Crime survey of England and Wales annex tables [online]. 23 April 2020. Available at: https://www.ons.gov.uk/peoplepopulationandcommunity/crimeandjustice/datasets/crimeinenglandandwalesappendixtables [Accessed 30 June 2020].

Phipps, A., 2014. The dark side of the impact agenda. *The Times Higher Education* [online]. 4 December. Available at: https://www.timeshighereducation.com/comment/opinion/the-dark-side-of-the-impact-agenda/2017299.article [Accessed 29 March 2020].

Poland, B., 2016. *Haters, Harassment, Abuse and Violence Online*. Lincoln: University of Nebraska Press.

Protection from Harassment Act 1997 (c. 40).

Protection of Freedoms Act 2012 (c. 9).

Public Order Act 1986 (c. 64).

Quinn, B., 2018. Met police chief backs call to focus on violent crime not misogyny. *The Guardian* [online]. 2 November. Available at: https://www.theguardian.com/uk-news/2018/nov/02/metropolitan-police-chief-cressida-dick-backs-call-focus-violent-crime-misogyny [Accessed 30 June 2020].

R v Nimmo and Sorley, 2014. Sentencing remarks [online]. Available at: https://www.judiciary.uk/wp-content/uploads/JCO/Documents/Judgments/r-v-nimmo-and-sorley.pdf [Accessed 20 June 2020].

R v Viscount St Davids, 2017. Sentencing remarks [online]. Available at: https://www.judiciary.uk/judgments/r-v-viscount-st-davids/ [Accessed 30 June 2020].

Schweppe, J., 2012. Defining characteristics and politicizing victims: a legal perspective. *Journal of Hate Studies*, 10(1), pp. 173–198. DOI: 10.33972/jhs.118.

Smith, G., 2015. From telegram to tweet: section 127 and all that [online]. *Cyberleagle.com*, 22 February. Available at: https://www.cyberleagle.com/2015/02/from-telegram-to-tweet-section-127-and.html [Accessed 30 June 2020].

Sobieraj, S., 2018. Bitch, slut, skank, cunt: patterned resistance to women's visibility in digital publics. *Information, Communication and Society*, 21(11), pp. 1700–1714. DOI: 10.1080/1369118X.2017.1348535.

Stein, M., 2008. Misogyny. In: Smith, B.G., ed. *Oxford Encyclopaedia of Women in World History*. Oxford: Oxford University Press. Available via: Oxford Reference [Accessed: 27 March 2020].

The Scotsman, 2020. Tory MP under fire after saying prejudice against men should be made a hate crime. *The Scotsman* [online]. 8 March. Available at: https://www.scotsman.com/news/politics/tory-mp-under-fire-after-saying-prejudice-against-men-should-be-made-hate-crime-2441112 [Accessed 30 June 2020].

UK Government, 2019. Online harms white paper [online]. Available at: https://assets.publishing.service.gov.uk/government/uploads/system/uploads/attachment_data/file/793360/Online_Harms_White_Paper.pdf [Accessed 20 June 2020].

Vaughan, H., 2019. Less than 1% of cases reported online hate crime unit resulted in charges. *The Independent* [online]. 30 December 2019. Available at: https://www.independent.co.uk/news/uk/home-news/online-hate-crime-report-charge-sadiq-khan-a9263316.html [Accessed 04 August 2020].

Wajcman, J., 2010. Feminist theories of technology. *Cambridge Journal of Economics*, 34(1), pp. 143–152. DOI: 10.1093/cje/ben057.

5 From sexism to misogyny
Can online echo chambers stay quarantined?

Alexandra Krendel

Introduction

In this chapter, I investigate the use of sexist language in five communities within the Reddit 'manosphere', and consider whether or not this language amounts to hate speech. I make a distinction between potentially prosecutable hate crime and hate speech which does not necessarily warrant a legal response but could still present a risk to women and girls, and thus necessitate a response from the platforms which host these communities. To do this, I utilise Manne's (2018) distinction between sexism and misogyny, where sexism is defined as the discriminatory beliefs about women that individuals hold, whereas misogyny is defined as seeking to enforce these beliefs by aiming to silence its victims. Thus, she argues that misogyny has a strongly disciplinary component whereas sexism does not. However, Manne (2018) also observes that sexist beliefs can lead to misogynist behaviour. Thus, examining sexism as well as misogyny is important because it considers the extent to which sexist beliefs and participating in sexist communities could lead to criminal acts which can be interpreted as misogynistic. The chapter will firstly discuss how sexist language is a prevalent issue online, and the ways it can affect women and feminists with a public profile. Then, I will describe the loose network of online platforms known as the 'manosphere', the differences between the five sub-groups of the 'manosphere', and the extent to which their beliefs and actions can be considered a solely online phenomenon. Then, I will discuss whether these groups pose a threat to women and girls, whether the speech of the 'manosphere' constitutes hate speech, and how this speech should be considered in comparisons to the other harms described in this volume.

Misogyny and sexism online

Much research into gender relations online has noted that the online realm is still regarded as a male-dominated domain (Banet-Weiser and Miltner 2016; Nicholas and Agius 2018), and mainstream online platforms such as Twitter and Reddit are used for both harassing women (defined as misogyny for our purposes) and expressing sexist opinions (sexism). For example, Mantilla (2013) used the term "gendertrolling" to refer to the gender-based insults, rape threats, threats of doxxing (revealing information about a person's offline identity such as their address), and physically aggressive language that women with a public profile are subjected to online. Citron (2014) noted that online harassment and cyber-stalking disproportionately affect women, that women in journalism across the political spectrum are regularly subjected to gender-based abuse, and that gender-based abuse is an expected phenomenon when maintaining an online presence. This is supported by the prevalence of online hate against female MPs on Twitter in the UK, with some female MPs citing online harassment as a reason for not re-standing in elections (Williams and Mishcon de Reya 2019).

This disciplinary phenomenon also applies to laypeople. Megarry (2014) conducted a content analysis of the #mencallmethings hashtag on Twitter, which women used to disclose the online harassment they had been subjected to from men. One key theme of these posts was that these abusive messages, and their sheer presence online, affected the freedom of expression of women, and encouraged them to self-silence for fear of being harassed. Sobieraj (2018) found similar results in her interviews with 38 female victims of online harassment, and interviews with industry professionals in content moderation. She found that the presence of women online is resisted in three ways through online misogyny: limiting women's public impact by shaming them, intimidating and discrediting women; others constructing femininity as a weakness; and calling attention to women's bodies.

Such online attacks are not always isolated acts conducted by a single person. Banet-Weiser and Miltner (2016) noted the prevalence of co-ordinated acts of misogyny on social media sites, which they refer to as instances of 'networked misogyny'. The content aggregation site Reddit, which is the sixth most popular website in the US, and has 330 million monthly active users per month (Archibald 2020), was central to two such 'networked misogyny' movements, colloquially referred to as 'Gamergate' and 'The Fappening'. On Reddit, individuals create discussion spaces known as subreddits, which are dedicated to sharing both original posts and external links on a specific topic, and then users comment on these posts. In Gamergate, which occurred in 2014, game developers Zoe Quinn and Brianna Wu, and feminist media critic Anita Sarkeesian, were the victims of an ongoing harassment campaign which included rape threats, death threats, and doxxing. This sexist movement could be tracked across multiple online platforms, including 4chan, 8chan, and Reddit, where the subreddit /r/KotakuInAction was created to facilitate discussions around Gamergate. In the same year, a cache of private photographs of nude female celebrities was leaked online without their consent, and the subreddit /r/TheFappening was created for sharing these photographs. This subreddit was allowed to function for months following the incident, and was banned to avoid copyright disputes rather than to protect the victims of image-based sexual abuse (Woollacott 2014).

In her ethnographic study of Reddit as a platform, Massanari (2015) observed that although subreddits are distinct from one another in terms of topic, Reddit as a whole has a culture which is developed by regular Reddit users, and that this culture is anti-feminist. For instance, she notes resistance to the woman-centred subreddit /r/TwoXChromosomes gaining popularity and space on Reddit's homepage, the popularity of subreddits which share and enjoy sexually explicit pictures of women while simultaneously judging the women negatively for participating, and the popularity of memes which stereotype women as either unreasonable feminists, overly demanding, or sexually promiscuous. Massanari (2015, p. 137) also noted the prevalence of subreddits hosting 'manosphere' content such as /r/MensRights, which discuss the discrimination that men face as a social demographic, and /r/seduction, which discuss seduction techniques for picking up women. Although 'manosphere' subreddits frame relations between men and women in problematic ways, these spaces typically facilitate discussions between 'manosphere' members as opposed to organising harassment attacks. Thus, I argue that the Reddit 'manosphere' can broadly be described as a sexist community, as opposed to an explicitly misogynist one like Gamergate, although it would be problematic to suggest that online discussions of sexism could not manifest in misogynistic acts elsewhere. Indeed, the following description of the 'manosphere' community below highlights this cline between sexism and misogyny.

The 'manosphere' in five parts

The 'manosphere' is a loose network of anti-feminist websites and communities, which are united in the masculinist (Blais and Dupuis-Deri 2012) belief that men are in crisis due to widespread feminism, and that feminism should be resisted in various ways. This perception of being in a crisis of masculinity leads to feelings of 'aggrieved entitlement' (Kimmel 2013), that is, not getting what one feels entitled to, experiencing anger and humiliation as a result, and seeking a way to reclaim what has been lost. For different aspects of the 'manosphere', elaborated on below, different entitlements are foregrounded; however 'aggrieved entitlement' in the context of the 'manosphere' broadly refers to a 'mythic past of fixed gender dynamics' (Kelly 2017, p. 73), before the second-wave feminist movement made gains towards women's economic and sexual freedom. However, unlike past offline masculinist movements which coalesced around collective action such as men's rights protests, Siapera (2019) described the 'manosphere' as a broadly connective movement, where offline calls to actions are not the norm, and instead, experiences of 'aggrieved entitlement' are shared online with other 'manosphere' members. Thus, the 'manosphere' has been conceptualised as a purely online phenomenon.

Ging (2017) identified five aspects of the 'manosphere': men's rights activists (who discuss socio-political change to benefit men), Men-Going-Their-Own-Way (or MGTOW, who seek to distance themselves from women to varying degrees), pick-up artists (who use formulaic tactics known as 'game' to seduce women), traditional Christian conservatives, and members of gamer/geek culture. Although overlap has been identified between these last two groups and 'manosphere' activity, the first three explicitly label themselves as part of the 'manosphere' and are considered more central themes. Additionally, Ribeiro et al. (2020) included involuntary celibates (hereafter referred to as incels) in their definition of the 'manosphere', who do not have romantic or physical relationships with women despite desiring to, and resent those who do have such relationships.

Although these four sub-groups of the 'manosphere' are distinct from one another in their prescribed approach towards women and wider society, 'manosphere' forums are characterised by essentialised statements about gender relations between men and women. Across websites which discuss men's rights issues and pick-up artist tactics, women are referred to in derogatory terms such as 'bitches', 'sluts', and 'whores' (Lilly 2016). Furthermore, to demonstrate the formulaic nature of the insults against women found in the 'manosphere', Jane (2018) developed a random rape threat generator to demonstrate the recurring themes of threats amongst men's rights activists, pick-up artists and a group of 'manosphere' members who are unaffiliated with a specific sub-group, which Jane (2018) refers to as 'sub-cultural trolls'. These themes are: unattractiveness, sexual promiscuity, sexual frigidity, unintelligence, mental illness, and misinformed political opinions.

Connections have been made by thinktanks and scholars alike between the 'manosphere', the far-right, and the online alt-right. For instance, the UK advocacy group 'Hope Not Hate' (2020, p. 9) aligned the 'manosphere' with far-right actors, and acknowledges that although the 'manosphere' is considered a fringe group, its existence is reflective of a broader culture war around "political correctness, the liberal establishment and gender equality". A report from the Anti-Defamation League (2018, p. 5) also noted this link between the manosphere and alt-right communities, observing that "white supremacist, incel and MRA (Men's Rights) orbits feed and inform one another's poisonous hatred of women". The report cites examples of alt-right figureheads who have also participated in men's rights groups online, such as a prominent participant in the Charlottesville 'Unite The Right' rally in 2017, as well as the founder of the neo-Nazi site 'The Daily Stormer' who is quoted as saying 'when you give women rights, they destroy absolutely everything around them' (2018, p. 7). Some commentators in the 'manosphere' movement have been dubbed members of hate groups by the Southern Poverty Law Center (2018), for their comments on men's rights activist and pick-up artist websites, such as "women should be terrorized by their men". Similarly, scholars such as Ging and Siapera (2019), Nicholas and Agius (2018), and Marwick and Lewis (2017) all observed a link between the 'manosphere' and the alt-right movement, which is mediated by hostile attitudes towards women.

In some instances, the connection between the 'manosphere' and the right manifests in the networked harassment of feminists online, as in the case of Gamergate discussed above. One such incident occurred as recently as April 2020, when an academic specialising in victim-blaming was targeted by a group "who align themselves with the "alt-right", men's rights activists, incel and MGTOW movements" (Flood 2020). However, the majority of 'manosphere' discourse is not directed outwardly at women and feminists (which would constitute misogyny as Manne (2018) defines it), but is shared in somewhat isolated communities such as dedicated websites, as well as subreddits. I will now consider the content of each of these sub-groups, and their manifestations on Reddit, in turn. I will also consider a fifth sub-group, referred to as TRP to maintain the anonymity of the originating community, which considers 'manosphere' members who do not conform to the norms on one sub-group, but nonetheless participate in 'manosphere' themed discussions.

Men's rights activists

Firstly, considering the topics discussed by men's rights activists online, LaViolette and Hogan (2019) argued that /r/MensRights was characterised by blaming women for the issues that men are framed as facing (such as bias in legal custody cases, alimony payments, and men being viewed as disposable), and that the subreddit has links to the alt-right community. Gotell and Dutton (2016) noted that attitudes towards rape was a salient topic across three men's rights activist websites, and found that users believed that statistics discussing the prevalence of sexual violence towards women were exaggerated for women's benefit, and that women habitually make false rape accusations against men for financial benefit. Gotell and Dutton (2016) also found that men are portrayed as victims of gender-based hostility at an equal rate of women, that rape culture is portrayed as a fictional concept made up by feminists, and that feminists seek to erase men's experiences of sexual violence. Rafail and Freitas (2019) observed that rape was the most discussed topic in /r/MensRights, suggesting that these conceptualisations of sexual violence are central to their ideology. Although sexual violence towards men is an importance issue in its own right, the attitudes espoused in the men's rights community arguably dismiss the lived experiences of women, and amount to rape apology i.e. denying the prevalence of the issue and excusing acts of rape.

Violence and hostility against women in men's rights communities are another common theme in the literature. Schmitz and Kazyak (2016) observed two types of men's rights activist in their content analysis of 12 dedicated men's rights activist websites: Cyber Lads, who expressed explicit aggression towards women (in some cases even advocating intimate partner violence); and Virtual Victims, who foregrounded anti-feminism and the social issues which affected them. Thus, a distinction is made between men's rights activists who could more likely cause harm towards women offline, and those who focus on the perceived legal and societal issues at hand. However, Cyber

Lads were found to be more common than Virtual Victims. Furthermore, Lumsden (2019) analysed how online violence and trolling was represented in /r/MensRights, and found that users denied that women were victims of online violence, claiming that women were overly emotional about statements with no offline consequences. For example, statements such as 'I want to kill you in front of your children' were defended by users as having no offline consequences and thus not constituting a threat to women. Thus, the online harassment of women is defended in these circles, which in turn could encourage others to participate in such behaviour.

Pick-up artists

Turning to the pick-up artist sub-group, as the online community is centred around sharing strategies for offline interactions with women and practising these strategies, it is inevitable that this language will have a material effect on women. Dayter and Rüdiger (2016) examined the practice of sharing 'field reports' (that is, offline experiences) in pick-up artist forums, and found that the reports were characterised by language from business (to reference the value of interlocutors) and from the military (e.g. target and obstacle to refer to women), as well as evaluating women's appearance on a scale from 1 to 10. This reflects a degree of dehumanisation, as users were interested in achieving physical intimacy at the expense of considering their partners as individuals deserving of mutual respect.

Discussions around rape and what constitutes consent are also prevalent in the pick-up artist community. Although there is naturally no problem with men learning how to flirt with women and build their confidence, the pick-up artist community present such strategies as infallible, and these strategies promote hostile behaviours towards women offline. One such strategy is "negging" (short for negative complimenting), which Rüdiger and Dayter (2019, p. 19) defined as "making negative statements about one's interlocutor to reduce their self-esteem", to make them seek the approval of the pick-up artist. Furthermore, Wright (2020) analysed a 26-million-word corpus from an online pick-up artist forum for discussions about resistance to sex. The forum posters argued that resistance was only expressed by women at the 'last minute' because they did not want to be seen as sexually promiscuous, rather than genuinely not wanting to engage in sex acts. Thus, resistance was seen as ingenuine and something to be overcome, as opposed to an opportunity to stop and make sure that their partner was comfortable. This concept of overcoming 'last-minute resistance' also arose in the prosecution of a pick-up artist from Glasgow in 2019, who filmed himself giving advice on how to overcome such resistance, and used pick-up tactics on women and girls in public, which constituted 'threatening and abusive behaviour' (BBC 2019)[1]. This demonstrates that pick-up artists perpetuate a problematic notion of consent as something to not be taken seriously. To an extent, this mirrors the discussions of false rape accusations found in the men's rights community, which disregard the prevalence of sexual violence towards women.

MGTOW

Turning to MGTOW, this group advocates distancing oneself from women to varying degrees, with some MGTOW abstaining from sex with women to avoid false rape accusations, and some abstaining from marriage to avoid divorce and potential subsequent alimony payments (Lin 2017). Thus, the sexism is apparent in the perception that women are dishonest, selfish, and seek to harm men. Wright et al. (2020) observed a paradoxical tendency in the MGTOW community for most conversations to discuss women, despite expressing a wish to live lives independent of women. In their analysis of 1,012 comments on a MGTOW forum with approximately 33,000 users, they found that 59% of comments mentioned women, with 33% being centred on women. 61% of these comments were sexist in nature, with women being portrayed in derogatory terms (e.g. sluts), and as manipulative and deceptive. As well as examining a dedicated MGTOW forum, Jones et al. (2019) analysed 1,688 tweets from the three most active MGTOW users on Twitter, and found that 483 (29%) were coded as either active or passive harassment. Only 4% of tweets constituted active harassment, which was defined as having a particular target, whereas 96% constituted passive harassment, and thus had many potential targets (i.e. women in general). The majority of these tweets referenced sexist statements, anti-feminism, and sexual harassment, although 7% of harassing tweets were found to reference violently controlling women.

By discussing passive harassment, Jones et al. (2019) acknowledge that 'manosphere' discourse can have reach outside the immediate community and cause harm. Furthermore, Vivenzi (2017) demonstrated that although MGTOW forum posters did not support offline action such as protests, they did seek to affect the actions of others offline by giving advice about offline relationships. This suggests that the content of such communities has the potential to negatively affect women outside the community, although such a connection must be tentatively made. Indeed, due to the relatively low rate of active harassment, Jones et al. (2019) utilise Manne's (2018) sexism/misogyny distinction to portray MGTOW as sexist. Contrastingly, they consider both men's rights activists and incels as misogynist as these communities utilise explicit calls to action to end the injustices they perceive.

Incels

Incels are arguably the most well-known sub-group of the 'manosphere', as they have received much negative attention in the press for perpetrating offline violence. Since 2014, incel-motivated incidents have resulted in approximately 50 fatalities (Hoffman et al. 2020). Incels are characterised by a fatalistic attitude that their perceived unattractiveness will result in a lifetime of unfulfilment and misery, as they argue that women only want to have sex with conventionally attractive men (referred to as Chads). Incels first came into public consciousness in 2014, when 22-year-old Elliot

Rodger murdered seven people and injured 14 in Isla Vista, California, after publishing an online manifesto in which he detailed violent fantasies of retribution towards men and women considered conventionally attractive. He argued that women rejecting him pushed him to target a sorority house. Other individuals aligned with the incel movement such as Christopher Harper-Mercer in 2015, Alek Minassian in Canada in 2018, and Cole Carini as recently as June 2020, have since committed or attempted to commit similar attacks inspired by Rodger, or explicitly in his name. Thus, incels arguably demonstrate Kimmel's (2013) concept of 'aggrieved entitlement' most explicitly. In these examples, the perpetrators themselves said that the online content of the 'manosphere' encouraged them to carry out offline violence. For instance, in Rodger's (2014, p. 118) manifesto, he noted that one incel website "confirmed many of the theories I had about how wicked and degenerate women really are". Similarly, in 2019, Minassian claimed that he was radicalised by online incel communities before carrying out the 2018 attack (Cecco 2019)[2]. However, it should be noted that although several perpetrators of violence have been identified as incels, this does not mean that all incels will necessarily become violent.

Although the main subreddit for incel activity was banned for inciting violence against women in November 2017, following an online petition, alternative spaces have appeared since. For instance, a replacement incel subreddit was allowed on the platform until it was banned in October 2018. In their analysis of a sample of 50 posts and comment threads from this subreddit, Heritage and Koller (2020) found that women were homogenously represented as deceptive, immoral, and capable of hurting men, whereas men were placed on a hierarchy of masculinity with incels near the bottom of this hierarchy. Additionally, in their analysis of a dedicated incel forum website, Baele et al. (2019) revealed that women are typically referred to as "femoids" or "foids", which suggests that women are robotic and thus incapable of controlling their actions, as well as "roasties", which was used to derogatorily refer to sexually promiscuous women.

Furthermore, Jaki et al. (2019) analysed the forum section of a dedicated incel website, and found that posts expressing a desire to abolish women's rights were prevalent, and pro-violence posts outnumbered anti-violence posts, with many posts referencing beating, raping or killing women, supporting the actions of previous incel mass murderers. Additionally, Baele et al. (2019) argued that the content in dedicated incel forums constitutes an extreme worldview, an interpretation which has since been shared by those informing legal policy (Zimmerman et al. 2018). Hoffman et al. (2020, pp. 576, 565) also argued that incel violence 'remains a grave terrorism threat', is intended to have 'far-reaching societal effects', and that the aspects of the incel community overlap with aspects of other extremist communities. For instance, they noted that perpetrators of incel attacks used racist and antisemitic language online, and also cited examples of far-right European terrorists who expressed incel beliefs but did not align themselves with the movement. They also observed that incels have a culture of martyrdom around perpetrators of incel violence who committed suicide following their attacks, such as Rodger. However, in May 2020, one incel-motivated machete attack in Toronto was treated as a domestic terrorism incident, the first of its kind to be categorised as such. This suggests that the incel subset of the 'manosphere' is the most extreme and is now being considered a matter of national security.

TRP

The last sub-group I will consider in this chapter is referred to as TRP, and encompasses 'manosphere' members who participate in discussions but do not fit into the other four sub-groups. The /r/TRP subreddit serves as a hub for these members, which seeks to 'generate consensus and belonging among the manosphere's divergent elements' (Ging 2017, p. 8). This subreddit has been referred to as "the online heart of modern misogyny" (Marche 2016), and has been associated with the alt-right consistently in the past literature (e.g. Mountford 2018; Dignam and Rohlinger 2019). Dignam and Rohlinger (2019) noted that the denigration of women is a salient feature of discussions in the subreddit, with women being referred to as "plates" (casual sexual partners), "cunts", "sluts", and "bitches", and although the community originally situated itself as an apolitical space, the community aligned itself with the Republican party for the 2016 US election. Furthermore, Krendel (2020) found that bare assertions about female social actors frequently occurred a corpus of TRP posts from Reddit, and that these actors were characterised as immoral, deceptive, wishing to harm men, and desiring hostile behaviour from men. She also found that the term 'girls' was used to refer to women in a romantic/sexual manner, and that 'girls' were represented as manipulating men into assaulting them, a finding which mirrors those of the men's rights and pick-up artist communities discussed above.

Van Valkenburgh (2018), who analysed 26 documents which are considered key readings in the community, notes that the beliefs of TRP are underpinned by evolutionary psychology, which argues that men and women are immutably different from each other. This foundation was used to argue that women are likely to manipulate and cheat on romantic partners in search of more masculine 'alpha' men, and that all women will do this, which was expressed using slogans such as "all women are like that" (Van Valkenburgh 2018, p. 13) (often abbreviated to AWALT). In turn, the documents promote an approach to women which dismisses their emotions as attempts at manipulation, and encourages men to become more 'alpha'. This is done by seeking casual sexual relationships with many women (a practice referred to as 'spinning plates'), and self-improvement through economic success and fitness (particularly weightlifting).

Krendel (2020) also noted that the terms 'hypergamy' (seeking high status partners, typically used to denote a caste system) and 'hybristophilia' (a paraphilia for criminal or dangerous partners), which use neo-classical compounding, are co-opted by TRP to signal academic rigour. These terms are used to argue that all women will cheat on their partners and are incapable of love, and that women desire violence from their partners. By co-opting these terms, and explicitly citing literature from the fields of psychology and economics (Van Valkenburgh 2018), as well as classical philosophers (Zuckerberg 2018), the community situates themselves as pseudo-academic actors focussed on self-improvement, which could in turn make their arguments seem more convincing, and mask the sexist beliefs which underpin their approach.

Considering all five of these sub-groups, Ribeiro et al. (2020) analysed 38 million posts from both dedicated 'manosphere' websites (8 million) and subreddits (30 million), and found that the MGTOW, incel, and TRP communities are characterised by more toxic and misogynistic language than the men's rights and pick-up artist communities. Ribeiro et al. (2020) also found that there was substantial migration from the men's rights and pick-up artist communities. This suggests that participation in a less controversial portion of the 'manosphere' could lead to radicalisation over time. Thus, the five communities may not be as separate as they first appear. This presents risks when we look at sites such as Reddit, as these five communities are treated differently on the Reddit platform. As mentioned above, the incel subreddits have been banned from the site. Contrastingly, the men's rights and pick-up artists have faced no sanctions, and TRP and MGTOW subreddits were 'quarantined' in October 2018 and January 2020 respectively. This means that the communities do not come up on search engines, and the communities can only be viewed after clicking through a content warning page. The quarantine reflects that the majority of Reddit would be expected to find this content 'shocking and highly offensive'. This is also reflected in the mainstream media's response to the 'manosphere', as multiple news articles have expressed shock at the language within these spaces (e.g. Marche 2016). However, the content is still available to view on Reddit.

Having demonstrated the sexist beliefs which underpin the 'manosphere', I now consider whether this language constitutes hate speech in the eyes of the law, and how the Reddit platform consider hate in their site rules.

Online hate speech and website regulations

Crucial to this discussion on hate is the distinction between what constitutes free speech and hate speech. Past international definitions of hate speech were formulated as exceptions to freedom of expression rights, and are focused on public order offences. For instance, Article 20(2) of the International Covenant on Civil and Political Rights (United Nations 1976, p. 178) defines hate speech as "[a]ny advocacy of national, racial or religious hatred that constitutes incitement to discrimination, hostility or violence".

However, the Committee of Ministers of the Council of Europe (1997, p. 107) recommend defining hate speech more broadly, as:

> covering all forms of expression which spread, incite, promote or justify racial hatred, xenophobia, anti-Semitism or other forms of hatred based on intolerance, including: intolerance expressed by aggressive nationalism and ethnocentrism, discrimination and hostility against minorities, migrants and people of immigrant origin. In this sense, hate speech covers comments which are necessarily directed against a person or a particular group of persons.

Notably, these definitions of hate speech do not mention gender, and gender is not currently a legislatively protected characteristic in the UK (Crown Prosecution Service 2020), an oversight which the current volume intends to address.

Barker and Jurasz (2018) acknowledged that it is unclear which existing hate speech legislation applies to online offences, and argue that online offences such as stalking and gendered harassment require specific legislation. However, Barker and Jurasz (2018) solely consider instances of misogynist abuse, as opposed to the sexist language which occurs in somewhat isolated communities. This approach suggests that misogynist speech, the targeted nature, and silencing aspect of hostility against women, could be considered hate speech, whereas sexist speech, which is not targeted towards women, could not. This is supported by Richardson-Self (2018), who, using Manne's (2018) definitions of sexism and misogyny, argued that sexist speech which occurs in public (e.g. a politician suggesting that women are weaker than men during a television broadcast) is not hate speech but misogynist speech is (e.g. threatening a woman with violence for not conforming to feminine standards), as it seeks to coerce its target into silence. However, I would argue that this ignores the role that allowing sexist speech in public spaces has in potentially influencing public opinion.

As anybody can access the 'manosphere' and read their content, this is arguably an online public space, and thus its influence should not be underestimated. For instance, the impact of the 'manosphere' is not limited to online spaces, as users can apply what they have learnt offline in some manner, such as in the case of pick-up artists and incels. Furthermore, Hope Not Hate (2020) provided evidence that 'manosphere' talking points such as explicit anti-feminist arguments and the victimisation of men are being mainstreamed, and that young boys are accessing this content. Their report cited examples of hostile encounters that female teachers have had in the classroom where teenage boys have echoed these 'manosphere' talking points when the teachers discussed issues such as gender equality. Therefore, despite some 'manosphere' communities being quarantined or banned on the Reddit platform, these ideas have achieved a wide reach. This is perhaps unsurprising, given the popularity of the Reddit platform, which contains the majority of online 'manosphere' content, according to Ribeiro et al. (2020). This demonstrates that sexist language, despite not being broadly considered a legal issue, can indirectly effect women, through the actions of the people who read such language.

Central to these definitions of hate speech is the concept of incitement, which is to 'stir up feelings of hatred, to discriminate or in some cases, to cause violence against others' (Sorial 2015). To an extent, this has been recognised in the Racial and Religious Hatred Act (2006), in which 'stirring up hatred' is considered an offence in its own right. However, this legislation has not been extended to other forms of hate, such as that against women. Thus, incitement exists on a cline, where at best an echo chamber full of like-minded hateful individuals is created, and at worst, individuals from these hate groups act on these hateful beliefs. In this definition of incitement, Sorial (2015) consciously accounted for Waldron's (2012) definition of hate speech: that the 'hate' in hate speech could refer to the feeling the speaker intends on evoking in others, meaning that ideological recruitment would come under his definition of hate speech. Waldron (2012) also posited that undermining the dignity of others is integral to hate speech, which is done by presenting hate speech as a factual claim (thus obscuring the truth), denigrating a whole group of people via character generalisation, dehumanising others, and finally using slogans to denigrate the group. Arguably, these four criteria are met by the 'manosphere' language presently discussed, through the use of pseudo-academic language (such as 'hypergamy' and 'hybristophilia' in TRP; Krendel 2020), assertions about women as a whole, reducing women to sexual objects, and slogans such as 'all women are like that' (Van Valkenburgh 2018).

Furthermore, UNESCO (2015, p. 10) also utilised this broader definition of hate and incitement, and, in their report on countering online hate speech, defined hate speech more broadly as 'to dehumanize and diminish members assigned to [a] group', and 'to reinforce a sense of an in-group that is (purportedly) under threat'. This definition is arguably more general, as no specific protected groups are mentioned, and hate speech does not need to be directed at a victim in order to be deemed hateful. Under this definition, the sexist language discussed in this chapter would constitute hate speech, as it constitutes the dehumanisation of women through derogatory terms, and is based on a concept of traditional masculinity under threat. However, this hate speech does not necessarily constitute criminal behaviour in the eyes of the UK Government, making it distinct from hate crime. Thus, we presently consider which actions would be appropriate to take to mitigate the effects of such language.

Acknowledging the danger of 'manosphere' language and its overlap with the alt-right, the Anti-Defamation League (2018) suggested that such language should be policed by both social media platforms and legal authorities. However, the Human Rights Council (cited in UNESCO 2015, p. 16) argued that three types of hateful expression should be differentiated, and thus handled in different ways:

> (a) expression constituting an offence under international law that can be prosecuted criminally; (b) expression not criminally punishable but that may justify a restriction and a civil suite; (c) expression that does not give rise to criminal or civil sanctions but still raises concerns in terms of tolerance, civility and respect for others.

UNESCO (2015) argued that the law should not be used to deal with expressions such as (c), which the expressions in online communities such as the 'manosphere' would be categorised as. However, they acknowledged that these sites contain hate speech, despite not directly addressing members of the out-group they denigrate.

Brown (2017) argued that although online hate speech is dangerous for its ease of access, anonymity, and the size of the potential audience, the unique danger of online hate speech comes from its ability to give people the opportunity to experiment with producing hate speech for the first time, and by doing so, interact with like-minded people. This is supported by Wojcieszak (2010), who found that participation in online hate groups strengthens the hateful opinions first held when beginning participation on hate sites. This suggests that deplatforming such communities would prevent such radicalisation from occurring. Indeed, Baele et al. (2019, p. 3) noted that "without a way to relate and discuss, these individuals would have had no way to recognize themselves as 'Incels' and learn the culture and particular idioms that cements the Incel worldview". This is supported by Zimmerman et al. (2018, p. 3), who posited that the incel subset of the 'manosphere' is comparable to other extremist groups due to their explicit incitement of violence, so preventing radicalisation should be considered a top priority.

When combined with Ribeiro et al.'s (2020) findings that 'manosphere' members move to more extreme subsets of the community over time, and the consideration that the 'manosphere' is united by underlying sexist beliefs, this suggests that efforts to limit the damage of 'manosphere' language should not be limited to its most extreme elements. This is supported by Allport (1954), whose five-point cline for how prejudice is enacted demonstrated that if left unchecked, prejudice can take on more extreme forms. This cline consisted of: antilocution (negative speech/hate speech about an out-group), avoidance, discrimination, physical attack, and finally, extermination. It could be argued that the 'manosphere' is generally characterised by the antilocution stage, although the MGTOW sub-group practices 'avoidance' to varying degrees, and some parts of the incel sub-group have carried out 'physical attack'. This would support deplatforming as a potential response to this phenomenon.

On the other hand, Eichhorn (2001) suggested that online hateful speech should not be taken as seriously as offline hateful speech, as there is a greater opportunity for counter-speech online and that hateful websites can be avoided. However, three main issues can be identified with this approach. Firstly, this ignores the cumulative effect that unregulated hate speech online can have on marginalised communities, such as self-censoring behaviours (Megarry 2014; Manne 2018). Secondly, the potential for counter-speech varies depending on the platform. As users on Reddit select which communities they want to see on a regular basis, this provides a self-selected filtered experience. Also, 'manosphere' moderators curate the subreddits by deleting posts which do not conform to their ideals. Therefore, the potential for counter-speech effectively reaching these users is low. Lastly, considering the online and offline as completely separate domains ignores the fact that our online and offline identities are not distinct, and that the sexism produced online has offline consequences.

Historically, mainstream social media platforms with wide-reaching audiences have been reluctant to regulate such language, because they position themselves as intermediary platforms for others to publish their individual opinions, and not responsible for the content on these platforms (Williams and Mishcon de Reya 2019). However, we are perhaps at a turning point, as social media platforms such as Facebook, YouTube, and Twitter have begun to take a more active role in regulating hate on their platforms by suspending the accounts of controversial right-wing figures. Furthermore, the UK Government's Online Harms White Paper (Department for Digital, Culture, Media & Sport 2019) indicates that online platforms will be expected to regulate for online abuse, extremist material, and illegal content in a timely and transparent manner, or risk facing fines. Reddit is no exception here, as at the end of June 2020, Reddit updated their content policy to explicitly forbid communities which 'incite violence or that promote hate based on identity or vulnerability' (Reddit 2020a). To an extent, this policy mirrors the definitions of hate and incitement which Waldron (2012) and Sorial (2015) apply respectively. Furthermore, this policy explicitly references 'marginalized or vulnerable groups include, but are not limited to, groups based on their actual and perceived race, colour, religion, national origin, ethnicity, immigration status, gender, gender identity, sexual orientation, pregnancy, or disability', and gives '[a] comment arguing that rape of women should be acceptable and not a crime' as a prototypical example of a rule violation (Reddit 2020b). This suggests that, despite Reddit's historically anti-feminist culture (Massanari 2015), gender is becoming increasingly recognised as a characteristic which should be protected.

Approximately 2,000 subreddits which were deemed hateful, including a popular pro-Trump subreddit and a trans-exclusionary subreddit, were banned following this change. However, the 'manosphere' subreddits, with the exception of the incel-specific ones which were banned previously, remain accessible. This could be due to the pseudo-academic language used to discuss such concepts (e.g. hybristophilia), which is indeed a feature of hate speech as Waldron (2012) defines it, and as Sorial (2015) argues, has the potential to mask its danger. As these subreddits arguably promote hostile attitudes towards women on the basis of gender, it could be argued that they are in violation of the new guidelines, and should be deplatformed as a result.

Conclusion

The majority of chapters in this edited volume focus on targeted instances of hate crime, by considering forms of gendered hostility which fall under the definition of misogyny. These include offline street harassment, online image-based sexual abuse, online verbal harassment, and doxxing. These are also the issues that the majority of academic literature focuses on (Powell and Henry 2017) as well as the issues that thinktanks and policymakers (e.g. Gender and Policy Insights 2019) foreground. However, in this chapter, I have argued that a cline exists between isolated sexism and targeted misogyny, as illustrated by the gradual radicalisation of the online anti-feminist 'manosphere' community, and that the online sharing of beliefs cannot be easily removed from the potential for offline action.

I have also argued that the sexist language which characterises the 'manosphere' can be defined as hate speech, as it aims to spread hateful beliefs about women as an entire social group using dehumanising language. This community is united by a feeling of 'aggrieved entitlement' (Kimmel 2013) to certain behaviours from women, which manifests in different behaviours across the five sub-groups, including negative representations, avoidance, and physical attack. However, the community as a whole refer to women in derogatory ways, and conceptualise women as being immutably different to men, believing that women are incapable of love, seek to cause men harm, and seek hostile behaviours from men. However, engaging in online hate speech in a closed space does not amount to hate crime.

To answer the titular question of the chapter, I have also demonstrated that such language does not stay isolated, especially in the case of the incel subset of the 'manosphere', which is increasingly being treated as an extremist group. By considering 'manosphere' attitudes towards relationships and sexual violence, one is able to draw a connection between such beliefs and the possibility of users applying this understanding of relationships in an offline context. Whilst it is incorrect to suggest that participating in the 'manosphere' inevitably leads to the mistreatment of women and girls, it cannot be ruled out that subscribing to such beliefs would affect one's relationships with, and attitude towards, women. In any case, although such language may not necessarily warrant a legal response, mainstream social media platforms, and websites are facing pressure to moderate their sites more strictly. Thus, it can be expected that in the coming months and years that social media and content platforms will recognise the risk that hateful language presents to others, and take a stronger stance against allowing such content on their platforms.

Notes

1 It should be noted that although this pick-up artist was originally sentenced to two years in prison, the ruling was quashed on appeal in September 2020. The three appeal judges ruled that there was not sufficient evidence for the original conviction, with one judge commenting that being approached in public could not be deemed threatening on the basis that it was unwelcome from the women in question. This illustrates that what constitutes prosecutable street harassment is currently ambiguous.
2 This claim was disputed in the court ruling on the attack. The ruling concluded that the perpetrator only claimed a connection with the incel movement, and specific individuals in the incel community, to increase his notoriety meaning. This is despite the perpetrator naming his identification with the incel movement and anger against women as motivating factors for the attack.

References

Allport, G., 1954. *The Nature of Prejudice*. Oxford: Addison-Wesley.
Anti-Defamation League, 2018. When women are the enemy: the intersection of misogyny and white supremacy [online]. Available at: https://www.adl.org/resources/reports/when-women-are-the-enemy-the-intersection-of-misogyny-and-white-supremacy [Accessed 06 July 2020].
Archibald, M., 2020. Reddit statistics for 2020 (demographics, usage and traffic data) [online]. Available at: https://foundationinc.co/lab/reddit-statistics/ [Accessed 06 July 2020].
Baele, S.J., Brace, L. and Coan, T.G., 2019. From 'incel' to 'saint': analyzing the violent worldview behind the 2018 Toronto attack. *Terrorism and Political Violence*, pp. 1–25. DOI: 10.1080/09546553.2019.1638256.
Banet-Weiser, S. and Miltner, K., 2016. #MasculinitySoFragile: culture, structure and networked misogyny. *Feminist Media Studies*, 16(1), pp. 171–174. DOI: 10.1080/14680777.2016.1120490.
Barker, K. and Jurasz, O., 2018. *Online Misogyny as Hate Crime: A Challenge for Legal Regulation?* London: Routledge.
BBC, 2019. YouTube terminates Addy A-game and street attraction channels [online]. Available at: https://www.bbc.com/news/uk-scotland-49957059 [Accessed 07 July 2020].
Blais, M. and Dupuis-Déri, F., 2012. Masculinism and the antifeminist countermovement. *Social Movement Studies*, 11(1), pp. 21–39. DOI: 10.1080/14742837.2012.640532.
Brown, A., 2017. What is so special about online (as compared of offline) hate speech? *Ethnicities*, 18(3), pp. 297–326. DOI: 10.1177/1468796817709846.
Cecco, L., 2019. Toronto van attack suspect says he was 'radicalized' online by 'incels'. *The Guardian* [online]. 27 September. Available at: https://www.theguardian.com/world/2019/sep/27/alek-minassian-toronto-van-attack-interview-incels [Accessed 07 July 2020].
Citron, D., 2014. *Hate Crimes in Cyberspace*. Harvard: Harvard University Press.
Committee of Ministers of the Council of Europe, 1997. Recommendation no. R (97) 20 [online]. Available at: https://search.coe.int/cm/Pages/result_details.aspx?ObjectID=0900001680505d5b [Accessed 07 July 2020].
Crown Prosecution Service, 2020. Hate crime [online]. Available at: https://www.cps.gov.uk/hate-crime [Accessed 07 July 2020].

Dayter, D. and Rüdiger, S., 2016. Reporting from the field: the narrative reconstruction of experience in pick-up artist online communities. *Open Linguistics*, 2(1), pp. 337–351. DOI: 10.1515/opli-2016-0016.

Department for Digital, Culture, Media and Sport, 2019. Online harms white paper [online]. Available at: https://assets.publishing.service.gov.uk/government/uploads/system/uploads/attachment_data/file/793360/Online_Harms_White_Paper.pdf [Accessed 27 July 2020].

Dignam, P. and Rohlinger, D., 2019. Misogynist men online: how the red pill elected trump. *Signs: Journal of Women in Culture and Society*, 44(3), pp. 589–612. DOI: 10.1086/701155.

Eichhorn, K., 2001. Re-in/citing linguistic injuries: speech acts, cyberhate, and the spatial and temporal character of networked environments. *Computers and Composition*, 18(3), pp. 293–304. DOI: 10.1016/S8755-4615(01)00057-3.

Flood, A., 2020. Author of book about victim blaming bombarded with misogynist abuse. *The Guardian* [online]. 24 April. Available at: https://www.theguardian.com/books/2020/apr/24/author-book-victim-blaming-misogynist-abuse-jessica-taylor [Accessed 06 July 2020].

Gender and Policy Insights, 2019. When technology meets misogyny: multi-level, intersectional solutions to digital gender-based violence [online]. Available at: https://gen-pol.org/wp-content/uploads/2019/11/When-Technology-Meets-Misogyny-GenPol-Policy-Paper-2.pdf [Accessed 07 July 2020].

Ging, D., 2017. Alphas, betas, and incels: theorizing the masculinities of the manosphere. *Men and Masculinities*, 22(4), pp. 1–20. DOI: 10.1177/1097184X17706401.

Ging, D. and Siapera, E., 2019. *Gender Hate Online: Understanding the New Anti-feminism*. London: Palgrave Macmillan.

Gotell, L. and Dutton, E., 2016. Sexual violence in the 'manosphere': antifeminist men's rights discourses on rape. *International Journal for Crime, Justice and Social Democracy*, 5(2), pp. 65–80. DOI: 10.5204/ijcjsd.v5i2.310.

Heritage, F. and Koller, V., 2020. Incels, in-groups, and ideologies: the representation of gendered social actors in a sexuality-based online community. *Journal of Language and Sexuality*, 9(2), pp. 153–180. DOI: 10.1075/jls.19014.her.

Hoffman, B., Ware, J. and Shapiro, E., 2020. Assessing the threat of incel violence. *Studies in Conflict and Terrorism*, 43(7), pp. 565–587. DOI: 10.1080/1057610X.2020.1751459.

Hope Not Hate, 2020. State of hate 2020: far-right terror goes global [online]. Available at: https://www.hopenothate.org.uk/wp-content/uploads/2020/02/state-of-hate-2020-final.pdf [Accessed 06 July 2020].

Jaki, S. et al., 2019. Online hatred of women in the Incels.me forum: linguistic analysis and automatic detection [online]. Available at: http://organisms.be/downloads/incels.pdf [Accessed 07 July 2020].

Jane, E., 2018. Systemic misogyny exposed: translating rapeglish from the manosphere with a random rape threat generator. *International Journal of Culture Studies*, 21(6), pp. 661–680. DOI: 10.1177/1367877917734042.

Jones, C., Trott, V. and Wright, S., 2019. Sluts and soyboys: MGTOW and the production of misogynistic online harassment. *New Media and Society*, pp. 1–19. DOI: 10.1177/1461444819887141.

Kelly, A., 2017. The alt-right: reactionary rehabilitation for white masculinity. *Soundings* 66(1), pp. 68–78.

Kimmel, M., 2013. *Angry White Men: American Masculinity at the End of an Era*. New York: Type Media Center.

Krendel, A., 2020. The men and women, guys and girls of the 'manosphere': a corpus-assisted discourse approach. *Discourse and Society*, pp. 1–24. DOI: 10.1177/0957926520939690.

LaViolette, J. and Hogan, B., 2019. Using platform signals for distinguishing discourses: the case of men's rights and men's liberation on reddit. *Proceedings of the International AAAI Conference on Web and Social Media, Munich, 11–14 July, 2019*, Germany. Available at: https://www.aaai.org/ojs/index.php/ICWSM/article/view/3357 [Accessed 06 July 2020].

Lilly, M., 2016. *The world is not a safe place for men: the representational politics of the manosphere* [online]. MA dissertation, University of Ottowa. Available at: https://ruor.uottawa.ca/bitstream/10393/35055/1/Lilly_Mary_2016_thesis.pdf [Accessed 06 July 2020].

Lin, J., 2017. Antifeminism online: MGTOW (men going their own way). In: Frömming, U., Köhn, S., Fox, S. and Terry, M., eds. *Digital Environments. Ethnographic Perspectives across Global Online and Offline Spaces*. New York: Columbia University Press, 2017, pp. 77–96.

Lumsden, K., 2019. 'I want to kill you in front of your children' is not a threat. It's an expression of a desire, not of an intent: discourses of trolling and gendered violence on r/MensRights. In: Lumsden, K. and Harmer, E., eds. *Online Othering: Exploring Violence and Discrimination on the Web*. Basingstoke: Palgrave Macmillan, pp. 91–115.

Manne, K., 2018. *Down Girl: The Logic of Misogyny*. Oxford: Oxford University Press.

Mantilla, K., 2013. Gendertrolling: misogyny adapts to new media. *Feminist Studies*, 39(2), pp. 563–570.

Marche, S., 2016. Swallowing the red pill: a journey to the heart of modern misogyny. *The Guardian* [online]. 14 April. Available at: https://www.theguardian.com/technology/2016/apr/14/the-red-pill-reddit-modern-misogyny-manosphere-men [Accessed 07 July 2020].

Marwick, A. and Lewis, R., 2017. Media manipulation and disinformation online [online]. Available at: https://datasociety.net/pubs/oh/DataAndSociety_MediaManipulationAndDisinformationOnline.pdf [Accessed 06 July 2020].

Massanari, A., 2015. *Participatory Culture, Community, and Play: Learning from Reddit*. New York: Peter Lang Publishing, Inc.

Megarry, J., 2014. Online incivility or sexual harassment? Conceptualising women's experiences in the digital age. *Women's Studies International Forum*, 47(1), pp. 46–55. DOI: 10.1016/j.wsif.2014.07.012.

Mountford, J., 2018. Topic modeling the red pill. *Social Sciences*, 7(3), pp. 1–16. DOI: 10.3390/socsci7030042.

Nicholas, L. and Agius, C., 2018. #Notallmen, #meninism, manospheres and unsafe spaces: overt and subtle masculinism in anti-'PC' discourse. In: Nicholas, L. and Agius, C., eds. *The Persistence of Global Masculinism*. London: Palgrave MacMillan, pp. 31–59.

Powell, A. and Henry, N., 2017. *Sexual Violence in a Digital Age*. London: Palgrave Macmillan.

Racial and Religious Hatred Act, 2006 (c. 1).

Rafail, P. and Freitas, I., 2019. Grievance articulation and community reactions in the men's rights movement online. *Social Media + Society*, 5(2), pp. 1–11. DOI: 10.1177/2056305119841387.

Waldron, J., 2012. *The Harm in Hate Speech*. Harvard: Harvard University Press.

Williams, M. and de Reya, M., 2019. Hatred behind the screens: a report on the rise of online hate speech [online]. Available at: https://hatelab.net/wp-content/uploads/2019/11/Hatred-Behind-the-Screens.pdf [Accessed 06 July 2020].

Wojcieszak, M., 2010. 'Don't talk to me' - effects of ideologically homogeneous online groups and politically dissimilar offline ties on extremism. *New Media and Society*, 12(1), pp. 637–665. DOI: 10.1177/1461444809342775.

Woollacott, E., 2014. Reddit gives mixed messages after pulling leaked celebrity photos [online]. Available at: https://www.forbes.com/sites/emmawoollacott/2014/09/08/reddit-gives-mixed-messages-after-pulling-leaked-celebrity-photos/#-2f16965980a5 [Accessed 06 July 2020].

Wright, D., 2020. The discursive construction of resistance to sex in an online community. *Discourse, Context and Media*, 36(1), pp. 1–9. DOI: 10.1016/j.dcm.2020.100402.

Wright, S., Trott, V. and Jones, C., 2020. 'The pussy ain't worth it, bro': assessing the structure and discourse of MGTOW. *Information, Communication and Society*, 23(6), pp. 908–925. DOI: 10.1080/1369118X.2020.1751867.

Zimmerman, S., Ryan, L. and Duriesmith, D., 2018. Recognizing the violence extremist ideology of 'incels' [online]. Available at: https://www.wiisglobal.org/wp-content/uploads/2018/09/Policybrief-Violent-Extremists-Incels.pdf [Accessed 07 July 2020].

Zuckerberg, D., 2018. *Not All Dead White Men: Classics and Misogyny in the Digital Age*. Harvard: Harvard University Press.

Reddit, 2020a. Reddit content policy [online]. Available at: https://www.redditinc.com/policies/content-policy [Accessed 07 July 2020].

Reddit, 2020b. Promoting hate based on identity and vulnerability [online]. Available at: https://www.reddithelp.com/en/categories/rules-reporting/account-and-community-restrictions/promoting-hate-based-identity-or [Accessed 07 July 2020].

Ribeiro, M. et al., 2020. From pick-up artists to incels: a data-driven sketch of the manosphere [online]. Available at: https://www.researchgate.net/publication/338737324_From_Pick-Up_Artists_to_Incels_A_Data-Driven_Sketch_of_the_Manosphere [Accessed 06 July 2020].

Richardson-Self, L., 2018. Woman-hating: on misogyny, sexism, and hate speech. *Hypatia: A Journal of Feminist Philosophy*, 33(2), pp. 256–272. DOI: 10.1111/hypa.12398.

Rodger, E., 2014. My twisted world: the story of Elliot Rodger [online]. Available at: https://assets.documentcloud.org/documents/1173619/rodger-manifesto.pdf [Accessed 07 July 2020].

Rüdiger, S. and Dayter, D., 2019. The language of pick-up artists. *Babel - The Language Magazine*, 27(1), pp. 16–20.

Schmitz, R. and Kazyak, E., 2016. Masculinities in cyberspace: an analysis of portrayals of manhood in men's rights activist websites. *Social Sciences*, 5(2), pp. 1–16. DOI: 10.3390/socsci5020018.

Siapera, E., 2019. Online misogyny as witch hunt: primitive accumulation in the age of techno-capitalism. In: Ging, D. and Siapera, E., eds. *Gender Hate Online: Understanding the New Anti-feminism*. London: Palgrave Macmillan, pp. 21–43.

Sobieraj, S., 2018. Bitch, slut, skank, cunt: patterned resistance to women's visibility in digital publics. *Information, Communication and Society*, 21(11), pp. 1700–1714. DOI: 10.1080/1369118X.2017.1348535.

Sorial, S., 2015. Hate speech and distorted communication: rethinking the limits of incitement. *Law and Philosophy*, 34(3), pp. 299–324. DOI: 10.1007/s10982-014-9214-9.

Southern Poverty Law Center, 2018. Male supremacy [online]. Available at: https://www.splcenter.org/fighting-hate/extremist-files/ideology/male-supremacy [Accessed 06 July 2020].

UNESCO, 2015. Countering hate speech online [online]. Available at: https://unesdoc.unesco.org/in/documentViewer.xhtml?v=2.1.196&id=p::usmarcdef_0000233231&file=/in/rest/annotationSVC/DownloadWatermarkedAttachment/attach_import_ec25fcc4-72f7-46c4-a8f4-5ad6a018f697%3F_%3D233231eng.pdf&locale=en&multi=true&ark=/ark:/48223/pf0000233231/PDF/233231eng.pdf#%5B%7B%22num%22%3A295%2C%22gen%22%3A0%7D%2C%7B%22name%22%3A%22XYZ%22%7D%2C%709%2C0%5D [Accessed 06 July 2020].

United Nations, 1976. International covenant on civil and political rights [online]. Available at: https://treaties.un.org/doc/publication/unts/volume%20999/volume-999-i-14668-english.pdf [Accessed 07 July 2020].

Van Valkenburgh, S., 2018. Digesting the red pill: masculinity and neoliberalism in the manosphere. *Men and Masculinities*, pp. 1–20. DOI: 10.1177/1097184X18816118.

Vivenzi, L., 2017. Infiltrating the manosphere: an exploration of male-oriented virtual communities from the inside [online]. Available at: https://www.diggitmagazine.com/articles/infiltrating-manosphere-exploration-male-oriented-virtual-communities-inside [Accessed 06 July 2020].

Part 3
Identities and lived experiences

6 Adolescent girls' experiences of street harassment

Emotions, comments, impact, actions and the law

Rachel Harding, Lucy Betts, David Wright, Sheine Peart and Catarina Sjolin

Introduction

The prevalence and range of street harassment (SH) incidents as experienced by adolescents[1] is an understudied area. SH can be defined as harassment behaviour in public places occurring both on-street (Fileborn 2014; Logan 2015; Vera-Gray 2017; Wånggren 2016) and when using public transport (Logan 2015; Gekoski et al. 2017). SH includes a range of behaviours such as, "Threat of physical harm, staring or watching, shouting, following or stalking, indecent proposals, name calling and verbal abuse" (Deakin 2006, p. 378). SH can also be seen as an act of violence (Gardner 1995), a public health issue (Bucchianeri et al. 2014) and a precursor to violent crime (Logan 2015). The advantage of a multi-disciplinary team such as the authors in this chapter is to examine girls' SH experiences from different perspectives. This is because girls' behaviour, well-being, coping strategies, safety, ability to learn and behaviour can all be affected when out and about in public.

In this chapter, our team of academics from sociology, psychology, linguistics, law and education present a multi-disciplinary perspective on a study undertaken with three secondary schools in the UK. Both quantitative and qualitative data of adolescent girls is analysed to discuss the impact of SH experiences on emotions, well-being, safety, coping strategies and ability to learn. The study also included adolescent boys; however, the focus of this chapter is on the SH experiences of adolescent girls. In this regard, some mention is made of the findings about boys' experiences to discuss how girls' SH experiences appear distinctive. The chapter discusses findings relating to adolescent girls' emotions when experiencing SH and the comments they make about these experiences including what actions they can take. We also consider what the impact of SH on their education, and implications for how far SH is covered by UK law.

DOI: 10.4324/9781003023722-6

Emotional reactions, perceived safety and changed behaviour – a literature context

The SH of adolescent girls can be understood by looking at the literature about women's experiences of SH, which has been well documented. For example, Gardner (1995), one of the key studies to analyse public behaviour, reported their entire sample of 293 women had experienced SH with only nine of the women reporting that their experiences of SH were not 'troublesome'. Furthermore, 65 of the women reported making a 'notable life decision' following their experiences such as moving to a new house or changing jobs to avoid the perceived or actual harassment in public places that they had experienced. In this way, although SH is a common experience for many women, the impact of such experiences varies (Fileborn 2014). However, the *emotional* impact of SH is significant, and the literature has documented a range of emotional responses associated with SH in adult females ranging from annoyance to fear (Bowman 1993).

Characteristic of the studies about adult females is that a link between experiencing SH and subsequent negative emotions has been reported (Fairchild and Rudman 2008). Research suggests that fear is a common response to SH experiences. For example, adult females are more likely to report experiencing fear following rude behaviour in public places and these experiences have an impact on their subsequent well-being compared to adult males (Bastomski and Smith 2017). Although Bastomski and Smith (2017) note that it is hard to tell without further research whether the experiences between adult females and males are quantifiably different or whether these differences reflect variance in how the event is perceived, other research has reported that it is important to recognise that adult males also experience SH (Laniya 2005). While it is beyond the remit of this chapter to cover the differences between girls' and boys' experiences of SH, this is discussed in our paper Betts et al. (2019).

Davidson et al. (2016) report an association between women's experiences of SH and their anxiety, with greater experiences of SH associated with elevated experiences of anxiety. Davidson et al. (2016) explore the mediating role of perceived public safety in both busy public places and isolated public places. The results highlight that while experiences of SH are likely to lead to a reduction in perceived levels of safety in isolated places and in busy public places, only perceived public safety in isolated public places predicted elevated levels of anxiety. Therefore, it seems that having experienced SH, women's perceptions of public safety are changed and that this is particularly impactful in isolated environments.

Moreover, evidence shows that the emotional responses associated with women experiencing SH can result in them changing their behaviour to avoid future incidents (Bowman 1993). Bowman, in one of the only studies about SH as social behaviour phenomenon, also discusses how although women may fear SH, their reactions can be considered to be counterproductive.

For example, women often ignore or give the impression that they are ignoring the situation. Although Bowman (1993) suggests the reasons for such behaviours may be complex, one possible motive is embarrassment while another is not wanting to 'reward' the person engaging in the behaviour by providing an obvious response. Therefore, SH also prompts changes in behaviour so women do not put themselves in situations where they may experience harassment again.

While studies have explored the emotional impact of experiences of SH in adult women, fewer studies have considered the emotional impact of SH on young people. Recent research with women aged 14–21 in the UK highlighted that young women experience similar emotional responses to SH to those reported by adult women (Southgate and Russell 2018). For example, feeling embarrassed and ashamed because they were drawn attention to; disorientated and confused because of the harassment; anger; fear because of how the situation may develop and helplessness. There is also evidence that the emotional response to SH occurs in cultures other than the UK. For example, when SH was operationalised and assessed as 'Eve teasing' (a euphemism in South Asia for sexual harassment in public places), Talboys et al. (2017) reported that adolescents and young adults – including both boys and girls from Punjab, India who experienced 'Eve teasing' – also experienced negative emotions. Specifically, of the 36 participants who experienced 'Eve teasing', the majority reported feelings of anger (61%) and feelings of shame or humiliation (47%). Participants also reported experiencing fear, worry or tension following experiencing 'Eve teasing'. Talboys et al. (2017) argue that their findings can be explained by the normative beliefs or victim blaming and the perceived association between 'Eve teasing' and more severe forms of sexual violence. In this way, the context of women's SH literature offers insight into the experiences of adolescent girls in the UK.

Street harassment and public safety – legal and educational contexts

Recognising SH as a safety issue for adolescent girls when out in public is critical. However, even though the UK is a signatory to the United Nations Convention on the Rights of the Child (United Nations 1989) and enshrines 'best interests of the child' considerations in both family[2] and criminal law[3] contexts and through the establishment of the Children's Commissioner[4], actually *listening* to children and adolescents still is not the norm. For example, Gearon (2019) has highlighted that the problems of the state response to child trafficking are immigration and prosecution-led rather than child-focused, leading to further victimisation of the children. Similarly, listening to what adolescent girls have to say about how they understand SH incidents is important in addressing the problem.

Crime statistics in relation to children and adolescents regarding SH are sparse. Office for National Statistics (ONS) reports rely on both recorded crime data and Crime Survey for England and Wales (CSEW) questionnaire responses, but both are limited. Recorded crime data comes from police forces (who do not all record crime in the same way) and requires a report to the police and the police to record it as a crime, so unreported crime and harassing behaviour short of criminal conduct is missed. The CSEW relies on a nationally representative sample survey asking people about their experience of crime in the preceding 12 months, but its comparatively small child (aged 10–15) section (around 2,398 compared to 33,735 adults, ONS (2020)) makes extrapolation difficult and it only collects experiences of serious offences (violence causing injury and theft, but not sexual offences) (ONS 2019b). Lower-level street harassment and sexual misconduct are not caught by the CSEW and the apparent tendency of respondents to downplay incidents (79% of respondents perceived the violence they suffered as not a crime in ONS (2019a, 2019b)) suggests that the CSEW could be hampered in gathering information on lower-level incidents by the label 'crime'. Further, the ONS statistics are not routinely broken down by gender.

Gallagher et al. (1998) examined victimisation outside the home, whether criminal or not, but the questionnaires focused on fear, thus potentially missing out behaviour which did not result in this emotional response, and there has been no follow-up study in the following 30 years.

The study discussed in this chapter seeks to establish what SH problems adolescents face and how they react to these. This is because adolescents, particularly but not exclusively groomed ones, do not necessarily react negatively to unacceptable behaviour. Understanding SH is therefore difficult for adolescents. Furthermore, adults need to understand and properly categorise what they are being told by adolescents about SH. Adolescents' experiences feed into the decision whether to criminalise, and also into the criminal justice system response to non-criminal behaviour which may in fact be pre-criminal (for example, identifying vulnerable children to target for exploitation) and society's response to the behaviour, even if it is not criminalised. There is a significant gender aspect to this (whether girls are targeted by particular behaviour and particular crimes, whether they report differently and whether they respond differently) which also informs whether adult responses need to differ. The responsibility to listen to adolescent girls' experiences of SH is therefore paramount.

Safety is also a significant aspect to the impact of SH experiences for adolescent girls regarding their education. Learning can be configured as a characteristic human condition, but specific circumstances (both internal and external) are more likely to support and facilitate learning. While 'natural learning' (Knowles et al. 2011) is a default state of living and occurs continuously "as the individual interacts spontaneously with the environment" (Knowles et al. 2011, p. 215), the ability to learn or study can be disrupted by different negative events, and this includes SH experiences. Bandura (1977) emphasises calm or low emotional arousal is more likely to produce success in learning, and Wallace (2007, p. 107) claims that it is important to build "self-concept in order to...achieve high performance" since learning cannot take place when young people feel de-motivated.

As a signatory to the UN Convention of the Rights of the Child, the UK has signalled its commitment to providing each child with automatic access to education which will "develop a child's personality, talents and abilities". However, to profit from education, young people need to be in a state of learning readiness. Such readiness has become more significant in contemporary education as increasingly schools require learners to be independent and to exhibit "agency (intentional behaviour) in a learning environment" (Khan et al. 2010, p. 95). In this regard, events which occur before learning are critical as these episodes may impact on a student's emotional well-being, their personal feelings of self-efficacy and their capacity to learn. The study discussed below explores the impact of SH on adolescent girls' ability to positively engage with education, since SH can undermine their ability to learn.

Methodology

The aim of the study was to examine adolescents' SH experiences. The objectives were to explore adolescents' emotional response following SH, to analyse their descriptions and reflections of SH and to consider the implications of these experiences for their education and legal rights. We undertook this study in two stages. Firstly, adolescents were asked to report SH to the team using either a bespoke mobile app or a paper copy of a print-out of the app. They were asked to indicate any SH incidents for example, whether there was any name calling or if any physical contact occurred, to report their emotions using the app about the SH incidents for example feeling 'active', 'frightened', 'smiley', 'upset' and to add any further description about the SH experiences in their own words. Secondly, two focus groups were held to explore further how adolescents understood SH. The study produced three datasets: reporting the incidents and emotions, free-text descriptions, focus group transcripts.

Our sampling strategy was as follows. We used a convenience sample of schools known through professional teaching contacts of the research team. We then only included those who volunteered to report SH using the app, which means that while we cannot claim a representative sample took part, the findings are still indicative of the SH experiences of adolescents in the UK. Three secondary school took part in the reporting of incidents and experiences, and two of these also participated in the focus groups. The schools were from the East Midlands and London, and using the English Indices of Deprivation 2015 (Gill 2015), the schools were 'inner-city very deprived', 'semi-rural deprived' and 'suburban very affluent' (thereby suggesting SH is not confined to deprived areas only). A total of 118 adolescents aged 11–15 years of which 68 identified as female (a further 43 identified as male and 7 did not give their gender) took part in reporting SH incidents and experiences over a six-week period using multiple-choice questions (MCQs) with additional free-text space for further descriptions. As part of the data collected about the incidents, adolescents were asked to report their emotional response to the SH incident/s using a modified version of the Positive and Negative Affect Schedule for Children (PANAS-C) (Ebesutani et al. 2012). The PANAS-C is a short measure of positive effect and negative effect. Participants were presented with a series of emotions as MCQs and asked to indicate which ones they felt following the episode of harassment. Informed consent was gained from the headteachers, parents and carers and the adolescent students. We also ran school assemblies to explain the project, provide an opportunity for questions, inform of rights to confidentiality and anonymity and encourage talking with families, tutors or ChildLine for support if necessary. Although our study featured boys and girls (Betts et al. 2019), as SH affects not only girls (Deakin 2006), this chapter focuses on the SH of adolescent girls of secondary school age.

Our sampling of the focus groups was from two of the three schools which had taken part in the reports. The schools acted as gatekeepers in asking if any of the adolescents who had made a SH report also wanted to be in a focus group. Using additional information and consent forms specifically for the focus groups, 13 adolescents took part, nine from an all girls' school ('Ash[5]') and four at a mixed-sex school ('Beech') where three participants were girls. The semi-structured focus group schedules covered: what 'SH' means, why people might harass others, whether being able to report SH was useful and what could be done if SH is experienced. Digital recordings by members of the research team were transcribed verbatim for analysis. The focus group and interview transcripts were analysed thematically (Mason 2002; Nowell et al. 2017) using a social constructionist epistemology (Burr 1995; Henwood 2014) to capture the thoughts and feelings of the participants (Sutton and Austin 2015). There were three main findings which showed the distinctiveness of SH for adolescent girls: (1) immediate effects of experiencing SH; (2) being able to identify SH from experiencing an incident and (3) the potential to disrupt their education.

The analysis from different academic disciplines shows how the SH of adolescent girls can be informed by multi-disciplinary team (Silberzahn et al. 2018; Urbanska et al. 2019) and promoting how social sciences and the humanities can work together (Arjomand 2016; Albert et al. 2017). The importance of a multi-disciplinary approach is that it lends itself to a phenomenon as complex as SH. SH has implications for psychology, social policy, education, law and linguists, and the analysis presented here from each academic discipline gives a multi-faceted approach.

Findings

The reports – the language of managing SH incidents

The emotional impact of experiencing SH in the UK was examined (Betts et al. 2019). The data revealed that adolescents reported experiencing very few positive emotions such as 'happy', 'glad' 'proud' following SH incidents. Both girls and boys reported experiencing negative emotions such as 'frightened', 'disgusted', 'ashamed' following incidents of SH, but the level of negative emotions was significantly greater in girls (as discussed in greater detail in Betts et al. 2019). However, when considering the findings, it is important to recognise that during adolescence, boys tend to increasingly restrict their emotional expression (Polce-Lynch et al. 2001). This demonstrates how adolescent girls' experiences of SH are associated with a range of negative emotions.

Participants were also invited to provide a written description when reporting an incident in the study: 'If you would like to tell us more about what happened and how you felt, please use your own words to describe the incident'. Of the 118 reports submitted, 61 included a free-text description. These descriptions averaged at 24.8 words in length, and around half of all girls (38/68) provided a description. 'Narrative' responses such as these "offer insights into people's private worlds" (Pavlenko 2007, p. 164) which are inaccessible to purely quantitative or MCQ-based methods. In addition, the language choices that the adolescent girls used when describing the SH event re-constructs their experience, providing an insight into the "meanings they attach to those experiences" (Barkhuizen 2015, p. 176). Analysis of the language used in the free-text descriptions offers unique insight into: (i) the sexualised dialogues experienced by adolescent girls, (ii) the way in which the girls describe their responses to the harassment and (iii) how the quantitative and qualitative data collected can be triangulated. Of particular interest is the way adolescent girls used coping strategies following SH incidents.

Details of sexualised dialogue were distinctive to adolescent girls' SH, and the dialogue details are not homogenous in nature. This extract shows a 15-year-old girl describing a taxi driver approaching her in the street:

> It was 5am and I was going to France and I was walking the vehicle slowed down to my speed and he asked me to go inside his car he showed me his taxi badge, convincing he was a taxi driver. He said to me he wanted to keep me 'safe' I had said no 3 times and he shrugged as if it was my fault like I was losing out. and then he drove out.

Although not explicitly sexual, this is unambiguously predatory, with the taxi driver attempting to coax the girl into his car. Whatever his motives, the girl indicated she felt 'frightened' and 'disgusted' at his approach in the MCQs. This sort of harassment is not widely reported in the literature on the harassment of adult women, and so may be unique to the harassment of adolescent girls. For example, studies of SH experienced by adult women does not indicate many men offering to 'keep them safe' (e.g. Kearl 2014; Mullany and Trickett 2018; Kearl et al. 2019). Promises to keep a young girl 'safe' fits within Lorenzo-Dus et al.'s (2016, p. 44) model of grooming discourse under 'deceptive trust development', in which "groomers hide their ulterior motive of wanting to engage the target in sexual activities by discursively building a trust-based bond with him/her" (Lorenzo-Dus 2019, p. 17). The fact that she 'said no 3 times' also suggests that there were multiple attempts by the man to get the girl into his car.

This extract, also submitted by another 15-year-old girl, shows a different sort of verbal harassment:

> I was walking to my friends' house and I got horned at and I looked and two guys (men) asked me 'how old are you babe?' It made me feel completely disgusted.

Here, the harassment is more explicitly sexualised, not least by the reference to the girl using the term of endearment 'babe'. Terms of address such as this are very commonly used by men to passing female strangers in "an attempt to conjure and impose a fleeing moment of heterosexual intimacy" (Bailey 2016, p. 599). However, requests for age are *not* commonly used in the harassment of adult women; the combination of such a request and the word 'babe' that makes this incident distinctive for adolescent girls. It may be assumed that asking about the girl's age to identify whether or not she is of the age of sexual consent (16 years of age in the UK). This suggests sexual intent pervades the entire exchange and is particularly predatory. This extract also reports a 14-year-old girl being complimented and asked her age:

> When me and my best mate was walking some man in a car went by us, turned around and came back to follow us in his car. He said 'How old are you' my mate said 'why' and he said your beautiful so then I rang my mum and we tried running away.

Compliments are an extremely common way in which men harass women and thereby "reinforce the right of all men to be rightful proprietors and legitimate commentators in public" (Gardner 1995, p. 147). 'Compliments' such as this are perceived by adult women as "rude and an invasion of privacy" (Kissling 1991, p. 453) and "objectively degrading, objectifying and frequently threatening in nature" (Sullivan et al. 2010, p. 238). Such effects and motives are exacerbated when the target of the harassment is an adolescent girl; during adolescence there is a "confusion between what is ordinary, what is complimentary and what is dangerous" (Vera-Gray 2017, p. 132). The analysis of these three extracts alone shows how SH of adolescent girls is distinct from that of adult women, while concerning in and of themselves, could be the precursor to much more serious crimes.

Although the text in the previous quote (14-year-old girl being complimented and asked her age) does not explicitly express any feeling or emotional response, the fact that the girls ran away and called their parents as a means of managing the incident indicates their feelings indirectly. However, when we look at the accompanying MCQ, the girl indicated that she felt 'upset', 'scared', 'frightened' and 'afraid' by the incident. This range of negative emotions emphasises the need to ask adolescents directly how incidents made them feel rather than assuming they would disclose it in accounts or statements about an event. Reports by others also shed more light on this:

> on the way back from school me and my friend Amy[6] was going home and a car was beep I was scared

> people just called me names that made me really upset

> it was just banta with my friends apart from one thing

When compared and triangulated with their accompanying MCQs, these quotes provide important insights into disclosure patterns of adolescent girls. In the first quote, the girl reports being 'scared', the only emotion selected in the MCQs. In others, however (such as the second quote), the girl expresses feeling 'really upset' in the written account, but had earlier responded to the multiple-choice questions that she felt a range of additional, perhaps more concerning, emotions: 'afraid', 'ashamed', 'frightened', 'lonely', 'miserable', 'moody', 'nervous', 'sad', 'scared' and 'upset'. In this case, saying that she felt 'upset' hides a number of emotional reactions that she disclosed when asked in a different way. The third quote is particularly telling, describing SH as 'just banta', while indicating she felt 'blue' in the MCQs, and reporting experiencing *five* types of harassment, selecting that 'I was called names', 'I was laughed at', 'I was pushed/hit', 'I was tripped up' and 'I had my bag taken/grabbed'. Attributing five different co-occurring behaviours to 'just banta with my friends' therefore appears problematic, with the 'apart from one thing', suggesting she distinguishes one event as not being 'banta'. By labelling the incidents as 'banta', the girl is possibly mitigating, downplaying and normalising what happened. The use of euphemistic terms such as 'banta' to describe potentially traumatic experiences can reflect a confusion as to whether threatening and dangerous behaviours will be taken seriously by adults (e.g. Hlavka 2014). It is important to have an understanding of the ways in which language is used to encode and attach meaning to experiences of adolescent girls' SH.

The girls who provided free-text extracts also often gave details of how they physically responded to and used coping strategies when experiencing SH.

> me and friend was from school then a car stopped and papped by a man in a car so we walked away

> I was in a shop in [town] and this man started staring at me and my friends and when we were about to leave he started to get his things and he started to follow us we ran away and we lost him

These two extracts show the girls managing SH by walking or running away. This mirrors the most common 'coping strategies' that adult women use as 'passive' (Fairchild and Rudman 2008; Saunders et al. 2016) or 'avoidance' (Magley 2002), to reduce, rather than escalate, potential danger or threat. This shows how avoidance or evasion as the primary response to SH is a coping strategy that girls develop at a young age.

The free-text descriptions also captured insights into public safety at all levels of SH behaviour, whether 'low level', or more serious, criminal incidents. By cross-referencing both the narrative text MCQs for each report with the elements of specific offences, it was possible to establish which incidents were criminal and which fell outside the law. It was also possible to show how girls' SH experiences are distinctive from that of boys', as girls were more likely to report SH using the app (Table 6.1).[7]

The types of crime experienced by adolescent girls and boys were also were also different (Table 6.2).

While boys were more likely to be the victims of street harassment which can be classified as acquisitive offences or driving offences, girls were much more likely to be the victims of minor public order offences and slightly more likely to be victims of minor offences against the person. Only one report each of sexual assault and threatening with a bladed article, and both victims were girls. While Deakin's (2006) analysis of Gallagher et al.'s (1998) results also found that girls suffered more harassment and sexual offending, it was also found that harassment formed the bulk of victimisation of both genders.[9]

The reports of non-criminal behaviour bore out the same pattern with perpetrators more ready to approach and interact with girls than boys. There were similar levels of being followed and/or stared at in concerning situations (three girls, two boys), but only girls reported being approached

Table 6.1 Breakdown of reports of crime by gender

	Girls	Boys
Reported SH using the app	68 (57% of all reports)	43 (36% of all reports)
Reported incident amounted to a possible crime	32 (47% of girls' reports, 27% of all reports)	19 (44% of boys' reports, 16% of all reports)

Table 6.2 Breakdown of crime reports by crime category and gender

Offence	Girls	Boys
Minor public order – s. 4, 4A or 5 Public Order Act 1986 (verbal)	20	5
Assault/battery/harassment (physical)	8[8]	4
Sexual assault	1	0
Threatening with a bladed article	1	0
Attempted/full theft/robbery	2	7
Careless/dangerous driving	–	3
Totals	32	19

and spoken to. It was also only girls (three) who reported being filmed or photographed, a change from Gallagher et al.'s research (1998), and likely driven by the proliferation of mobile phones with cameras, as well as the ability to use and share images.

Currently, even where an offence can be identified, it is often not possible to prosecute due to the paucity of evidence, particularly when the perpetrator is a stranger as highlighted by Bowman (1993). Where the incident is serious, such as a robbery, the police may be willing to devote time and resources to investigating it, but the tendency of young people to underplay the importance of incidents makes reporting is unlikely in the first place; adults need to be able to bridge this reporting gap and support young people to understand what has happened to them. Police investigation is significantly less likely when the incident amounts to, at most, a minor public order matter. However, the incidents of girls being approached may well be precursors to offending, for example, child abduction, child sexual offences or exploitation. Adults could help prevent grooming and victimisation (Turnbull et al. 2012; James et al. 2017), but this is dependent on listening to adolescents, understanding SH and knowing how to act. As Bowman (1993) argues, the law can fail to support where SH incidents occur, leaving the safety of adolescent girls at risk.

The focus groups – confusion, unpredictability and a negative impact on learning

The focus groups with adolescent girls took place at two of the participating schools: 'Ash' (an all girl's school) and 'Beech' (a mixed-sex school).

Firstly, SH was described in terms of confusion and fear:

> …probably that scared…you just want to get out of that place ('Mia' yr8 'Beech').

The girls described SH as a traumatic experience with the potential to harm, as reported by adult women (Vera-Gray 2015, 2017; Jones et al. 2018). Feeling confused can follow experiencing unexpected, disturbing and traumatic incidents (Davidson et al. 2016), affecting the ability of individuals to process emotion (Clapp et al. 2015). The confusion caused by experiencing SH is therefore significant for adolescent girls.

Secondly, SH was seen as unpredictable public disorder incidents that can happen anywhere and at any time:

> …you could erm be street harassed any time… ('Ayah' yr9 'Ash').

Avoiding what seem to be unsafe routes can be about *feeling* safer, rather than necessarily *being* safer when out in public (Buckley 2016). However, the girls regarded limiting their movements in public to try and minimise the risk of experiencing SH as neither healthy nor preferable (Fernandez 2016), and possibly 'victim blaming' (Vera-Gray 2017). However, in managing their experiences, the girls emphasised recognising and naming SH:

> Not many people know how to deal with being street harassed...if I got street harassed I wouldn't of classified it as SH I would of just thought it was a random thing ('Hana' yr7 'Ash').

The naming of traumatic experiences is a political act (Swartz 2017). The danger of *not* identifying SH is that of accepting incidents as normal experiences when out in public, with students developing potential risky coping strategies from becoming 'desensitised' (Mellgren et al. 2018). Two girls from 'Ash' school commented:

> ...as a teenager, you might just brush it under the carpet thinking it's a minor issue... ('Barbara' yr8 'Ash')
> ...yeah I think that that's right I think it's quite easy to sort of think 'Oh this happens, I'll just shrug it off' or 'I'm not too sure what to do so I'll carry on' kind of thing ('Chloe' yr8 'Ash').

Other ways of managing SH involved reporting incidents to the police as 'Amy' from 'Ash' school described:

> Do you know how the police might respond if you were to report street harassment? (Researcher)
> Erm if you described how the person looked they could go on a search... ('Barbara' yr 8 'Ash')
> Erm my situation wasn't taken seriously. I was with my little sister and my friend and she was also younger than me... ('Amy' yr7 'Ash')
> ...you informed the police did you? (Researcher)
> Yeah but nothing happened ('Amy' yr7 'Ash')
> And nothing happened? And what did they say to you?.. (Researcher)
> Nothing really. They just said like 'we're on it go home' and stuff, and nothing happened. They didn't contact us back or anything ('Amy' yr7 'Ash').

The girls from 'Ash' school were not confident in reporting to the police, and much more likely to speak with their parents or friends in the first instance (Hamilton et al. 2016). They regarded talking about their experiences with people they knew and trusted to be a healthy way of dealing with the distress of SH (Malin et al. 2019):

> I would say that if you do get street harassed that erm you shouldn't let it affect you like in your later life you should still stay confident when you're going out and about and still be happy when you're going like to places ('Sara' yr9 'Ash')

> ...Erm you should always talk to people if you feel like erm your upset or if you if it happens like frequently you should talk to someone and hopefully sort it out ('Sara' yr9 'Ash')
>
> Erm I think that erm like be friends with the right people because if something happens to you then you need someone to talk to or someone to be there for you ('Niyati' yr7 'Ash').

Similarly, the focus group at 'Beech' school expressed the same views with an emphasis on being able to trust the right people:

> I'm sure everyone's got like a good friend that that they know wouldn't judge them on everything, and if they don't have that, there's like parents and family and stuff, that may be a cousin or sommat like that. That you know someone that, that you're close to them, you know won't like, after finding that out, like they won't leave you, don't want to stay and help you through it... ('Lilly' yr 7 'Beech')
>
> ...like a sibling... ('fire-breathing-dragon' yr 8 'Beech')
>
> ...they want to help you and stay with you through it ('Lilly' yr 7 'Beech').
>
> ...Erm, yeh. Don't be afraid to tell anyone ('fire-breathing-dragon' yr8 'Beech').
>
> If they, if you tell someone if that if there's like a friend if they, like, if they were truly close to you they wouldn't change their mind, they wouldn't say anything like, they wouldn't tell anyone, they would just like keep it like a secret, and like, they wouldn't want you to get hurt... ('Mia' yr 8 'Beech').

Reluctance in contacting the police included not thinking SH was serious enough to be reported, they feared being blamed for over-reacting and they were not confident they would be believed about their experiences. As Vera-Gray (2017) writes, reporting to the police can be disappointing, compounding the distress of the original harassment incident for the individual.

Thirdly, both focus groups also demonstrated SH had a direct (and often immediate) impact on adolescents affecting their learning. The girls discussed a heightened emotional state, and that the incidents made them feel 'really scared and worried', 'confused' and 'really annoyed', all of which counter the calm state, which Bandura (1977) claims is more suited for productive and positive learning. Others stated SH caused them to feel 'sad', 'disgusted', 'upset' and 'bad about yourself', at odds with Wallace's assertion (2007) for the need to have a positive sense of self and your personal abilities when learning. As 'Mia' and 'Lilly' at 'Beech' school commented, SH incidents were not easily forgotten and can lead to very negative thinking and harmful behaviour.

> ...days or like months...it might like flash back into your mind, you might just start thinking about it again ('Mia' yr8 'Beech')

> And the thing is you'll start thinking about like if street harassment or something does happen to you, then you don't speak to someone about it, and you don't tell anyone, then you, and then you're always thinking about it, you'd just be like ashamed of it, because you might think, and especially if its like happened to you more than once, you would like start to think why do people like pick on me or something [inaudible] and stuff, that would start to like self-harm and suicide and stuff like that ('Lilly' yr7 'Beech')
> ...So you need to like tell people... ('Lilly' yr7 'Beech')
> ...And then if you don't have many friends anyway, like if that does happen to someone like that doesn't have any friends, then that could lead to like self-harming ('Mia' yr8 'Beech').

Furthermore, these feelings had the potential to resurface and, by distracting, continue to exert a negative impact on learning readiness. This high level of emotional turmoil did not help adolescents to learn, and their comments indicate SH left them feeling shaken and preoccupied with the exchange.

Interestingly, the girls at 'Beech' school appreciated they may need some time to recover,

> Until you're like ready to talk about it ('Fire-breathing-dragon' yr8 'Beech'),

and even considered that specialist help might be necessary,

> speak to someone about it...a bit like a therapist...never be afraid to talk ('Fire-breathing-dragon' yr8 'Beech'),
> Yeh. Don't bottle it up cause it doesn't help ('Mia' yr8 'Beech').

Conclusions

Significant aspects emerge from examining how adolescent girls experience SH. The negative emotions experienced by adolescent girls following SH incidents are more severe than those of boys, and the SH incidents experienced by girls also appear different to that of boys (Betts et al. 2019), for example, the incidents reported were more likely to be criminal than those reported by boys, with girls only reporting being spoken to or being filmed or photographed. Furthermore, girls can 'mask' their negative feelings. This indicates that SH puts their safety and well-being at risk due to the impact of SH, for example being asked their age, with obvious sexual connotations, is not something reported by adult women. While their coping strategies are similar to that of adult women, girls only respond with avoidance or evasion. The confusion experienced following SH incidents, and the unpredictability of when and where SH might occur emphasises the difficulties for girls in developing successful coping strategies. Of most concern is that of the impact experiencing SH can have on learning, namely disruption and distraction. If, as Kramer (cited in Rogers 1961, p. xiii) asserts, self-actualisation is the highest order of learning and being, then reporting SH incidents is to start a hugely positive response. It is the role of parents, teachers, academics, educators, law enforcement and adult members of the community to listen, support and address the risks that SH poses for adolescent girls.

Notes

1 In our study, 'adolescent' refers to children ages 11–15 years.
2 Children Act 1989 s. 1.
3 Children and Young Persons Act 1933 s. 44(1).
4 Children Act 2004 Part 1.
5 Pseudonyms have been used to protect the anonymity of the individual participants and their respective schools; the pseudonyms for the individual participants were self-selected by those at 'Beech' school and ascribed to those at 'Ash'.
6 All names used in these reports are pseudonyms.
7 There were also seven reporters who either did not identify as a particular gender or chose not to give their gender.
8 Three of the reports appeared to be of the same incident, all experienced by girls.
9 Vehicle-based behaviour was not captured by Gallagher et al. (1998).

References

Albert, M., Paradis, E. and Kuper, A., 2017. Interdisciplinary fantasy: social scientists and humanities scholars working in faculties of medicine. In: Frickel, S., Albert, M. and Prainsack, B., eds. *Investigating Interdisciplinary Collaboration: Theory and Practice across Disciplines*. New Brunswick: Rutgers University Press, pp. 84–103.

Arjomand, S., 2016. The rise of interdisciplinary studies in social sciences and humanities and the challenge of comparative sociology. *European Journal of Social Theory*, 20(2), pp. 292–306. DOI: 10.1177/1368431016646112.

Bailey, B., 2016. Street remarks to women in five countries and four languages: impositions of engagement and intimacy. *Sociolinguistic Studies*, 10(4), pp. 589–609. DOI: 10.1558/sols.28020.

Bandura, A., 1977. *Social Learning Theory*. Englewood Cliffs, NJ: Prentice Hall.

Barkhuizen, G., 2015. Narrative inquiry. In: Paltridge, B. and Phakiti, A., eds. *Research Methods in Applied Linguistics: A Practical Resource*. London: Bloomsbury, 2015, pp. 169–185.

Bastomski, S. and Smith, P., 2017. Gender, fear, and public places: how negative encounters with strangers harm women. *Sex Roles*, 76, pp. 73–88. DOI: 10.1007/s11199-016-0654-6.

Betts, L.R., Harding, R., Peart, S., Sjölin, C., Wright, D. and Newbold, K.R., 2019. Adolescents' experiences of street harassment: creating a typology and assessing the emotional impact. *Journal of Aggression, Conflict and Peace Research*, 11, pp. 38–46. DOI: 10.1108/jacpr-12-2017-0336.

Bowman, C.G., 1993. Street harassment and the informal ghettoization of women. *Harvard Law Review*, 106, 517–580. DOI: 10.2307/1341656.

Bucchianeri, M.M. et al., 2014. Multiple types of harassment: associations with emotional well-being and unhealthy behaviours in adolescents. *Journal of Adolescent Health*, 54(6), pp. 724–729. DOI: 10.1016/j.jadohealth.2013.10.205.

Buckley, N., 2016. *Sexual harassment on public transit and the influence of perceptions of safety on travel behaviour.* Doctoral dissertation, University of Texas in Austin.

Burr, V., 1995. *An Introduction to Social Constructionism.* London: Routledge.

Children Act 2004 (c. 41).

Children and Young Persons Act 1933 (c. 12).

Clapp, J., Patton, S. and Beck, J., 2015. Expressive inhibition in response to stress: implications for emotional processing following trauma. *Journal of Anxiety Disorders*, 29, pp. 109–118. DOI: 10.1016/j.janxdis.2014.11.008.

Davidson, M. et al., 2016. The mediating role of perceived safety on street harassment and anxiety. *Psychology of Violence*, 6(4), pp. 553–561. DOI: 10.1037/a0039970.

Deakin, J., 2006. Dangerous people, dangerous places: the nature and location of young people's victimisation and fear. *Children and Society*, 20(5), pp. 376–390. DOI: 10.1111/j.1099-0860.2006.00011.x.

Ebesutani et al., 2012. The 10-item positive and negative affect schedule for children, child and parent shortened versions: application of item response theory for more efficient assessment. *Journal of Psychopathology and Behavioral Assessment*, 34(2), pp. 191–203. DOI: 10.1007/s10862-011-9273-2.

Fairchild, K. and Rudman, L., 2008. Everyday stranger harassment and women's objectification. *Social Justice Research*, 21(3), pp. 338–357. DOI: 10.1007/s11211-008-0073-0.

Fernandez, N., 2016. *Street harassment effects on women: an exploratory study.* Masters Dissertation, California State University.

Fileborn, B., 2014. Online activism and street harassment: digital justice or shouting into the ether? *Griffith Journal of Law and Human Dignity*, 2, pp. 32–51.

Gallagher, B., Bradford, M. and Pease, K., 1998. *The Children and Young People's Safety Survey (CYPSS) Final Report to the ESRC.* Manchester: University of Manchester.

Henwood, K., 2014. Qualitative research. In: Teo, T., ed. *Encyclopedia of Critical Psychology.* New York: Springer, pp. 1611–1624.

Gardner, C., 1995. *Passing By: Gender and Public Harassment.* Berkeley: University of California Press.

Gearon, A., 2019. Child trafficking: young people's experiences of front-line services in England. *British Journal of Criminology*, 59(2), pp. 481–500. DOI: 10.1093/bjc/azy042.

Gekoski, A. et al., 2017. The prevalence and nature of sexual harassment and assault against women and girls on public transport: an international review. *Journal of Criminological Research, Policy and Practice*, 3(1), pp. 3–16. DOI: 10.1108/JCRPP-08-2016-0016.

Gill, B., 2015. The English indices of deprivation 2015 [online]. Department for Communities and Local Government. Available at: https://assets.publishing.service.gov.uk/government/uploads/system/uploads/attachment_data/file/465791/English_Indices_of_Deprivation_2015_-_Statistical_Release.pdf [Accessed 17 January 2021].

Hamilton, P. et al., 2016. *Street Aware Evaluation: Final Report into the Effectiveness of a School-Based Knife, Gun and Gang Crime Educational Intervention.* Nottingham: Nottingham Centre for Children, Young People and Families, Nottingham Trent University.

Hlavka, H.R., 2014. Normalizing sexual violence: young women account for harassment and abuse. *Gender and Society*, 28(3), pp. 337–358. DOI: 10.1177/0891243214526468.

James, D. et al., 2017. New challenges in adolescent safeguarding. *Postgraduate Medical Journal*, 93, pp. 96–102. DOI: 10.1136/postgradmedj-2016-134426.

Jones, L., Mitchell, K., Turner, H. and Ybarra, M., 2018. Characteristics of bias-based harassment incidents reported by a national sample of US adolescents. *Journal of Adolescence*, 65, pp. 50–60. DOI: 10.1016/j.adolescence.2018.02.013.

Kearl, H., 2014. *Unsafe and Harassed in Public Spaces: A National Street Harassment Report*. Reston. Available at: http://www.stopstreetharassment.org/wp-content/uploads/2012/08/2014-National-SSH-Street-Harassment-Report.pdf [Accessed 15 December 2021].

Kearl, H., Johns, N.E. and Raj, A., 2019. *Measuring #MeToo: A National Study on Sexual Harassment and Assault*. UC San Diego Centre on Gender Equity and Health. Available at: http://www.stopstreetharassment.org/wp-content/uploads/2012/08/2019-MeToo-National-Sexual-Harassment-and-Assault-Report.pdf [Accessed 15 December 2021].

Khan, F.A. et al., 2010. Identifying and incorporating affective states in web-based learning management systems. *Interaction Design and Architecture Journal – IxD&A*, 9–10, pp. 85–103.

Kissling, E.A., 1991. Street harassment: the language of sexual terrorism. *Discourse and Society*, 2(4), pp. 451–460. DOI: 10.1177/0957926591002004006.

Knowles, M.S., Holton, E.F. and Swanson, R.A., 2011. *The Adult Learner, The Definitive Classic in Adult Education and Human Resource Development*. 7th ed. Oxford: Butterworth-Heinnemann.

Laniya, O.O., 2005. Street smut: gender, media, and the legal power dynamics of street harassment, or "hey sexy" and other verbal ejaculations. *Columbia Journal of Gender and Law*, 14(1), pp. 91–130. DOI: 10.7916/cjgl.v14i1.2503.

Logan, L.S., 2015. Street harassment: current and promising avenues for researchers and activists. *Sociology Compass*, 9(3), pp. 196–211. DOI: 10.1111/soc4.12248.

Lorenzo-Dus, N., Izura, C. and Pérez-Tattam, R., 2016. Understanding grooming discourse in computer-mediated environments. *Discourse, Context and Media*, 12, pp. 40–50. DOI: 10.1016/j.dcm.2016.02.004.

Lorenzo-Dus, N. and Kinzel, A., 2019. 'So is your mom as cute as you?': examining patterns of language use by online sexual groomers. *Journal of Corpora and Discourse Studies*, 2(1), pp. 1–30. DOI: 10.18573/jcads.31.

Magley, V.J., 2002. Coping with sexual harassment: reconceptualizing women's resistance. *Journal of Personality and Social Psychology*, 83(4), pp. 930–946. DOI: 10.1037/0022-3514.83.4.930.

Malin, H., Morton, E., Nadal, A. and Smith, K., 2019. Purpose and coping with adversity: a repeated measures, mixed-methods study with young adolescents. *Journal of Adolescence*, 76, pp. 1–11. DOI: 10.1016/j.adolescence.2019.07.015.

Mason, J., 2002. *Qualitative Researching*. London: Sage.

Mellgren, C., Anderson, M. and Ivert, A.K., 2018. 'It happens all the time': women's experience and normalization of sexual harassment in public space. *Women and Criminal Justice*, 28(4), pp. 262–281. DOI: 10.1080/08974454.2017.1372328.

Mullany, L. and Trickett, L., 2018. *Misogyny Hate Crime Evaluation Report*. Nottingham Women's Centre. Available online: https://www.nottinghamwomenscentre.com/wp-content/uploads/2018/07/Misogyny-Hate-Crime-Evaluation-Report-June-2018.pdf.

Nowell, L. et al., 2017. Thematic analysis: striving to meet the trustworthiness criteria. *International Journal of Qualitative Methods*, 16, pp. 1–13. DOI: 10.1177/1609406917733847.

ONS, 2019a. Improving victimisation estimates derived from the Crime Survey of England and Wales [online]. 24 January. Available at: https://www.ons.gov.uk/peoplepopulationandcommunity/crimeandjustice/articles/improvingvictimisationestimatesderivedfromthecrimesurveyforenglandandwales/2019-01-24 [Accessed 15 December 2021].

ONS, 2019b. The nature of violent crime in England and Wales: year ending March 2018 [online]. 7 February. Available at: https://www.ons.gov.uk/peoplepopulationandcommunity/crimeandjustice/articles/thenatureofviolentcrimeinenglandandwales/yearendingmarch2018 [Accessed 17 January 2021].

ONS, 2020. Crime in England and Wales: year ending March 2020 [online]. July 2020. Available at: https://www.ons.gov.uk/releases/crimeinenglandandwalesyearendingmarch2020 [Accessed 15 December 2021].

Pavlenko, A., 2007. Autobiographic narratives as data in applied linguistics. *Applied Linguistics*, 28(2), pp. 163–188. DOI: 10.1093/applin/amm008.

Polce-Lynch, M. et al., 2001. Adolescent self-esteem and gender: exploring relations to sexual harassment, body image, media influence, and emotional expression. *Journal of Youth and Adolescence*, 30(2), pp. 225–244. DOI: 10.1023/A:1010397809136.

Rogers, C., 1961. *On Becoming a Person. A Therapist's View of Psychotherapy.* New York: Houghton Mifflin Company.

Saunders, B.A. et al. 2016. Contending with catcalling: the role of system-justifying beliefs and ambivalent sexism in predicting women's coping experiences with (and men's attributions for) stranger harassment. *Current Psychology*, 36(2), pp. 324–338. DOI: 10.1007/s12144-016-9421-7.

Silberzahn, R. et al. 2018. Many analysts, one data set: making transparent how variations in analytic choices affect results. *Advances in Methods and Practices in Psychological Science*, 1(3), pp. 337–356. DOI: 10.1177/2515245917747646.

Southgate, J. and Russell, L., 2018. *Street Harassment: It's Not Ok.* London: Plan International UK. Available at: https://plan-uk.org/file/plan-uk-street-harassment-reportpdf/download?token=CyKwYGSJ [Accessed 15 December 2021].

Sullivan, H.B., Lord, T.L. and Mchugh, M.C., 2010. Creeps and casanovas: experiences, explanations, and effects of street harassment. In: Paludi, M. and Denmark, F., eds. *Victims of Sexual Assault and Abuse: Incidence and Psychological Dimensions.* Santa Barbara, CA: Praeger, pp. 237–258.

Sutton, J. and Austin, Z., 2015. Qualitative research: data collection, analysis, and management. *Canadian Journal of Hospital Pharmacology*, 68(3), pp. 226–231. DOI: 10.4212/cjhp.v68i3.1456.

Swartz, S., 2017. Collectively speaking: the many meanings of naming and sharing group trauma. *Psychoanalytic Dialogues*, 27(2), pp. 156–163. DOI: 10.1080/10481885.2017.1284506.

Talboys, S.L. et al., 2017. What is eve teasing? A mixed methods study of sexual harassment of young women in the rural Indian context. *Sage Open*, 7(4), pp. 1–10. DOI: 10.1177/2158244017697168.

Turnbull, M., Davies, R. and Brown, C., 2012. *Caught in a Trap: The Impact of Grooming.* London: NSPCC/Childline. Available at: https://www.basw.co.uk/system/files/resources/basw_21744-2_0.pdf [Accessed 15 December 2021].

United Nations, 1989. Convention on the rights of the child [online]. Available at: https://www.unicef.org.uk/what-we-do/un-convention-child-rights/ [Accessed 17 January 2021].

Urbanska, K., Huet, S. and Guimond, S., 2019. Does increased interdisciplinary contact among hard and social scientists help or hinder interdisciplinary research? *PLoS ONE*, 14(9), pp. 1–20. DOI: 10.1371/journal.pone.0221907.

Vera-Gray, F., 2017. *Men's Intrusion, Women's Embodiment: A Critical Analysis of Street Harassment*. London: Routledge.

Wallace, S., 2007. *Getting the Buggers Motivated in FE*. London: Continuum.

Wånggren, L., 2016. Our stories matter: storytelling and social justice in the Hollaback! Movement. *Gender and Education*, 28(3), pp. 401–415. DOI: 10.1080/09540253.2016.1169251.

7 Misogyny, hate crimes and gendered Islamophobia

Muslim women's experiences and responses

Amina Easat-Daas

Introduction

Muslim women across the globe consistently find themselves disproportionately impacted by gendered Islamophobia. For example, in the UK 721 of the overall 1,444 cases of Islamophobia reported to Tell Mama (Islamophobia monitoring organisation) were incidents targeting Muslim women (Tell Mama 2019a).[1] Similarly, in France the *Collectif contre l'Islamophobie en France* (the Counter Islamophobia Collective in France – CCIF) has highlighted an overall increase in reported Islamophobic hate crimes, with 70% of the 789 cases reported targeting Muslim women (CCIF 2020).[2]

Along similar lines, the *Collectif contre l'Islamophobie en Belgique* (the Counter Islamophobia Collective in Belgium – CCIB) highlighted a general increase in reported Islamophobic hate crimes towards Muslim women; 90.6% of the hate crime cases that it reviewed were against Muslim women (CCIB 2020). This represented a marked increase in gendered Islamophobic hate crimes in Belgium in the previous year. In the preceding year, the CCIB reported that 75% of Islamophobic hate crimes were against Belgian women (CCIB 2020);[3] nonetheless, this figure similarly represents an alarmingly high rate of gendered Islamophobic hate crimes. These examples are repeated across Europe (Easat-Daas 2019a; Mason-Bish and Zempi 2019). Whilst the statistical evidence is alarming, as with all hate crime statistics, these figures represent just the 'tip of the iceberg'. The scale of hate crimes rooted in Islamophobia and its gendered manifestations is likely to well exceed the statistical evidence available.

This statistical evidence pertaining to gendered Islamophobic hate crimes begs the question: Why are Muslim women disproportionately impacted by Islamophobia across the globe? Here the reasons are numerous, complex, diverse and interlocking. This chapter seeks to map and analyse the current state of gendered Islamophobia via selected examples from my own geographical areas of expertise – namely, France, Belgium and the UK – to highlight the multiple factors and narratives that give rise to this highly gendered phenomenon. The chapter begins by defining the key terms employed within the work including misogyny, hate crime and Islamophobia. The chapter then

DOI: 10.4324/9781003023722-7

continues to establish the theoretical frameworks applied within the chapter namely those relating to Orientalism and Intersectionality. A discussion of Muslim women's experiences of gendered Islamophobia, misogyny and hate crime is then presented. This is then problematised vis-à-vis the external signals and systems that seemingly legitimise the disproportionate targeting of Muslim women as victims of gendered Islamophobia. The chapter then goes on to discuss the ways in which Muslim women respond to the issues pertaining to and arising from misogyny and gendered Islamophobia. The chapter concludes by discussing potential ways of working towards effectively countering the disproportionate gendered Islamophobia and misogyny towards Muslim women.

Defining the terms

Like other chapters in this edited collection, the current chapter focuses primarily on misogyny but through the lens of gendered Islamophobia. Here, I employ the following definition and frame misogyny as "the dislike of, contempt for, or ingrained prejudice against women" as per the UK Hate Crime (Misogyny) Bill 2019–2021. The definition of misogyny put forward in the UK as part of the aforementioned Bill constitutes part of a wider national project to formally recognise misogynistic abuse as a hate crime. This follows the adoption of the Misogyny Hate Crime Policy by Nottingham police in 2016 and the data that arose from this was subsequently evaluated by Mullany and Trickett (2018) (see also Chapter 14 in this book). The debate on the classification of misogyny as a hate crime in the UK was led by former Member of Parliament for Greater Grimsby, Melanie Onn although was trivialised by some parliamentary figures (Davies 2018). This perhaps indicates the hostile climate in which the proposed legislation was made and demonstrates the ways in which misogyny is downplayed as well as ways in which it remains a serious and pressing problem both in the UK and further across the globe.

The term 'hate crime' emerged in the 1980s in the US political arena and gained traction in the media sphere post-1985 before becoming a significant field of academic study from the 1990s onwards (Jacobs and Potter 2000). Jacobs and Potter (2000) argue that hate crimes are rooted in prejudice (such as racism or misogyny) and that there is a causal link between prejudice and the hate crime. Hate crime is a visible manifestation of prejudice. Whilst hate crime data can often quantifiably demonstrate the severity and extent of prejudices and racisms within a given society, using hate crime statistics simultaneously presents limitations: as noted throughout this edited collection, hate crime statistics are limited by the fact that they can only represent those who have come forward to report their experiences. Naturally this is mitigated by individual differences; for example, do those who experience hate crimes always perceive their experiences as such? Even when those who experience a hate crime recognise it as such the likelihood of their reporting to monitoring bodies is shaped by their confidence and trust in these organisations as well as having the confidence to report. Furthermore, when the individual who has experienced hate crime has multiple identity facets that are typically 'othered' and subject to prejudice in a given society, their intersectional identities may mean that disaggregation of hate crime motivations and effective recording of hate crimes bases may be difficult. In other words, whilst hate crime statistics provide useful insight into the nature of Islamophobic hate crime and its prevalence, it is important to note that this statistical evidence presents only a partial picture or just the 'tip of the iceberg'. In reality, it is highly likely that Islamophobia (or any other type of prejudice) is far more prevalent than currently anticipated.

As noted earlier, this chapter focuses heavily on Islamophobia and in particular gendered Islamophobia. Here the definition of Islamophobia, as put forward by the British All Party Parliamentary Group (APPG) on British Muslims, is employed to best define the phenomenon. The British APPG on British Muslims (2018) report entitled *Islamophobia Defined*, frame Islamophobia as follows: '*Islamophobia is rooted in racism and is a type of racism that targets expressions of Muslimness or perceived Muslimness*'. I argue that this definition is most appropriate since it focuses heavily on the racialisation of Muslims meaning that 'Muslimness' as a category is broad. Consequently, the broadness of the definition means that those who convert to Islam are often similarly racialised in the same way as those who are perceived to be born in Islam. Equally importantly, this definition also recognises the experiences of those who face Islamophobia on the grounds that they are perceived to be Muslims. Indeed, members of various 'otherised' and marginalised communities have also borne the consequences of Islamophobia because they were perceived to be Muslim. This was apparent in the research by Awan and Zempi (2018) that investigated the Islamophobic experiences of non-Muslim men. Furthermore, the Southern Poverty Law Centre reports that the basis of hate-based murders that were committed in response to the 9/11 attacks was motivated by the (perceived) shared identity of the victims with those who carried out the 9/11 attacks (Southern Poverty Law Centre 2002).

The definition of Islamophobia as put forward by the APPG on British Muslims (2018) has been accepted by numerous local British councils including Oxford, Manchester, Brent, Harrow, Birmingham. Additionally, this definition has also been accepted by many UK political parties, including the Labour Party, the Scottish National Party (SNP), Plaid Cymru, the Scottish Greens and the Scottish Conservatives (APPG on British Muslims 2018). However, the definition was rejected by the current UK government and ruling party, the Conservative party. Given their stance as a centre right political party, the risk here is that this decision by the Conservative party sends a signal to the wider public, namely that Islamophobia is not taken seriously from the perspective of the government and thus Islamophobia is acceptable in the wider public.

The concept of gendered Islamophobia implies that it disproportionately targets one gender over another; however, in the scope of this chapter I am focusing on the experiences of Muslim women and the disproportionate ways in which they are impacted by Islamophobia, as established at the outset of this chapter. Gendered Islamophobia intersects with misogyny, and this will be explored further within the chapter.

Theoretical frameworks

In order to understand the nature of gendered Islamophobia, associated hate crimes and their connectedness to misogyny, this chapter employs the following theoretical frameworks: Orientalism and Intersectionality. Orientalism facilitates the historical basis and understanding of gendered Islamophobia in particular, whilst intersectionality underlines the importance of the multiple layers of marginalisation that Muslim women often encounter.

In his 1978 book Palestinian scholar, Edward Said, established basis of his critique of the Western study of the Orient within which he outlines the ways in which the Western gaze has framed and constructed women from the 'Orient'. Said (1978, p. 1) argued that 'the Orient was almost a European invention, and had been since antiquity a place of romance, exotic beings, haunting memories and landscapes, remarkable experiences'. The exoticisation of the Oriental woman has led to the sexualisation of the Muslim woman with a sense of intrigue and mystery surrounding her. Furthermore, Said (1978, p. 6) explained the ways in which the Oriental woman was often infantilised, 'a widely influential model of the Oriental woman; she never spoke of herself, she never represented her emotions, presence, or history. He spoke for and represented her'. Consequently, the figure of the Orientalised woman is both sexualised and infantilised. When we juxtapose this simultaneous infantilisation and sexualisation, with an understanding of misogyny that primarily prejudices women, the Orientalised woman or Muslim woman emerges as a vulnerable figure, an 'easy' target for the misogynist in today's society.

Similarly, Said (1978, pp. 59–60) highlights the Orientalist perception of Islam, he writes that Islam came:

> ... to symbolize terror, devastation, the demonic, hordes of hated barbarians. For Europe, Islam was a lasting trauma. Until the end of the seventeenth century the "Ottoman peril" lurked alongside Europe to represent for the whole of Christian civilization a constant danger, and in time European civilization incorporated that peril and its lore, its great events, figures, virtues, and vices, as something woven into the fabric of life.

As Said (1978) elucidates, Europe became fixated on the perceived threat posed by Islam and this narrative was woven into the fabric of European culture. As such, it is perhaps unsurprising that we see these narratives persist within modern day dominant narratives of Islamophobia, as documented by Law et al. (2018). This work mapped the dominant Islamophobic perceptions of Muslims across Europe and in spite of context-based specificities, there was apparent convergence in dominant Islamophobic narratives, namely as Law et al. (2018, p. 6) state:

> These narratives were found to fix Muslims collectively as in descending order of prevalence, a threat to security, unassimilable, a demographic threat, an Islamisation threat, a threat to local, national and European identity, responsible for … women's oppression, essentially different and violent, incomplete citizens and a risk to the majority, and essentially homophobic.

This empirical evidence points to a continuation of Orientalised narratives around Islam and Muslimness; however, this fixation now takes place both within the Western boundaries and in relation to the 'Orient'. As highlighted above, increasingly in the contemporary world the Orientalised Muslim woman is simultaneously seen as sexualised and infantilised, but also paradoxically as a source of 'threat'. Her visible Muslimness comes to symbolise this contradictory simultaneous threat, infantilisation and sexualisation. As such, this double embodiment marks the figure of the Muslim woman out for both the misogynist and the Islamophobe.

This double narrative that places the Muslim woman between being helpless and sexualised has been employed on numerous occasions throughout history to legitimise the disproportionate legislative targeting of Muslim women. For example, we might consider the implementation of the 2004 *Loi Stasi* in France. The law prohibits the presence of 'ostentatious faith symbols' in French state schools (Legifrance 2004). However, the implementation of the ban follows years of so-called *affaires* around Muslim women's dress in the country, something which cyclically continues in France over 30 years since the initial *affaire* in Creil in 1989 (Hargreaves 2007; Winter 2008). Notwithstanding, the implementation of the 2004 law was preceded by a commission review within which the voices of visibly Muslim women, and particularly those who contested the position of the French state vis-à-vis the increasing Islamophobic instrumentalisation of *laïcité* or secularism, were all but absent (Baubérot 2012; Easat-Daas 2020a). Subsequent to the implementation of the ban on ostentatious faith symbols in French schools, the evidence points to visibly Muslim women bearing the brunt of the ban (Hargreaves 2007).

The narrative constructed around the ban employed the tropes of French secularism, or *laïcité,* and also the Orientalised framing of needing to protect or 'save' the young Muslim women from the alleged perceived perils of covering. Muslim covering has been demonstrated to be seen in conflict to western feminist ideas (Fayard and Rocheron 2009). This law and the wider debate around the position of visible gendered Muslimness in France, and in particular in relation to the construction of French Muslim women's infantilisation, recalls the argument of the decolonial scholar, Gayatri Chakravorty Spivak, who in her piece 'Can the Subaltern Speak', states 'White men saving the brown women from the brown men' (Spivak 1988, p. 93). Here we see the way in which the subaltern (brown and colonised) woman is infantilised by the coloniser, speaks simultaneously to her gender (and the dominant misogynistic perception that exists around this) and her racialised position as a then colonised person. This intersection of multiple disadvantaging positionalities corresponds to the experience of hate crime among Muslim women, who are likely targeted for multiple intersecting prejudices.

Regarding intersectionality, lawyer and critical race theory scholar, Kimberlé Crenshaw, theorised intersectionality via her legal practice and contributed to understanding the experiences of Black women in the USA. In her 1991 paper, 'Mapping the Margins: Intersectionality, Identity Politics, and Violence against Women of Color', Crenshaw (1991, pp. 1243–1244) writes:

> Via the consideration of male violence against women – battery and rape – I consider how the experiences of women of color are frequently the product of intersecting patterns of racism and sexism and how these experiences tend not to be represented within the discourses of either feminism or antiracism.

Whilst it is often perceived that an 'otherised' individual's experiences of marginalisation will correspond to either category, she writes '...women of color are marginalized with both' (Crenshaw 1991, p. 1244). In short, intersectionality, as a theoretical model, allows us to understand the numerous disadvantages that marginalised individuals experience. In the case of Muslim women, their alterity is multifold; namely as women, they face marginalisation and prejudice on the grounds of their gender. Often, but not always, Muslim women are racialised both on the grounds of their Muslimness and also frequently on the grounds of their perceived ethnic difference. These intersecting marginalities are apparent even before we begin to consider less visible or explicit multiple and further intersecting marginalisations that Muslim women may encounter, such as those around ablism or agism among many others. Notwithstanding, it is via the consideration of these intersecting facets of Muslim women's identities that we may begin to understand the multiple and interlocking forms of prejudice they experience.

Having established a definition of the key terms (hate crime, Islamophobia, misogyny) and having mapped dominant Islamophobic narratives – with insight to their historical bases, the final section of this chapter examines the way in which these elements are brought together through a view of the evidence pertaining to Muslim women's experiences of gendered Islamophobia and their responses.

Gendered Islamophobia

Central to this chapter is the statistical evidence pointing to the fact that Muslim women face disproportionally high rates of Islamophobic attacks. As stated, the recently published report by the CCIB (2020) underlines that 90% of the cases reported to them pertained to hate crimes against Muslim women. Similarly, evidence demonstrates the targeted victimisation of Muslim women globally (Easat-Daas 2019a, Mason-Bish and Zempi 2019), but what is the nature of these highly gendered Islamophobic hate crimes? This section of the chapter explores and maps the nature of gendered Islamophobia and examines the environment within which it takes place.

Regarding the environment in which gendered Islamophobia spikes, the statistical evidence points to an overall significant increase in gendered Islamophobia around terror attacks. For example, following the terrorist attacks in January 2015 on the Charlie Hebdo office and a nearby supermarket, and the November 2015 terrorist attacks on the Bataclan, France saw a distinct increase in Islamophobic hate crimes (CCIF 2016). Overall, Islamophobic hate crimes in France during 2015 were two and a half times higher than the preceding year, whilst Islamophobic incidents on the whole were up by 18.5% (CCIF 2016). The CCIF highlight the perceived link between terror and Islam in writing on reports of Islamophobia that they have dealt with during 2015: 'The rise of Islamophobic acts demonstrates a confusion between terrorism and Islam' (CCIF 2016, p. 21), before continuing to highlight the double punishment faced by Muslims given that Muslims as French citizens face the consequences of terror in the country and also, they face retaliation-based Islamophobic attacks following terrorist attacks.

Within the scope of the CCIF's 2015 report, the organisation also highlights that during this period, 74% of recorded Islamophobic attacks were directed at French Muslim women and comprised physical attacks as well as discrimination (CCIF 2016). Whilst the proportional rates of gendered Islamophobia in the country remain consistently high and continue to disproportionately affect Muslim women, it is important to underline that the overall level of Islamophobic acts, including physical Islamophobic hate crimes, have persistently increased following suspected terrorism and Muslim women have consistently faced the consequences of this rise. More recently, and perhaps comparatively less well documented, following the abhorrent murder of Samuel Paty, two Muslim women were attacked and stabbed in Paris by two inebriated French women. The attackers similarly called the visibly Muslim women 'dirty Arabs' and that 'France was not their home' (Al Jazeera 2020). This attack demonstrates the nature of Islamophobic hate crimes that Muslim women face in France, and the ways in which these attacks intersect with their gender, ethnic alterity and Muslimness. Whilst the aforementioned incident was carried out by women, it is important to highlight that the majority of Islamophobic attacks against Muslim women are perpetrated by white men (Tell Mama 2016). However, it is also important to recognise that Muslim women face misogyny from within their own communities, such as I encountered in my work around Muslim women's political participation in Belgium, illustrated here:

> They [Muslim men] were really open to women's participation... [but] I saw that there were lots of stereotypes still, even young men with progressive ideas who still held stereotypes, saying they [Muslim women] are women, they have children, how can they participate... I said come on that is not coherent.
> (Easat-Daas 2020a, p. 153)

Furthermore, the rise of Islamophobic hate crimes is also apparent in Belgium. For example, following the terrorist attacks on the Zavantem Airport in Brussels and on the Brussels Metro Maelbeek Station in March 2016 – in which notable Muslims such as Loubna Lafquiri lost their lives (El Bachiri and van Reybrouck 2017) – there was a marked growth in Islamophobic acts, especially towards Muslim women (Easat-Daas 2018). Where there is a clear conflation by the lay public of Muslimness and terror, consequently we see a rise in Islamophobic attacks; perhaps as a retaliatory measure and a means of disciplining Muslimness in the context where the terror attacks have occurred. Following the far-right terror attacks on Muslims in Christchurch, New Zealand in March 2019 which resulted in the killing of 51 Muslims and the injury of a further 49 (Tell Mama 2019b), Muslims across the globe faced Islamophobic reprisals. For example, in the UK in the week following the far-right inspired terror attacks in New Zealand in 2019, reports to Tell Mama increased by 695% (Tell Mama 2019b). These statistics highlight that regardless of who commits acts of terror, Muslimness and Islam have been so frequently conflated with terror that Muslims – and particularly those who are visibly Muslim such Muslim women who wear the hijab (headscarf) or niqab (veil) – are likely to be targeted and face hate crimes in the immediate period following acts of terror.

Regarding the nature of gendered Islamophobic hate crimes, these are diverse. Gendered Islamophobia ranges from verbal to physical attacks but can also be more nuanced and include the denial of service or access. Denial of service, when not legally reasonable and where this is motivated by misogyny, racism and/or ethnic difference, may constitute a hate crime. Examples of this type of denial of service experienced by Muslim women include the case of a Muslim woman – who wore the niqab – and her child who were denied access to public transport in London. The London bus driver is alleged to have continued to make Islamophobic, misogynistic remarks stating "I can't hear you, I don't want to speak to you with that thing on your face" before attempting to shut the doors on the Muslim woman and her child (Tell Mama 2019c). This type of denial of service is echoed across the continent and furthermore, Muslim women are, on occasion, denied the right to carry out their legal obligations – for example in Belgium, where voting is compulsory by law, a Belgian Muslim mother and daughter who wore the hijab were denied access to the polling station in Bressoux, Belgium in May 2014 (SudInfo 2014).

Further denial of access to services include Islamophobic acts that are also within the legal framework of a nation and as such are not direct examples of hate crimes, but indicate the emergence of 'institutional gendered Islamophobia' – which undoubtedly draws on Islamophobic, racist and misogynistic discourses. To illustrate this, consider the French *Loi Stasi* implemented in 2004 prohibits the presence of 'ostentatious symbols of faith' (Legifrance 2004). This legislative measure has disproportionately impacted young Muslim girls in French education (Hargreaves 2007). Furthermore, the law may lead to the exclusion of young Muslim girls from education. As such, it deprives Muslim women of their futures, their right to the tools to effectively join the workforce and also limits their potential to contest Islamophobic legislation and the gendered Islamophobia that they may face in life. Indeed, the extent to which the 2004 legal measure was implemented primarily to target Muslim women is debated in French society. Whilst the official state narrative and its apparent legitimisation lie within its framing as being part of the national legally enshrined concept *laïcité* and therefore this makes the 2004 law somehow incontestable, there is growing consensus particularly among scholars who critically engage with French secularism that it has increasingly become weaponised to specifically target expressions of Muslimness in the nation (Laachir 2008). Not only such legal measures target Muslimness in France, they also demonise and even criminalise gendered expressions of Muslimness in France and elsewhere in the West. This signal from the state stands to legitimise hate crimes in the field. Therefore, there is a cyclical link between political Islamophobic narrative, legislation and gendered Islamophobic hate crimes.

Regarding the proliferation of Islamophobic political discourse and the rise of gendered Islamophobia, it is important to highlight that hate crimes committed against Muslim women do not occur in a vacuum; rather, gendered hate crime is among the few visible and quantifiable manifestations of gendered Islamophobia that is predicated by wider systems and signals of gendered Islamophobia and misogyny. A clear example of such systemic signals is apparent in the comments of the current UK prime minister and then Foreign Secretary, Boris Johnson, who wrote in his newspaper column in the Telegraph comparing Muslim women who wear the niqab to letterboxes – a common gendered Islamophobic insult which resulted in a 375% spike Islamophobic hate crimes (Tell Mama 2019d), many of which were towards Muslim women. Reported examples of gendered Islamophobia following the publication of Johnson's column included Muslim women being called 'letterbox' (Ali and Whitham 2020). According to Ali and Whitham (2020, p. 15), 'This illustrates the mutual constitution of structural and direct forms of racism'. In addition, the presence of gendered Islamophobic political discourse and the legislation that has arisen in this climate demonstrates an attempt to police Muslim women's bodies at the state level, arguably highlighting the way in which misogynistic attitudes intersect with racism and subsequently give rise to state-mandated gendered Islamophobia – particularly apparent in France but followed by many others.

Furthermore, whilst Muslim women are generally more impacted by Islamophobic hate crimes, it must be noted that their visible Muslimness increases the likelihood of experiencing Islamophobic hate crime. In the case of Muslim women wearing the hijab or niqab, visible Muslimness gives rise to an increased likelihood of experiencing Islamophobic hate crime (Tell Mama 2016). Nonetheless, examples such as the discrimination of those who have Muslim sounding names in the search for employment, regardless of their actual religiosity (Valfort 2017), highlights the way in which explicit visibility of one's Muslimness is not the sole factor in determining experiences of discrimination and hate. In terms of the nature of gendered Islamophobic hate crime, Muslim women often experience verbal hate speech. Examples might include microaggressions, such as the following experienced by a French Muslim politician: "One day I arrived at parliament they [staff in parliament] had never seen the elected politicians and she said to me 'down there, the service entry is down there, here is for the parliamentarians'" (Easat-Daas 2020a, p. 147). This highlights the way in which ethnic difference, and arguably perceived Muslimness, led to others assuming and verbalising the assumption that she could not possibly be a politician; rather, she must be part of the service staff. More explicit examples include two Muslim women who were verbally attacked in Uccle, Belgium in March 2019 by a driver who stated: 'I am a racist and I hate women who wear the headscarf' (Easat-Daas 2019b, p. 124).

Notwithstanding, physical gendered Islamophobic hate crimes often clearly intersect with violent gendered Islamophobic hate crimes such as visibly Muslim women having their headscarves pulled off from their heads – a clear example of the intersection of ethnic and Islamophobic racism with the misogynistic need to control women's bodies. Cases of Muslim women having their hijabs removed include a case which took place on the 20th of February 2018 whereby a Belgian Muslim woman in Charleroi had her headscarf forcibly removed (Easat-Daas 2019b), and that of a young Muslim girl who had her headscarf removed from her head whilst on a school trip to Ostende, Belgium in April 2018 (Easat-Daas 2019b). More violent examples of gendered Islamophobic hate crimes include the forced removal of Muslim women's headscarves, which is apparent in the 2019 case of a visibly Muslim woman in her 60s being pushed onto the tracks of the Brussels metro by a 51-year old inebriated homeless woman. This gendered Islamophobic attack was not the first carried out by a woman. This attack and the previously discussed attack on two Muslim women in Paris that took place earlier in 2020 show cases of gendered Islamophobic hate crimes perpetrated by women. When considered vis-à-vis misogyny this may initially appear problematic, but here it is helpful to consider the limitations of dominant white feminist narratives that have been criticised in their failure to account for and protect the experiences of racialised women. Similarly, if misogyny pertains to the prejudice against women, when factoring in the intersectional identities of Muslim women, a woman's identity as a woman does not limit her from being prejudiced towards racialised women. This intersection of racialised women's identities – here as Muslim women – recalls the work of Moya Bailey on Misogynoir, a term used to describe the 'anti-black misogyny that Black women experience' (Bailey and Trudy 2018, p. 762). However, whilst Bailey and Trudy's (2018) work pertains to the experiences of Black women, I would argue that this term can be developed further to better understand the experiences of racialised Muslim women, perhaps here Islamo-misogynism may best explain the current nature of gendered Islamophobia, this is an area for further theoretical study.

As highlighted previously, Orientalised narratives frame the so-called Oriental or Muslim woman as hypersexualised whilst also being helpless, yet also 'off limits'. Winter (2008) critically considers the way in which the figure of the Muslim woman is problematised in the French context. Winter (2008) describes the way in which the visibly Muslim woman is seen as anti-feminist, oppressed and since she is 'off limits' she becomes the hypersexualised 'forbidden fruit' and as such becomes more alluring. Within the framework of gendered Islamophobic attacks that intersect with misogyny, Muslim women face sexualised hate crimes. These range from cat calling to calls to see their faces and hair under their hijab or niqab, as documented by Mason-Bish and Zempi (2019). Women who are visibly Muslim also experience hate crimes that comprise verbal, physical and sexual attack simultaneously. For example, in Anderlues in Belgium in 2018 a teenage Muslim woman was attacked by two men in an alleyway, the attackers removed her headscarf and clothing, whilst cutting her body with a sharp object and calling her a 'dirty Arab' (Easat-Daas 2018). Here there is a clear intersection of explicit ethnicity-based racism in the attackers' hate speech, whilst the removal of her headscarf demonstrates gendered Islamophobic hate crime, and the removal of clothes and exposure of her body show evidence of sexual assault and misogyny.

Such examples are not unique or limited to any one context and gendered Islamophobia, along with more generalised Islamophobia, show no signs of abating; rather, gendered Islamophobia continues to proliferate globally. Nonetheless, it is important to note that Muslim women themselves undertake significant efforts to counter gendered Islamophobia. In particular, Muslim women's efforts to counter gendered Islamophobia are diverse and widespread across the continent. For example, the Brussels-based pan-European umbrella organisation, European Forum of Muslim Women, routinely document and research the position of Muslim women in Europe as well providing capacity building opportunities.[4] Other examples include Muslim women-led collectives such as *Mamans toutes égales*[5] (Mothers are all equal) campaign in France for the rights of Muslim mothers to drop off and collect their children from schools or accompany them on school trips. Similarly, groups such as *Les Cannelles*[6] (formerly *Bruxelloise et voilée*) use media to combat negative stereotypes about Islam and Muslim women. Despite gendered Islamophobias, Muslim women successfully and meaningfully participate in all aspects of life, from politics to civic society, and education to the arts among countless others.

Conclusion

In spite of Muslim women's diverse engagement and resilience, regrettably they continue to find themselves reduced to tired Orientalist and Islamophobic tropes and to this end, being silenced and spoken for by others. It remains crucial to define and document the intersections of misogyny and Islamophobia that Muslim women are increasingly facing. Furthermore, it is essential that Muslim women's voices, experiences and endeavours are foregrounded, rather than the persistent silencing of gendered Muslimness that is currently apparent. Regarding gendered Islamophobia and misogynistic hate crimes, again the recognition and documentation of these is key, alongside the foregrounding of Muslim women's voices. Nonetheless, given the intersectional nature of these women's identities as racialised individuals, within the framework of hate crime reporting recording becomes problematic – essentially how does one effectively disaggregate the motivations behind gendered Islamophobic hate crimes? In spite of these potential limits, given the nature and scope of gendered Islamophobic hate crimes and the wider hostile Islamophobic environment that exists, the legal conceptualisation of misogyny as a hate crime would contribute to deterring gendered hate crimes against Muslim women, as well as women more broadly and thus should be welcomed.

Notes

1 Tell Mama is one of many Islamophobia monitoring organisations in the UK, such as MEND among others. These organisations differ in terms of public perceptions and scope, for example within its remit MEND also focuses heavily on advocacy and capacity building among affected communities.
2 In France, the CCIF is arguably the principal Islamophobia monitoring and advocacy group. Notwithstanding France is also home to noteworthy groups such as the Muslim feminist collective, *Lallab*, who work on intersectional issues faced by French Muslim women including Islamophobia. The CCIF now operates supranationally as the CCIE - Collectif centre l'islamophobie en Europe following the 2020 French government crackdown on Muslim humanitarian, charity and counter-Islamophobia organisations in France.
3 The CCIB, like the CCIF, is arguably the principal Islamophobia monitoring group in Belgium. Importantly, the CCIB works with and utilises statistical information from the state funded organisation, The Interfederal Centre for Equal Opportunities – UNIA, to compile the CCIB's Islamophobia statistics.
4 See the European Forum of Muslim Women's website for further details: https://efomw.eu.

5 See *Mamans toutes égales* for more information: https://sites.google.com/site/mamanstoutesegalestest/.
6 See *Collectif les Cannelles* for more details: https://www.facebook.com/collectiflescannelles/.

References

Al Jazeera, (2020). Two women charged over racist stabbing of veiled Muslims [online]. Available at: https://www.aljazeera.com/news/2020/10/22/two-french-women-charged-over-racist-stabbing-of-veiled-muslim [Accessed 1 December 2020].

All Party Parliamentary Group on British Muslims, 2018. *Islamophobia Defined: The Inquiry into a Working Definition of Islamophobia*. London: UK Parliament. Available at: https://static1.squarespace.com/static/599c3d2febbd1a90cffdd8a9/t/5bfd1ea3352f531a6170ceee/1543315109493/Islamophobia+Defined.pdf [Accessed 1 December 2020].

Ali, N. and Whitham, B., 2020. Racial capitalism, Islamophobia, and austerity. *International Political Sociology*, 0, pp. 1–22. DOI: 10.1093/ips/olaa023.

Awan, I. and Zempi, I., 2020. 'You all look the same': non-Muslim men who suffer Islamophobic hate crime in the post-Brexit era. *European Journal of Criminology*, 17(5), pp. 585–602. DOI: 10.1177/1477370818812735.

Bailey, M. and Trudy, 2018. On misogynoir: citation, erasure, and plagiarism. *Feminist Media Studies*, 18(4), pp. 762–768. DOI: 10.1080/14680777.2018.1447395.

Baubérot, J., 2012. *La Laïcité Falsifiée*. Paris: Éditions la Découverte.

CCIB, 2020. *Rapport Chiffres 2019*. Brussels: CCIB.

CCIF, 2016. *Report 2016*. Paris: CCIF.

CCIF, 2020. *Rapport du Collectif contre l'Islamophobie en France sur l'année 2019*. Paris: CCIF.

Crenshaw, K., 1991. Mapping the margins: intersectionality, identity politics, and violence against women of color. *Stanford Law Review*, 43(6), pp. 1241–1300. DOI: 10.2307/1229039.

Davies, P., 2018. 'Misogyny as hate crime'. HC Deb 07 March 2018 vol 637 cc132–134WH. Available at: https://hansard.parliament.uk/Commons/2018-03-07/debates/92236C51-2340-4D97-92A7-4955B24C2D74/MisogynyAsAHateCrime [Accessed 1 December 2020].

Easat-Daas, A., 2018. Islamophobia in Belgium: national report 2017. In: Bayraklı, E. and Hafez, F., eds. *European Islamophobia Report 2017*. Istanbul: SETA, pp. 85–108.

Easat-Daas, A., 2019a. Gendered dimensions of Islamophobia in Belgium. In: Zempi, I. and Awan, I., eds. *The Routledge International Handbook of Islamophobia*. Abingdon: Routledge, pp. 123–134.

Easat-Daas, A., 2019b. Islamophobia in Belgium: national report 2018. In: Bayraklı, E. and Hafez, F., eds. *European Islamophobia Report 2018*. Istanbul: SETA, pp. 141–166.

Easat-Daas, A., 2020a. *Muslim Women's Political Participation in France and Belgium*. London: Palgrave Macmillan.

Easat-Daas, A., 2020b. Islamophobia in Belgium: national report 2019. In: Bayraklı, E. and Hafez, F., eds. *European Islamophobia Report 2019*. Istanbul: SETA, pp. 115–139.

El Bachiri, M. and Van Reybrouck, D., 2017. *A Jihad for Love*. London: Head of Zeus.

Fayard, N. and Rocheron, Y., 2009. *Ni Putes ni Soumises*: a Republican Feminism from the *Quartiers Sensibles. Modern and Contemporary France*, 17, pp. 1–18. DOI: 10.1080/09639480802639736.

Hargreaves, A.G., 2007. *Multi-ethnic France: Immigration, Politics, Culture and Society*. Abingdon: Routledge.

Hate Crime (Misogyny) Bill 2019–2021 (2019). *Parliament: House of Commons*. London: UK Parliament. Available at: https://services.parliament.uk/Bills/2019-21/hatecrimemisogyny.html.

Jacobs, J.B. and Potter, K., 2000. *Hate Crimes: Criminal Law and Identity Politics*. Oxford: Oxford University Press.

Laachir, K., 2008. State Islamophobia in France. In: Sayyid, S. and Vakil, A., eds. *Thinking Thru' Islamophobia 2008 University of Leeds, 7 May 2008*. Leeds: Centre for Ethnicity and Racism Studies, University of Leeds, pp. 23–25.

Law, I., Easat-Daas, A. and Sayyid, S., 2018. *Counter-Islamophobia Kit: Briefing Paper and Toolkit of Counter Narratives to Islamophobia*. Leeds: Centre for Ethnicity and Racism Studies, University of Leeds. Available at: https://cik.leeds.ac.uk/wp-content/uploads/sites/36/2018/09/2018.09.17-Job-44240.01-CIK-Final-Booklet.pdf [Accessed 1 December 2020].

Legifrance, 2004. *Loi du 15 mars 2004–228 encadrant, en application du principe de laïcité, le porte de signes ou de tenues manifestant une appartenance religieuse dans les écoles, collèges et lycées publics* (France). Paris: Legifrance.

Mason-Bish, H. and Zempi, I., 2019. Misogyny, racism, and Islamophobia: street harassment at the intersections'. *Feminist Criminology*, 14(5), pp. 540–559. DOI: 10.1177/1557085118772088.

Mullany, L. and Trickett, L., 2018. *Misogyny Hate Crime Evaluation Report*. Nottingham Woman's Centre [online]. Available at: http://www.nottinghamwomenscentre.com/wp-content/uploads/2018/07/Misogyny-HateCrime-Evaluation-Report-June-2018.pdf [Accessed 5 January 2021].

Said, E., 1978. *Orientalism*. London: Routledge.

Southern Poverty Law Centre, 2002. Remembering victims of hate crimes [online]. Available at: https://www.splcenter.org/fighting-hate/intelligence-report/2002/remembering-victims-hate-crimes?page=0%2C6 [Accessed 5 January 2021].

Spivak, G. C., 1988. Can the subaltern speak? In: Nelson, C. and Grossberg, L., eds. *Marxism and the Interpretation of Culture*. London: Macmillan, pp. 66–111.

SudInfo, 2014. Liège: Karima et sa maman, voilées, refusées dans un bureau de vote de Bressoux. Available at: https://www.sudinfo.be/art/1015149/article/2014-05-25/liege-karima-et-sa-maman-voilees-refusees-dans-un-bureau-de-vote-de-bressoux [Accessed 1 December 2020].

Tell Mama, 2016. *The Geography of Anti-Muslim Hatred: Tell Mama Annual Report 2015*. London: Faith Matters. Available at: https://www.tellmamauk.org/wp-content/uploads/pdf/tell_mama_2015_annual_report.pdf [Accessed 1 December 2020].

Tell Mama, 2019a. *Normalising Hatred: Tell Mama Annual Report 2018*. London: Faith Matters. Available at: https://tellmamauk.org/wp-content/uploads/2019/09/Tell%20MAMA%20Annual%20Report%202018%20_%20Normalising%20Hate.pdf [Accessed 1 December 2020].

Tell Mama, 2019b. *The Impact of the Christchurch Terror Attack: Tell Mama Interim Report 2019*. London: Faith Matters. Available at: https://www.tellmamauk.org/wp-content/uploads/2020/03/The-Impact-of-the-ChristChurch-Attack-Tell-MAMA-Interim-Report-2019-PP.pdf [Accessed 1 December 2020].

Tell Mama, 2019c. Muslim woman in niqab denied entry onto bus with her child in London [online]. Available at: https://tellmamauk.org/muslim-woman-in-niqab-denied-entry-onto-bus-with-her-child-in-london/ [Accessed 5 January 2021].

Tell Mama, 2019d. Islamophobic attacks in UK rose 'significantly' after Boris Johnson's controversial comments comparing veiled Muslim women to letterboxes, watchdog reveals [online]. Available at: https://tellmamauk.org/press/islamophobic-attacks-in-uk-rose-significantly-after-boris-johnsons-controversial-comments-comparing-veiled-muslim-women-to-letterboxes-watchdog-reveals/ [Accessed 5 January 2021].

Valfort, M.-A., 2017. Has France a problem with Muslims? Evidence from a field experiment in the labour market. Work Paper. Available at: http://conference.iza.org/conference_files/CREST_OECD_2017/valfort_m5542.pdf [Accessed 5 January 2021].

Winter, B., 2008. *Hijab and the Republic: Uncovering the French Headscarf Debate.* Syracuse: Syracuse University Press.

8 The intersection of antisemitism and misogyny

Lesley Klaff

Introduction

The time is ripe to develop a policy argument to recognise gendered antisemitism as a unique sub-category of misogynistic hate crime. The term 'gendered antisemitism' is used to refer to the abuse that occurs at the intersection of antisemitism and misogyny. Taking an intersectional approach to misogynistic hate crime is important because women's experience of abuse appears to differ according to their different intersectional identities. Sociologist and antisemitism scholar, Dr David Hirsh, believes that the expression of sexual violence against women becomes far worse when an element of conscious antisemitism enters it, but there has been very little empirical sociological work done to support his belief (Hirsh 2019). In fact, although gendered antisemitism is an important issue, nothing significant, including nothing that is empirically well supported, has been written about it. The 2018 Sara Conference Against Misogyny and Antisemitism[1] noted that research on women and antisemitism has hitherto largely only focused on the "Jewish Princess" or "Jewish American Princess" ("JAP") stereotype (Sara Conference 2018). This stereotype has been described as a combination of antisemitism and misogyny because it remodels the traditional antisemitic tropes into a female form: she is materialistic, money-grabbing, manipulative, shallow, crafty, and ostentatious (Antisemitism Policy Trust 2019, p. 2). Other empirical work, albeit limited, has focused on the experience of Jewish women at the hands of the Nazis. In her 2018 book, *Women's Experiences in the Holocaust: In Their Own Words*, Agnes Grunwald-Spier narrates the personal experiences of Jewish women in the Shoah to show how they were different, and in many respects, were worse than the experiences of Jewish men (Grunwald-Spier 2018). Women were disproportionately chosen for the death camps, for example, to prevent Jews from breeding (Felstiner 1994, p. 205 in Grunwald-Spier 2018, p. 10). Other than the attention that has been given to the JAP stereotype, and one book on female Shoah victims, there is no available academic work on the nature, function, and impact on the victims of gendered antisemitism.

DOI: 10.4324/9781003023722-8

There are several possible reasons for the lack of attention given to gendered antisemitism. One may be that the theory of intersectionality, which recognises that people are often disadvantaged by multiple sources of discrimination, only burst onto the academic scene in 1989 and has been slow to garner mainstream interest (Crenshaw 1989). Feminist sociologist and antisemitism scholar, Professor Karin Stoegner (2020), believes that antisemitism is rarely included in intersectional theory because the latter relies on binary markers, such as white-black, male-female, hetero-lesbian/gay, and antisemitic theory places Jews beyond binary categorisation. She further suggests that the vehement anti-Zionist orientation of some feminist, anti-racist social movements contributes to the exclusion of antisemitism from the intersectionality framework (Stoegner 2020).[2] It may also be the case that antisemitism scholars have lacked a general interest in women and their experiences.

The function of this chapter will be to attempt, in a preliminary and limited way, to start the social–scientific ball rolling in the area of gendered antisemitism by considering some of the places where evidence of it exists, and where one might expect further enquiries and research to reveal interesting results. This will be done by noting carefully at each point where evidence of gendered antisemitism requires further research on its nature, function, and impact.

Understanding antisemitism

To consider the nature and function of gendered antisemitism, an elementary understanding of antisemitism is necessary. Whilst a good place to start is with the definition, defining antisemitism is problematic because the concept of antisemitism is contested. This was evident in the political dispute that arose within the Labour Party when its National Executive Committee (NEC) refused to adopt the International Holocaust Remembrance Alliance (IHRA) Definition of Antisemitism in July 2018 (Harpin 2018), claiming that it stifles free speech on Israel and allows antisemitism to be weaponised for political reasons. This was because the definition recognises that antisemitism can "also target the State of Israel, conceived as a Jewish collectivity" (Holocaust Remembrance 2016). When the NEC finally adopted the definition in September 2018 following considerable pressure from centrists within the Labour Party, as well as from Jewish communal bodies, it did so subject to a caveat that its adoption would in no way constrain criticism of Israel (BICOM 2018).[3] This effectively rendered several of the definition's examples of antisemitism redundant and allowed the Labour Party to extricate itself from accusations of antisemitism by altering the definition of the term (MacEoin 2018).

Nevertheless, the IHRA Definition of Antisemitism has been widely adopted overseas and within the UK[4] and is therefore frequently referred to as the "International Definition" (Porat 2011). It defines antisemitism as "a certain perception of Jews, which may be expressed as hatred toward Jews. Rhetorical and physical manifestations of antisemitism are directed toward Jewish or non-Jewish individuals and/or their property, toward Jewish community institutions and religious facilities" (Holocaust Remembrance 2016). This statement is then followed by 11 examples which "could taking into account the overall context" manifest antisemitism in public life, the media, schools, the workplace, and religious institutions (Holocaust Remembrance 2016). The examples include making "mendacious, dehumanizing, demonizing, or stereotypical" claims about Jews as a collectivity; charging Jews individually or as a people with inventing or exaggerating the Holocaust; or accusing Jews of dual-loyalty with respect to Israel. In addition, there are several more explicit examples of how antisemitism can be manifested, when context is taken fully into account, with respect to the State of Israel. These include denying the Jewish people the right to self-determination; applying double standards by expecting from Israel a behaviour not expected of any other state; applying the images and symbols of traditional antisemitism (e.g. the blood libel) to Israel; comparing contemporary Israeli policy to that of the Nazis; or holding Jews collectively responsible for actions of the State of Israel. The IHRA Definition emphasises that criticism of Israel similar to that levelled against any other country is not a manifestation of antisemitism (Holocaust Remembrance 2016).

It is not only the hard left of the Labour Party that opposes the IHRA Definition of Antisemitism. It has plenty of other critics, too (Harrison and Klaff 2020, 2021). The controversy that surrounds it, as is evident from the controversy within the Labour Party, is because of its explicit acknowledgement, by means of its short list of examples that refer to Israel, that there are historical continuities between traditional antisemitism and contemporary, or post 1948, anti-Zionism. Critics of the definition claim that it wrongly stigmatises contemporary anti-Zionism as antisemitic. They argue that anti-Zionism is not antisemitic because it is merely in opposition to Zionism, and Zionism is a political movement or ideology that is independent of, and unrelated to, a person's race or religion. They frequently point to anti-Zionist Jews to support their claim. Zionists and proponents of the IHRA Definition disagree with them. They assert that antisemitism is implicated in contemporary anti-Zionism because it is in opposition to Zionism, which is the Jewish project of establishing, developing, and protecting the State of Israel as the ancestral homeland of the Jews. Further, this opposition is frequently expressed in the language of prejudice against Israel or the Zionist project. It is this meaning of anti-Zionism that is found in the official 2002 definition contained in the report of the Berlin Technical University's Centre for Research on Antisemitism, drafted for the European Union Monitoring Centre on Racism and Xenophobia (EUMC) (Bergmann and Wetzel 2003). The report defines anti-Zionism as "the portrayal of Israel as a state that is fundamentally negatively distinct from all others and which therefore has no right to exist" (Bergmann and Wetzel 2003, p. 18). Thus, the controversy surrounding the IHRA Definition is directly related to the fact that anti-Zionism, like antisemitism, is a contested concept.

Anti-Zionism's relationship to antisemitism can be explained by the fact that an affinity with Israel and the Zionist project is an aspect of the identity of the majority of British Jews who assume an obligation to support Israel and to ensure its survival as the ancestral homeland of the Jewish people (Graham and Boyd 2010). This affinity does not equate to unconditional or unstinting support for the government of Israel or its policies; rather it amounts to a sense of connection with Israel and a sense of its importance in the context of Jewish history and the persecution of the Jewish people. For this reason, hostility to Israel engages Jews not only in conventional political terms but also because Israel is an aspect of their identity. It is also the case that hostility towards Israel is frequently directed at individual Jews who, because of their assumed role in the creation of the State of Israel and their support for its continued existence, are collectively taken to be "Nazis", "racists", "warmongers", and "apologists for settler-colonialism and apartheid". Such expressions of hostility towards Jews are often serious and sometimes violent. This is why the IHRA Definition stigmatises as antisemitic certain expressions of hostility towards Israel which characterise the country as an essentially racist, Nazi state, and settler-colonial society that poses a permanent threat to peace, both in the region and in the world (Klaff and Harrison 2020; Harrison and Klaff 2021).

The fact that much contemporary anti-Israel hostility shrouds significant continuities with traditional antisemitism is because of the nature of antisemitism: it is not reducible to a single essence. Instead, there are many antisemitisms. This is because antisemitism is protean and capable of shifting its shape in response to different events, milieus, contexts, and cultural anxieties. Critical social theorists, Theodor Adorno and Max Horkheimer, understood antisemitism as ever changing, as an evolving social phenomenon (Fine and Spencer 2017, p. 62), while lawyer, writer, and antisemitism scholar, Anthony Julius, has described antisemitism as an "heterogeneous phenomenon, the site of collective hatreds..." (Julius 2011, p. xliii) and as "a repertoire of attitudes, myths and defamations in circulation at any given time" (Julius 2011, p. xliv). It is because of the plurality of its forms of existence that antisemitism is, in the words of the late historian Robert Wistrich, the world's "longest hatred" (Wistrich 1994).

Julius's description of antisemitism as a collection of defamations in circulation at any given time is useful to explain antisemitism without specific reference to the IHRA Definition. This is because all versions of antisemitism libel Jews, whether as individuals or as a collective (Julius 2011, p. 69). These libels may be grouped under three headings: the blood libel, the conspiracy libel, and the economic libel. All three libels substantially derive from three distinct aspects of Christian thinking and practice and share the premise that Jews hate or despise non-Jews (Julius 2011, p. 69). The blood libel, which originated in 12th Century England, holds that Jews entertain homicidal intentions towards non-Jews (at first Christians and now predominantly Muslims). The principal charge is that Jews kill non-Jewish children. The blood libel has become the governing trope in the characterisation of Israel and the Zionist project, with Israelis and Zionists frequently described or characterised as child-murderers (Julius 2011, pp. 96–97).

The conspiracy libel supposes that Jews act as one, in pursuit of goals inimical to the interests of non-Jews. A good example is the assertion that the Jews were behind 9/11 or that Jews control Hollywood or the media. For antisemitic conspiracy theorists, the Jews are everywhere and are well-organised. Their goal is world domination, and their actions are clandestine and sinister. *The Protocols of the Elders of Zion*, a Russian forgery first published in 1903 which told of a secret meeting of Jewish leaders who were plotting world domination, is perhaps the most notorious example of antisemitic conspiracy theory.[5]

Research conducted by Cambridge University in 2018 indicates that as many as 60% of Britons believe in conspiracy theories of one sort or another (Rogers de Waal 2018). Evidence from recent antisemitic incident reports published in Britain, Europe, and America indicates that there has been a significant rise in antisemitic conspiracy theories on both the left and the right of the political spectrum (European Union Agency for Fundamental Rights 2019; Anti-Defamation League 2020a; The Community Security Trust 2020a). On the hard left, the tendency is to see "the hand of Israel" behind everything that is bad in the world. Examples include the actress Maxine Peake's claim in an interview and subsequently tweeted that the Israeli Secret Service trained the American police in the knee-on-the-neck tactic that killed George Floyd (Pollard 2020). Another hard-left example is the claim by the actress Miriam Margolyes that former Labour Party leader Jeremy Corbyn was "forced" to resign due to "a conspiracy within the party motivated from Israel" (Campaign Against Antisemitism 2020). The tendency of the far right, on the other hand, is to regard the Jews as destroying white nations (Community Security Trust 2019c). This conspiracy myth involves the idea that Jews control migration flows and are therefore responsible for the immigration of people regarded as ethnically and culturally inferior, resulting in the destruction of 'native' identity. Known as "white genocide", the famous Jewish investor and philanthropist, George Soros, is frequently accused of being its mastermind (BBC News 2019). It was a delusional belief in the 'white genocide' conspiracy myth that drove a white supremacist named Robert Bowers to shoot dead 11 worshippers and injure six others in the Tree of Life Synagogue in Pittsburgh in October 2018. More recently, the coronavirus pandemic has sparked a wave of antisemitic conspiracy theories which blame Jews for spreading the disease and profiting from it (Zonshine 2020). A recent report by the government's independent advisor on antisemitism, Lord John Mann, reveals that anti-vaxxers on both the left and the right of the political spectrum are spreading online hate linking the pandemic to "Jews plotting to take over the world" (Tominey

2020). Sara Khan of the Commission for Countering Extremism summarises antisemitic COVID-19 conspiracy theories as the claim that:

> the virus is fake and part of a Jewish plot to mislead the public, that it's real and was deliberately created for malevolent purposes, that the Jews are the primary spreaders of the virus, that Jewish people are dying in disproportionately higher numbers, and posts that incite others to deliberately spread the virus to Jews.
>
> (Harpin 2020a)

The economic libel supposes that Jews, who are self-interested, acquisitive, and unproductive by nature, financially exploit non-Jews. Stereotypes of Jews as greedy, miserly, stingy, wealthy, and connected to money lending and usury have stoked antisemitic sentiment throughout history and still influence the perception of Jews today.[6] Often the economic libel is bound up with the conspiracy libel in the same expression of antisemitic sentiment. Examples may be found in the following tweets reported to the Community Security Trust in March and April 2018 respectively: "There is no argument here. Global banks are ripping everyone off because they are run by Jews…" (The Community Security Trust 2019c) and "Jews make money out of the gas chambers and six million supposedly dead cadavers. Can you imagine any other ethnic group profiting from the dead?" (The Community Security Trust 2019c; see also Finkelstein 2000). Another example of the operation of the economic libel in conjunction with the conspiracy libel may be found in the anti-vaxxer claims that Jews created the coronavirus and are colluding behind the scenes to destabilise banks and countries through its spread (Harpin 2020b).

An understanding of traditional and contemporary antisemitism is needed to recognise and assess the gravity of the abuse that occurs at the intersection of antisemitism and misogyny. Evidence of this abuse will be offered throughout the chapter and will be referred to as 'gendered antisemitism'. The chapter begins with a consideration of the published experience of Jewish female politicians who spoke out about antisemitism in the Labour Party during Jeremy Corbyn's leadership.

Gendered antisemitism directed at Jewish female politicians

While there has been no shortage of antisemitism within the left tradition historically, its emergence into the mainstream of the Labour Party under Jeremy Corbyn's leadership has provided the opportunity for a more extensive public debate about left antisemitism (Fine and Spencer 2017, pp. 4–7). It is in this context that experiences of antisemitism combined with misogyny were reported to the House of Commons by Jewish female politicians during its first general debate about antisemitism on April 17, 2018 (HC Deb 17 April 2018), and to the subsequent Sara Conference Against

Antisemitism and Misogyny in October 2018 (Sara Conference 2018). The Sara Conference was organised to specifically examine the intersectionality of antisemitism and misogyny and this was the first time that attention had been given to gendered antisemitism in the UK. The following section will therefore focus on three specific examples of abuse that were reported by Jewish female politicians to the House of Commons and to the Sara Conference following their complaints about antisemitism in the Labour Party during Corbyn's tenure as leader.

These three examples provide an opportunity to consider the nature and impact of gendered antisemitism. In considering the experiences of Jewish female politicians it should be remembered that there is nothing new about misogyny in politics. Defined as "dislike of, contempt for, or ingrained prejudice against women" (Lexico 2021), misogyny is thought to consistently feature in politics because of male resentment against women taking positions of political power. The Sara Conference noted that both antisemitism and sexism involve notions of power, control, and domination, and that Jewish women are at the intersection of both (Antisemitism Policy Trust 2019, pp. 2–3). Such notions of power, control, and domination are even more concentrated in the case of Jewish women who hold political power. This may help to explain the vicious abuse that was directed at Jewish female politicians who spoke out about antisemitism in the Labour Party while Corbyn was its leader. This chapter will focus on three of these women, namely, Ruth Smeeth, Dame Margaret Hodge, and Luciana Berger.[7] All three were, at the relevant time, Labour members of parliament.

The first example involves Ruth Smeeth and Dame Margaret Hodge. They reported to the House of Commons and the Sara Conference in 2018 that they were accused on Twitter by a Labour Party member of being "a couple of shit stirring cum buckets bought and paid for by Israel" (HC Deb 17 April 2018; Antisemitism Policy Trust 2019, pp. 2–3). This short statement manages to be profoundly disparaging of both women and Jews. The term "cum bucket" is a synonym for "slut". The Urban Dictionary's top definition for a "cum bucket" is "one whom you would imagine to be containing enough semen within various orifices of their body to fill a receptacle of some kind, such as a bucket" (Urban Dictionary 2021). Smeeth described this language as "obscene" (Antisemitism Policy Trust 2019, pp. 2–3). What primarily makes this social media attack on Smeeth and Hodge antisemitic is the suggestion that they are not only traitors to the Labour Party because they complained about antisemitism, but that they are also traitors to the country because they are paid servants of a foreign power ("paid for by Israel"). It is the thought that each woman is paid, as a whore is paid, that is then presumably taken by the abuser to "justify" the sexual abuse. In other words, it is by way of the thought that Smeeth and Hodge are paid for by Israel – the great whoremaster of the world in far-left thinking – that their abuser arrives at the thought that these women are literally whores, "cum buckets". Thus, the sexual abuse in this social media attack on Smeeth and

Hodge appears to be driven by antisemitism. Had their abuser said, "Ruth Smeeth and Margaret Hodge are Blairite cum buckets", the logic of the thought – the nature of the connection supposed to obtain between being a follower of Tony Blair and being a cum bucket – would have been much less easy to follow and therefore much less effective as a means of abuse. It would appear, therefore, that the antisemitism, the verbal violence, and the sexual obscenity are all intrinsically connected in this attack on Smeeth and Hodge. Research on the connection between antisemitic and misogynistic ways of thinking is necessary to develop a sound policy position advocating the legal adoption of gendered antisemitism as a sub-category of misogynistic hate crime.

There are other examples of the link between antisemitic and misogynistic ways of thinking. For instance, Smeeth reported that in early 2018 she received the following abusive tweet: "The gallows would be a fine and fitting place for this dyke piece of yid shit to swing from" (Antisemitism Policy Trust 2019, pp. 2–3). The use of the word "dyke" is interesting. Its most obvious use is its original sense as a homophobic and misogynistic slur to denote a masculine or a butch woman. However, the term might also have been used in an antisemitic sense as many images in the late 19th and early 20th century portrayed Jews as having an ambiguous sexuality and gender. Antisemitism has traditionally considered Jewish men to be effeminate and Jewish women to be masculinised (Stoegner 2020). The debasement and antisemitism inherent in the description of Ruth Smeeth as a "piece of yid shit" needs no explication: it is well known that the word "yid" is a derogatory term for a Jew and the suffix "shit" is considered the height of incivility when making a personal attack. The suggestion that Smeeth deserves to swing from the gallows likens her to the criminal who was hanged as punishment for his crime. It could be interpreted as a death threat because it deploys violent language. Indeed, Smeeth told the House of Commons that she experienced this abusive tweet as threatening and as undermining of her sense of personal security (Antisemitism Policy Trust 2019, pp. 2–3). One is left with no doubt that the intention behind the language was to cause distress, humiliation, and fear.

It should be acknowledged that the use of violent language in relation to female politicians is not new. Theresa May as prime minister, for example, experienced violent rhetoric in the form of certain lynch mob sentiments expressed by her own party members, such as the suggestion that she "bring her own noose" to a forthcoming meeting of the backbenchers 1922 Committee (Elgot and Walker 2018). The language of politics has reputedly always been aggressive, often drawing on the metaphors of battles and big guns, especially during heated political debates. In the case of the female Jewish MPs who voiced concerns about antisemitism in Corbyn's Labour Party, the violent rhetoric they reported was invariably coupled with misogynistic and sexually violent references to their Jewishness. For example, Ruth Smeeth, Dame Margaret Hodge, and Luciana Berger told of repeated rape threats accompanied by the terms "Zionist bitch" and "Zionist cunt" (HC Deb 17 April 2018). Feminists have argued that the words "bitch" and "cunt" act to reinforce the dehumanisation of women by reducing them to the image of a dog or to a mere body part, the female genitalia.[8] As before, the language used in these examples of gendered antisemitism is evidence of a connection between sexual obscenity, verbal violence, and antisemitism. The antisemitism resides in the use of the pejorative term "Zionist" to characterise a Jewish person as a "racist", a "Nazi", a "white supremacist", a "coloniser", and an "imperialist".[9] This derogatory use of "Zionist" to mean "Jew" is the result of the perceived connection between Jews, Israel, and the Zionist project, and the far-left anti-Zionist narrative which portrays Israel as a racist, colonialist, imperialist, Nazi state.

UN women have emphasised that online violence against women, as in the case of the rape threats described above, can be just as harmful and damaging as physical violence (UN Women 2015). Research on the harm and damage caused to women by offline threats is also needed. Jewish MP Luciana Berger reported feeling physically ill following the receipt of violent threats that were delivered to her Wavertree constituency office in Liverpool when she was a Labour MP (Kentish 2019). One such threat was in the form of a hand-written letter in September 2018 which was signed by people describing themselves as "Corbyn supporters". It opened with the words, "Hello Luciana, You nasty, stinking, lying, Zionist, 'Jew-Bitch'" and ended with, "Attached is correspondence of what Brother Lewis (sic) Farrakhan thinks about you stinking Jews. Have a good read, cunt…. And see you later!! Yeah!!" (Antisemitism Policy Trust 2019, p. 4). This letter provides further evidence of the connection between antisemitism and misogyny. Not only did it use dehumanising and degrading misogynistic words like "bitch" and "cunt", the Medieval antisemitic stereotype of Jews as liars (Luther 1543), and the antisemitic stereotype of Jews as "stinking" made popular in Nazi Germany, but it also included correspondence by Louis Farrakhan, the Nation of Islam leader whose antisemitism is well-documented. According to the Anti-Defamation League which monitors antisemitism in North America, Louis Farrakhan has railed against Jews for over 30 years, accusing them of all manner of conspiracies, of being "Satanic", of being "termites" (Anti-Defamation League 2020b), and describing Hitler as "a great man" (JNS 2020). It was Farrakhan's antisemitic Independence Day sermon on 4 July 2020 that was responsible for the public embrace of antisemitic sentiments by several African American football players, musicians, and celebrities (Anti-Defamation League 2020c), as well as for the claim made by British grime artist Wiley that Black people are the "real children of Israel" (Anti-Defamation League 2020c).

There is evidence in this abusive incident of an intention on the part of the perpetrators to offend, insult, and intimidate Berger as both a woman and a Jew. Other hand-written letters to Berger's constituency office threatened that she would be "raped, stabbed, and covered in acid" (Kentish 2019). Not only were these violent threats profoundly intimidating, but the effort required to hand-deliver them to her place of work might have suggested to Berger that the offenders not only wished her serious harm, but that they possessed the inclination and means to carry it out. It might well be the case, therefore, that Berger felt her physical safety to be more threatened by the receipt of these hand-delivered letters than by the receipt of the threats online, however bad they happened to be. Research on the difference, if any, between the impact on Jewish women of offline as opposed to online threats is necessary to understand the range and nature of the harms that arise in the context of gendered antisemitism. This is important to argue for gender antisemitism's criminalisation.

The next section will address what is already known about gendered antisemitism and online abuse. This section also provides a further opportunity to consider examples of gendered antisemitism directed at Jewish women who are in the public eye.

Gendered antisemitism and online abuse

According to the limited data available it appears that online abuse involving a combination of antisemitism and misogyny is directed at specific female politicians, television journalists, and entertainers who are known to be Jewish rather than at women who are not involved in public life (Antisemitism Policy Trust 2019, p. 4). It is likely, however, that Jewish women who are not in the public eye are also the victims of online targeted abuse and that the absence of available data is a reflection of the lack of research on non-public-life women, whether Jewish or otherwise. Elsewhere it has been shown that the so-called "gender trolling phenomenon" is targeted at women who assert their opinion, whether they are in the public eye or not (Mantilla cited in European Women's Lobby 2017).

Some statistics on online abuse and women are in order. Research by a UN Commission in 2015 found that globally, women are 27 times more likely than men to be harassed online (UN Women 2015); and a report entitled, "Hidden Hate: What Google Searches Tell Us About Antisemitism Today", published jointly by the Antisemitism Policy Trust and the Community Security Trust in 2019, stated that Jewish female politicians are the subject of more antisemitic Google searches than Jewish male politicians (The Community Security Trust 2019a, 2019b). Moreover, Jewish female politicians are more likely to be the subject of an antisemitic Google search than a search about a political issue. For example, there are more searches for "Luciana Berger Jew" than for "Luciana Berger policy", "Luciana Berger votes", or "Luciana Berger Brexit" (The Community Security Trust 2019a, 2019b). Only about 3.3% of searches for Luciana Berger are looking for information relating to mental health, even though this was a policy area of particular interest to Berger when she was in parliament and which she represented in Labour's shadow cabinet from September 2015 to June 2016 (The Community Security Trust 2019a, 2019b).

The website Stormfront, a far-right internet hate site, shows a clear connection between antisemitism and misogyny: the two Jewish parliamentarians with the most mentions on Stormfront are Luciana Berger and Dame Margaret Hodge, and in the history of Stormfront there have been 14% more mentions of Jewish female MPs than Jewish male MPs (The Community Security Trust 2019a, 2019b). On the other hand, British Jewish female entertainers do not get as many mentions on Stormfront as British Jewish male entertainers do (The Community Security Trust 2019a, 2019b). The conclusion drawn from this is that Jewish women with political power are particularly subject to antisemitic abuse (The Community Security Trust 2019a, 2019b). This reflects the fact that women in positions of political power cause male resentment and Jewish women with political power combine the notions of power associated with both sexism and antisemitism. A 2019 report based on the Sara Conference concluded that for politically active Jewish women, online abuse acts as a direct barrier to their freedom of expression and political participation because it undermines their sense of personal security (Antisemitism Policy Trust 2019, p. 3). This, in turn, has an "anti-democratic impact" (Akiwowo 2018).

Overall, there are more than 9,000 threads on the far-right Stormfront website related to feminism, 60% of which also mention Jews (The Community Security Trust 2019a, 2019b). To put this statistic into context, Jews are mentioned in 39% of all Stormfront threads on any subject, while black people are mentioned in 33% (The Community Security Trust 2019a, 2019b). Stormfront members appear to believe that Jews are leading the feminist movement. A common theme is the claim that "feminism is a Zionist conspiracy" and one thread called feminism "an entirely Jewish invention" (The Community Security Trust 2019a, 2019b). Margaret Hodge told the Sara Conference that she received messages via social media claiming that "feminism is a Zionist conspiracy" (Antisemitism Policy Trust 2019, p. 4). This again shows that there is a clear connection between antisemitism and misogynistic attitudes towards Jewish women, as do Stormfront's negative comments about the appearance of Luciana Berger who is described as an "equine-faced Zionist" (Antisemitism Policy Trust 2019, p. 4). Berger's appearance is also a major theme of Google searches about her, but unlike Stormfront, they tend to be more positive with the most common Google search being "Luciana Berger is hot" (Antisemitism Policy Trust 2019, p. 4).

Researchers at American media watchdog MediaMatters looked at 4chan – an online forum with a reputation for racism and antisemitism as well as misogyny, homophobia, and transphobia – and found that the number of antisemitic posts that were also misogynistic had drastically risen, growing by 180% between 2015 and 2017 (Meaker 2019). Given its prevalence on Stormfront and 4chan, it is inevitable that the harmful combination of antisemitism and misogyny would filter into the more mainstream social media sites like Facebook. In April 2018 *The Sunday Times* (Ungoed-Thomas 2018) reported that not only was Luciana Berger a frequent victim of pro-Corbyn Facebook trolls with comments like "She is a vile Zionist"[10] and "Deselect the cunt"[11] but BBC political editor, Laura Kuenssberg, who is not Jewish, was the victim of comments such as, "I wonder what vested interests this confirmed Zionist might be protecting?"[12] and "She is an evil lackey, sold to the big money and corporations".[13] The context for these antisemitic and misogynistic comments, of which there were many more on Corbyn-supporting Facebook sites (Ungoed-Thomas 2018), was that Corbyn supporters perceived Luciana Berger as deliberately manufacturing a crisis within the Labour Party by making false accusations about antisemitism. They also believed Laura Kuenssberg to be biased against Jeremy Corbyn following a BBC Trust ruling in 2017 that she had inaccurately reported his views (Martinson 2017).

Much antisemitic discourse is expressed in subtle and coded ways, especially online (Becker 2019). The belief that Berger was acting in bad faith to smear the Labour Party when she raised concerns about antisemitism is antisemitic because it is based on the conspiracy belief among Corbyn supporters that the allegations of antisemitism in the Labour Party were a smear or a witch-hunt invented by Zionists, Tories or Blairites (Labour Party 2020). This belief was best summed up by the celebrity Corbyn supporter, director Ken Loach, when he wrote that "exaggerated or false charges of antisemitism have coincided with the election of Jeremy Corbyn as leader" (Loach 2017). The ECHR Report, released on 29 October 2020, concluded that the culture of denial of antisemitism in the Labour Party, coupled with the allegation that antisemitism was being exaggerated for instrumental purposes, was itself evidence of institutional antisemitism (Equality and Human Rights Commission 2020, p. 28). The claim that Kuenssberg is a "confirmed Zionist" protecting vested interests and in the pay of "the big money and corporations", is antisemitic because it replicates the conspiracy belief that the BBC is a Zionist-controlled enterprise, and it deploys the economic libel which associates Jews and Zionists with money and influence. The impact of this online antisemitism is made even more powerful by the misogynistic descriptions of Berger and Kuenssberg as "vile" and "evil" women. It has been suggested that the allegation that Kuenssberg is biased in her reporting about Labour, when the same was never alleged in relation to any of her male BBC colleagues or her predecessor, Nick Robinson, is merely because she is a woman (Media Mole 2016). Moreover, the claim that Kuenssberg is a "lackey, sold to the big money and corporations", denies her any female agency.

Other victims of online antisemitic and misogynistic abuse, such as the actress Tracy-Ann Oberman and the *Countdown* co-presenter, Rachel Riley, have experienced the internet as a toxic place where intersectional abuse is used as a weapon to punish women for speaking out about political issues (Meaker 2019). It is no coincidence that Luciana Berger, Ruth Smeeth, and Dame Margaret Hodge experienced such abuse following their emotional speeches to the House of Commons about their experiences of antisemitism in the Labour Party on 17 April 2018 (Tapsfield and Ferguson 2018). Following the published findings of the Equality and Human Rights Commission on Labour Party antisemitism in October 2020, Luciana Berger experienced further online abuse, including a message that threatened that she 'would pay' for Jeremy Corbyn's suspension from the party (Harpin 2020c). As Tracy-Ann Oberman explained, "The misogyny I found, the hatred and vitriol that came towards me as a Jewish woman, the rape threats, the death threats, the sexualisation – all of it was so pointed" because "I stuck my head above the entertainment parapet and spoke out" about antisemitism in the Labour Party (Comerford 2020).

The goal behind gendered antisemitism appears to be to dehumanise, scare, threaten, humiliate, embarrass, and silence. It is abundantly clear that online technology enables many channels for its personal public expression. It is all too easy to produce a storm of antisemitic and misogynistic tweets and posts aimed at a specific Jewish woman or group of women in the public arena. Targeted campaigns directed at individual victims often involve dozens of social media accounts and hundreds, or even thousands, of anonymous tweets, images, and posts (The Community Security Trust 2020a). Not only does the internet permit a huge economy of scale, but the anonymity it provides allows for the proliferation of gendered antisemitic abuse which, as illustrated in this chapter, uniquely combines graphic, sexualised, and gendered insults with age-old canards about the malevolence of the Jew. At best, gendered antisemitism risks silencing its victims by threatening their security and morale and at worst, it encourages physical assaults on them. Its perpetrators, moreover, corrupt public discourse. These individual and societal harms are good reasons to argue that gendered antisemitism should be deterred. Deterrence can only be achieved by the threat of criminal sanctions for its commission. This is further justification for making gendered antisemitism a sub-category of misogynistic hate crime.

Gendered antisemitism directed at Jewish females in public spaces

While online antisemitism has become the single biggest contributing factor to the increasing number of antisemitic incidents recorded by the Community Security Trust (2020a, p. 1), the single highest category of offline antisemitic incident type involves abusive behaviour directed at (perceived) Jewish people in public spaces.[14] This includes, but is not limited to, verbal abuse using threatening language. Typically, in around one-half of these cases, the victim is visibly Jewish and can be identified by their religious or traditional clothing, the wearing of religious symbols such as a Star of David, or by the wearing of a Jewish school uniform. In the remaining cases, the victim is presumed to be Jewish, generally because the area has a high concentration of Jews. The spontaneous, verbal abuse of strangers who are identifiably Jewish or presumed to be Jewish as they go about their

168 *Lesley Klaff*

lives in public spaces is often associated with anti-social behaviour or local patterns of street crime rather than with political activism or ideologies (The Community Security Trust 2020a, p. 22).

In terms of the gender breakdown of the victims of antisemitic abuse in public spaces for the first six months of 2020, which are the only available figures for 2020 at the time of writing, 58% were male, 33% were female, and 9% were mixed groups of male and female (The Community Security Trust 2020b). This data is in line with that produced for the year 2019, when the Community Security Trust recorded 57% of victims as male, 37% as female, and 6% as a mixed group of males and female (The Community Security Trust 2020b, p. 23). These 2019 figures are also consistent with those recorded for 2018 where 60% of the victims were male, 34% were female, and 7% were mixed groups of females and males (The Community Security Trust 2019c).

The section below illustrates the fact that Jewish female victims in public spaces tend to experience a combination of antisemitism and misogyny. This contrasts with Jewish male victims who only experience antisemitism. Unfortunately, there is no available data on the effects of this. The relative impact on Jewish women and Jewish men of the abuse that they are subjected to in public spaces is an area that needs research attention. Data on the harm caused to Jewish women who are abused in public spaces is important to construct a persuasive policy position advocating the criminalisation of gendered antisemitism.

In terms of the gender of the offender for the first half of 2020, it was male in 83% of cases, female in 15% of cases, and a mixed group of male and female in 2% of cases (The Community Security Trust 2020b). In 2019, the gender of the offender was male in 82% of cases, female in 16% of cases, and a mixture of male and female in 2% of cases (The Community Security Trust 2020a). These figures are in line with the figures recorded for 2018, where of the cases in which gender was reported, 84% of offenders were male, 14% were female, and 2% were a mixture of male and female (The Community Security Trust 2019c).

Accordingly, the picture that emerges is one of incidents of offline antisemitic abuse typically involving a male perpetrator and a female victim, with the female victim experiencing misogynistic abuse alongside the antisemitism. This is evident in the two sections below, which consider those antisemitic incidents reported to the Community Security Trust by women and girls between 2016 and 2020. It should be noted that no research has been done on the nature of the gendered antisemitism that occurs in public spaces, or on the harm it causes.

Abuse targeting Jewish schoolgirls

Data on the incidence and nature of antisemitic and misogynistic abuse experienced by Jewish schoolgirls is limited. As most schools were closed on 20 March 2020 as a direct consequence of the COVID-19 outbreak, there were only 20 recorded incidents of antisemitic abuse in the school sector for the period January to June 2020 (The Community Security Trust 2020b). Further, while the figures for the school sector are higher for the two previous years, with a total of 122 recorded antisemitic incidents in 2019[1] and a total of 96 in 2018 (The Community Security Trust 2019c), there has never been a breakdown of incident according to the victim's gender. This means that to consider the nature of any possible intersectional abuse of Jewish schoolgirls, it is necessary to comb through the Community Security Trust's antisemitic incident reports to look for concrete examples. This exercise reveals that the antisemitic abuse of Jewish schoolgirls typically involves an element of misogyny.

Two separate incidents reported to the Community Security Trust in 2018 concerning the abuse of girls at a Jewish school in Hertfordshire involved the word "cunt" coupled with the word "Jewish". Specifically, it was reported that in May 2018, a group of Jewish girls from the school were verbally and physically attacked by girls from another local school who shouted slurs such as "you Jewish cunts!" and pulled their hair (The Community Security Trust 2019c). One month earlier, in April 2018, it was reported that two girls from the same school witnessed girls from another school fighting on a public bus. Upon spotting the Jewish girls the offending individuals shouted at them, "What are you fucking looking at you Jewish cunts?" (The Community Security Trust 2019c). The fact that the perpetrators of abuse in both incidents were also female is not entirely surprising given their relatively young age and the popular use of the word "cunt" as a generic insult in contemporary youth culture (Livingstone 2020). It has also been noted that some females are just as prone to using misogynistic language as their male counterparts (Brogaard 2019). A third incident reported to the Community Security Trust in April 2017 involved a Jewish girl in school uniform standing on the pavement waiting to cross the road when she was abused with the words, "Jewish cunt" from a passing car (The Community Security Trust 2018). On this occasion, the perpetrator was described as male.

Abuse targeting Jewish women

As with Jewish schoolgirls, there is no independent data analysing the quantity and quality of the abuse that targets Jewish women. A consideration of recent antisemitic incident reports produced by the Community Security Trust over the last few years reveals that the antisemitic abuse of Jewish women is invariably accompanied by misogyny. For example, an incident that took place in Manchester in June 2016 involved a visibly orthodox Jewish woman walking home when a white female shouted at her, "You fucking Jewish whore!" (The Community Security Trust 2017). The use of "whore" in this context was presumably intended to be disparaging and offensive.

An example of antisemitic abuse that was less obviously accompanied by misogynistic abuse occurred in Scotland in August 2018. A woman who was going through a conversion to Judaism was wearing a Star of David. She was riding on a bus in Edinburgh when a male passenger boarded the bus and spat in her face as he walked past her, calling her a "Jew" (The Community Security Trust 2019c). While the offender's act of spitting into the victim's face could have been to merely express hatred and contempt for her as a Jew, it is reasonable to assume that the act also involved an element of misogyny because of the phallic significance of spitting (Gomberg 1981), as well as the disrespect that spitting signifies. It would be interesting to know whether the perpetrator would have been equally inclined to spit in the face of a Jewish passenger who was male.

There are instances, albeit infrequent, where the antisemitism is not directed at the female victim but where we nevertheless see a link between the misogyny that is directed at her and antisemitism. For example, an incident reported to the Community Security Trust in January 2018 involved a non-Jewish woman travelling on the London underground. A man struck up a conversation with her during which he began to make racist remarks. When the woman protested, the man said, "I suppose you are a Jew-loving cunt!" (The Community Security Trust 2019c). This phenomenon is referred to as "intersectional discourse" because a link is made between the female identity of the victim and Jewish identity and both are disparaged (The Community Security Trust 2019c).

Other instances of gendered antisemitism do not start out as antisemitic and misogynistic but become so during the exchange. An incident of this nature was reported to the Community Security Trust in February 2016. A Jewish woman was at a pub with two female friends. She accidentally bumped into a man on her way back from the toilet and after she apologised to him, he said, "You should be sorry, you Jewish looking cunt". He then poured drinks over her and her two friends (The Community Security Trust 2017). This was an aggravated act of antisemitic and misogynistic verbal abuse because it also entailed physical assault.

In the final example, an incident recorded by the Community Security Trust in London in June 2016 once again shows the coupling of the word "Jewish" with the word "cunt". In this case, a Jewish woman told a man to stop shouting in the street and he responded with, "Fuck off you Jewish cunt" (The Community Security Trust 2017).

To conclude this section on gendered antisemitism in public spaces, all but one example of reported antisemitic abuse that targeted a female between 2016 and 2020 included misogynistic words like "cunt" and "whore", while an example of misogynistic abuse directed at a non-Jewish woman also included an antisemitic reference to Jews. The one example of antisemitic abuse which did not contain a misogynistic word involved the misogynistic act of spitting. The abuse experienced by Jewish men in public spaces, on the other hand, is very different. The majority of antisemitic abuse Jewish men experience takes place online but that which takes place in public spaces tends to occur in the context of a football match, or in the form of a direct physical attack on the street (The Community Security Trust 2017, 2018, 2019c, 2020a, 2020b). The antisemitic rhetoric used in these instances generally involves the word "Yid" or the phrase "Dirty Jew" (The Community Security Trust 2017, 2018, 2019c, 2020a, 2020b). There are no recorded instances of antisemitic rhetoric using gendered abusive terms like "cunt" where the victim is male. It appears, therefore, that a Jewish woman's experience of antisemitic abuse is shaped by her female identity.

Conclusion

There is very little available work on the topic of gendered antisemitism. The goal of this chapter has been to examine such evidence of it that does exist, and to locate within that evidence points at which future research might usefully be directed. Limited though the evidence is, it is sufficiently indicative to suggest that David Hirsh's belief that the expression of sexual violence against women becomes far worse when an element of conscious antisemitism enters it, is basically sound. Further research into the intersection of the two is urgently needed to provide empirically supported data on the nature, function, and impact of gendered antisemitism. Once such data becomes available, it will hopefully be a relatively small step to the legal recognition of antisemitism as an aggravating factor in misogynistic hate crime.

Notes

1 This was organised and hosted by the All-Party Parliamentary Group Against Antisemitism with support from the Antisemitism Policy Trust (AST) and the UK Government. The AST is a charity which focuses on educating and empowering decision-makers in the UK to effectively address antisemitism.
2 These movements include Women's March on Washington, Chicago Dyke March, and Black Lives Matter. Linda Sarsour, organiser of the Women's March on Washington, argues that Zionism (the belief in the existence of a Jewish state) and feminism exclude and contradict each other.
3 It was stated that 'This does not in any way undermine the freedom of expression on Israel and the Palestinians' (BICOM 2018).
4 The IHRA Definition has been adopted by the British Government, over 260 councils in England and Wales, the judiciary, the Crown Prosecution Service, the police, 85 universities, the National Union of Students, and the Labour, Conservative and Liberal-Democrat Parties, while versions of it have been adopted by the U.S. Department of State, the U.S. Commission of Civil Rights, the Organisation for Security and Cooperation in Europe, and other agencies, as well as by 35 countries.
5 The Protocols of the Elders of Zion was influenced by the publication in 1806 of the 'Simonini Letter' which falsely alleged that the Jews had conspired to bring about the French Revolution, see Oberhauser (2020).
6 See, for example, Logue and Gallagher (2017).
7 There is other evidence of gendered antisemitism in the Labour Party during Corbyn's tenure as leader, but limited space permits only a close examination of the chosen three. See Fraser (2019).

8 Other online threats of physical violence against Luciana Berger were reminiscent of acts of domestic violence. These included the threat of 'a good kicking' coupled with the offensive characterisation of her as a 'Zionist Extremist MP ... who hates civilised people', see Philpot (2019).
9 Jewish actress Tracy-Ann Oberman tweeted on 6 August 2020, that she and Jewish Countdown co-presenter, Rachel Riley, were the victims of a campaign in which they are being smeared as 'white supremacists' for speaking out about antisemitism among Corbyn supporters (Oberman 2020).
10 Facebook group *Jeremy Corbyn True Socialism* reported in Ungoed-Thomas (2018).
11 Facebook group *Supporting Jeremy Corbyn and John McDonnell* reported in Ungoed-Thomas (2018).
12 Facebook group *We Support Jeremy Corbyn* reported in Ungoed-Thomas (2018).
13 Facebook group *Supporting Jeremy Corbyn and John McDonnell*, reported in Ungoed-Thomas (2018).
14 Other antisemitic incidents recorded by the Community Security Trust include violent assaults, direct antisemitic threats, antisemitic graffiti, one-off cases of hate mail, abusive behaviour other than verbal abuse, and damage and desecration of Jewish property (The Community Security Trust 2020a, p. 1).

References

Akiwowo, S., 2018. Intervention notes at the UN Human Rights Council (38th session). 21 June. Available at: https://seyiakiwowo.com/2018/06/21/founder-director-glitchuk-seyi-akiwowos-intervention-notes-at-un-human-rights-council/ [Accessed 1 December 2020].

Anti-Defamation League, 2020a. Hate, conspiracy theories and advertising on Facebook [online]. 22 June. Available at: https://www.adl.org/blog/hate-conspiracy-theories-and-advertising-on-facebook [Accessed 1 December 2020].

Anti-Defamation League, 2020b Farrakhan: in his own words [online]. Available at: https://www.adl.org/education/resources/reports/nation-of-islam-farrakhan-in-his-own-words [Accessed 1 December 2020].

Anti-Defamation League, 2020c. Farrakhan remains most popular antisemite in America [online]. 15 July. Available at: https://www.adl.org/blog/farrakhan-remains-most-popular-antisemite-in-america [Accessed 1 December 2020].

Antisemitism Policy Trust, 2019. Misogyny and antisemitism. sexist abuse: online, offline and antisemitic [online]. April 2019. Available at: https://www.antisemitism.org.uk/wp-content-uploads/2019/055982-Misogyny-and-Antisemitism-Breifing-April-2019-v1.pdf [Accessed 1 December 2020].

BBC News, 2019. Why is billionaire George Soros a bogeyman for the hard right? 6 September. Available: https://www.bbc.com/news/amp/stories-49584157 [Accessed 1 December 2020].

Becker, M.J., 2019. Understanding online antisemitism: towards a new qualitative approach [online]. *Fathom*. Available at: http://fathomjournal.org/understanding-online-antisemitism-towards-a-new-qualitative-approach/ [Accessed 1 December 2020].

Bergmann, W. and Wetzel, J., 2003. Manifestations of anti-semitism in the European Union [online]. Synthesis Report, Berlin Technical University Centre for Research on Antisemitism, First Semester 2002 (Draft February 2003). Available at: www.infopartisan.net/document/antisemitismusstudie.pdf [Accessed 1 December 2020].

BICOM, 2018. Labour adopts antisemitism definition, but guarantees free speech on Israel [online]. 5 September. Available at: https://www.bicom.org.uk/news/labour-adopts-antisemitism-definition-but-guarantees-free-speech-on-israel/ [Accessed 1 December 2020].

Brogaard, B., 2019. 12 ways to spot a female misogynist. *Psychology Today* [online]. 12 August. Available at: https://www.psychologytoday.com/gb/blog/the-mysteries-love/201908/12-ways-spot-female-misogynist%3famp [Accessed 1 December 2020].

Campaign Against Antisemitism, 2020. Miriam Margolyes says a conspiracy within the party motivated from Israel forced Jeremy Corbyn to stand down as Labour leader. July 13. Available at: https://antisemitism.uk/miriam/margolyes-says-a-conspiracy-within-the-party-motivated-from-israel-forced-jeremy-corbyn-to-stand-down-as-labour-leader/ [Accessed 1 December 2020].

Comerford, R., 2020. Tracy-Ann Oberman: my experiences of anti-semitism will inform how I play Shylock. *The Stage* [online]. 26 February. Available at: https://www.thestage.co.uk/news/tracy-ann-oberman-my-expereinces-of-anti-semitism-will-inform-how-i-play-shylock [Accessed 1 December 2020].

Crenshaw, K., 1989. Demarginalizing the intersection of race and sex: a black feminist critique of antidiscrimination doctrine. Feminist theory and antiracist politics. *University of Chicago Legal Forum*, 140, pp. 139–167.

Elgot, J. and Walker, P., 2018. Calls to remove Tory whip after 'disgraceful' remarks about May. *The Guardian* [online]. 22 October. Available at: https://www.theguardian.com/politics/2018/oct/22/tories-identify-mps-vile-language-theresa-may-yvette-cooper [Accessed 1 December 2020].

Equality and Human Rights Commission, 2020. Investigation into antisemitism in the labour party. Available at: https://www.equalityhumanrights.com/sites/default/files/investigation-into-antisemitism-in-the-labour-party.pdf [Accessed 1 December 2020].

European Union Agency for Fundamental Rights, 2019. Experiences and perceptions of antisemitism – second survey on discrimination and hate crime against Jews in the EU [online]. 8 March. Available at: https://fra.europa.eu/en/news/2018/persistent-antisemitism-hangs-over-eu [Accessed 1 December 2020].

European Women's Lobby, 2017. #HerNetHerRights report [online]. Available at: https://www.womenlobby.org/IMG/pdf/hernetherrights_report_2017_for_web.pdf [Accessed 1 December 2020].

Fine, R. and Spencer, P. 2017. *Antisemitism and the Left: On the Return of the Jewish Question*. Manchester: Manchester University Press.

Finkelstein, N., 2000. *The Holocaust Industry: Reflections on the Exploitation of Jewish Suffering*. London: Verso.

Fraser, J., 2019. In Britain's Labour Party, Jewish women endure the worst abuse. *Hadassah Magazine* [online]. March 2019. Available at: https://www.hadassahmagazine.org/2019/03/06/britains-labour-party-jewish-women-endure-worst-abuse/ [Accessed 1 December 2020].

Gomberg, H.L. 1981. A note on the phallic significance of spitting. *Psychoanalitic Quarterly*, 50(1), pp. 90–95. DOI: 10.1002/j.2167-4086.2007.tb00293.x.

Graham, D. and Boyd, J., 2010. Committed, concerned and conciliatory: the attitudes of Jews in Britain towards Israel [online]. JPR Report. Available at: https://archive.jpr.org.uk/download?id=1509 [Accessed 1 December 2020].

Grunwald-Spier, A., 2018. *Women's Experiences in the Holocaust: In Their Own Words*. Stroud: Amberley Publishing.

Harpin, L., 2018. Labour rejects full IHRA antisemitism definition – but is accused of 'fudge' for pledging review. *The Jewish Chronicle* [online]. 17 July. Available at: https://www.thejc.com/news/uk/labour-rejects-ihra-definition-antisemitism-nec-1.467291 [Accessed 17 January 2021].

Harpin, L., 2020a. Community facing 'five dangerous categories of conspiracy theories' blaming it for Covid 19, new report warns. *The Jewish Chronicle* [online]. 9 July. Available at: https://www.thejc.com/news/uk/community-facing-five-dangerous-categories-of-conspiracy-theories-blaming-it-for-covid-19-new-report-warns-1.501396 [Accessed 17 January 2021].

Harpin, L., 2020b. New report warns that 79% of anti-vaccination networks host Jew-hate. *The Jewish Chronicle* [online]. 21 October. Available at: http://www.thejc.com/new-report-warns-that-79-of-anti-vaccination-networks-host-jew-hate-1.507742 [Accessed 17 January 2021].

Harpin, P., 2020c. Threats to Berger include online message saying she 'would pay' for Corbyn suspension. *The Jewish Chronicle* [online]. 1 November. Available at: https://www.thejc.com/news/uk/threats-to-berger-include-online-message-saying-she-would-pay-for-corbyn-suspension-1.508123 [Accessed 17 January 2021].

Harrison, B. and Klaff, L., 2020. In defence of the IHRA definition [online]. *Fathom*. Available at: https://fathomjournal.org/in-defence-of-the-ihra-definition/ [Accessed 17 January 2021].

Harrison, B. and Klaff, L., 2021. The IHRA definition and its critics. In: Rosenfeld, A.H., ed. *Contending with Antisemitism in a Rapidly Changing Political Climate*. Bloomington: Indiana University Press, pp. 9–43.

HC Deb 17 April 2018 vol 639 c247–292 [online]. Available at: https://hansard.parliament.uk/commons/2018-04-17/debates/9D70B2B4-39D7-4241-ACF8-13F7DFD8AEB2/Anti-Semitism [Accessed 17 January 2021].

Hirsh, D., 2019. Labour's intersection of antisemitism and misogyny. *The Times of Israel* [online]. April 2019. Available at: https://blogs.timesofisrael.com/labours-intersection-of-antisemitism-and-misogyny/ [Accessed 17 January 2021].

Holocaust Remembrance, 2016. Working definition of antisemitism [online]. Available at: https://www.holocaustremembrance.com/working-definition-antisemitism [Accessed 17 January 2021].

JNS, 2020. Petition to remove Farrakhan from Twitter gains signatures. *The Jewish Voice* [online]. August 2020. Available at: https://thejewishvoice.com/2020/08/petition-to-remove-farrakhan-from-twitter-gains-signatures/ [Accessed 17 January 2021].

Julius, A., 2011. *Trials of the Diaspora: A History of Antisemitism in England*. Oxford: Oxford University Press.

Kentish, B., 2019. 'The abuse made me physically ill': Luciana Berger reveals toll of fighting antisemitism while Labour MPs refused to stand by her. *Independent* [online]. 9 November. Available at: https://www.independent.co.uk/news/uk/politics/luciana-berger-labour-antisemitism-jeremy-corbyn-election-latest-liberal-democrats-finchley-a9196696.html%3famp [Accessed 1 December 2020].

Klaff, L. and Harrison, B. 2020. Why Facebook must adopt IHRA. *The Jewish Chronicle* [online]. 16 October. Available at: https://www.thejc.com/comment/opinion/why-facebook-must-adopt-ihra-1.507619 [Accessed 1 December 2020].

Labour Party, 2020. *Work of Labour Party's Governance and Legal Unit in Relation to Antisemitism 2014–2019*. London: Labour Party.

LEXICO, 2021. Misogyny. Available at: https://www.lexico.com/en/definition/misogyny [Accessed 1 December 2020].

Livingstone, J., 2020. What's so bad about the C-word? *The New Republic* [online]. 5 June. Available at: https://newrepublic.com/article/148713/whats-bad-c-word [Accessed 1 December 2020].

Loach, K., 2017. Letter clarifying my comments on the Holocaust. *New York Times* [online]. 13 October. Available at: https://www.nytimes.com/2017/10/13/opinion/ken-loach-holocaust-anti-semitism.html [Accessed 1 December 2020].

Logue, P. and Gallagher, C., 2017. Sunday Times drops Kevin Myers and apologises for offensive article. *The Irish Times* [online]. 30 July. Available at: https://www.irishtimes.com/business/media-and-marketing-/sunday-times-drops-kevin-myers-and-apologises-for-offensive-article-1.3171421%3fmode=amp [Accessed 1 December 2020].

Luther M., 1543. *On the Jews and Their Lies.* Wittenberg.

MacEoin, D., 2018. The British Labour Party's new definition of anti-semitism [online]. Gatestone International Policy Council. 6 September. Available at: https://www.gatestoneinstitute.org/12965/labour-party-antisemitism [Accessed 1 December 2020].

Martinson, J., 2017. BBC Trust says Laura Kuenssberg report on Corbyn was inaccurate. *The Guardian* [online]. 18 January. Available at: https://www.google.co.uk/amp/s/amp.theguardian.com/media/2017/jan/18/bbc-trust-says-laura-kunessberg-report-on-jeremy-corbyn-was-inaccurate-labour [Accessed 5 January 2021].

Meaker, M., 2019. No, antisemitic abuse against women is not OK. *Stylist* [online]. 31 January. Available at: www.stylist.co.uk/long-reads/rachel-riley-antisemitism-abuse-online-holocaust-research-survey-eu-brxit-opinion/249219/amp [Accessed 5 January 2021].

Media Mole, 2016. Why do people hate Laura Kuenssberg so much? *New Statesman* [online]. 10 May. Available at: https://www.newstatesman.com/politics/media/2016/05/why-do-people-hate-laura-kuenssberg-so-much [Accessed 5 January 2021].

Oberhauser, C., 2020. Simonini's letter: the 19th century text that influenced antisemitic conspiracy theories about the Illuminati [online]. 31 March. Available at: https://theconversation.com/simoninis-letter-the-19th-centurytext-that-influenced-antisemitic-conspiracy-theories-about-the-illuminati-134635 [Accessed 5 January 2021].

Oberman, T., 2020. Thread: there is an organised smear campaign going on against me and @RachelRileyRR [Twitter]. 6 August. Available at: https://twitter.com/TracyAnnO/status/1291292356004773888 [Accessed 5 January 2021].

Philpot, R., 2019. A 'Zionist extremist who hates civilised people', Luciana Berger's labour ordeal. *The Times of Israel* [online]. 18 February. Available at: https://www.timesofisrael.com/jewish-mps-resignation-puts-claims-of-uk-labour-anti-semisitsm-back-in-spotlight/amp/ [Accessed 5 January 2021].

Pollard, A., 2020. Maxine Peake: 'people who couldn't vote Labour because of Corbyn? they voted Tory as far as I'm concerned'. *The Independent* [online]. 25 June. Available at: https://www.independent.co.uk/arts-entertainment/films/features/maxine-peake-interview-labour-corbyn-keir-starmer-black-lives-matter-a9583206.html [Accessed 5 January 2021].

Porat, D., 2011. The international working definition of antisemitism and its detractors. *Israel Journal of Foreign Affairs*, 3(5), pp. 93–101. DOI: 10.1080/23739770.2011.11446474.

Rogers de Waal, J., 2018. Brexit and Trump voters more likely to believe in conspiracy theories. [online]. *YouGov*. 14 December. Available at: https://yougov.co.uk/topics/international/articles-reports/2018/12/14/brexit-and-trump-voters-are-more-likely-believe-co [Accessed 5 January 2021].

Sara Conference, 2018. *Sara Conference against Misogyny and Antisemitism*, 26 November 2018. Antisemitism Policy Trust, Westminster.

Stoegner, K., 2020. Intersectionality and antisemitism – a new approach. *Fathom*. Available at: https://fathomjournal.org/intersectionality-and-antisemitism-a-new-approach/ [Accessed 5 January 2021].

Tapsfield, J. and Ferguson, K., 2018. Labour MPs suffer online abuse after speaking out on antisemitism. *Daily Mail* [online]. 18 April. Available at: https://www.dailymail.co.uk/news/article-5628845/amp/Labour-MPs-suffer-wave-online-abuse-speaking-anti-Semitism.html [Accessed 5 January 2021].

The Community Security Trust, 2017. Antisemitic incidents report 2016 [online]. 2 February. Available at: https://cst.org.uk/news/blog/2017/02/record-number-of-hate-incidents-in-the-uk-in-2016 [Accessed 5 January 2021].

The Community Security Trust, 2018. Antisemitic incidents report 2017 [online]. 1 February. Available at: https://cst.org.uk/news/blog/2018/02/01/antisemitic-incidents-report-2017 [Accessed 1 December 2020].

The Community Security Trust, 2019a. Hidden hate: what Google searches tell us about antisemitism today [online]. 11 January. Available at: https://cst.org.uk/news/blog/2019/01/11/hidden-hate-what-google-searches-tell-us-about-antisemitism-today [Accessed 1 December 2020].

The Community Security Trust, 2019b. Hidden hate: what Google searches tell us about antisemitism today. Available at: https://cst.org.uk/public/data/file/a/b/APT%20Google%20Report%202019.pdf [Accessed 1 December 2020].

The Community Security Trust, 2019c. Antisemitic incidents report 2018 [online]. 7 February. Available at: https://cst.org.uk/news/blog/2019/02/07/antisemitic-incidents-report-2018 [Accessed 1 December 2020].

The Community Security Trust, 2020a. Antisemitic incidents report 2019 [online]. 6 February. Available at: https://cst.org.uk/news/blog/2020/02/06/antisemitic-incidents-report-2019 [Accessed 1 December 2020].

The Community Security Trust, 2020b. Antisemitic incidents report January-June 2020 [online]. 30 July. Available at: https://cst.org.uk/public/data/file/e/7/IncidentsReportJan-June2020-Embargo.pdf [Accessed 1 December 2020].

Tominey, C., 2020. Conspiracy theories link pandemic to Jewish plot. *The Telegraph* [online]. 21 October. Available at: https://digitaleditions.telegraph.co.uk/data/394/reader/reader.html?#!preferred/0/package/394/pub/394/page/21/article/94765 [Accessed 1 December 2020].

Ungoed-Thomas, J., 2018. Inside Labour's hate factory: targets of the trolls. *The Sunday Times* [online]. 1 April. Available at: https://www.thetimes.co.uk/article/targets-of-the-trolls-h28k3l2mw [Accessed 1 December 2020].

UN Women, 2015. Combatting online violence against women and girls: a worldwide wake-up call [online]. 24 September. Available at: http://unwomen.org/media/headquarters/attachments/sections/library/publications/2015/cyber_violence_gender%20report.pdf?vs=4295 [Accessed 1 December 2020].

Urban Dictionary, 2021. Cum bucket. Available at: https://www.urbandictionary.com/define.php?term=cum+bucket&amp=true [Accessed 1 December 2020].

Wistrich, R., 1994. *Antisemitism: The Longest Hatred*. New York: Schocken Books.

Zonshine, I., 2020. Far-right extremists spreading antisemitic conspiracies about COVID-19. *The Jerusalem Post* [online]. 14 June. Available: https://www.google.co.uk/amp/s/m.jpost.com/diaspora/antisemitism/far-right-extermists-spreading-antisemitic-conspiracies-about-covid-19-631209/amp [Accessed 1 December 2020].

9 An exposition of sexual violence as a method of disablist hate crime

Jane Healy

Introduction

> The voices and experiences of minority victims of hate crime have not played a sufficiently central role in the debates.
> (Boeckmann and Turpin-Petrosino 2002, p. 222)

Earlier chapters have explicated the nature and extent of policy and legislation about hate crime in England and Wales; this chapter will not revisit these in detail, suffice to say that disability is one of the five current legally protected characteristics, or *strands*, of hate crime. Disability, in the context of this chapter, is understood as a physical, mental, psychological or sensory impairment or condition that, in interaction with an individual's environment, has a long-term adverse effect on that individual's ability to conduct day to day activities.[1] Official police recorded figures suggest there were 8,469 disability hate crimes during 2019/2020, an increase of 9% on the previous year (Home Office 2020), although these figures are considered unreliable. Despite some recent improvement, disability-motivated hate crimes are believed to be significantly under-reported and research is urgently needed as to why disabled people are less likely to report their experiences of hate crime to the police (Sin et al. 2012; Sin 2013; Richardson et al. 2016). Crime Survey for England and Wales data suggests that occurrences of disability hate crimes could be as high as 52,000 per year (Home Office 2020), based on self-reported data. These figures may also be an underestimate, as even in self-report studies not everyone will be aware or willing to report hate crime victimisation (Walters and Brown 2016).

The reasons for under-reporting are varied. A number of studies suggest the possible relationship between perpetrator and victim as a significant factor in under-reporting (Petersilia 2000; Sin et al. 2009b; Clement et al. 2011). Other factors include: fear of reprisals or possible recriminations (e.g. Sin et al. 2009a; Vincent et al. 2009; Sin 2013); a lack of diversity and disability awareness within criminal justice organisations in responding to disabled people's experiences (Mason-Bish 2013; Macdonald et al. 2017) and police stereotypes about certain disabilities and impairments resulting in

DOI: 10.4324/9781003023722-9

reports being trivialised, particularly for those with learning disabilities and/or mental health conditions (Roulstone and Sadique 2013; Sin 2013). A general lack of disability awareness combined with diagnostic overshadowing (the tendency to make assumptions about certain impairments and conditions) can 'doubly' disadvantage disabled people who experience crime (Sin et al. 2009b). In addition, there are practical and "structural" barriers to reporting hate crimes (Sin 2015) such as accessibility barriers to police stations and reporting systems, lack of interpreters, communication limitations, lack of access to an advocate, inaccessible reporting systems, lack of consideration of special measures, poor wheelchair access and a lack of training for frontline staff (Petersilia 2000; Cunningham and Drury 2002; Vincent et al. 2009; Balderston 2013b; Sin 2013). These must be understood in terms of existing welfarist assumptions around disabled people, culminating in a risk-averse response to them and a focus on harm avoidance, often underpinned by assumptions about a disabled person's vulnerability (Perry 2004; Sin 2015). A common response to disabled people, 'protectionism' assumes all disabled persons are vulnerable and in need of protection or help, rather than considering alternative criminal justice or human rights approaches situated with a social model approach to disability (Perry 2008; Sin et al. 2009a).

Existing literature also indicates that many disabled people report experiencing cumulative, repeated incidents of abuse, harassment, physical violence, sexual violence and withdrawal of support (Sin et al. 2009a; Pettitt et al. 2013; Sherry 2013a; Williams and Tregidga 2014; Chakraborti et al. 2014b; Richardson et al. 2016; Healy 2020). Disability hate crime also has significant impact upon victims' physical and mental health and well-being (Shapland and Hall 2007; Sin et al. 2009b). This can include hospitalisation and, in some cases, attempted suicide or suicidal ideation (Pettitt et al. 2013; Chakraborti et al. 2014b). The impact of this risks being magnified when combined with the effects of misogyny. The next section will look explicitly at crimes against disabled women and it also draws on other elements of victimisation by way of comparison.

Disability hate crime against women

The focus of this chapter is on disabled women's experiences of hate crime but this is framed within wider discourses of violence against women.[2] The World Health Organization (WHO 2018) reports that violence against women is a global 'epidemic' health problem. One in three women globally will experience violence, which presents a significant social, economic and criminal justice challenge in many societies. However women are not a homogeneous group (Balderston 2013a). It is acknowledged that both men and women can be victims of domestic violence but this chapter is concerned with disabled women's experiences.

Numerous studies have found that disabled women are at greater risk of victimisation than non-disabled women and disabled men, that they are more likely to experience domestic violence or abuse, and are at increased risk of sexual assault and stalking (Marley and Buila 2001; Barclay and Mulligan 2009; Hughes et al. 2012; Balderston 2013a; Coleman et al. 2013; Pettitt et al. 2013; Thiara and Hague 2013; McCarthy 2017). These experiences are nuanced, with some disabled women at greater risk than others: for example, Petersilia (2000) and Bruder and Kroese (2005) found high rates of sexual assault against women with learning disabilities, and Marley and Buila (2001) found higher rates of sexual offending against women with mental health conditions. The intersection of both gender and disability together appears to be contributing and escalating factors for disabled women.

Early studies in victimology emphasised the importance of investigating the relationship between victim and offender (Petersilia 2000). Historically, however, hate crime was understood as a 'stranger' crime (Stanko 2001; Mason 2005a; Chakraborti and Garland 2009). A typical image of hate crime involves a victim who is a complete stranger to the perpetrator, as with popular images of sexual assault, rather than abuse coming from people with whom they have an intimate or regular relationship (Mason 2005b). Evidence points to the contrary, with many perpetrators of disability hate crimes having a relationship with their victim (Brownridge 2006; Landman 2014). Consequently, disabled women are particularly vulnerable to victimisation from those they are in a relationship with (Sobsey and Doe 1991; Petersilia 2000; Marley and Buila 2001; Magowan 2003). Disability-related factors can also limit disabled women's abilities to leave such relationships, both in terms of individual limitations and structural inequalities in service provision (Thiara and Hague 2013; McCarthy 2017). The limited routes to safety for disabled women and their reliance upon their abusers to perform caring tasks mean they are effectively forced to stay in abusive relationships. This dependence upon partner-carers, many of whom use the woman's impairment as a target for abuse, compounds victims' experiences and challenges their ability to seek help. There is often a gap in refuge service provision for disabled women (Thiara and Hague 2013), as they have inadequate provision for disabled women, meaning they have no route out. Consequently, disabled women may be at increased risk of *repeat* victimisation from their partners or family members.

The dominant but misleading image of hate crime as stranger-crime therefore risks excluding or ignoring those cases where both victim and perpetrator know each other. Although the literature suggests that hate crimes have a significant impact on disabled victims and their engagement with society (Williams and Tregidga 2014) the impact can be even more pernicious in cases where there is a relationship between perpetrators and victims (Petersilia 2000; Thomas 2011, 2013; Landman 2014). Consideration must be given to the decreased likelihood of victims' reporting experiences of hate crime by those close to them, particularly those that involve crimes of a sexual or intimate nature, suggesting that numbers are in fact much higher than those reported. Understanding the relationships involved in hate crime is therefore crucial to its interpretation and response, as well as explaining why reporting figures remain low and providing insight into how they can be improved.

Furthermore, there is a scarcity of research on the interaction of disability with other elements of identity, and little on the situational context of violence against disabled people (Balderston and Roebuck 2010; Balderston 2013a; Sherry 2013b; Emerson and Roulstone 2014; Sin 2015). This chapter contributes to that gap in knowledge by considering the experiences of disabled women in particular.

Methodology

The research presented herein is part of a wider study exploring the experiences of victims of disability hate crimes through the criminal justice system (Healy 2019, 2020). Data was collected between 2013 and 2016 using focus groups, an online survey with disabled people, interviews with key informants and policy makers, as well as with disabled victims themselves. The research focused particularly on the disparity in the criminal justice system's response to reports of disability hate crimes and explored victims' experiences of reporting to police and other services. This section provides findings from interviews and the online survey.

The research framework was participatory in approach, with an inclusive research design that aimed to be collaborative with disabled communities within a social constructivist perspective. Participatory research with disabled groups is particularly challenging (Cameron and Murphy 2006; Aldridge 2014) but it is important to ensure that disabled participants are engaged in the research, rather than researched 'on' (for example, see Beazley et al. 1997). Disabled participants were engaged with, in line with a social model approach, by contributing to research design in focus groups (Dupont 2008; Aldridge 2014; Nind 2017). Significant time was spent establishing relationships with the narrative interview participants before their interview was conducted, so that there was a degree of openness and collaboration in the approach to interview. Participants who were interviewed were given copies of their transcripts for review and amendments. The project was approved by Middlesex University's School of Law, Sociology, Criminology and Social Science Ethics Sub-Committee, and was in accordance with the British Society of Criminology's Code of Ethics (BSC 2015).

Each participant was given a pseudonym, as outlined in Table 9.1 below, which also includes a description of their disability or impairment. As can be seen, participants had a variety of impairments and conditions, in line with the pan-disability design of the study. Whilst not representative due to the small sample size, this research provides an excellent exploratory study into victims' experiences in a marginalised area (Sin 2015; Tyson et al. 2015).

182 Jane Healy

Table 9.1 Female participant interview details

Participant number (of 12)	Pseudonym	Type of disability, impairment or condition	Interview in person (IP) or by phone/skype (PS)
1	Amy	Physical impairments and a wheelchair user	(IP)
2	Anne Marie	CDG, congenital disorder and physical impairments	(IP)
3	Ciara	Learning and physical disabilities	(IP)
5	Gemma	Sensory impairment (blind) and medical conditions	(PS)
6	Grace	Auto-immune disease with physical impairments and a wheelchair user	(PS)
7	Hayley	Medical conditions and genetic disorders	(PS)
9	Ruby	Cerebral Palsy, Asperger's Syndrome, PTSD and a brain tumour	(PS)
10	Sarah	Myalgic encephalomyelitis (ME), physical and mental health conditions	(IP)

Intersectionality as a research framework

Intersectionality within research involves the concurrent analyses of multiple, intersecting elements of identity, based on the principle that the impact on one form of subordination or oppression may differ depending on its combination with other potential elements. By considering multiple, intersecting layers of oppression or subordination, the impact of experiences of hate crime may vary. Liasidou (2013) and Balderston (2013a) advocate that intersectionality is a suitable method for interpreting experiences of disability hate crime, as it explores the way in which social and cultural categories inter-weave and compound forms of oppression and marginalisation. Although intersectionality is at odds with hate crime policy, it acknowledges overlapping 'layers', or elements of identity, but considers that traditional, simplistic analyses fail to make sense of the lived experience of victims (Horvath and Kelly 2007; Healy 2019). This approach offered the opportunity to acknowledge the contribution of more than one element of the participants' identities.

The research framework drew upon McCall's (2005, p. 1777) intracategorical approach to intersectional analysis with disability and/or impairment the 'master category' or element of identity to be researched. The participants had self-identified as disabled or impaired and it was a dominant category in their descriptions of themselves. This approach allowed for other categories of identity to emerge from the fieldwork though 'self-categorisation' (Crenshaw 1993). The process of categorisation is in itself an exercise of power and a method of resistance for members of subordinated groups. Self-categorisation subverts unequal power relations by enabling "some degree of agency that people can and do exert in the politics of naming" (Crenshaw 1993, p. 1297). Therefore the research instruments did not ask participants for their race, ethnicity or sexual orientation, for example, as the opportunity for those to be identified and prioritised through participants' *own* self-categorisation was available through this design.

Many participants self-identified through the interview process as having one or more categories of identity or "dimensions of social life" (McCall 2005, p. 1772) which were important to them. These included: a female participant who was a victim of both homophobic and disablist violence; female participants describing their experiences as both disablist and misogynist and many participants recounting experiences of discrimination because of their social status and disability combined. Drawing upon feminist scholarship in this way engaged with the problematic nature of researching the complex lives of others whilst avoiding essentialising them through potentially tokenistic, objectifying or voyeuristic means (Crenshaw 1993). It recognised their own categorisation, not just to the 'master category' of disability, but to other, equally valid elements of identity and social life. Through their narratives, participants naturally and authentically indicated how multiple dimensions of identity shaped their experiences.

A hate crime model informed by intersectionality therefore is able to engage on a multi-rather than single-strand level and reduce the "real risks of oversimplifying the victim experience" (Perry 2009, p. 9). There is limited evidence of the experiences of those who occupy multiple positions of inferiority, such as disabled women (Sin et al. 2009a), although there are some exceptions (Brownridge 2006; Barclay and Mulligan 2009; Williams and Tregidga 2014). This research contributes to the gap in knowledge.

Women's experiences of disability hate crimes

The majority of hate crimes reported by the female participants of this study involved verbal abuse, in or near their home, in public spaces and online. Offensive words or phrases were extremely common, supporting existing literature (Sin et al. 2009a; Piggott 2011; Scope 2011; Chakraborti et al. 2014a, 2014b). Some of the abuse was misogynistic and homophobic as well as disablist (see Healy 2019).

A significant finding from the interviews was that disabled women were more likely to be targeted by young men (in contrast to male participants who reported being targeted by both older women and men), and particularly groups of young men. Ciara, Grace, Gemma, Ruby and Amy all talk of groups of young men being typical perpetrators, supporting findings by Chakraborti et al. (2014b), Roberts et al. (2013) and Iganski et al. (2011). Further research is needed to explore this area in relation to disabled women as it suggests there is a contributing factor of misogyny at play here.

Additionally, three of the eight interview participants reported experiencing sexual abuse and assaults, including rape, from their abusers. Anne Marie was sexually assaulted at a bus stop by a stranger, when returning home from a class. Anne Marie reported her experience to the police and initially said they were helpful. However, she blamed herself for her victimisation. She says she was targeted "because I was vulnerable". She talked about how frequently strange men think she is 'drunk' because of her gait and say "stuff, horrible stuff" to her. Following the sexual assault, she introduced avoidance strategies to reduce her risk of future victimisation, changing her route home and she does not go out in the dark unless she has someone with her. This evidence of routine acceptance and management of risk aligns with Stanko's (1995) work on the ordinariness of violence for women. Additionally, these strategies and responses are typical of many disabled people's reactions to their victimisation, yet do nothing to address offender behaviour.

Sarah described two incidents of attempted rape and rape, the first when she was a young woman (dragged into a van), the second by a man she met on a social networking site more recently. She reports experiencing such poor response from the police in regards to her first experience that she chose not to report the rape later on. She describes a victim-blame culture by the police in response to her first experience, which left her feeling responsible for the later events. She says:

> the first time I've actually had to go and report anything and basically it was: we're not interested, they told my employers that I'd willingly got in the van – who then phoned up my parents and told them the same.

In her interview, Sarah described her experiences as being targeted because she was a disabled *woman*. Similarly, Ruby was assaulted as a teenager, which she believed was as a direct consequence of her being targeted because of her disability, and because her perpetrator knew she would not be believed. Additionally, she was later threatened with sexual assault as a method of harassment and abuse from a group of young men who lived near her home, with language indicative of gendered sexual violence. She describes how: "the kids threatened to rape and stab me" and their language included: "I'm gonna stick you with my great big 12 inch cock, I'm gonna stab you..." and "I'm gonna stab you up the arse".

The stories by these participants support the literature regarding sexual assault as a method of disability hate crime against women (for example, Barclay and Mulligan 2009; Coleman et al. 2013; Sherry 2013b). It is disappointing but not surprising that only one of the participant's reports, Anne Marie's, was taken seriously by police although the perpetrator was not identified or charged. On the contrary, Sarah's early experience of attempted rape and sexual violence was laughed at by police officers at the time when she reported it, and directly contributed to her decision not to report a very violent rape to police at a later date. Ruby was also told by the police to ignore the 'anti-social behaviour' she was experiencing, which was in actuality disability hate crime.

Although this research presented here focuses predominantly on the narrative interviews conducted with disabled women, it must be noted that disabled women in focus groups also contributed evidence of their experiences of sexual violence. A wheelchair user described how she was sexually assaulted by the warden of her building and had no means to escape because of the nature of her impairment (as mentioned above, it is not unusual for disabled people to be targeted by those in a position of trust).

Research by Chakraborti et al. (2014a) reported that 22% of their disabled respondents had experienced sexual violence, suggesting that this is a dominant method of disability hate crime. None of the survey participants in this research selected "sexual assault" as an experience of hate crime, yet these three participants all completed the survey. They openly disclosed these experiences during the interview; their stories emerged through the narrative interview process itself. This suggests that reliance on a survey method alone could fail to capture these experiences, and the benefits of using a qualitative approach to research. It also suggests there could be a significant underestimation of sexual violence and assaults in research surveys.

Intersections of misogyny, disability and hatred

Mason-Bish (2015, p. 25) highlights the frustration that can be felt when a victim experiences more than one form of victimisation, such as the experiences reported by disabled women here. She urges policy to "understand the fluidity of identity and the multiple ways in which prejudice and violence might be experienced". This is compounded in the case of gender and disability as misogyny is not a recognised form of hate crime, despite evidence supporting its introduction (Gill and Mason-Bish 2013). An inability to recognise the increased risk disabled women face as a result of their gender could result in a failure to recognise, label and respond to experiences as hate crimes. Consequently, victims may not report their experiences as they fear they will not be recognised and respected as such, as in Sarah's experiences described above. Sherry (2013b) advocates for greater recognition of rape as a gendered hate crime, without which he argues disabled women may lack recognition or identification as hate crime victims. The evidence here provides support for this.

Further evidence for this comes from one of the key practitioners who was interviewed in another part of the study. Emily (a housing officer) cited a number of cases of domestic violence where disability was a contributing factor to the victimisation. Because of the constraints of their in-house recording system, cases can only be logged within one primary classification. As such a number of her cases are logged as domestic violence rather than as disability-related abuse, and potential hate crimes. Emily emphasises that regardless of how it is logged, her priority is to address *all* contributing elements to her residents' victimisation and support will target multiple areas, according to need. However, although she concedes that disability is potentially involved in several cases, Emily did not appear to consider the increased risk that *disabled women* are placed at in terms of domestic and interpersonal violence.

This complimentary intersection of gender with disability was therefore a particularly strong theme within the research findings. This is not unexpected, given the argument that disabled women face double disadvantage through both gender and disability, making them particularly vulnerable to sexual violence and exploitation (Brownridge 2006; Balderston 2013a; Sherry 2013b). Many studies show that disabled women are at greater risk of victimisation than disabled men (for example, Balderston 2013a; Coleman et al. 2013; McCarthy 2017). Indeed, female survey respondents reported being threatened and bullied more than men, as well as reporting more name-calling, verbal abuse and physical assaults. Thus, women reported more types of violence and abuse than their male counterparts. This study contributes to the literature around women's increased risk of victimisation.

In an attempt to understand why women reported more victimisation than men, Waxman (1991) describes how disabled women are labelled as morally suspect and more dangerous than disabled men because disability is perceived as preventing women from embracing traditional female roles such as nurturing and sexual desirability. In addition, sexual stereotypes of women exist around the assumed passivity of disabled people and of women generally; dependency, vulnerability and frailty are dominant, and women are represented in negative and passive ways (Hague et al. 2008; Barclay and Mulligan 2009; Murray and Powell 2009).

Consequently, disabled women in this study resorted to blaming themselves for their victimisation:

"I'm quite vulnerable" (Grace)
"I was vulnerable" (Anne Marie)
"I've very vulnerable" (Gemma)

This evidence shows how the experience of disability is compounded when combined with gender (Clement et al. 2011; Coleman et al. 2013). The introduction of intersectionality as a methodological framework here illustrated this, and many academics agree that consideration of hate crime on an individual strand basis fails to recognise the interplay of these elements of identity with other social and situational characteristics (Walters and Hoyle 2012; Chakraborti 2015; Chakraborti and Garland 2015; Mason-Bish 2015). Researching hate crime through a wider lens, beyond simple constructions of identity, acknowledges the roles other factors have to play in experiences of victimisation.

Efforts to tackle disability hate crime may benefit from a critical examination of the lessons generated from discourse on violence against women. Balderston (2013a) proposes that there is a blurring between violence in private spaces and hate crime in public spaces, demonstrating how experiences may be misconstrued as domestic violence in the home but hate crime externally. Reframing this violence against women as a human rights issue has placed individual experiences within a wider pattern of inequality, reflecting a broader, gendered, construct of society and requiring cultural change. Barclay and Mulligan (2009) propose that lessons can be drawn for tackling targeted violence against disabled people, such as conceptualising targeted violence against women as a cause and consequence of their inequality. Whilst conceding that there are differences between groups, areas of commonality between constructions of violence against women and hate crimes include the structural context of inequality and its link to violence as part of a wider pattern of behaviour that reinforces such inequality. However, as Murray and Powell (2009) warn in their research on domestic violence, tensions can arise between situating responses within a discourse on rights to participate equally in society, and framing women as vulnerable and in need of protection. The same argument can be applied to disability issues. Protectionist discourses have tended to pathologise women (and disabled people) as vulnerable or helpless victims in order to legitimise policy responses. A protectionist response is one that emphasises 'care' rather than empowerment, contributing to the cultural expectation that disabled people are dependent and ultimately inherently vulnerable and in need of protection (Edwards 2014; Sin 2014).

Within the policy field of Violence Against Women and Girls, Sexual Assault Referral Centres (SARC) bring a bespoke service together for victims of sexual violence and assault. Evidence has shown how officers trained in sexual offences investigation techniques (SOIT) in combination with SARC services have produced increases in victim confidence, and improved reporting and attrition rates, supported by successful cost-benefit and service-user evaluations (Lovett et al. 2004; van Staden and Lawrence 2010; Angiolini 2015; Hohl and Stanko 2015). Furthermore, when SARC service users report being treated with care and respect, they report that negative outcomes, such as court acquittals, have a less devastating impact (Lovett et al. 2004; van Staden and Lawrence 2010; Angiolini 2015; Hohl and Stanko 2015). A holistic hate crime response can learn lessons from such specialisms, which highlight the positive impacts of successful multi-agency work (Robinson et al. 2008). Unfortunately, without the confidence to report disablist sexual violence, disabled women and girls may be unable to avail themselves of these services. If a response to these experiences is to categorise experiences as either sexual violence *or* hate crimes, victims will receive different support via different pathways. A common understanding of the nuances of experiences of disability hate crime is therefore essential for building trust. However, the onus is also on the criminal justice system to identify and collect evidence to support victims' or community members' perceptions of hate crimes, whether they are motivated by disablism or misogyny. The sustained and repeated nature of the victimisation reported by these participants, combined with a lack of response by criminal justice agencies, has significant psychological effects on victims. There is a need to evaluate how all forces are responding to disability hate crime and establish clearer protocols and policies that reflect an improved understanding of disability, embedded within the social model, and a recognition of the increased risk disabled women face in particular. Currently, there is little consensus across forces in their approach to hate crime investigations however, on the basis of this evidence, criminal justice agencies must develop more proactive, specialist and knowledgeable approaches to disability hate crime.

Conclusion: the perfect storm

This chapter has shown how disabled women experience distinct forms of hate crime when compared to disabled men, and women. It has identified increasing evidence of a pattern of sexual assault and violence as gendered hate crime, and yet misogyny is not a recognised hate strand at present. The evidence demonstrates how experiences of disability hate crime by female victims can be conceptualised within wider structural patterns of violence against women but it requires greater awareness and better training and recognition of those experiences. Victims are targeted for being disabled *and* female, compounding their experiences and resulting in a reluctance to report to police and a willingness to blame themselves.

Challenges for researchers and practitioners remain: how best can we interpret, understand and respond to experiences of disabled women as victims, whether of hate crime, or any other crime, without contributing to a victim-blame or protectionist narrative. The challenge for academics is to continue to produce evidence-based research such as this which locates and exposes the holistic experiences of disabled people in context. The challenge for government is to acknowledge these marginalised voices of disabled people within policy frameworks and to provide them with an opportunity to be heard and influence change. The challenge for criminal justice agencies is to see beyond a single label or strand.

Notes

1 This was the definition used in the study, and is similar to that presented within the Equality Act 2003 and the World Health Organization (2003) classification of health and disability and a Social Model approach (Miller et al. 2006).
2 This research recognises that violence is not simply physical but also encompasses sexual, emotional, psychological violence and neglect and financial abuse. See Boyle (2019) for a discussion on the problematic use of language in researching violence against women.

References

Aldridge, J., 2014. Working with vulnerable groups in social research: dilemmas by default and design. *Qualitative Research*, 14(1), pp. 112–130. DOI: 10.1177/ 1468794112455041.

Angiolini, E., 2015. Report of the independent review into the investigation and prosecution of rape in London. 30 April 2015. London. Available at: https://www.cps.gov.uk/sites/default/files/documents/publications/dame_elish_angiolini_rape_review_2015.pdf [Accessed 10 May 2021].

Balderston, S., 2013a. Victimized again? Intersectionality and injustice in disabled women's lives after hate crime and rape. In: Texler Segal, M. and Demos, V., eds. *Gendered Perspectives on Conflict and Violence: Part A (Advances in Gender Research, Volume 18A)*. Bingley: Emerald Group Publishing Limited, pp. 17–51.

Balderston, S., 2013b. After disablist hate crime: which interventions really work to resist victimhood and build resilience with survivors? In: Roulstone, A. and Mason-Bish, H., eds. *Disability, Hate Crime and Violence*. London: Routledge, pp. 177–192.

Balderston, S. and Roebuck, E., 2010. *Empowering People to Tackle Hate Crime: Trans Women and Disabled People Working together with Victim Services in North East England*. Manchester: EHRC; Gay Advice Darlington and Durham; Victim Support; Vision Sense.

Barclay, H. and Mulligan, D., 2009. Tackling violence against women – lessons for efforts to tackle other forms of targeted violence. *Safer Communities*, 8(4), pp. 43–50. DOI: 10.1108/17578043200900037.

Beazley, S., Moore, M. and Benzie, D., 1997. Involving disabled people in research: a study of inclusion in environmental activities. In: Barnes, C. and Mercer G., eds. *Doing Disability Research*. Leeds: The Disability Press, pp. 142–157.

Boeckmann, R.J. and Turpin-Petrosino, C., 2002. Understanding the harm of hate crime. *Journal of Social Issues*, 58, pp. 207–225. DOI: 10.1111/1540-4560.00257.

Boyle, K., 2019. What's in a name? Theorising the Inter-relationships of gender and violence. *Feminist Theory*, 20(1), pp. 19–36. DOI: 10.1177/1464700118754957.

British Society of Criminology (BSC), 2015. Statement of ethics [online]. Available at: http://www.britsoccrim.org/documents/BSCEthics2015.pdf [Accessed 26 October 2017].

Brownridge, D.A., 2006. Partner violence against women with disabilities: prevalence, risk, and explanations. *Violence against Women*, 12(9), pp. 805–822. DOI: 10.1177/1077801206292681.

Bruder, C. and Kroese, B, 2005. The efficacy of interventions designed to prevent and protect people with intellectual disabilities from sexual abuse: a review of the literature. *Journal of Adult Protection*, 7(2), pp. 13–27. DOI: 10.1108/14668203200500009.

Cameron, L. and Murphy, J., 2006. Obtaining consent to participate in research: the issues involved in including people with a range of learning and communication disabilities. *British Journal of Learning Disabilities*, 35, pp. 113–120. DOI: 10.1111/j.1468-3156.2006.00404.x.

Chakraborti, N., 2015. Framing the boundaries of hate crime. In: Hall, N., Corb, A., Giannasi, P. and Grieve, J.G.D., eds. *The Routledge International Handbook on Hate Crime*. Oxon: Routledge, pp. 13–23.

Chakraborti, N. and Garland, J., 2009. *Hate Crime: Impact, Causes, Consequences*. London: Sage.

Chakraborti, N. and Garland, J., 2015. *Hate Crime: Impact, Causes and Responses*. 2nd ed. London: Sage.

Chakraborti, N., Garland, J. and Hardy, S.-J., 2014a. *The Leicester Hate Crime Project: Findings and Conclusions*. University of Leicester [online]. Available at:

https://www2.le.ac.uk/departments/criminology/hate/documents/fc-full-report [Accessed 18 August 2016].
Chakraborti, N., Garland, J. and Hardy, S.-J., 2014b. *The Leicester Hate Crime Project: Briefing Paper1: Disablist Hate Crime: Victims' Perspectives.* University of Leicester [online]. Available at: https://www2.le.ac.uk/departments/criminology/hate/documents/bp1-disablist-hate-crime/view [Accessed 18 August 2016].
Clement, S. et al., 2011. Disability hate crime and targeted violence and hostility: a mental health and discrimination perspective. *Journal of Mental Health*, 20(3), pp. 219–225. DOI: 10.3109/09638237.2011.579645.
Coleman, N., Sykes, W. and Walker, A., 2013. *Crime and Disabled People: Baseline Statistical Analysis of Measures from the Formal Legal Inquiry into Disability-Related Harassment.* Research Report 90. London: EHRC/Independent Social Research.
Crenshaw, K., 1993. Mapping the margins: intersectionality, identity politics, and violence against women of color. *Stanford Law Review*, 43(6), pp. 1241–1299. DOI: 10.2307/1229039.
Cunningham, S. and Drury, S., 2002. *Access All Areas: A Guide for Community Safety Partnerships on Working More Effectively with Disabled People.* London: Nacro.
Dupont, I., 2008. Beyond doing no harm: a call for participatory action research with marginalized populations in criminological research. *Critical Criminology*, 16, pp. 197–207. DOI: 10.1007/s10612-008-9055-7.
Edwards, C., 2014. Pathologising the victim: law and the construction of people with disabilities as victims of crime in Ireland. *Disability & Society*, 29(5), pp. 685–698. DOI: 10.1080/09687599.2013.844099.
Emerson, E. and Roulstone, A., 2014. Developing an evidence base for violent and disablist hate crime in Britain: findings from the life opportunities survey. *Journal of Interpersonal Violence*, 29(17), pp. 3086–3104. DOI: 10.1177/0886260514534524.
Gill, A.K. and Mason-Bish, H., 2013. Addressing violence against women as a form of hate crime: limitations and possibilities. *Feminist Review*, 105(1), pp. 1–20. DOI: 10.1057/fr.2013.17.
Hague, G. et al., 2008. *Making the Links: Disabled Women and Domestic Violence. Final Report.* Women's Aid. Available at: https://www.womensaid.org.uk/wp-content/uploads/2015/12/Disabled-women-Making_the_Links_-_full_length_report_large_print11.pdf [Accessed 10 May 2021].
Healy, J., 2019. Thinking outside the box: intersectionality as a hate crime research framework. *Papers from the British Criminology Conference*, 19, pp. 60–83. Available at: https://www.britsoccrim.org/pbcc2019/.
Healy, J.C., 2020. 'It spreads like a creeping disease': experiences of victims of disability hate crimes in austerity Britain. *Disability and Society*, 35(2), pp. 176–200. DOI: 10.1080/09687599.2019.1624151.
Hohl, K. and Stanko, E.A., 2015. Complaints of rape and the criminal justice system: fresh evidence on the attrition problem in England and Wales. *European Journal of Criminology*, 12(3), pp. 324–341. DOI: 10.1177/1477370815571949.
Home Office, 2020. *Hate Crime, England and Wales 2019/20. Statistical Bulletin 29/20.* Available at: https://www.gov.uk/government/statistics/hate-crime-england-and-wales-2019-to-2020 [Accessed 1 December 2020].
Horvath, M.A.H. and Kelly, L., 2007. *From the Outset: Why Violence Should be a Priority for the Commission for Equality and Human Rights.* A briefing paper

by the End Violence against Women Campaign and the Roddick Foundation. Available at: https://www.equallyours.org.uk/wp-content/uploads/2007/06/From-the-outset-.pdf [Accessed 10 May 2021].

Hughes, K. et al., 2012. Prevalence and risk of violence against adults with disabilities: a systematic review and meta-analysis of observational studies. *The Lancet*, 379(9826), pp. 1621–1616. DOI: 10.1016/S0140-6736(11)61851-5.

Iganski, P. et al., 2011. *Rehabilitation of Hate Crime Offenders*. Scotland: Equality and Human Rights Commission.

Landman, R.A., 2014. "A counterfeit friendship": mate crime and people with learning disabilities. *Journal of Adult Protection*, 16(6), pp. 355–366. DOI: 10.1108/JAP-10-2013-0043.

Liasidou, A., 2013. Intersectional understandings of disability and implications for a social justice reform agenda in education policy and practice. *Disability and Society*, 28(3), pp. 299–312. DOI: 10.1080/09687599.2012.710012.

Lovett, J., Regan, L. and Kelly, L., 2004. *Sexual Assault Referral Centres: Developing Good Practice and Maximizing Potentials*. Home Office Research Study 285. London: Home Office.

Macdonald, S., Donovan, C. and Clayton, J., 2017. The disability bias: understanding the context of hate in comparison with other minority populations. *Disability and Society*, 12(4), pp. 483–499. DOI: 10.1080/09687599.2017.1304206.

Magowan, P., 2003. Nowhere to run, nowhere to hide: domestic violence and disabled women. *Safe: Domestic Abuse Quarterly*, 5, pp. 15–18.

Marley, J.A. and Buila, S., 2001. Crimes against people with mental illness: types, perpetrators, and influencing factors. *Social Work*, 46(2), pp. 115–124. DOI: 10.1093/sw/46.2.115.

Mason, G., 2005a. Hate crime and the image of the stranger. *British Journal of Criminology*, 45(6), pp. 837–859. DOI: 10.1093/bjc/azi016.

Mason, G., 2005b. Being hated: stranger or familiar? *Social and Legal Studies*, 14(4), pp. 585–605. DOI: 10.1177/0964663905057596.

Mason-Bish, H., 2013. Conceptual issues in the construction of disability hate crime. In: Roulstone, A. and Mason-Bish, H., eds. *Disability, Hate Crime and Violence*. London: Routledge, pp. 11–24.

Mason-Bish, H., 2015. Beyond the silo: rethinking hate crime and intersectionality. In: Hall, N., Corb, A., Giannasi, P. and Grieve, J.G.D., eds. *The Routledge International Handbook on Hate Crime*. Oxon: Routledge, pp. 24–33.

McCall, L., 2005. The complexity of intersectionality. *Signs*, 30(3), pp. 1771–1800. DOI: 10.1086/426800.

McCarthy, M., 2017. 'What kind of abuse is him spitting in my food?': reflections on the similarities between disability hate crime, so-called 'mate' crime and domestic violence against women with intellectual disabilities. *Disability and Society*, 32(4), pp. 595–600. DOI: 10.1080/09687599.2017.1301854.

Miller, P., Gillinson, S. and Huber, J., 2006. *Disablist Britain: Barriers to Independent Living for Disabled People in 2006*. London: Scope/Demos.

Murray, S. and Powell, A., 2009. "What's the problem?" Australian public policy constructions of domestic and family violence. *Violence against Women*, 15(5), pp. 532–552. DOI: 10.1177/1077801209331408.

Nind, M., 2017. The practical wisdom of inclusive research. *Qualitative Research*, 17(3), pp. 278–288. DOI: 10.1177/1468794117708123.

Perry, B., 2009. The sociology of hate: theoretical approaches. In: Levin, B., ed. *Hate Crimes Volume I: Understanding and Defining Hate Crime*. Westport, CT: Praeger, 2009, pp. 55–76.

Perry, J., 2004. Is justice taking a beating? *Community Care*, 1–7 April 2004, pp. 44–45. Available at: https://www.communitycare.co.uk/2004/04/02/is-justice-taking-a-beating/.

Perry, J., 2008. The 'perils' of an identity politics approach to the legal recognition of harm. *Liverpool Law Review*, 29, pp. 19–36. DOI: 10.1007/s10991-008-9034-9.

Petersilia, J., 2000. Invisible victims: violence against persons with developmental disabilities. *Human Rights*, 27(1), pp. 9–13.

Pettitt, B. et al., 2013. *At Risk, Yet Dismissed: The Criminal Victimisation of People with Mental Health Problems*. London: Victim Support and Mind.

Piggott, L., 2011. Prosecuting disability hate crime: a disabling solution. *People, Place and Policy Online*, 5(1), pp. 25–34. DOI: 10.3351/ppp.0005.0001.000.

Richardson, K. et al., 2016. "I felt that I deserved it" – experiences and implications of disability hate crime. *Tizard Learning Disability Review*, 21(2), pp. 80–88. DOI: 10.1108/TLDR-03-2015-0010.

Roberts, C. et al., 2013. *Understanding Who Commits Hate Crime and Why They Do It*. Social Research Report Number 38/2013. Merthyr Tydfil: Welsh Government.

Robinson, A., Hudson, K. and Brookman, F., 2008. Multi-agency work on sexual violence: challenges and prospects identified from the implementation of a Sexual Assault Referral Centre (SARC). *The Howard Journal*, 47(4), pp. 411–428. DOI: 10.1111/j.1468-2311.2008.00531.x.

Roulstone, A. and Sadique, K., 2013. Vulnerable to misinterpretation: disabled people, 'vulnerability', hate crime and the fight for legal recognition. In: Roulstone, A. and Mason-Bish, H., eds. *Disability, Hate Crime and Violence*. London: Routledge, pp. 25–39.

Scope, 2011. Deteriorating attitudes towards disabled people [online]. Available at: http://www.scope.org.uk/news/attitudes-towards-disabled-people-survey [Accessed 19 May 2011].

Shapland, J. and Hall, M., 2007. What do we know about the effects of crime on victims? *International Review of Victimology*, 14(2), pp. 175–217. DOI: 10.1177/026975800701400202.

Sherry, M., 2013a. International perspectives on disability hate crime. In: Roulstone, A. and Mason-Bish, H., eds. *Disability, Hate Crime and Violence*. London: Routledge, pp. 80–91.

Sherry, M., 2013b. Feminist reflections on disability hate crime. Gendered perspectives on conflict and violence, Part A. *Advances in Gender Research*, 18(A), pp. 53–66.

Sin, C.H., 2013. Making disablist hate crime visible: addressing the challenges of improving reporting. In: Roulstone, A. and Mason-Bish, H., eds. *Disability, Hate Crime and Violence*. London: Routledge, pp. 147–165.

Sin, C.H., 2014. Using a 'layers of influence' model to understand the interaction of research, policy and practice in relation to disablist hate crime. In: Chakraborti, N. and Garland, J., eds. *Responding to Hate Crime: The Case for Connecting Policy and Research*. Bristol: Policy Press, pp. 99–112.

Sin, C.H., 2015. Hate crime against people with disabilities. In: Hall, N., Corb, A., Giannasi, P. and Grieve, J.G.D., eds. *The Routledge International Handbook on Hate Crime*. Oxon: Routledge, pp. 193–206.

Sin, C.H. et al., 2009a. *Disabled People's Experiences of Targeted Violence and Hostility.* EHRC Research Report 21. EHRC and Office for Public Management. Available at: https://www.equalityhumanrights.com/sites/default/files/research_report_21_disabled_people_s_experiences_of_targeted_violence_and_hostility.pdf [Accessed 10 May 2021].

Sin, C.H. et al., 2009b. Disabled victims of targeted violence, harassment and abuse: barriers to reporting and seeking redress. *Safer Communities*, 8(4), pp. 27–34.

Sin, C.H., Sheikh, S. and Khanna, M., 2012. Police readiness for tackling hate crime against people with learning disabilities – areas for improvement and examples of good practice. *Safer Communities*, 11(3), pp. 145–153.

Sobsey, D. and Doe, T., 1991. Patterns of sexual abuse and assault. *Sexuality and Disability*, 9(1), pp. 243–259. DOI: 10.1007/BF01102395.

Stanko, E., 1995. *Everyday Violence: How Women and Men Experience Sexual and Physical Danger.* London: Pandora.

Stanko, E., 2001. Reconceptualising the policing of hatred: confessions and worrying dilemmas of a consultant. *Law and Critique*, 12, pp. 309–29. DOI: 10.1023/A:1013784203982.

Thiara, R.K. and Hague, G., 2013. Disabled women and domestic violence: increased risk but fewer services. In: Roulstone, A. and Mason-Bish, H., eds. *Disability, Hate Crime and Violence.* London: Routledge, pp. 106–117.

Thomas, P., 2011. 'Mate crime': ridicule, hostility and targeted attacks against disabled people. *Disability and Society*, 26(1), pp. 107–111. DOI: 10.1080/09687599.2011.532590.

Thomas, P., 2013. Hate crime or mate crime: disablist hostility, contempt and ridicule. In: Roulstone, A. and Mason-Bish, H., eds. *Disability, Hate Crime and Violence.* London: Routledge, pp. 135–146.

Tyson, J., Giannasi, P. and Hall, N., 2015. Johnny come lately? The international and domestic policy context of disability hate crime. In: Shah, R. and Giannasi, P., eds. *Tackling Disability Discrimination and Disability Hate Crime.* London: Jessica Kingsley, pp. 20–35.

van Staden, L. and Lawrence, J., 2010. *A Qualitative Study of a Dedicated Sexual Assault Investigation Unit.* Research Report 48: Key Implications. London: Home Office.

Vincent, F. et al., 2009. Hate crime against people with disabilities: a baseline study of experiences in Northern Ireland [online]. Available from: http://www.ofmdfmni.gov.uk/hate_crime_against_people_with_disabilities__pdf_760kb_.pdf [Accessed 1 December 2020].

Walters, M. and Brown, R., 2016. *Preventing Hate Crime: Emerging Practices and Recommendations for the Improved Management of Criminal Justice Interventions.* Sussex Crime Research Centre and INHS. Available at: http://sro.sussex.ac.uk/id/eprint/64925/1/Interventions%20for%20Hate%20Crime%20-%20FINAL%20REPORT_2.pdf [Accessed 10 May 2021].

Walters, M. and Hoyle, C., 2012. Exploring the everyday world of hate victimization through community mediation. *International Review of Victimology*, 18(1), pp. 7–24. DOI: 10.1177/0269758011422472.

Waxman, B.F., 1991. Hatred: the unacknowledged dimension in violence against disabled people. *Sexuality and Disability*, 9(3), pp. 185–199. DOI: 10.1007/BF01102392.

Williams, M.L. and Tregidga, J., 2014. Hate crime victimization in Wales: Psychological and physical impacts across seven hate crime victim types. *British Journal of Criminology*, 54(5), pp. 946–967. DOI: 10.1093/bjc/azu04.

World Health Organization (WHO), 2003. *ICF Checklist Version 2.1a Clinician Form for International Classification of Functioning, Health and Disability.* Geneva: WHO.

World Health Organization (WHO), 2018. *Addressing Violence against Women: Key Achievements and Priorities.* WHO/RHR/18.18. Switzerland.

10 Trans identities, cisgenderism and hate crime

Michaela Rogers

Introduction

Globally, recognition of the human rights and equality concerns for trans and non-binary people is in the nascent stage of being addressed through research, policy and practice. Despite this, there is a growing evidence-base that highlights the high levels of discrimination, marginalisation and victimisation that trans and non-binary people experience. This chapter will explore everyday experiences of hate crime and violence in trans and non-binary people's lives. The concept of cisgenderism (a prejudicial ideology which is rooted to notions of gender normativity) will be employed as a lens to explore the ways in which transphobic hate crime manifests (Ansara and Hegarty 2011, 2014; Rogers 2017a, 2017b). Informing this discussion, a conceptual framework will be employed which is underpinned by Serano's (2007, 2013, 2016) thesis which illuminates the workings of gender normativity as instrumental in sustaining different forms of sexism and cisgender privilege (the power and privilege utilised by people who identify in a gender corresponding to that which was assigned at birth). These ideas inform an understanding of trans and non-binary people's exposure to hate, violence and victimisation.

The chapter begins by clarifying key terminology in the theoretical framework employed throughout. This includes gender, trans, non-binary and cisgender. This is followed by a discussion that explains key concepts (cisgenderism, transphobia, transmisogyny) helping to elucidate the ways in which trans and non-binary people experience inclusion/exclusion and belonging/non-belonging, as well as experiences of hate, violence and victimisation. Using the example of ongoing conflict between some feminists (specifically, Trans-Exclusionary Radical Feminists (TERFs)) and queer activists and scholars (as well as other feminists who identify as trans allies), this chapter will illustrate how prejudicial ideologies (namely, cisgenderism) operate in contemporary times (e.g. through social media) to maintain the phenomena of hate, violence and victimisation. The chapter ends by providing a snapshot of transphobic hate crime in the UK.

DOI: 10.4324/9781003023722-10

Theorising gender, trans and non-binary identities

Gender is multi-dimensional. It can be articulated in different ways. For example, gender can be understood on a micro-basis as an aspect of one's identity or, on a macro-level, gender can be conceived as a form of social classification or organising device which categorises and orders people according to their behaviours and biological, sexed bodies (Monro 2007; Rogers and Ahmed 2017). Whilst in scholarship it is generally understood that gender is socially constructed, and relates to a person's sense of self as a gendered person and that this is separate from sex (which is signified by a body's biological characteristics), the distinctions between gender and sex can still be opaque and entwined (see the discussion below on theoretical paradigms). In this chapter, gender is considered to be a form of identification as people can be ascribed an identity by others (external ascription) or adopt a gender identity (internal identification) (Jenkins 2000). In addition, gender is an aspect of positionality which shapes social location (Rogers and Ahmed 2017). The notion of positionality is helpful as it combines an understanding social positioning (as process, practice or action) as well as social position (as outcome). A consideration of positionality requires an analysis of people and everyday experience not in terms of fixed identities, but relative to an individual's location across shifting networks of relationships (Anthias 2002). Such relationships are imbued with varying degrees of power and privilege and can, therefore, provide the conditions for practices of hate, violence and victimisation in public and personal life.

Two processes of identification are indisputably integral to this analysis, those of similarity and difference. Jenkins (2014, p. 22) comments on similarity and difference claiming that 'neither makes sense without the other, and identification requires both'. Similarity and difference function through the existence of borders and another process: belonging (and its opposite, non-belonging). Such borders and the processes of belonging do not work independently, both are bound up with the intersecting workings of similarity and difference. In the case of gender identity, the processes of similarity and difference largely call upon an understanding of gender as binary (that is, it offers two options; man or woman) or, in the case of non-binary gender, as something that is other. The term *other*, or *othering*, refers to the attitude towards or treatment of a person (or group) as fundamentally different from and alien to oneself (Wilkinson and Kitzinger 1996); this has clear relevance in an analysis of hate crime. These processes operate to shape experiences of gender, delimit the options for identification and affect an individual's experience of inclusion (belonging) or exclusion (non-belonging). Doan (2010, p. 635) names these processes as the 'tyranny of gender' using examples of how public space is ordered and controlled to reinforce the notion that binary gender is dominant and the norm.

Notwithstanding, there has been a notable expansion in the recognition of trans and non-binary identities throughout the last decade (LGBT Foundation 2017). This acknowledgement supports the premise that identity does not have a predetermined or fixed essence and has resulted in a paradigm shift moving beyond binary thinking towards an understanding of gender as a spectrum, or continuum, of indeterminate possibilities (see Rogers and Ahmed 2017). In this paradigm, 'trans' is an umbrella term to describe a person whose self-identification in relation to gender is different to that which was ascribed at birth. It can include those which align with the binary identities of man or woman including: trans woman; trans man; transsexual woman; transsexual man; Male to Female (MtF); Female to Male (FtM); a woman or man with a transgender history (Bachmann and Gooch 2018).

The term 'non-binary' is also a catchall term that falls under the trans umbrella. The term 'non-binary' distinguishes identities that do not conform to the man/woman binary including: queer; genderqueer; genderfluid; gender neutral; gender diverse and gender non-conforming (Bachmann and Gooch 2018). The identities listed here are merely indicative, not exhaustive, and it is important to acknowledge the multiplicity and complexity of trans identities (Dargie et al. 2014). Further, no attempt is made to further contextualise or homogenise these identities as Serano's (2016) ethical stance is taken in that experience of gender identity is subjective and should not be reducible to the biological or physical presentation of a sexed body nor to a set of social or cultural norms. Lastly, another identity term is important: that of 'cisgender', or 'cis', which describes a person whose self-identity conforms to their gender assigned at birth (Schilt and Westbrook 2009).

The increased global recognition of trans identities is salient because in terms of belonging, or not belonging, often this entails identifying with and, importantly, being accepted by a particular community or group (May 2013). The possibilities and restrictions resulting from the processes of individual identification, external ascription and collective belonging are particularly germane for minority groups. This is because the processes of belonging, or not belonging, are influenced by a range of structural, systemic and physical conditions outside of individual identification including norms, values, law, economics and spatial dimensions to name a few. Across academic disciplines, research has been undertaken to explore these dynamics of gender in relation to trans and non-binary identities. For example, geographic scholarship has found that most public space is constructed as gender normative and heterosexual, and, more importantly, the fear of violence is a key aspect of the gendering of this space (Pain 1997; Lubitow et al. 2017). There is an important link between this scholarship and other disciplinary research which suggests that violence and harassment are commonplace for trans and non-binary people in public spaces (Grant et al. 2011; Walters et al. 2017; GEO 2018).

Understanding cisgenderism and related concepts

All societies and communities have dominant norms, values, traditions and ideologies that underpin social structures, systems and institutions. In relation to gender, more specifically, most societies have integrated the notion that this is binary; that it is constituted by two possibilities, man or woman.

Globally, there is a shift in binary thinking about gender. However, we are at the beginning of this shift. As such, long-standing and normative structures persist and maintain systems of inequality and marginalisation by cataloguing and organising people through the processes of identification, assigning those who belong and those who do not (invoking recognition through similarity or difference). To understand this in relation to gender, it is useful to employ a conceptual lens which explores the predominance of binary thinking and helps to clarify the ways in which people who are trans or non-binary are catalogued as *different* in this process. The lens of cisgenderism enhances the analysis in this respect.

Cisgenderism is a prejudicial ideology akin to racism and sexism (Rogers 2017a, 2017b). It draws on the notion of gender normativity or cisnormativity. Both refer to the way in which social constructions of binary gender operate as the norm, positioning any divergence from this as abnormal (Blumer et al. 2013; Stryker and Aizura 2013). Gender or cisnormativity is undergirded by a set of ideas about cis identities as natural and fixed, as well as heterosexual coupling, marriage and procreation between a cis man and a cis woman as the norm (Schilt and Westerbrook 2009). Cisgenderism integrates these fixed notions of gender identities, practices and institutions positioning people who do not conform to this cisnormative ideal as deviant, unnatural and less than equal (Ansara and Hegarty 2011, 2014). By implication, the machinery of cisgenderism invokes notions of belonging (inclusion), or non-belonging (exclusion), and can underscore the means by which people are accepted or marginalised. Cisgenderism is strongly correlated with transphobia. Betcher (2007, p. 46) defines transphobia as: 'any negative attitudes (hatred, loathing, rage, or moral indignation) harboured towards trans people on the basis of enactments of [their] gender'.

By definition, transphobia involves the irrational hatred or disgust of people who identify under the trans umbrella and whose presentation and expression clearly reflects their trans or non-binary identity. This definition reflects the gender and cisnormative attitudes and beliefs that underpin cisgenderism; chiefly, that gender is biologically determined and fixed. It is important to acknowledge the difference between cisgenderism and transphobia; the latter can be thought of as active whereas cisgenderism can be either active or passive (an inadvertent act or phenomenon).

Scholarship on cisgenderism has departed from its initial position of theorising trans in opposition to cis, acknowledging the crude way that this homogenised a diverse set of identities that fall under the trans umbrella. This earlier work was focused too heavily at a micro-level centring on personal experiences (Serano 2016), rather than on collective experience or macro-level phenomena. It is now broadly accepted that cisgenderism operates at micro, meso and macro levels (across individual relationships, communities, institutions and social structures) (Ansara and Hegarty 2014; Rogers 2017a, 2017b). This wider lens enhances an analysis of trans people's experiences of hate, violence and victimisation across these levels (Rogers

2017b). This is because at any level, the processes of gender identification can promote the *norm*, identifying those who belong (cis people), positioning those people who identify outside of the *norm* and as not belonging (trans or non-binary people). These processes and effects are reinforced by dominant and authoritative cultural discourses (Ansara and Hegarty 2011) and can invisibilise, silence and invalidate trans and non-binary people's identities and experiences; a systemic practice known as 'trans-erasure' (Serano 2007, p. 189; Rogers 2017a, 2017b).

Throughout this edited collection, all the chapters centre women's experiences of hate crime and, as such, it is useful to end this section by considering trans women's experiences drawing from the conceptual ideas of Serano (2007) on transmisogyny (the intersection of transphobia and misogyny). First, Serano (2007, 2016) approaches an analysis of gender by discerning different forms of sexism operating in everyday life. She defines *traditional sexism* as the belief that men and masculinity are superior to women and femininity. She proposes another type as *oppositional sexism* (the idea that male and female are rigid, mutually exclusive gender categories) identifying its effects for trans and non-binary identities: the positioning of trans people in the lower strata of a gender hierarchy. When combined, these definitions have another effect: the positioning of trans women at the very bottom of this hierarchy. Serano (2007, 2013, 2016) provides several examples of transmisogyny to support her assertions, for example, highlighting the entrenched barriers to healthcare, social justice and safety. Supporting Serano's thesis, empirical research on public violence and hate crime shows that trans women and non-binary people who present as feminine are the most vulnerable to hate crime and violence (Lubitow et al. 2017; Matsuzaka and Koch 2019).

Cisgenderism, transphobia and hate crime

It is important to recognise the motivations that lie behind hate crime as cisgenderist action or speech can be either inadvertent or intentional (Ansara and Hegarty 2011, 2014). It is difficult to make or sustain an argument that unintended cisgenderism is hate-fuelled. When it is intentional, enactments of cisgenderism and transphobia can lead to the abuse and harassment of people who Hill and Willoughby (2011, pp. 533–534) label 'gender non-conformists' through the activity of hate-motivated violence they term 'gender bashing'. Witten and Eyler (1999, p. 461) describe transphobic hate crime as 'gender terrorism' which integrates an underlying motivation to maintain the systems of binary gender and patriarchy. Trans and non-binary people can experience transphobic hate-motivated crime or incidents as:

- physical, sexual and verbal abuse;
- sexual exploitation;
- financial and material abuse;

- misgendering (the intentional use of erroneous gendered language which does not reflect a person's self-identification);
- pathologising (the intended action of labelling or treatment of a person's self-identified gender, body, presentation and practice as abnormal or deviant)
- and other types of microaggressions (Ansara and Hegarty 2011, 2014; Nadal et al. 2014; Rogers 2017a, 2017b, 2020; Arayasirikul and Wilson 2019).

Hate-motivated behaviour and victimisation can take place at micro or meso levels and be compounded by macro-level policy, institutions or structures. For example, misgendering can occur on a micro-level as an individual can experience hate through the refusal by partners, family members, peers or strangers to use their chosen name and appropriate pronoun (instead persisting in using their former name and inaccurate gender pronouns). Hate-motivated behaviour and victimisation can result from the differences or difficulties in an individual's ability to pass in their chosen gender (Chakraborti and Garland 2015). It may also differ in terms of the quality and degree of violence and victimisation for trans men, trans women and non-binary people (Doan 2007).

At a meso (community or organisational) level, there is some evidence to show that trans and non-binary people's experiences of hate victimisation is likely to be exacerbated when they pursue legal redress with some studies suggesting that police officers frequently expose trans victims to direct and secondary victimisation (Turner et al. 2009). This argument can be scaled up into a macro-level analysis of the police as an institution which is tied to particularly rigid notions of gender identity. Walters et al. (2017, p. 8) observe that 'not only have the police represented male officers as traditionally masculine, powerful, and tough, but it has also, as an institution, been active in policing the gender of others'. Various studies have suggested that the gendered nature of policing in this regard has resulted in the reinforcement of entrenched power inequalities and resulted in trans and non-binary people's view of policing as unhelpful and even dangerous (Perry and Dyck 2014).

Whilst small, there is a growing body of literature which illuminates the ways in which trans people experience misgendering and pathologising as microaggressions (Nadal et al. 2014). These are not rare occurrences, but permeate routine life for marginalised groups and are found within everyday interactions (Thurber and DiAngelo 2018). Microaggressions include verbal, nonverbal and symbolic communications, such as derogatory remarks or terminology, facial expressions, body language or environmental slights that communicate hostility or offence (Sue 2010; Arayasirikul and Wilson 2019). Microaggressions serve to denigrate, humiliate and exclude people (Thurber and DiAngelo 2018). Whilst not inherently 'violent', microaggressions can be experienced as a form of hate-motivated action or speech.

When cisgenderism undergirds microaggressions, hate-motivated behaviour or speech, the effects can be wide-ranging. On an individual level, this can include physical injury, stress and stress-related physical and mental ill health, emotional and psychological harm, loss of relationships, loss of status, loss of employment, economic and/or housing issues. Fundamentally, cisgenderist and transphobic hate crimes marginalise and delegitimise people's self-identification in terms of gender and their self-designation of the body as one thing or another (Rogers 2017b).

Of great concern, is the growing evidence-base detailing transphobic hate crime worldwide which has led to it being designated as a global public health concern (Jauk 2013). The Fundamental Rights Agency (FRA) (2015) conducted an extensive study of LGBT people's experiences publishing a report that specifically explored 'being trans in the European Union'. The analysis was drawn from survey data of 6,771 trans-identified respondents across 28 European member states and is illuminating:

> The results reveal that trans people face frequent infringements of their fundamental rights: discrimination, violence and harassment, all to a degree more intense than those suffered by other lesbian, gay or bisexual survey respondents.
> (FRA 2015, p. 1)

The study found that respondents experienced a high level of violence, hate-motivated attacks and harassment as one in three trans respondents (34%) experienced violence or was threatened with violence in the five years preceding the survey (FRA 2015). These experiences resulted in persistent feelings of fear and led some trans persons to avoid certain locations or disguise their gender identity when in public space. These experiences also led people to live in hiding and effectively exclude themselves from public life as far as possible. In addition to the experiences of hate and harassment, this self-directed isolation further curtailed their rights as citizens. This lack of visibility and presence, coupled with an absence of public awareness and cisgenderist attitudes, perpetuates the challenges of recognition and acceptance for trans and non-binary identities within public life (FRA 2015). This results in sustaining a circularity in which fear, bias and intolerance lead to hate-motivated action and speech.

It is important to note that just as gender identity overlaps with sexual orientation in studies of LGBT people's experiences, there are additional intersecting aspects of social location and difference that affect trans people's experiences of hate crime and violence (Lombardi 2009; Lubitow et al. 2017). Indeed, an intersectional analysis can illuminate how different forms of privilege intersect with notions of cisgenderism and transphobia to mitigate or aggravate experiences of hate crime. For example, Schilt (2010) has argued how whiteness, particularly for trans men, can lessen experiences of discrimination. In particular, there are several studies which illuminate the interlocking effects of cisgenderism and racism. These studies expose the degree to which minority ethnic trans people experience greater levels of violence, abuse, discrimination and hate crime than their white counterparts (Gordon and Pratama 2017; Jaime 2017; Vähäpassi 2019). Studies have shown that age is another intersecting social characteristic that can represent a risk factor in trans and non-binary young people's lives (Perry and Dyck 2014). A study by Perry and Dyck (2014, p. 50) found that trans and non-binary young people are regularly afflicted by a fear of victimisation which results in an almost constant "hyper-vigilance" in public space and multiple subjective definitions of what constitutes "safety" existed for young victims. Moreover, Perry and Dyck (2014) claimed that trans and non-binary young people are particularly vulnerable to a lack of safe space as their gender is policed in both public space by strangers and in the privacy of the home by family members.

Finally, it is important to consider the extremity of hate crime and the potential for fatalities. Trans-related homicides have received global attention with high profile cases brought to life through social media and other means. What unites these cases is the explicit presence of cisgenderism, transphobia and hate. For example, the murder of 21-year-old Brandon Teena, a trans man, has been widely reported and later the subject of the award-winning film, *Boys Don't Cry* (1999). In 1993 Teena was gang raped and later, along with two others, murdered in Humboldt, Nebraska. The attitudes and actions of the murderers, as well as the circumstances leading up to and after Teena's violent death, are all heavily imbued with transphobia and notions of gender/cisnormativity. Since Teena's murder there has been a continued growth in reporting of trans people's murder across the world. Overall, a significant proportion of these homicides are trans women of colour with the Washington Post claiming in 2019 that the "murder of black transgender women is becoming a crisis" (Dvorak 2019).

In recognition of the high levels of transphobic homicide across the world, the Trans Murder Monitoring Project (TMM) was established in 2009 to systematically monitor, collect and analyse homicide reports (TGEU 2020). At the same time, the International Day of Trans Remembrance was established in November 2009 and has been in operation ever since. Whilst the data collected by the TMM is alarming, it is not comprehensive for a multitude of reasons including: lack of reporting; problems in capturing worldwide data and reports and the problem that not all trans and non-binary people who are murdered are identified as trans or non-binary. In addition, the TMM notes that the classification of the murder of a trans or non-binary person as a hate crime is often difficult, due to a lack of information in the reports as well as the lack of national monitoring systems (TGEU 2020). Notwithstanding, the brutality of violence and contextual information in reported cases suggests that almost all can be designated as transphobic hate crimes (TGEU 2020). The monitoring of reported cases in the UK, between 2008 and 2018, has resulted in the identification of ten cases where trans or non-binary people have been murdered where transphobia was present (Transrespect 2018).

Theorising transphobic hate crime: queer theory and feminism

It is fruitful to consider the ways in which two theoretical perspectives have influenced scholarship pertaining to trans identity and experiences over the last few decades. These perspectives, queer theory and feminism, can be employed to analyse transphobic hate crime as both are concerned with, amongst things, identity, positionality and the body as well as issues of power and inequality. At its core, queer theory takes a deconstructionist approach to gender and sexuality. A queer paradigm assumes that both are fluid and transgress societal and cultural boundaries that exist and which sustain and promote normative gender and sexual identities. As such, queer theorising has utility in an analysis of trans identity and experience. Similarly, there are several scholars who have examined the connections and overlaps between trans and feminism advocating for an acknowledgement of the shared experiences of gender inequality, violence, discrimination and other rights-based issues (Monro 2005; Hines 2005, 2013). This theoretical and empirical work illuminates the value of a queer feminist theoretical framework which combines queer subject matters and feminist theory (Marinucci 2016).

Queer theorists question rigid gender and sexual categories, and their relationship, as well as the gender hierarchy that embeds such categories. Queer theory also problematises the ways in which normative ideas about sexed bodies are fixed to certain gender and sexual categories; for example, that most male bodies produce a particular type of heterosexual masculinity. It is important to note, however, that queer theorists do not treat gender and sexuality as inextricably entwined, nor equal; they privilege sexuality, analytically separating it out from gender (Taylor 2008).

These theoretical and conceptual ideas are presented earlier in this chapter and the theoretical and conceptual framework adopted in this discussion is similar in that both propose that gender is socially constructed, subject to transformation and not inevitably tied to the sexed, physical body. Similarly, queer theory is useful in illuminating the marginalisation and violence for those at the bottom of gender and sexual hierarchies and for those who do not identify with essentialist and rigid gender categories. However, there are limitations as queer theorising can reinforce the invisibilisation that occurs for trans people by the privileging of sexual orientation over gender identity and lack of recognition for individuals identifying as trans within the context of the binary identities of 'man' and 'woman'.

Similarly, feminist theorising has value in an analysis of trans, but there is a small, yet vocal, faction within feminist scholarship which has a contentious history with trans communities and scholarship. Lasting several decades, the work of this faction has resulted in a dogged hostility towards trans people: see, for example, Janice Raymond in the 1980s (Raymond 1979), Sheila Jeffreys in the 1990s (Jeffreys 1997) and Julie Bindel since the 2000s (Bindel 2007). These feminists have used essentialist perspectives to denigrate trans identities propagating ideas that such identities and practices problematically serve to reinforce patriarchy by mirroring normative gender identities and boundaries. Trans women have been criticised for reinforcing female gender stereotypes (adopting *uber* femininity) referencing the male privilege that they were born with. Similarly, trans men have been accused of seeking that male privilege and power. Both have had their gendered authenticity challenged.

The topic of public space has been at the forefront of these many arguments and exchanges. Subsequently, there is a well-documented history of trans women being ideologically and physically excluded from women-only events (particularly in the US) in addition to being positioned as outsiders more broadly at discursive and political levels (Hines 2013). Some radical feminists have argued for women-only spaces to be reserved for women born and raised female, that is, cis women (Gottschalk 2009). In 2008 the term Trans-Exclusionary Radical Feminist (TERF) emerged and has now become an established, yet controversial, aspect of the lexicon of feminist and trans movements and discourse (Hines 2019). The philosophical and political standpoint of TERFs can be mapped to the writings of Raymond, Jeffreys and Bindel. A more recent example of TERF derived transphobic discourse is exemplified by the emergence on Twitter, in 2014, of the hashtag #NoUnexpectedPenises. This appeared in defence of women-only spaces and the narrative accompanying #NoUnexpectedPenises argued vehemently that women-only spaces (namely public toilets, prisons, health services and refuges) should be reserved for cis women (Hines 2019). Hines (2019) illuminates the central thrust of #NoUnexpectedPenises as being tied to the specious notion that the presence of a penis is synonymous with violence. Phipps (2016, p. 31) articulates this: "the penis [is] imagined as a separate entity which is itself responsible for sexual violence rather than being, as Serano reminds us, merely someone's genital organ".

Phipps, Serano and Hines all illuminate the ways in which TERF narratives and activism are inflammatory and have potential to both reflect and induce hate that has been directed towards trans people, especially trans women. One of the ongoing claims by TERFs is that the inclusion of trans women, within female spaces, creates an unsafe environment for cis women, increasing their risk of violence. The irony is that the problem of public violence against trans people is considerably higher than that for cis people (Stotzer 2009). Matsuzaka and Koch (2019) claim that trans women are at a higher risk of sexual victimisation than any other subset of the US population. Further, much of the transphobic rhetoric emanating from TERF activity goes unsupported by evidence.

Transphobic hate crime in the UK

In the UK, whilst transphobic hate crime represents one of the five strands of monitored hate crime (in addition to race, religion, sexual orientation and disability), it has received little academic attention (Chakraborti and

Garland 2015). It is, however, important to acknowledge that formal definitions of hate crime and the five categories currently monitored in the UK can result in the neglect of other aspects of difference and vulnerability (such as misogyny, age or homelessness) as people often experience hate crime from an intersectional, not singular, construction of identity (Chakraborti and Garland 2015). Additionally, depicting the scope and nature of transphobic hate crime can be challenged by the limited sources available for analysis and, more generally, it is reported that trans and non-binary people are often invisible in official statistics (Biblarz and Savci 2010; Rogers 2016b, 2017a). Where sources exist, locating and exploring the experiences of trans and non-binary people can be particularly problematic as they are subsumed into the lesbian, gay, bisexual and trans (LGBT) umbrella (Biblarz and Savci 2010; Rogers 2016b, 2017a). This homogenising tendency means that differences and similarities between LGB and T people are not routinely or sufficiently analysed (Walters et al. 2017).

In 2015, the Government Equalities Office (GEO) commissioned the National Institute of Economic and Social Research (NIESR) to conduct a wide-ranging, critical assessment of the evidence-base that details the inequality experienced by LGBT people in the UK (Hudson-Sharp and Metcalf 2016). Aligning with other studies, the review found that the most common form of hate crime experienced by LGBT people was verbal abuse and this mostly occurred in public space (Browne et al. 2011; Guasp 2013). Whilst neglecting to highlight the subsuming of trans people's experiences into the LGBT umbrella, the review's authors did note that the dearth of comparative research on trans and non-binary people's experiences of hate crime meant that there was little evidence to ascertain whether they are at greater risk of victimisation than L, G or B people (Hudson-Sharp and Metcalf 2016). They also acknowledged the chronic problem of under-reporting. This was similarly reported by Galop who conducted a study into hate crime experiences of LGBT people in the UK identifying various barriers to reporting and help-seeking (Antjoule 2016).

Following Hudson-Sharp and Metcalf's review, in 2017, the GEO launched a nationwide survey to gather more information about the experiences of LGBT people in the UK. This resulted in 108,100 valid responses which the GEO claimed was 'the largest national survey of LGBT people in the world to date' (GEO 2018, p. 5). A total of 13% of the respondents identified as trans: 6.9% as non-binary; 3.5% as trans women and 2.9% were trans men. One of the survey topics was safety, and respondents were asked about negative incidents involving 'people that they did not live with'. This included questions around: verbal harassment; threats of outing; threat of physical or sexual harassment or violence; physical harassment or violence; sexual harassment or violence.

The GEO (2018) study found that trans respondents (53%) were considerably more likely to report having experienced at least one incident that threatened their safety than cisgender respondents (38%). Queer trans respondents (66%) were especially more likely to have experienced an incident compared to heterosexual trans respondents (46%). For example, 49% of queer trans respondents had been verbally harassed by someone they did not live with due to being LGBT, or being thought to be LGBT, in the 12 months preceding the survey, compared to 31% of heterosexual trans respondents. It is unsurprising that 67% of trans respondents said that they avoided being open about their gender identity for fear of a negative reaction from others, and non-binary respondents (76%) were particularly likely to avoid being open about their identity. In a different study, Jauk (2013) found that trans women experienced violence more frequently than trans men, asserting that trans women may experience more violence as women and trans men may benefit from some protection through male privilege.

Across the GEO (2018) dataset for all respondents, more than 9 in 10 of the most serious incidents went unreported. Reasons for not reporting incidents to the police were because respondents thought the incident 'was too minor, not serious enough, or it happens all the time', that 'it would not be taken seriously enough' and/or that 'nothing would happen or change' (GEO 2018, p. 74). It is difficult to dispute that the available prevalence figures represent a small proportion of the actual number of hate crimes, particularly as it is well documented that trans and non-binary victims do not routinely report their experiences of violence or harassment (Rogers 2016a). This claim is supported in research as several studies have found that trans people are reluctant to engage with statutory or public services for fear of a discriminatory response that is transphobic or cisgenderist (FRA 2015; Hudson-Sharp and Metcalf 2016; Rogers 2016a). This is especially the case in relation to the criminal justice system (Duggan 2014). The lack of confidence to report hate crime is concerning as, in line with other research findings on hate crime, transphobic hate crime is highly likely to be repetitive in nature (Walters et al. 2017) and Antjoule (2013) claims that trans-identified victims can be targeted up to 50 times per year.

In the GEO (2018) study, when incidents were reported to the police, almost half (45%) of respondents were dissatisfied with the management of their report. When incidents were experienced by trans respondents, similar patterns of not reporting to the police were identified. Trans respondents were even less likely than cis respondents to have reported physical harassment or violence (33%) and sexual harassment or violence (38%) due to feelings of shame, embarrassment or not wanting anyone to know. Furthermore, trans respondents were more likely than cis respondents to have had a previous poor experience of reporting physical harassment or violence (28%) and sexual harassment or violence (21%). A UK-based study by Galop identified similar factors in non-reporting including: the feeling that reporting would not be worthwhile; there are low standards of police training on LGBT issues; fears that police would react negatively to their identity; discomfort about having to disclose their identity (fear of outing oneself) (Antjoule 2016). In Galop's study several trans respondents claimed that reporting had 'previously caused them more problems than it solved and that they used non-reporting as a strategy to protect information about their identify from being shared without their consent' (Antjoule 2016, p. 10).

Despite the problems with under-reporting, transphobic hate crime has been monitored by police forces in England and Wales since 2008 and through the Crime Survey for England and Wales since 2009. Notwithstanding the widely acknowledged limitations of prevalence data, according to recent statistics, the police in England and Wales recorded 105,090 hate crimes in 2019/2020, continuing an upward trend year on year (Home Office 2019) (see Table 10.1). Of these, a total of 2,540 were recorded under the 'transgender' strand. This showed a 16% increase in the previous reporting period, but still represents the smallest figure in the five different groupings.

As indicated throughout this chapter, transphobic hate crime results in a range of social, emotional, health, mental health and behavioural outcomes. The perception of threat (whether this is actual or symbolic) can have a powerful effect invoking heightened levels of fear, anxiety, stigma and/or anger. These emotions can result in social and spatial behaviours that are proactive (joining community groups) or avoidant (staying at home) (Brown and Walters 2016; Walters et al. 2017). Trans and non-binary people may feel unsafe in public and may try to conceal or moderate their gender identity and expression, or avoid public space altogether, in efforts to reduce the risk of hate crime victimization (FRA 2015; Perry and Dyck 2014). As noted earlier, trans and non-binary young people are especially susceptible to being denied safe space as their gender identity is policed in public and private spaces resulting in "hyper-vigilance"; the intense alertness to the omnipresent possibility for violence (Perry and Dyck 2014, p. 58). Finally, the multiple barriers to reporting transphobic hate crime noted above can also result in impacts. Not reporting hate crime can manifest in a lack of support, increased social isolation and feelings of marginalisation and rejection. Such experiences can lead to additional effects as the emotions tied to perceptions of social rejection can be internalised resulting in heightened feelings of anger, low self-worth and significant mental health impacts such as depression and a greater risk of suicidal ideation and/or attempted suicide than non-trans victims (Williams and Tregidga 2013; Perry and Dyck 2014).

Table 10.1 Transphobic hate crimes in the UK 2011–2020 (Home Office 2019)

Hate crime strand	2011/ 2012	2012/ 2013	2013/ 2014	2014/ 2015	2015/ 2016	2016/ 2017	2017/ 2018	2018/ 2019	2019/ 2020	% Change 2018/2019 to 2019/2020
Transgender	313	364	559	607	858	1,248	1,703	2,333	2,540	16

Conclusion

This chapter has provided an overview of the theoretical and conceptual framework that can be employed to explore the problem of transphobic hate crime. By describing the socially constructed nature of gender in relation to notions of identity, positionality and processes of identification (via understandings of similarity and difference), I have provided a backdrop to the subject of hate, violence and victimisation for people who do not conform to normative gender identities and who do not belong. The concepts of cisgenderism and transphobia are useful in this respect as these help illuminate the ways in which dominant and normative ideas – which are embedded in structures and systems – sustain phenomena such as individual and collective fear, ignorance and hate. These ideas help contextualise the conditions that result in transphobic hate crime. The chapter integrates the findings from empirical studies to bolster these arguments, and these data illustrate the scale and nature of hate-motivated violence and harassment when experienced by trans and non-binary people. However, there is also an acknowledgement of the paucity of academic research and theoretical development in relation to transphobic hate crime and so this chapter presents a call for further research in this regard. Finally, whilst UK figures suggest small numbers of trans and non-binary people experience hate crime, as noted earlier, the problem of under-reporting is significant and there are complex reasons for this including the expectations of a transphobic response by trans and non-binary victims.

References

Antjoule, N., 2013. *The Hate Crime Report: Homophobia, Biphobia and Transphobia in London*. London: GALOP.
Antjoule, N., 2016. *The Hate Crime Report: Homophobia, Biphobia and Transphobia in London*. London: GALOP.
Ansara, Y.G. and Hegarty, P., 2011. Cisgenderism in psychology: pathologising and misgendering children from 1999 to 2008. *Psychology and Sexuality*, 3(2), pp. 137–160. DOI: 10.1080/19419899.2011.576696.
Ansara, Y.G. and Hegarty, P., 2014. Methodologies of misgendering: recommendations for reducing cisgenderism in psychological research. *Feminism and Psychology*, 24(2), pp. 259–270. DOI: 10.1177/0959353514526217.
Anthias, F., 2002. 'Where do I belong': narrating collective identity and translocational positionality. *Ethnicities*, 2(4), pp. 491–514. DOI: 10.1177/14687968020020040301.
Arayasirikul, S. and Wilson, E.C., 2019. Spilling the T on trans-misogyny and microaggressions: an intersectional oppression and social process among trans women. *Journal of Homosexuality*, 66(10), pp. 1415–38. DOI: 10.1080/00918369.2018.1542203.
Bachmann, C.L. and Gooch, B., 2018. *LGBT in Britain: Trans Report*. London: Stonewall.
Betcher T.M., 2007. Evil deceivers and make-believers: on transphobic violence and the politics of illusion. *Hypatia*, 22(3), pp. 43–65. DOI: 10.1111/j.1527-2001.2007.tb01090.x.

Biblarz, T.J. and Savci, E., 2010. Lesbian, gay, bisexual, and transgender families. *Journal of Marriage and Family*, 72, pp. 480–497. DOI: 10.1111/j.1741-3737.2010.00714.x.

Bindel, J., 2007. My trans mission. *The Guardian*. 1 August 2007.

Blumer, M.L.C., Ansara, Y.G. and Watson, C.M., 2013. Cisgenderism in family therapy: how everyday clinical practices can delegitimize people's gender self-designations. *Journal of Family Psychotherapy*, 24, pp. 267–285. DOI: 10.1080/08975353.2013.849551.

Boys Don't Cry, 1999. [Film] Directed by Kimberly Peirce. USA: Fox Searchlight.

Brown, R. and Walters, M.A., 2016. *Findings from The Sussex Hate Crime Project. Submission to the Parliamentary Inquiry into Hate Crime and Its Violent Consequences*. London: House of Commons.

Browne, K., Bakshi, L. and Lim, J., 2011. 'It's something you just have to ignore': understanding and addressing contemporary lesbian, gay, bisexual and trans safety beyond hate crime paradigms. *Journal of Social Policy*, 40(4), pp. 739–756. DOI: 10.1017/S0047279411000250.

Chakraborti, N. and Garland, J., 2015. *Hate Crime: Impact, Causes and Responses*. 2nd ed. London: Sage.

Dargie, E. et al., 2014. Somewhere under the rainbow: exploring the identities and experiences of trans persons. *The Canadian Journal of Human Sexuality*, 23(2), pp. 60–74. DOI: /10.3138/cjhs.2378.

Doan, P.L., 2007. Queers in the American city: transgendered perceptions of urban space. *Gender, Place and Culture*, 17(5), pp. 635–654. DOI: 0.1080/09663690601122309.

Doan, P.L., 2010. The tyranny of gendered spaces: reflections from beyond the gender dichotomy. *Gender, Place and Culture*, 17(5), pp. 635–54. DOI: 10.1080/0966369X.2010.503121.

Duggan, M., 2014. Working with lesbian, gay, bisexual and transgender communities to shape hate crime policy. In: Chakraborti, N. and Garland, J., eds. *Responding to Hate Crime: The Case for Connecting Policy and Research*. Bristol: Policy Press, pp. 87–98.

Dvorak, P., 2019. The murder of black transgender women is becoming a crisis [online]. *The Washington Post*. 17 June 2019. Available at: https://www.washingtonpost.com/local/the-murder-of-black-transgender-women-is-becoming-a-crisis/2019/06/17/28f8dba6-912b-11e9-b570-6416efdc0803_story.html [Accessed 1 December 2020].

FRA, 2015. *Being Trans in the European Union - Comparative Analysis of EU LGBT Survey Data – Summary*. Vienna: The European Union Agency for Fundamental Rights.

Gordon, D. and Pratma, M.P., 2017. Mapping discrimination experienced by Indonesian trans* FtM persons. *Journal of Homosexuality*, 64(9), pp. 1283–1303. DOI: 10.1080/00918369.2016.1244446.

Gottschalk, L.H., 2009. Transgendering women's space: a feminist analysis of perspectives from Australian women's services. *Women's Studies International Forum*, 32(3), pp. 167–78. DOI: 10.1016/j.wsif.2009.05.001.

Government Equalities Office, 2018. *National LGBT Survey: Research Report*. London: Government Equalities Office.

Grant, J.M. et al., 2011. *Injustice at Every Turn: A Report of the National Transgender Discrimination Survey: Executive Summary*. Washington, DC: National Center for Transgender Equality and the National Gay and Lesbian Taskforce.

Guasp, A., 2013. *Homophobic Hate Crime: The Gay British Crime Survey.* London: Stonewall.

Hill, D.B. and Willoughby, B.L.B., 2011. The development and validation of the genderism and transphobia scale. *Sex Roles*, 53(7/8), pp. 531–44. DOI: 10.1007/s11199-005-7140-x.

Hines, S., 2005. 'I am a feminist but...': transgender men, women and feminism. In: Reger, J., ed. *Different Wavelengths: Studies of the Contemporary Women's Movement.* London and New York: Routledge, pp. 57–77.

Hines, S., 2013. *Gender Diversity, Recognition and Citizenship: Towards a Politics of Difference.* Basingstoke: Palgrave Macmillan.

Hines, S., 2019. The feminist frontier: on trans and feminism. *Journal of Gender Studies*, 28(2), pp. 145–157. DOI: 10.1080/09589236.2017.1411791.

Home Office, 2019. *Hate Crime: England and Wales, 2019/20.* London: Home Office. https://www.gov.uk/government/publications/hate-crime-england-and-wales-2019-to-2020/hate-crime-england-and-wales-2019-to-2020 [Accessed 1 December 2020].

Hudson-Sharp, N. and Metcalf, H., 2016. *Inequality among Lesbian, Gay, Bisexual and Transgender Groups in the UK: A Review of Evidence.* London: NIESR.

Jaime, K., 2017. 'Chasing rainbows': black cracker and queer, trans afrofuturity. *TSQ: Transgender Studies Quarterly*, 4(2), pp. 208–218. DOI: 10.1215/23289252-3815009.

Jauk, D., 2013. Invisible lives, silenced violence: transphobic gender violence in global perspective. In: Segal, M.T. and Demos, V., eds. *Gendered Perspectives on Conflict and Violence: Part A.* Binley: Emerald, pp. 111–136.

Jeffreys, S., 1997. Transgender activism: a feminist perspective. *The Journal of Lesbian Studies*, 1, pp. 55–74. DOI: 10.1300/J155v01n03_03.

Jenkins, R., 2000. Categorization: identity, social process and epistemology. *Current Sociology*, 48(3), pp. 7–25. DOI: 10.1177/0011392100048003003.

Jenkins, R., 2014. *Social Identity.* 4th ed. Abingdon: Routledge.

LGBT Foundation, 2017. Transforming outcomes: a review of the needs and assets of the trans community [online]. Available at: https://s3-eu-west-1.amazonaws.com/LGBT-media/Files/acd2bcc5-a2d4-4203-8e22-aed9f4843921/TransformingOutcomesLGBTFdn.pdf [Accessed 1 December 2020].

Lombardi, E., 2009. Varieties of transgender/transsexual lives and their relationship with transphobia. *Journal of Homosexuality*, 56(8), pp. 977–92. DOI: 10.1080/00918360903275393.

Lubitow, A. et al., 2017. Transmobilities: mobility, harassment, and violence experienced by transgender and gender nonconforming public transit riders in Portland, Oregon. *Gender, Place and Culture*, 24(10), pp. 1398–1418. DOI: 10.1080/0966369X.2017.1382451.

Marinucci, M., 2016. *Feminism is Queer: The Intimate Connection between Queer and Feminist Theory.* 2nd ed. London: Zed Books.

Matsuzaka, S. and Koch, D.E., 2019. Trans feminine sexual violence experiences: the intersection of transphobia and misogyny. *Affilia: Journal of Women and Social Work*, 34(1), pp. 28–47. DOI: 10.1177/0886109918790929.

May, V., 2013. *Connecting Self to Society: Belonging in a World.* Basingstoke: Palgrave Macmillan.

Monro, S., 2005. *Gender Politics: Citizenship, Activism and Sexual Diversity.* London: Pluto Press.

Monro, S., 2007. Transmuting gender binaries: the theoretical challenge. *Sociological Research Online*, 12(1). Available at: http://www.socresonline.org.uk/12/1/monro.html [Accessed 1 December 2020].

Nadal, K.L. et al., 2014. Emotional, behavioral, and cognitive reactions to microaggressions: transgender perspectives. *Psychology of Sexual Orientation and Gender Diversity*, 1(1), pp. 72–81. DOI: 10.1037/sgd0000011.

Pain, R., 1997. Whither women's fear? Perceptions of sexual violence in public and private space. *International Review of Victimology*, 4(4), pp. 297–312. DOI: 10.1177/026975809700400404.

Perry, B. and Dyck, D.R., 2014. 'I don't know where it is safe': trans women's experiences of violence. *Critical Criminology*, 22, pp. 49–63. DOI: 10.1007/s10612-013-9225-0.

Phipps, A., 2016. Whose personal is more political? Experience in contemporary feminist politics. *Feminist Theory*, 17(3), pp. 303–21. DOI: 10.1177/1464700116663831.

Raymond, J., 1979. *The Transsexual Empire*. London: The Women's Press.

Rogers, M., 2016a. Breaking down barriers: exploring the potential for social care practice with trans survivors of domestic abuse. *Health and Social Care in the Community*, 24(1), pp. 68–76. DOI: 10.1111/hsc.12193.

Rogers, M., 2016b. Transphobic 'honour'-based abuse: a conceptual tool. *Sociology*, 51(2), pp. 225–240. DOI: 10.1177/0038038515622907.

Rogers, M., 2017a. Challenging cisgenderism through trans people's narratives of domestic violence and abuse. *Sexualities*, 22(5–6), pp. 803–820. DOI: 10.1177/1363460716681475.

Rogers, M., 2017b. The intersection of cisgenderism and hate crime: learning from trans people's narratives. *The Journal of Family Strengths*, 17(2). Available at: http://digitalcomMons.library.tmc.edu/jfs/vol17/iss2/5 [Accessed 1 December 2020].

Rogers, M., 2020. Exploring trans men's experiences of intimate partner violence through the lens of cisgenderism. In: Gottzén, L., Bjørnholt, M. and Boonzaier, F., eds. *Men, Masculinities and Intimate Partner Violence*. London: Routledge, pp. 112–126.

Rogers, M. and Ahmed, A., 2017. Interrogating trans and sexual identities through the conceptual lens of translocational positionality. *Sociological Research Online*, 22(1). Available at: http://www.socresonline.org.uk/22/1/contents.html [Accessed 1 December 2020].

Schilt, K., 2010. *Just One of the Guys? Transgender Men and the Persistence of Gender Inequality*. Chicago, IL: University of Chicago Press.

Schilt, K. and Westbrook, L., 2009. Doing gender, doing heteronormativity: 'gender normals', transgender people, and the social maintenance of heterosexuality. *Gender and Society*, 23(4), pp. 440–464. DOI: 10.1177/0891243209340034.

Serano, J., 2007. *Whipping Girl: A Transsexual Women on Sexism and the Scapegoating of Femininity.* Berkeley, CA: Seal Press.

Serano, J., 2013. *Excluded: Making Feminist and Queer Movements More Inclusive.* Berkeley, CA: Seal Press.

Serano, J., 2016. *Whipping Girl: A Transsexual Women on Sexism and the Scapegoating of Femininity.* 2nd ed. Berkeley, CA: Seal Press.

Stotzer, R.L., 2009. Violence against transgender people: a review of United States data. *Aggression and Violent Behavior*, 14(3), pp. 170–179. DOI: 10.1016/j.avb.2009.01.006.

Stryker, S. and Aizura, A., 2013. *The Transgender Studies Reader 2*. London: Routledge.

Sue, D.W., 2010. *Microaggressions in Everyday Life: Race, Gender, and Sexual Orientation*. Hoboken, NJ: Wiley.

Taylor, Y., 2008. Sexuality. In: Richardson, D. and Robinson, V., eds. *Introducing Gender and Women's Studies*. 3rd ed. Basingstoke: Palgrave Macmillan, pp. 106–122.

TGEU, 2020. Trans murder monitoring project [online]. Available at: https://tgeu.org/tmm/ [Accessed 1 December 2020].

Thurber, A. and DiAngelo, R., 2018. Microaggressions: intervening in three acts. *Journal of Ethnic and Cultural Diversity in Social Work*, 27(1), pp. 17–27. DOI: 10.1080/15313204.2017.1417941.

Transrespect, 2018. *TvT TMM Update: Trans Day of Remembrance 2018*. Available at: https://transrespect.org/wp-content/uploads/2018/11/TvT_TMM_TDoR2018_Tables_EN.pdf [Accessed 1 December 2020].

Turner, L., Whittle, S. and Combs, R., 2009. *Transphobic Hate Crime in the European Union*. London: Press for Change.

Vähäpassi, V., 2019. User-generated reality enforcement: framing violence against black trans feminine people on a video sharing site. *European Journal of Women's Studies*, 26(1), pp. 85–98. DOI: 10.1177/1350506818762971.

Walters, M.A. et al., 2017. Hate crimes against trans people: assessing emotions, behaviors, and attitudes toward criminal justice agencies. *Journal of Interpersonal Violence*, 35(21–22), pp. 1–31. DOI: 10.1177/0886260517715026.

Wilkinson, S. and Kitzinger, C., 1996. *Representing the Other: A Feminism and Psychology Reader*. London: SAGE.

Williams, M. and Tregidga, J., 2013. *All Wales Hate Crime Project*. Cardiff: Race Equality First and Cardiff University. Available from: http://orca.cf.ac.uk/60690/ [Accessed 1 December 2020].

Witten, T.M. and Eyler, A.E., 1999. Hate crimes and violence against the transgendered. *Peace Review*, 11(3), pp. 461–468. DOI: 10.1080/10402659908426291.

11 "Not the right kind of woman"

Transgender women's experiences of transphobic hate crime and trans-misogyny

Ben Colliver

Introduction

Historically, transphobia has gained little attention academically, politically and socially. However, in recent years, a spotlight has been cast on to the lives of transgender and non-binary people: their existence, authenticity and lives have become subject to public 'debate'. The 'debate' has centred around a number of socially constructed binary trade-offs, but has centred most specifically around 'gender-based rights' vs. 'sex-based rights'. At the very core of this 'debate' is the question of whether growing recognition and protection of transgender people is inherently dangerous, granted at the expense of the rights of cisgender women and girls. The rights which are claimed to be infringed upon relate most commonly to the provision of 'single sex services', participation in sports and the claimed erasure of lesbian identities.

Whilst these 'debates' have been happening for some time, they have been fuelled recently by Government announcements to reform the 'Gender Recognition Act (2004)' (GRA) in order to make the process of acquiring legal recognition for transgender people's gender identity more humane, and less intrusive (Women and Equalities Committee 2018). Social media has become a hotbed of harassment, abuse and the targeting of individuals who engage in these conversations, experienced by those on both sides of the debate. It is important to note that a significant amount of concern and around reforms to the GRA centres on the consequences this may have for the Equality Act (2010) which designates the need for 'sex-specific' services and spaces. Although the focus of these conversations has centred on cisgender men being able to abuse this reform, by easily self-identifying as female to access female-only spaces, a significant amount of the narrative developed has transphobic undertones, and at times, explicit transphobia. The construction of 'gender-neutral' spaces as sites of significant risk and danger for women and girls has been engaged with academically (See Colliver and Coyle 2020). Furthermore, the use of transphobic discourse is often employed by those who seek to claim a 'victim position', and therefore delegitimising transgender people is central to this function (Colliver 2021).

DOI: 10.4324/9781003023722-11

Transgender men have been much less of a concern in online exchanges and are often overlooked completely. This is likely to be due to them not gaining access to spaces designed to protect a socially disadvantaged group whilst, or after, transitioning. This is unsurprising, as historically political, social and religious framings of danger have centred on men and transgender women (Stone 2019).

This chapter provides a critical exposé of the ways in which transgender women experience transphobic hate crime and trans-misogyny within the UK. This is achieved by drawing on data collected through semi-structured interviews with trans people living in the UK. This chapter does not devote significant space to engaging with theoretical and conceptual discussions around gender identity, as Chapter 10 has eloquently outlined the most significant concerns. However, a brief outline of some of the concerns shared within hate crime scholarship is detailed, before framing this within the context of the 'tyranny of gender' (Doan 2010). The chapter then explores the methodological approaches adopted throughout the research process that gave rise to the qualitative data collected. Finally, this chapter presents empirical evidence that illustrates the ways in which transgender women experience both transphobia and misogyny simultaneously and the impact this can have. It is also important to note that it is not the purpose of this chapter to debate the existence, authenticity or validity of transgender people. This chapter is situated firmly within the claim that transgender people do exist, are valid and worthy of respect. In doing so, it is hoped that this chapter frames some of the conceptual and theoretical debates outlined in Chapter 10 within empirical data that outline the reality for transgender women.

Transphobic hate crime

Research on transphobic hate crime within the UK is in its infancy, although there is some research and literature that has included transgender participants and lives (Antjoule 2013; Chakraborti et al. 2014). More recently, there has been a significant contribution to existing literature within the UK with the publication of Jamel's (2018) *'Transphobic Hate Crime'*, which centres on the lives of transgender people. As seen in the previous chapter, recorded incidents of transphobic hate crime are increasing annually (Home Office 2019). Whilst the Home Office claim that this increase is mainly due to improved reporting and recording mechanisms (which the author does not contend is a contributing factor), it is unlikely that this accounts solely for the increased levels of hate crime. It is likely that there has also been a material rise in incidents of transphobic hate crime (Chakraborti 2018). As seen in Chapter 10, research often documents high levels of discrimination, abuse and hate crime experienced by transgender people (METRO Charity 2014; Government Equalities Office 2018).

In 2012 the Legal Aid, Sentencing and Punishment of Offenders Act amended the Criminal Justice Act (2003). This amendment made the monitoring of transphobic hate crime mandatory within England and Wales. As such, transgender identity became a characteristic to be considered as an aggravating factor during sentencing if the offence was motivated by hostility or prejudice based on the individuals' transgender identity. Misogyny is not recognised under any of the various legislative provisions that criminalise hate and therefore crimes motivated by misogyny are not nationally recorded and reported with hate crime statistics. However, some police forces have begun to monitor incidents of misogyny, with Nottinghamshire Police recording incidents of misogyny from 2017 and North Yorkshire Police following suit (BBC News 2016). As outlined earlier in the book, the Law Commission is currently reviewing the adequacy of protections afforded to groups who may be victimised through hate crime. It is therefore possible that misogyny will be centrally monitored in the UK in the near future.

However, it is important to consider the legal implications this will have for transgender people who may experience incidents motivated by transphobia and misogyny. The Criminal Justice Act (2003) as it currently stands does not appreciate intersecting systems of oppression and marginalisation. Therefore, transgender people who currently experience victimisation fuelled by transphobia and racism cannot have both characteristics considered during sentencing. Therefore, we must question how effective legislation will be at addressing transgender people's experiences of trans-misogyny, or whether the current 'isolated, silo' approach will continue. If multiple forms of victimisation, oppression and marginalisation can be acknowledged in legal frameworks, then the unique experiences of transgender women may be fully acknowledged.

Academically, issues of hate crime have been engaged with for some time (Perry 2001; Iganski 2008; Chakraborti and Garland 2012). The difficulties associated with defining and conceptualising hate crime have been well documented (Jacobs and Potter 1998; Hall 2005). However, in academic writing, it is Perry's (2001, p. 10) definition of hate crime that has emerged as key, and she notes that:

> Hate crime ... involves acts of violence and intimidation, usually directed towards already stigmatised and marginalised groups. As such, it is a mechanism of power and oppression, intended to reaffirm the precarious hierarchies that characterise a given social order. It attempts to re-create simultaneously the threatened (real or imagined) hegemony of the perpetrator's group and the 'appropriate subordinate identity of the victim's group. It is a means of marking both the Self and the Other in such a way as to re-establish their 'proper' relative positions, as given and reproduced by broader ideologies and patterns of social and political inequality.

This conceptualisation of hate crime suggests that these incidents are best understood as extreme forms of discrimination. As such, incidents of hate crime will target those already ostracised, oppressed and marginalised within society, distinctively marked as 'different', as the 'Other'. Perry (2001) argues that this is cultivated by cultures of segregation. If we apply this conceptualisation of hate crime to transphobia, it can be argued that the 'Other', transgender people, are socially constructed in negative relation terms. In this sense, cisgender is marked as normal, unremarkable and as the identity through which everyone is measured against. Therefore, cisgender identities rarely experience the same level of interrogation and 'debate' that transgender identities do. It can therefore be argued that there is an 'expectation that all people are cissexual, that those assigned male at birth always grow up to be men and those assigned female at birth always grow up to be women' (Bauer et al. 2009, p. 356). Consequently, those who do not conform to this linear expectation of gender presentation may be socially marked as 'different'.

The 'difference' that the 'Other' present may lead to feelings of fear and insecurity within the dominant majority about their position within social hierarchies. The construction of transgender, and LGBTQ+ communities more broadly becoming the 'dominant voice' within society has been central in cisgender communities claiming a victim position (Colliver 2021). The dominant group must therefore find ways to 'police' minority communities in order to ensure that the perceived subordinate group remains subordinate. Perry (2001, p. 2) argues that this can leave 'minority members vulnerable to systemic violence'. In this sense, the power dynamic is therefore maintained through the process of 'gender policing', which may manifest in incidents of discrimination and violence. Jauk (2013, p. 808) argues that 'violence against trans people is often triggered by gender non-conformity and violence is a form of gender policing'. In this sense, transphobic hate crimes can be conceptualised as 'message crimes' (Perry 2001). Resultantly, incidents of transphobic hate crime function to send a wider message to transgender communities that gender deviance will not be tolerated (Burgess et al. 2013).

Consequently, it can be argued that hate crime targeting transgender people functions as a mechanism of 'intimidation and control exercised' by dominant groups who sense a need to reaffirm their position in fluctuating social hierarchies (Perry 2001, p. 2). However, in relation to discrimination, abuse and hate crime targeting transgender women specifically, Serano (2007, pp. 14–15) argues that they 'become the victims of a specific form of discrimination: *trans-misogyny*'. As such, transgender women do not simply experience transphobia as a result of deviating from expected gender norms that are dictated by cis-normative expectations. They also experience misogyny simultaneously resulting from embodying 'femininity', or at least, the perception that they embody femininity. In a patriarchal society which stipulates women, and therefore femininity, are 'less than', the perceived 'choice' to embody femininity presents a unique set of challenges and experiences for transgender women.

This can also be seen in media representations of transgender people, which have increased in recent years and have tended to focus on transgender women. Media representations have often been misleading and defamatory (See, for example, Express 2020). These media narratives are regularly drawn upon in discussions about the rights transgender people, and transgender women in particular, deserve. Therefore, irresponsible media reporting often fuels transphobic narratives that seek to delegitimise transgender identities. Media narratives often present transgender women as dangerous, drawing upon sexual offending and physical violence to delegitimise their female identity and construct them as 'men wearing dresses' (Serano 2007, p. 15). In constructing transgender women in this way, cis-normative gender roles are reinforced that construct men as physically dominant and women as vulnerable and weak (Connell 1987).

Methodology

This chapter draws upon data collected through semi-structured interviews with transgender people living in the UK. The data were collected over a 9-month period between 2017 and 2018. All participants identified as transgender, were over 16 years old at the time of interview and lived within the UK. The semi-structured interviews formed part of a wider research project that sought to explore transgender and non-binary people's experiences of abuse, discrimination and hate crime. The wider research project also consisted of an online survey completed by 396 transgender and non-binary people, and a discourse analysis of comments posted to *YouTube* in response to videos, which had a focus on 'gender-neutral toilets'.

A total of 32 semi-structured interviews were completed as part of this research project; however, this chapter draws specifically on 14 interviews that were conducted with transgender women. Participants were primarily recruited through social media, although the researcher attended various Pride events around the UK in order to advertise the research. Literature advertising the research was also sent to every Gender Identity Clinic in the UK and a number of charity and support organisations that work with transgender people. Whilst a diverse sample was obtained in relation to age, ethnicity, religion and disability status, it is likely that the sampling method has resulted in only transgender people being recruited who openly disclose their trans history.

The qualitative data was analysed thematically, guided by the process outlined by Braun and Clarke (2006). An inductive approach was adopted when analysing the data, as the scarcity of research into transgender people's conceptualisation of their experiences created difficulty in trying to locate pre-existing themes. Using an inductive approach also avoided many of the pitfalls associated with deductive analysis including the reframing and exclusion of key themes by relying on predetermined frameworks (Thomas 2008). In order to ensure the most accurate representation of participants narratives, participants were involved throughout the analysis process, including checking and verifying codes developed and reading the initial analysis. This allowed participants the opportunity to reflect on the research process and clarify any points of uncertainty. Three central themes were developed from the data: 'Normalcy and the Everyday', 'The Hierarchical Nature of Hate Crime Victimisation' and 'Space, Place and Belonging'. Incidents of trans-misogyny ran throughout all of the themes developed, and therefore this chapter does not focus on one key theme. Rather, all themes are discussed, with a specific focus on incidents of trans-misogyny experienced.

A diverse sample was recruited for all elements of the research project, and the interview participants all had different life experiences. However, in relation to the 14 interviews drawn upon for this chapter, all participants identified as female. 65% of these participants identified as heterosexual, 28% identified as bisexual and 7% identified as lesbian. Participants were also able to self-identify their ethnicity and seven of participants identified as White British, one identified as Black British, one identified as Thai, one identified as an Irish Traveller, one identified as White European, one identified as Asian Bangladeshi and two identified as dual-ethnicity. Six of these participants also identified as having a religion or faith, with two women identifying as Muslim and four women identifying as Christian. Six of the participants also identified as living with a disability, ranging from learning disabilities to sensory impairments. A range of age categories also participated in the research, with the youngest female participant being 17 and the oldest female participant being 67.

Findings and discussion

This chapter now moves on to present empirical data collected throughout this research project to provide an overview of the ways in which trans-misogyny manifests. It will be demonstrated that transgender women experience trans-misogyny in a range of spaces and contexts. This chapter explores these experiences within two central spaces: LGBTQ spaces and 'sex-segregated spaces'.

"Sorry, you are way too femme" – trans-misogyny in LGBTQ spaces

Ideas around misogyny within LGBTQ+ spaces have been well-documented, focusing primarily on gay men's relationship with femininity (Richardson 2009; Hale and Ojeda 2018). Whilst work has been done that explores 'femmephobia' and the impact this has on feminine, cisgender gay men, less attention has been paid to the experiences of transgender women specifically in LGBTQ spaces (Richardson 2009; Hoskin 2019). Whilst commonly referred to as 'LGBTQ spaces', these spaces are often shaped and dominated by gay men, and may therefore not be as inclusive, or safe for the broader spectrum of gender and sexual minorities (Casey 2004; Nash 2013). Therefore, when discussing trans-misogyny within LGBTQ spaces, these are actually experiences within gay, male spaces. Gay male communities have a complex relationship with notions of masculinity and femininity (Sánchez and Vilain 2012). In relation to establishing a gay identity, issues of gender presentation may be a central feature.

Significant work has been conducted around gay masculinities, the rejection of femininity and consequently the exclusion of feminine gay men from LGBTQ+ spaces, friendships and romantic and sexual relationships. It has been argued that the 'straight acting', masculine identity has been constructed as the 'gold standard' of gay identities. As such, other forms of gender expression are judged unfavourably against masculinity, which has come to symbolise the marker by which desirability and attractiveness are measured against (Bailey et al. 1997; Phua 2007). Masculinity certainly appeared to be a feature in participants narratives regarding their experiences within LGBTQ+ spaces.

> So I was in the smoking area chatting with my friend, a really hot gay guy, he gets loads of attention. Almost to the point where it is annoying because we can never talk in private without someone coming over and hitting on him. He is like, the perfect gay boyfriend, he is masculine, ripped, facial hair, beautiful eyes... These guys come over, both muscle guys, and I realise I used to see them a lot before I transitioned. We are standing there talking for a while and they obviously don't recognise me. Anyway, I decided to come out to them, so I reminded them who they would previously have known me as. The first guys response was 'why would you choose to do that? You were so hot and manly before'. The second guy chipped in and agreed and then really annoyed me. He was like 'OH MY GOD, yes! I remember you, you were the beautiful black guy that we all wanted to fuck!'
>
> (Deena, 34)

There are a number of points made in the excerpt above that are worth attention. Firstly, even though Deena no longer identifies with a masculine gender identity or expression, her description of her friend directly feeds into the narrative around masculinity to be consumable and desirable. This narrative is reinforced by comments made to her that position Deena as 'hot and manly before', in which manly signifies an identification with masculinity. Deena is simultaneously constructed as previously desirable and therefore currently undesirable for her move away from masculine ideals. This is also steeped within socially recognisable motifs of transgender people consciously 'choosing' a gender identity. In this sense, the perception that Deena has 'chosen' to associate with more traditionally feminine identity markers can be used to isolate and exclude her. The construction of transgender people 'choosing' to live a particular 'lifestyle' is a key rhetoric in justifying transphobic discourse (Colliver et al. 2019).

However, it is not just the trans-misogyny that Deena experiences that is worth comment. Whilst it is clear from her description that there are underlying tones of transphobia, femmephobia and a lack of interest in her romantically or sexually, she also experiences the racist, fetishisation of black men (McKeown et al. 2010). This adds a complex layer to gay communities' relationship with masculinity, which is situated within racialised expectations of narratives and the hyper-sexualisation of black men. It is important to acknowledge that social configurations of masculinity and femininity may also be culturally situated in which gendered expectations are not universal. It is important to note here that Deena is constructed as not only betraying her gendered expectation of masculinity, but for betraying a specific, racialised masculinity.

What also became clear throughout participants' narratives is the acceptance of femininity within LGBTQ+ spaces within the context of entertainment, comedy and a particular cultural configuration of femininity that is consumable for some cisgender, gay men:

> I was in my local gay pub, it is quite a small venue, not a crazy party pub, more like the place you go to socialise, catch-up with friends etc... Sunday is always cabaret at [the pub]. I am standing at the bar, talking to two guys, they were a couple I think. They were happily chatting away and then they asked me what time I would be performing. I must have instantly look confused as the other one instantly asked 'oh, sorry, are you not the drag queen?'. I was quite taken aback, I know my make-up was a bit messy, but I didn't think I looked like a drag queen. So I confirmed that I wasn't the drag queen, trying to be as polite as possible. Then one of them turns around and just bluntly says 'ooooh, you're a tranny'. It was said in a way that was posed as a question. I replied and told them I was a woman and one of them just laughed. The one standing next to me just turned his back on me. It was clear that conversation was over.
>
> (Piper, 42)

The experience described by Piper above illustrates the ways in which femininity is sometimes perceived as 'acceptable' within LGBTQ+ spaces, particularly with cisgender gay men. In the excerpt above, Piper describes an exchange in which she is initially perceived to be a drag queen. Within this context, the exchange is friendly, with the patrons consuming this 'acceptable femininity'. In this sense, there are appropriate ways to 'do difference' (Perry 2001). This emphasises the ways in which performative femininity, which is often rooted within comedic values is somewhat socially accepted within gay male culture, providing a distance is maintained between the performer and audience (Berkowitz et al. 2007). However, the reaction to Piper when she discloses her trans identity illustrates the juxtaposition of femininity within gay spaces. As such, to be perceived to cross the 'gender binary' permanently is deemed an inappropriate way to 'do difference'. Whereas, the temporary 'crossover' that is satirical in nature is deemed an appropriate way to 'do difference'.

Performative femininity may be acceptable 'on stage' and in performance areas. However, this is harshly juxtaposed with the experiences of transgender women when they try to authentically occupy social space designed for LGBTQ+ people, which tend to be dominated by cisgender, gay men (Pritchard et al. 2002). It can therefore be argued that femininity, when remaining within the confines of performance and comedy is socially accepted. However, transgender people experience trans-misogyny when attempting to occupy 'inclusive' space, which is regulated and policed by cisgender men. Additionally, the use of the term 'tranny', which in itself, signifies a contempt, disdain or hostility towards transgender people. The term itself is also highly gendered, and is most commonly used to denigrate transgender women. This is a more explicit, overt example of the trans-misogyny participants faced.

"Not the right kind of woman" – trans-misogyny and gender policing in 'sex-segregated spaces'

Finally, this chapter will explore the ways in which transgender women experience abuse in sex-segregated spaces, perpetrated by other women who seek to 'police' the authenticity of transgender women. Until this point, the data that has been presented has focused on transgender women's experiences of trans-misogyny as a result of embodying perceived femininity. In this section, transgender women's experiences in 'women-only' spaces are explored and it will be demonstrated that transgender women often experience discrimination and abuse as a result of failing to conform to cis-normative expectations of femininity.

For the participants in this study, this was most strongly felt in 'sex-segregated toilets', in which they felt an element of 'hyper-vigilance' in relation to gender. The spatial design of public toilets has been explored and it has been argued that public toilets are designed in such ways that facilitate surveillance (Cavanagh 2010; Bender-Baird 2016). This certainly matched the experiences of participants in this study:

> I came out of the cubicle, minding my own business, went to the sink area to wash my hands, check my appearance in the mirror. Anyway, I'm standing there washing my hands and there are two women beside me talking to each other. All of a sudden, their voices get lower, but I can still roughly hear what they are saying. They are now standing there, making assumptions about me, talking about the size of my hands, saying that I must have only recently started to wear make-up because it wasn't that good. I only had lipstick and mascara on, how bad can that be? Anyway, I just remember leaving the bathroom as quickly as I could, making my excuses to leave the meal, getting in the car and crying. I just remember sitting there feeling like I would never be the right kind of woman that people accepted.
>
> (Rose, 67)

The excerpt above is one that was fairly common across participants narratives of their time within public toilets. Rose experienced a situation in which the authenticity of her identity as a woman is under surveillance and being questioned because of 'stereotypically' masculine features. In this sense, Rose experiences trans-misogyny in a unique way, as a result of being identifiable as transgender, and also for failing to conform to expected gender norms for women. Doan (2010, p. 635) argues that transgender people experience a 'special kind of tyranny – the tyranny of gender – that arises when people' fail to confirm to, and actively challenge expected, dominant gendered behaviour within Western society. This may happen so frequently within public toilets as they represent the ultimate sex-segregated spaces within Western society (Doan 2010; Greed 2019).

Failing to meet appropriately ascribed gender expectations was a common theme that underlined participants' narratives that they perceive motivated the abuse, discrimination and hate crime they experienced. However, it is important to note that conforming to socially prescribed gender norms was not the ultimate goal for all transgender women who participated in this research:

> So I walk in to the toilet, there is a group of women, all drunk and loud standing by the sinks. I feel their eyes on me as soon as I walk in. I get myself in to a cubicle, sit down, go to the toilet, I can hear them all talking. I wait for a while hoping they will leave. After what seemed like forever, I flush the toilet and walk out. I walk over to the sink, and the question comes. 'Are you a man?' I look them up and down, turn back to the mirror and continue washing my hands. They then decide to have an open conversation about me, obviously I must be a man, look at what I was wearing, no woman would ever wear that. Of course I was a man, I was obviously wearing a bra that I had stuffed as I didn't have real boobs. I did by the way, I had undergone surgery at this point. Obviously I was a man, I wasn't wearing any make-up. Obviously I was a man, I had short hair. It just went on and on… I was attacked by all of them, well the men they were with as I left the pub.
>
> (Isa, 58)

Isa experienced a verbally and physically violent attack as a result of failing to conform to expectations around femininity. In this case, traits associated with femininity (make-up, fashion choices, long hair) were all drawn upon as a way to delegitimise her identity as a woman. This is inherently transphobic, in that it denies the material existence of transgender women being able to authentically occupy a female social identity, but it is also fuelled by misogynistic narratives that construct women in ways which are easily identifiable and sexualised (make-up, attire). In the situation described above, Isa experiences a form of 'genderism' – that is, 'a hostile reading of gender ambiguous bodies' (Browne 2004, p. 332). However, it should be noted that these assumptions and expectations surrounding 'appropriate' gender presentation do not just permeate society, but are prevalent within healthcare systems. Healthcare professions within gender identity clinics 'have the power to determine what constitutes an appropriate or 'trans enough' patient' (Pearce 2018, p. 60). These expectations may pressure trans women into dressing and presenting in hyper-feminine ways associated with particular clothing items and make-up (Ellis et al. 2015). Therefore, it is clear to see that cis-normative expectations of gender identity, expression and presentation permeate through various levels and institutions at a societal level. As Isa does not seek to conform to traditional notions of femininity that are associated with a specific physical presentation of a gendered body. This feeds in to a narrative that cisgender people can 'always tell' who is transgender and who is not (Colliver et al. 2019).

Whilst transgender people may experience gender surveillance within different spaces, given then segregated nature of public toilets, it is unsurprising to find that public toilets are sites of significant anxiety for transgender women (Faktor 2011). However, transgender women experience heightened levels of 'gender scrutiny' in not just public toilets. Other spaces in which women's gender presentation may be scrutinised include changing rooms in retail stores:

> I was shopping with my mum, I had only recently come out to her, and I had done well in my A-levels so she took me shopping. Anyway, we went in to a couple of shops, we bought a few things. I was able to go in to a few changing rooms with no problem. Then we went in to one shop, I picked some stuff up, went to the changing room, and the woman that worked in the shop told me I couldn't go in. My mum asked why, and she basically said that the changing rooms were for women only, and I was obviously a boy. I don't know why she assumed she knew what was between my legs, but I'm guessing that because I was wearing jeans and a jumper, I have short hair, I was wearing trainers. I had to walk off in the end, my mum was standing there arguing with her, because she said that the changing rooms were for real women, not boys who want to play dress up. We put in a complain, they gave us some vouchers, that's it.
> (Rachel, 18)

Rachel experienced a hostile reading of her gendered body when trying to access a public changing room. Whilst fears around sexual violence to women and girls in sex-segregated spaces is documented (Colliver et al. 2019), the refusal of access seemed to relate primarily to her authenticity as 'female'. In this sense, her experience is similar to that of Rose, in that she is marked as 'not the right kind of woman'. Rachel therefore does not benefit from cissexual privilege which 'is typically given to those who are not trans and thus more able to orchestrate a normative concord between their gender identities and the sex of their bodies, as perceived by others' (Cavanagh

2010, p. 54). It is evident that there is a disconnect between Rachel's sense of self, and the perception of her gender, and thereby her biological sex.

The narrative of 'men wearing dresses' and 'boys playing dress up' is also evident in Rachel's account of her experience. Serano (2007) specifically outlines this narrative as an example of trans-misogyny and links this to the pathologisation and fetishisation of transgender women. What is also interesting in these accounts of abuse and discrimination is the perceived gender of the perpetrator. Whilst it is documented that most perpetrators of hate crime are men (Chakraborti et al. 2014), instances of gender policing, trans-misogyny and holding transgender women to account for failing to meet cis-normative gender expectations are primarily perpetrated by women. This strongly coincides with a wider societal awareness around transgender women and the need for cisgender women to 'protect' their 'safe spaces' from men (Colliver and Coyle 2020; Colliver 2021). As a result of this, bodies may be subject to heightened levels of surveillance. However, it is important to note that the impact of this is not limited to transgender women, as a number of gender non-conforming women have experienced gender policing and attempted expulsion from 'women-only' spaces as a result.

Conclusion

The empirical data presented in this chapter has illustrated different contexts within which trans-misogyny operate. Trans-misogyny is not exclusive to heteronormative, cis-normative spaces and this chapter has demonstrated the complex, harmful relationship that exists between cisgender, gay male culture and femininity. It is therefore vital that issues of transphobia, femmephobia and trans-misogyny are not solely located outside of LGBTQ+ communities, as this risks overshadowing the toxicity within and between communities. Furthermore, transgender women are often judged unfavourably in relation to stereotypical, cis-normative expectations around gender. Therefore, they experience trans-misogyny in unique ways for 'attempting' to embody a feminine presentation and identity, but 'failing' to achieve the required criteria. Of course, this is not to say that achieving a stereotypical feminine presentation is the goal for all transgender women. However, it is clear throughout these narratives that this is the perception of cisgender women when reading gender ambiguous bodies.

This chapter has also noted that the very nature of trans-misogyny appears to be gendered in relation to perpetrators. Mainstream LGBTQ+ venues tend to be dominated by cisgender, white, gay men. Consequently, transgender women's experiences in these spaces can be significantly impacted by the attitudes, and gender policing of gay men. In these spaces, transgender women may experience trans-misogyny as a result of a disdain and discomfort with femininity in an authentically, embodied manner. On the other hand, in sex-segregated spaces, and when transgender women occupy 'women-only' space, they experience trans-misogyny as a result of not being the 'right type of woman'. Given that research illustrates that perpetrators of hate crime are predominantly male, and perpetrators of misogyny are male, it is important not to overshadow the experiences of transgender people who experience trans-misogyny perpetrated by women.

As discussed at the beginning of this chapter, existing legislation fails to acknowledge the often-intersecting forms of oppression that individuals experience. This failure within legal provision is demonstrated within participants narratives explored in this chapter. Participants in this research project often experienced transphobia, racism and trans-misogyny simultaneously. Failure to legally recognise these simultaneous experiences of oppression, marginalisation and discrimination means that the experiences of transgender people, transgender women in particular, cannot be fully acknowledged or responded too. Whilst it is significant that misogyny is currently being considered within the Law Commission Review, it is also important to push for a more reflective legal system that is capable of recognising trans-misogyny.

References

Antjoule, N., 2013. *The Hate Crime Report: Homophobia, Biphobia and Transphobia in London*. London: GALOP.

Bailey, J.M. et al., 1997. Butch, femme, or straight acting? Partner preferences of gay men and lesbians, *Journal of Personality and Social Psychology*, 73(5), pp. 960–973. DOI: 10.1037//0022-3514.73.5.960.

Bauer, G.R. et al., 2009. 'I don't think this is theoretical; this is our lives': how erasure impacts health care for transgender people. *Journal of the Association of Nurses in AIDS Care*, 20(5), pp. 348–361. DOI: 10.1016/j.jana.2009.07.004.

BBC News, 2016. Nottinghamshire police records misogyny as a hate crime [online]. Available at: https://www.bbc.co.uk/news/uk-england-nottinghamshire-36775398 [Accessed 3 March 2020].

Bender-Baird, K., 2016. Peeing under surveillance: bathrooms, gender policing, and hate violence. *Gender, Place and Culture*, 23(7), pp. 983–988. DOI: 10.1080/0966369X.2015.1073699.

Berkowitz, D., Belgrave, L. and Halberstein, R., 2007. The interaction of drag queens and gay men in public and private spaces. *Journal of Homosexuality*, 52(3–4), pp. 11–32. DOI: 10.1300/J082v52n03_02.

Braun, V. and Clarke, V., 2006. Using thematic analysis in psychology. *Qualitative Research in Psychology*, 3(2), pp. 77–101. DOI: 10.1191/1478088706qp063oa.

Burgess, A., Regehr, C. and Roberts, A., 2013. *Victimology: Theories and Applications*. 2nd ed. Burlington: Jones and Bartlett Learning.

Browne, K., 2004. Genderism and the bathroom problem: (re)materialising sexed sites, (re)creating sexed bodies. *Gender, Place and Culture*, 11(3), pp. 331–346. DOI: 10.1080/0966369042000258668.

Casey, M., 2004. De-dyking queer space(s): heterosexual female visibility in gay and lesbian Spaces. *Sexualities*, 7(4), pp. 446–461. DOI: 10.1177/1363460704047062.

Cavanagh, S., 2010. *Queering Bathrooms: Gender, Sexuality and the Hygienic Imagination*. Toronto: University of Toronto Press.

Chakraborti, N., 2018. Responding to hate crime: escalating problems, continued failings. *Criminology and Criminal Justice*, 18(4), pp. 387–404. DOI: 10.1177/1748895817736096.

Chakraborti, N. and Garland, J., 2012. Reconceptualizing hate crime victimization through the lens of vulnerability and 'difference'. *Theoretical Criminology*, 16(4), 499–514. DOI: 10.1177/1362480612439432.

Chakraborti, N., Garland, J. and Hardy, S., 2014. *The Leicester Hate Crime Project: Findings and Conclusions*. Leicester: University of Leicester.

Colliver, B. 2021, Claiming victimhood: victims of the transgender agenda, In: Bailey, J., Flynn, A. and Henry, N., eds. *Handbook on Technology-Facilitated Violence and Abuse: International Perspectives and Experience*. Bingley: Emerald Publishing

Colliver, B. and Coyle, A., 2020. Constructing 'risk of sexual violence against women and girls' in gender-neutral toilets: a discourse analysis of comments on YouTube videos. *Journal of Gender-Based Violence*, 4(3), pp. 359–376. DOI: 10.1332/239868020X15894511554617.

Colliver, B., Coyle, A. and Silvestri, M., 2019. The online 'othering' of transgender people in relation to 'gender neutral toilets'. In: Lumsden, K. and Harmer, E., eds. *Online Othering: Exploring Digital Violence and Discrimination on the Web*. London: Palgrave Macmillan, pp. 215–237.

Connell, R., 1987. *Gender and Power: Society, the Person and Sexual Politics*. Berkeley: University of California Press.

Criminal Justice Act 2003 (c. 44).

Doan, P.L., 2010. The tyranny of gendered spaces: reflections from beyond the gender dichotomy. *Gender, Place and Culture*, 17(5), pp. 635–654. DOI: 10.1080/0966369X.2010.503121.

Ellis, S.J., Bailey, L. and McNeil, J., 2015. Trans people's experiences of mental health and gender identity services: a UK study. *Journal of Gay and Lesbian Mental Health*, 19(1), pp. 4–20. DOI: 0.1080/19359705.2014.960990.

Equality Act 2010 (c. 15).

Express, 2020. Correction – 'Call me Lian', Soham murderer Ian Huntley gives himself FEMALE name [online]. Available at: https://www.express.co.uk/news/clarifications-corrections/1234109/ian-huntley-correction [Accessed 3 March 2020].

Faktor, A., 2011. Access and exclusion: public toilets as sites of insecurity for gender and sexual minorities in North America. *Journal of Human Security*, 7(3), pp. 10–22.

Gender Recognition Act 2004 (c. 7).

Government Equalities Office, 2018. *National LGBT Survey: Research Report*. London: Government Equalities Office.

Greed, C., 2019. Join the queue: including women's toilet needs in public space. *The Sociological Review Monographs*, 67(4), pp. 908–926. DOI: 1177/0038026119854274.

Hale, S. and Ojeda, T., 2018. Acceptable femininity? Gay male misogyny and the policing of queer femininities. *European Journal of Women's Studies*, 25(3), pp. 310–324. DOI: 10.1177/1350506818764762.

Hall, N., 2005. *Hate Crime*. Cullompton: Willan Publishing.

Home Office, 2019. *Hate Crime: England and Wales, 2018/19*. London: Home Office.

Hoskin, R.A., 2019. Femmephobia: the role of anti-femininity and gender policing in LGBTQ+ people's experiences of discrimination. *Sex Roles*, 81(11), pp. 686–703. DOI: 10.1007/s11199-019-01021-3.

Iganski, P., 2008. *Hate Crime and the City*. London: Policy Press.

Jacobs, J. and Potter, K., 1998. *Hate Crimes: Criminal Law and Identity Politics*. Oxford: Oxford University Press.

Jamel, J., 2018. *Transphobic Hate Crime*. London: Palgrave Macmillan.

Jauk, D., 2013. Gender violence revisited: lessons from violent victimization of transgender identified individuals. *Sexualities*, 16(7), pp. 807–825. DOI: 10.1177/1363460713497215.

Legal Aid, Sentencing and Punishment of Offenders Act 2012 (c. 10).

McKeown, E., et al., 2010. Disclosure, discrimination and desire: experiences of Black and South Asian gay men in Britain. *Culture, Health and Sexuality*, 12(7), pp. 843–856. DOI: 10.1080/13691058.2010.499963.

METRO Charity, 2014. *Youth Chances*. London: METRO Charity.

Nash, C., 2013. Queering neighbourhoods: politics and practice in Toronto. *International E-Journal for Critical Geographies*, 12(2), pp. 193–213.

Pearce, R., 2018. *Understanding Trans Health: Discourse, Power and Possibility*. Bristol: Policy Press.

Perry, B., 2001. *In the Name of Hate: Understanding Hate Crimes*. London: Routledge.

Phua, V.C., 2007. Contesting and maintaining hegemonic masculinities: gay Asian American men in mate selection. *Sex Roles*, 57, pp. 909–918. DOI: 10.1007/s11199-007-9318-x.

Pritchard, A., Morgan, N. and Sedgley, D., 2002. In search of lesbian space? The experience of Manchester's gay village. *Leisure Studies*, 21(2), pp. 105–123. DOI: 10.1080/02614360110121551.

Richardson, N., 2009. Effeminophobia, misogyny and queer friendship: the cultural themes of Channel 4's Playing it Straight. *Sexualities*, 12(4), pp. 525–544. DOI: 10.1177/1363460709105718.

Sánchez, F.J. and Vilain, E., 2012. 'Straight-acting gays': the relationship between masculine consciousness, anti-effeminacy, and negative gay identity. *Archives of Sexual Behaviour*, 41(1), pp. 111–119. DOI: 10.1007/s10508-012-9912-z.

Serano, J., 2007. *Whipping Girl: A Transsexual Women on Sexism and the Scapegoating of Femininity*. Berkeley, CA: Seal Press.

Stone, A., 2019. Frame variations in child protection claims: constructions of gay men and transgender women as strangers. *Social Forces*, 97(3), pp. 1155–1176. DOI: 10.1093/sf/soy077.

Thomas, R., 2008. A general inductive approach for analysing qualitative evaluation data. *American Journal of Evaluation*, 27, pp. 237–246. DOI: 10.1177/1098214005283748.

Women and Equalities Committee, 2018. *Reform of the Gender Recognition Act: Government Consultation*. London: Government Equalities Office.

Part 4
Practice and activism

12 A call to feminist praxis
The story of Nottinghamshire's misogyny hate crime policy

Zaimal Azad and Sophie Maskell

Introduction

"What about women?"

As Centre Manager at Nottingham Women's Centre, Mel Jeffs found herself asking this question quite often: "What about women?" Mel asked it yet again on a drizzly April afternoon in 2014 when she met with George, the organiser for the Nottingham branch of Citizens UK: a non-partisan alliance of civil society institutions, comprising trade unions, faith groups, charities, schools and universities. Nottingham Citizens was about to launch a Commission into hate crime in Nottingham, having conducted a listening and scoping exercise to identify it as an issue that mattered to Nottingham's diverse communities. The 2011 Census reported that 35% of the population of the City were from BAME backgrounds (Nottingham Insight 2020).

Nottingham Citizens understood that hate crime impacts women differently, and therefore had approached Nottingham Women's Centre to ensure that women's experiences were included and reflected in the research. However, Mel was referring to something else when she posed the question, "What about women?": What about the things that women experience *because* they are women? In her role at Nottingham Women's Centre and as a lifelong feminist campaigner, Mel had conversations with women every day. She had heard time and again about women's experiences of being shouted at, harassed, threatened, cat-called, groped and objectified when out in public spaces. These were – and continue to be – behaviours that most women experienced, normalised to such a degree that there was no appropriate language or framework to talk about them outside of academic or activist spheres. Instead, there was an understanding that this was just 'part and parcel' of being a woman. Nottingham Citizens invited Mel to be one of the Commissioners leading this inquiry into hate crime – and so began the journey of misogyny being recognised as a hate crime in Nottinghamshire.

DOI: 10.4324/9781003023722-12

Standing on the shoulders of giants

Two years on in 2016, Nottinghamshire Police became the first police force in the UK to include 'misogyny' as a category for *recording* hate crime. To put this in context, when an incident is reported as 'hate crime' in the UK, police forces are required to add a 'flag' or 'prejudice marker' to the recording of the incident. Nationally, the Home Office monitors the recording of race, religion, disability, sexual orientation and gender identity-based hate crime. This means that every police force in the country is required to record these and add the relevant 'flags'. Police forces, however, also have the option to add categories based on local needs and priorities. These additional categories are solely at the recording level within the police force and do not garner any further recognition in the broader criminal justice system. Therefore the 'misogyny as hate crime' policy is a reporting and recording exercise – it has implications for how the police respond to such incidents but does not change the response of other parts of the criminal justice process. For their policy, Nottinghamshire Police (2016) define misogyny as:

> Incidents against women that are motivated by the attitude of men towards women, and includes behaviour targeted at women by men simply because they are women. Examples of this may include unwanted or uninvited sexual advances; physical or verbal assault; unwanted or uninvited physical or verbal contact or engagement; use of mobile devices to send unwanted or uninvited messages or take photographs without consent or permission.

This specifically excludes domestic violence and abuse which is dealt with elsewhere in Nottinghamshire Police's overall strategy. Therefore in practice, the behaviours being dealt with under this framework in Nottinghamshire are what are commonly referred to as 'street harassment'. In tackling street harassment, Nottinghamshire stands on the shoulders of giants. Street harassment has been faced by women and girls all over the world who have found ways to express and resist it long before this work began in Nottinghamshire. Indeed, it is worth exploring the language that has been created over time by activists, academics and policy makers to articulate and frame this behaviour. It is within this context of decades of activism, research and campaigning that the misogyny as hate crime policy presents a new response and way of framing these behaviours.

Speaking out: the evolving language and activism on street harassment

The feminist consciousness-raising of the 1970s and 1980s – a period that started conversations on the many forms of violence against women – has been identified as the beginning of women's articulation of these everyday forms of harassment as part of the wider picture of women's oppression (Langelan 1993). Liz Kelly (1987, 1988) formally theorised this for the first time in her concept of a 'continuum of sexual violence'. Kelly's (1988) continuum includes 'commonplace intrusions' such as those which happen on the streets, and extends to rape, domestic violence and femicide. Kelly (1988) places these in the context of "men's power and women's resistance". This approach was a critical development in understanding women's experiences of violence. It recognised that women's experiences of gendered violence could not be contained within the rigid legal parameters that defined sexual offences.

In contemporary discourse, the language of 'harassment' has since been identified as the most common framing of gendered violence in public settings (Vera-Gray 2014; Logan 2015). Social media has played an important role in restarting conversations about everyday forms of harassment. In 2005, Hollaback! was launched as a US based blog collecting stories of women and LGBTQI people who had been harassed on the streets. It is now a global movement with chapters in over 15 countries (Hollaback! 2020). Stop Street Harassment is another campaign against street harassment which started in 2008 as a blog, and now runs as a global resource with projects such as International Street Harassment Week (Stop Street Harassment 2020).

In the UK, street harassment exploded into the public consciousness with the launch of the Everyday Sexism project in 2012. The project initially started as a website, Twitter and Facebook account to record and share women's stories of 'sexism faced on a daily basis, by ordinary women in ordinary places' (Everyday Sexism Project 2020). Starting at approximately the same time that the Everyday Sexism movement was taking off, the campaign has sat alongside multiple ongoing conversations nationally and globally about harassment, women in public space and the power dynamics that shape women's experiences. While the policy change happened before the #MeToo movement gained prominence, #MeToo has undoubtedly also been a factor in pushing the conversation forward. Events such as the tragic murder of Jo Cox and the ongoing online abuse of women MPs, especially Black women MPs, have all formed part of the picture the campaign is situated in.

While feminist activists have organised around this issue for a long time, policies or laws that specifically target or acknowledge street harassment – and name it as such – are rare. However, many existing laws have clauses that certain 'street harassment' behaviours can be reported under (Hollaback!; DLA Piper and Thomas Reuters Foundation 2014; Logan 2015). In England and Wales, different forms of verbal street harassment can be reported under the Public Order Act 1986 or the Protection from Harassment Act 1997. Behaviours such as groping are covered under 'Common Assault' under the Criminal Justice Act 2003 or the Sexual Offences Act 2003 which also covers flashing. Whether these laws are fully utilised depends upon whether women realise that legislation covers normalised, everyday 'street harassment'. Furthermore, these isolated offences as they appear in law do not recognise the broader continuum of men's violence against women that Kelly (1987, 1988) and many academics and activists have identified. It is in this context that the activists in Nottinghamshire set to work in providing women with another framework to articulate and resist these everyday experiences of violence and intrusion. This framework is not an alternative to the Violence Against Women and Girls (VAWG) framework – instead it proposes a parallel policy response that sits alongside it.

"Misogyny": naming the problem

As discussed, the hate crime framework does not in itself create additional laws that provide legal redress to those victimised. What it does is provide the opportunity to record and respond to crimes that already exist in law in a different way, whilst also enabling a shift in how incidents are *framed* and perceived by society at large. If hate crime is a "message crime" (Chakraborti 2012) used to send a message to all members of the group being targeted, then the framework which enables the naming and addressing of these behaviours has a powerful symbolic function of determining what is acceptable, or not, in a society. By including "misogyny" in this framework and enabling it to be reported and made visible in a way not done previously, the same symbolic function is carried out – of making these previously normalised behaviours explicitly unacceptable.

The decision to name "misogyny" as the category as opposed to "gender" further emphasises this. Having worked closely with the Women's Centre, Nottinghamshire Police explained this decision in their official submission to the Women and Equalities Committee's Inquiry into Sexual Harassment of Women and Girls (2018):

> After taking evidence feedback locally and nationally, Nottinghamshire Police took the decision to identify Misogyny specifically to identify the problem for what it is – behaviour by men against women… the decision to record Misogyny was taken to be clear and upfront in identifying the real and present problem faced routinely by half of the population through application of the same principles that apply to other strands of hate crime – that they are victimised simply through their identity as women.

Nottinghamshire Police go on to argue that they had chosen the framing of misogyny over gender-based hate crime as they considered it far more likely to reach the public consciousness. Had they not, they question whether the same level of awareness – and reporting – would have been achieved (Nottinghamshire Police 2018). Crucially, they had evidence for this:

> Nottinghamshire Police has been able to identify additional forms of hate crime to the nationally monitored strands on its call handling

system using "qualifiers" for approximately 10 years. Included in the qualifiers available has been Gender. Contact Management staff are used to applying these qualifiers and are familiar with the concept of gender-based prejudice. The relative numbers of reports pre and post "Misogyny" are therefore pertinent to the debate around terminology... From 2014 to the force's introduction of Misogyny, call handlers qualified 24 gender hate crimes. Of these, eight were hostility to gender in context of sexual orientation whilst 13 were hostile to gender identity in context of gender reassignment. The remaining three were reports of gender that would now be classed as Misogynistic – workplace harassment of a woman and gender-based abuse of two women following driving incidents. For Nottinghamshire Police, the conclusion derived from this was that our staff have had the ability to record gender hate crime and have demonstrated the ability to do so, but the reports have not been forthcoming; three "Misogyny" reports in 30 months. The level of reporting following the decision to identify Misogyny suggests to the force that this explicit identification is necessary to encourage women to report the hate crime they experience purely because of their gender.

In this way, the hate crime framework provided feminist activists and Nottinghamshire Police an opportunity to re-frame the everyday misogynistic street harassment of women in our collective imaginary. No longer did those experiences exist in isolation from one another in little-known legal clauses, but in a powerful, socially symbolic framework that recognised their breadth, everydayness and wider patterns of oppression, adding another layer to the existing understandings of the continuum of violence against women.

Feminist praxis and the power of framing

Through employing the hate crime framework to tackle misogyny, Nottinghamshire put 'strategic framing' into practice (McAdam et al. 1996; Benford and Snow 2000). Benford and Snow (2000) claim that social movements mobilise around what they perceive to be a problem, and present possible solutions to that problem. The concept of 'strategic framing' necessitates the 'deliberate deployment of concepts and categories in political contests to achieve particular goals' (Bacchi 2009). 'Strategic framing' assumes conscious and strategic decision making in the choice of frames by agentic actors who are aware of the repertoire of ideas and discourses available to them. Nottingham Citizens' Commission into hate crime provided an opportunity to the activists in Nottingham, making available the frame of hate crime as a possible policy response to street harassment – a local solution to a global problem.

This approach is not without its issues. Bacchi (2009) argues that frames that are consciously and strategically chosen by movement actors are shaped – to a certain degree, at least – by hegemonic discourses and routine understandings of the world. Re-framing misogyny within the hate crime schema is no exception. The hate crime framework, in its legal construction and its translation into practice, is problematic on many levels. For example, it can emphasise individualistic understandings of discrimination over perspectives of structural oppression, diverting focus on 'incidents' rather than institutions and power. There are also concerns about who feels able to report and who doesn't. In instances where communities have poor relationships with law enforcement agencies, they are less likely to report their experiences to the police. In this way, especially when considering misogynistic hate crime, the framework can inadvertently perpetuate existing power structures by recording – and therefore centring – white women's experiences over those of black women, since white women are more likely to have confidence to report (ONS 2020). It can be argued though that this holds true for any law or policy that relates to the criminal justice system and is not a limitation of the hate crime framework *per se*.

At the same time, in some ways the hate crime framework facilitates an intersectional approach by enabling multiple prejudices to be captured at the reporting stage (for example, a Muslim woman targeted for her hijab in Nottinghamshire can report it as an incident based on misogyny, race and religion and all three types of prejudice would be recorded). However, this does not remain the case further along in the criminal justice system and when it comes to enhanced sentencing (which in its current form is itself only applicable to certain kinds of hate crime), one form of 'hostility' has to be chosen.

However, this does not mean that strategic frames cannot be transformative. Using available and existing discourses is not simply operating within them – processes of resistance and transformation also take place within these discourses (Lombardo et al. 2009). Bacchi (2009, p. 27) terms this critical frame analysis 'reflexive framing', and 'calls upon feminist activists and researchers to subject their own frames to critical scrutiny'. The process of 'reflexive framing' in a way that centres the diverse voices of women and girls has the potential to be radical across all levels of policy making and community building. In its intersectionality with race, religion, (dis)ability, class, sexuality, gender and age, misogyny as hate crime is the practice of what bell hooks (1984) might term, "bringing the margins to the centre" – an absolute tenet of the practice and the production of equality. It is by taking this approach to the implementation of the policy that some of the limitations described above can be overcome.

We describe this union of feminist theory and pragmatic practice as 'feminist praxis', and we call upon all policy makers, researchers and community-based practitioners to continuously re-centre the voices of women and girls across all of their praxis. Here is Nottinghamshire's story.

"Because I am a woman"

"Today I want to ask you something. I want to ask you why is it okay that I was threatened with rape for no reason other than that I am a woman who a man had access to? I want to ask you why this hatred for women is something I am supposed to just accept as part of my life? More importantly I want to ask you what you're going to do about this. Will you start a conversation with us about misogyny so that the next time a woman is physically, verbally or sexually assaulted for being a woman she is able to report it? Or will you tell me to get over it because I am a woman and living in fear comes with the territory?'"[1]

This testimony was given when the *No Place for Hate Commission* was officially launched in June 2014 at a gathering attended by more than 250 people at St. Nic's, a church in the heart of Nottingham. It was an unlikely alliance led by faith leaders, disability groups, feminists and LGBTQ+ campaigners, and no one was quite sure where it would go.

After the launch of the Commission, the first stage of the process began: research. Under the direction and supervision of academics from Nottingham's two universities, a survey was launched in an attempt to uncover the scale and nature of hate crime in Nottingham, followed by individual and focus group interviews. Alongside this process, expert submissions were requested and received from dozens of organisations, and contact made with local authorities, police forces and civic agencies across the country to seek out best practice. Whilst this was going on, the team at Nottingham Women's Centre carried out their own background research, looking at what had been done elsewhere on women and hate crime. Crucially, they undertook consultation with the women's sector in Nottingham, a city that has developed a strong women's sector engaging in effective partnerships with statutory services. This has resulted in a robust approach to Domestic and Sexual Violence and Abuse (DSVA) and it was imperative that the voices of the local women's sector were heard.

This research and consultation conducted by the Women's Centre quickly showed that there are no easy answers to where hate crime fits – if at all – within the VAWG agenda (Gill and Mason-Bish 2013). Locally there were fears that creating an additional process may hinder the established good practice for DSVA on both a practical and operational level. This intersection between hate crime and the VAWG agenda has been an issue practitioners, academics and policy makers have been grappling with across the globe – indeed the debate is still ongoing. For the campaign, it was still unclear at this stage how the two might effectively come together.

What remained clear was the overwhelming prevalence of normalised misogyny (Anonymous quoted in Nottingham Citizens 2014) and the need to provide women with some form of recourse:

I have been repeatedly shouted at in the street since 13 years of age and this continues to this day. The shouts at times have been very sexually explicit and have caused me to fear for my personal safety, to take a different route, quicken pace, telephone for help etc. I have been followed by strangers and had to take a different more public route to avoid risk of assault I feared may otherwise occur...I have been repeatedly sexually assaulted in clubs and pubs. If I go out in Nottingham it happens on at least 50% of the nights I have been out socialising. Some episodes far more severe than others...I believe all of these incidents happened because of my gender and because of the attitudes of some towards my gender – i.e. they consider my bodily integrity to be unimportant because I am female.[2]

As the research stage progressed, it quickly became apparent that women's experiences of hate crime were markedly different from men in two ways (Nottingham Citizens 2014):

1. Women experiencing hate because of other elements of their identity (e.g. race, religion, disability) experienced this hate differently and in an obviously gendered way.
2. Women who did not experience hate crime based on any of the recognised strands were reporting being targeted solely because of their gender.

The gendered nature of other strands of hate crime is well documented and studied (Chakraborti and Zempi 2012; Mason-Bish and Zempi 2019), and the intersections of misogyny, racism, Islamophobia, transphobia, homophobia and disability-based prejudice were highlighted through the research conducted by the Commission. Women identifying as lesbians spoke of being threatened with 'corrective rape'; women with mobility issues reported not being able to get away from sexual assault; Muslim women were more likely to be targeted with Islamophobic hate crime than Muslim men; and Black women were targeted with abuse that was both misogynistic and racist. The online survey found that 38% of women reporting a hate crime explicitly linked it to their gender (Nottingham Citizens 2014).

The collection of women's stories gathered by the Commission led to Citizens recommending that Nottinghamshire Police work with Nottingham Women's Centre and the wider women's sector to monitor incidents motivated by misogyny (Nottingham Citizens 2014):

> Furthermore, Nottinghamshire Police should work with Nottingham Women's Centre and other groups specialising in gender equality to monitor crimes and incidents motivated by misogynistic intent. Nottinghamshire Police is ground breaking in much of its work to tackle domestic violence and it can break new ground by moving to properly categorise and monitor the substantial volumes of incidents, particularly public harassment, perceived by women to be motivated by a hatred of their gender as documented in this report. Nottinghamshire Police should clarify their current recording systems and ensure that there are processes in place to pick up the wider spectrum of misogynistic offences that women experience (such as by implementing similar changes to those implemented by the British Transport Police).[3]

Policy into practice

This recommendation marked the start of what became a partnership between Nottingham Women's Centre and Nottinghamshire Police to introduce and implement the ground-breaking policy. However, it was not all plain sailing. There were reservations on all sides – including within Nottinghamshire's women's sector – about how this fit within the wider VAWG agenda and whether there was a need for this new intervention to record incidents against women.

Nevertheless, the Commission's report and accompanying lobbying was enough to convince Police and Crime Commissioner Paddy Tipping to give a grant to the Women's Centre in March 2015 to work with the police to explore this further. In September 2015, using the grant from the PCC, Nottingham Women's Centre and Nottingham Citizens organised the first Safer for Women summit. At this event, in front of decision makers from Nottinghamshire Police, the Office of the Police and Crime Commissioner, and Nottingham City and County Councils, women stood up and shared their experiences of being targeted on the street, in parks, in educational institutions, in bars and nightclubs. The question posed again and again was – *'should I have to put up with this because I am a woman'?* The answer that came back from decision makers was a clear 'no'.

The brave and powerful testimony of local women had made it clear that there was a whole range of harassing and misogynistic behaviours that women were experiencing every day that made them feel unsafe in their city. This harassment, which women did not feel able to report, forced them to change their behaviour. Some of these behaviours targeted at women were criminal offences but unreported due to the normalisation of such behaviours. Others were incidents that did not break the law but formed part of the picture of women's experiences of intrusion and violence. Recognising misogyny as a hate crime was one way of beginning to monitor and record these incidents and identify the scale of the problem. Perhaps more importantly, it was a way of saying to women of Nottingham that their experiences were valid and would be heard.

With agreement reached on recording misogynistic hate crime, work began on putting this policy into practice. Apart from logistical and operational challenges of introducing a new policy that had not been delivered elsewhere, there were also huge cultural challenges for this agenda within and outside Nottinghamshire Police. Both hate crime and VAWG are policy areas with considerable issues, historically and in the present, relating to attitudes of police officers, buy-in at various levels of the criminal justice system, treatment of victims and backlash from certain parts of the media (Hardy and Chakraborty 2017; Centre for Women's Justice, End Violence against Women Coalition, Rape Crisis England and Wales 2020). Now, these two challenging issues were being brought together and no one expected it to be easy. In 2016, with Sue Fish becoming Chief Constable of

Nottinghamshire Police and a champion for the policy, the project was fully green-lit – but the hard work was just getting started.

Hate crime is hugely under-reported for many reasons, one of the most significant being that the communities most likely to experience it are often the ones with historically poor relationships with the police and other statutory services. In this context, endeavours to increase reporting have to go alongside efforts to develop understanding and sensitivity within the police to ensure an appropriate response. It was imperative to recognise the low trust and confidence women often have in the criminal justice system, especially when reporting sexual violence, and the fear women carry of being disbelieved, dismissed or ridiculed. This is exacerbated with other marginalised strands of identity. Women from BAME backgrounds, for example, have even lower confidence to report any crime to the police than white women (ONS 2020). Therefore, due to the need to improve trust and confidence in the police and ensure positive experience for victims, one of the first priorities – before making the policy public – was training for Nottinghamshire Police staff, from call handlers to front line officers.

A video was developed with recordings of women speaking about their experiences directly to officers, with a preface by the Chief Constable emphasising the importance of the policy. The video was accompanied by a training session developed by Nottingham Women's Centre, Nottinghamshire Police and Hollaback! Nottingham. This was delivered first to control room staff to enable them to identify misogynistic hate incidents being reported, then to officers and other staff, such as front desk personnel. It is not known to the authors whether senior officers also received this training, which would be an interesting point to explore in relation to cultural change within institutions. Feedback on the training was mixed and this has since been corroborated by the impact evaluation of the policy (Mullany and Trickett 2018). Whilst it was a powerful tool in communicating experiences of women and the impact of those experiences, it was felt that it did not speak to staff in the way it could have done if there had been more input from those with policing experience, either as co-trainers or involved in the development of the training product. This highlights a key learning from the pilot about consistently seeking the voices involved at all levels of the process. It is, once again, that reflexive feminist praxis that is based on reflection, critique, co-production and listening.

Having laid the groundwork, on 1 April 2016 Nottinghamshire Police made history – quietly at first – by becoming the first police force in the country to begin recording misogyny as a hate crime. It was only in July 2016, after the policy had been in place for a quarter of a year, that it was made public. The decision to delay the public announcement and publicity of the policy was made to ensure that the systems set in place were functioning and that women would receive the response they were promised when reporting.

Misogyny unleashed: backlash to the policy

A media storm followed. With sensationalist headlines fiercely debating the policy and singling out the 'harmless, complimentary wolf-whistler' as being under threat from criminal law (Brown 2016; Collins 2016; Retter 2016), it was only a matter of time before the news went from local to national to international. Nottinghamshire had not, in fact, made wolf-whistling illegal. It had drawn a line in the sand. It had said that it would no longer tell women to put up with behaviours they found intrusive, abusive and harmful just for being women. The focus on wolf-whistling by swathes of the media served to minimise women's experiences of everyday gendered violence. Nottinghamshire Police's policy was not criminalising acts that were not previously criminal, it was giving women an opportunity to report behaviour that was targeted at them because of their gender.

This simple but radical shift brought forth an avalanche of fury that proved the need for the policy. The women involved in the campaign received a torrent of horrific abuse and threats (Ridley 2016). Mel – as a key spokesperson for the campaign – was told by men online that she was "not attractive enough" to speak about street harassment. Another man told her she should get cancer. An American man even wrote a post saying that if he ever visited the UK he would "make sure every woman I see there is treated like shit". Another man threatened to stab her with a dagger in one particularly graphic post. Protection in the form of police patrols was placed around Nottingham Women's Centre. Large parts of traditional and social media debated whether women should or should not have to put up with street harassment. Questions arose as to whether this was the end of flirting and courtship as we know it. The misogyny unleashed in response to a local policy change – one that simply sought to validate and record women's experiences – brought to the fore the consequences women face for speaking out. It highlighted the culture of acceptability and trivialisation around misogyny. The prospect of national rollout suddenly became all the more tempting to the women activists.

From Nottingham to nation

"I don't think it's sexual. It's not an attraction thing, it's a power thing. To me – unconsciously perhaps – but men seem to own public space more than women, just in the way I see even young boys behaving like that. And that's not their fault but it needs to be sorted out at quite a young age. I think there's a distinction; it's like when a man, in a car on his own, deliberately slows down and genuinely, deludedly thinks that they've got some actual chance with you by being creepy. But with the groups of men it's more intimidation, it's more power. It's ownership of public space."[4]

As one Nottingham woman testifies in the evaluation report (Mullany and Trickett 2018), misogyny is "a power thing," and the practice of utilising the hate crime framework for a local policing policy enabled Nottinghamshire to re-frame that power. The policy made something that is an everyday experience for women – behaviour that is at once violent and mundane – everyone's business. In placing women's experiences front and centre of policy making, it shows the possibilities for feminist praxis. Through its process of coalition-building, listening and organising, the misogyny hate crime campaign highlights feminist ways of working for the future. With the announcement of the Law Commission review of hate crime in 2018, we now have the opportunity to review and re-frame the power structures that generate, reinforce and perpetuate misogyny across the country. This section focuses on the importance of sustainable, community-building practices in the disempowerment of misogyny, and how Nottingham's conversation about misogyny went from local to national.

For women, misogynistic incidents do not happen in a theoretical framework. They happen in real time and space; a violation of body and self, and a violation of 'community' and the safety net one's community should provide. Indeed, the role of community has been critical for Nottingham's feminist praxis of misogyny as hate crime. The pilot itself was borne from women working at the grassroots and community organising. Without the buy-in of communities, it was recognised that a local policing policy could only go so far. The question of where to begin will always be daunting. However, Nottingham Women's Centre knew that robust evidence would be central to evolving the feminist praxis of misogyny as hate crime. We therefore went back to the community to evaluate the impact of the pilot and set its direction for the future.

Evaluation of the policy: back to community

Funded again by the PCC, the Women's Centre commissioned Louise Mullany of the University of Nottingham and Loretta Trickett of Nottingham Trent University to conduct an evaluation in order to assess the impact that the policy has had on the everyday lives of the general public living in Nottinghamshire (Mullany and Trickett 2018). The detailed findings and recommendations can be found in the evaluation report and also in Chapter 14, but key to this chapter are the following:

- Misogyny Hate Crime is highly prevalent. Of the 679 people who participated, 93.7% had experienced or witnessed street harassment in Nottinghamshire.
- High percentages of women have experienced harassment at the higher end of the crime continuum. This includes unwanted sexual advances (48.9%), groping (46.2%), sexually explicit language (54.3%) and indecent exposure (25.9%). A quarter of respondents reported that they had

experienced sexual assault (24.7%) and a fifth of respondents reported that they had experienced online abuse (21.7%).
- Women from Black and Minority Ethnic groups often experience Misogyny Hate Crime and Race Hate Crime simultaneously and report feeling doubly vulnerable to attack.
- 45.6% of respondents thought educational strategies should be implemented to change societal attitudes.
- Many of the male respondents found the behaviour characteristic of Misogyny Hate Crime completely unacceptable and wanted to prevent it from happening. They valued the opportunity to be consulted and wanted to help by being integrated and included in discussions and training.

Based on these findings, Nottingham Women's Centre worked with the researchers to set recommendations, some of which are:

- Roll out the policy nationally to increase publicity and reporting – there was clear support for the policy from men and women in the Nottinghamshire general public, as well as victims who have reported their experiences to the police.
- Raise awareness of the policy through sustained publicity campaigns that are intersectional in their approach.
- Change negative attitudes and behaviours that perpetuate misogyny hate crime through educational campaigns. Include campaigns that actively and positively engage boys and men.
- Use a multi-agency approach to work alongside the Police to bring about sustained social and cultural change.
- Review the wording of the policy. Members of the public and the police viewed the term 'misogyny' as too elitist or academic. Many of those surveyed thought 'hate crime' was an unhelpful term. Consideration should therefore be given as to whether the policy needs to be renamed to 'gender hate crime' or similar, or whether education about what the terms mean would be a better approach.

These findings and recommendations are a starting point. The recommendations are broad but by no means exhaustive. One common thread is that effective education – within community spaces, institutions and education settings – will be the key to acknowledging misogyny as a form of hate crime in the short term, and dismantling misogyny in the long-term. This education must be radical in the approach it takes and intersectional in its nature. It must take a whole community approach. And it must be unapologetic in its feminist praxis whilst remaining accessible to those it seeks to reach.

In spite of decreasing funding, Nottingham Women's Centre was able to trial some of the recommendations locally. For the educational work with young people, Nottingham Women's Centre partnered with local domestic abuse charity Equation who are experienced in delivering feminist education packages in local schools. Together, they developed a misogyny awareness session for students and teachers centred around the experiences of young people. In a four-month trial, the partnership delivered this to almost 2,000 students and members of staff. Staff were key to the success of this approach because of their role in ensuring a sustainable culture change within the school. For broader awareness-raising, Nottingham Women's Centre continued to engage with local and national media, as well as delivering talks to a wide range of audiences. This included university students, MPs, local authorities, police, policymakers, schools, academics, campaigners, community practitioners and local grassroots groups. Nottingham Women's Centre also conducted marketing campaigns that promoted the policy across local transport networks and social media. Reporting rates were small – in line with all strands of hate crime – but steadily rising.

Importantly, the launch of the evaluation report (Mullany and Trickett 2018) and the attention this received rejuvenated the conversation on a national rollout of misogyny as hate crime. This secured the support of Stella Creasy MP who then tabled the recommendation as an amendment to the Voyeurism Bill (particularly known for banning 'upskirting') in 2018. Whilst the amendment did not go through, a Law Commission review was announced in its place. With the support of Citizens UK, Nottingham Women's Centre and Sue Fish coordinated the Law Commission's visit to Nottingham in June 2019 (Anon 2019). A range of community voices were invited to present evidence, with representatives from the Police, the Councils, Nottingham's two universities, community groups working on Hate Crime locally and, of course, Nottingham Women's Centre. The overwhelming plea to the Commission was to use Nottinghamshire as the start of this conversation about misogyny, not the end. Most importantly, the Women's Centre invited and supported local women to share their stories of misogyny with the Law Commission. Over 30 women gave written testimony, and several women bravely stood up and spoke aloud the most intimate and profound impacts that misogyny had on their lives.

These were stories of everyday microaggressions, street harassment, groping, being told they could not pursue their dreams, childhood abuse, so called 'honour'-based abuse, transphobia, racism, police brutality and rape, to name but some. The women stood together before the Commission, united in their demand for change. Tears were shed, not only by these women but throughout the audience of police officers, academics, lawyers, practitioners and campaigners. A social transgression had been made: 'a veil torn down'. For when the visceral, identity-destroying nature of misogynistic hate was laid bare, suddenly it did not feel very normal at all. As the last woman to speak concluded (Anon 2019): "This has happened to my mother, her mother and me. Will this happen to my daughter too?"[5]

Despite their determination and enthusiasm, one Women's Centre in Nottingham could never do it all. The Centre has faced multiple barriers in not only securing the policy pilot, but in continuing its momentum so that it translates into real, everyday change. They experienced significant challenges in making those daily decisions on how to prioritise resources, workloads, staffing and time for an organisation on the frontline. From barriers relating to funding cuts and capacity, to counter-action and counter-rhetoric, the work needing to be done to engage the public to buy-in and take action often felt insurmountable. This is another reason why the methodology of community organising, building allies and partnership working becomes even more important. Change cannot be achieved alone.

Into the future: a feminist call to action

"Misogyny is the soil in which violence against women and girls grows."

The misogyny as hate crime policy was never meant to be the full and singular answer to street harassment and broader forms of VAWG, and the path that has led to it has always recognised both the challenges and limitations of this policy. It is one tool of many that are needed to tackle the deep rooted misogyny and sexism that exist in our society, one of the manifestations of which is the violence and intrusion that many women experience on an almost-daily basis.

Through giving women an opportunity to report and name experiences they had previously been told to 'get over', acknowledging misogyny as a form of hate crime has shifted the narrative and validated those experiences. The organising and activism that led to this policy has enabled dialogue and discussion of concepts such as rape culture, victim blaming and the continuum of VAWG, in spaces where this language did not exist. Through centring and amplifying women's voices, we have seen the creation of a new generation of activists locally and nationally who are continuing to fight for this agenda in a myriad of different ways. In spite of concerns that framing misogyny as hate crime places it in opposition to the VAWG framework, locally it has enabled the women's sector to build on existing good practice and move from a structure that focused on DSVA, to a broader VAWG strategy and early intervention model.

The journey of this campaign offers a blueprint for feminist praxis and lessons in successful campaigning and policy making that centres the voices of those it impacts. The story of misogyny being recognised as a hate crime is one of allies and partnerships, of give and take, of community organising and community building, of listening and amplifying the voices of those least heard. The partnerships were not always easy and the allies were not always those you might expect for a feminist campaign. It was only through an openness and commitment to working together in order to make real change happen for local women that the policy change was achieved. It was done so with a recognition that the hate crime framework may not be perfect but it does provide an opportunity to change the narrative in a way that makes a difference to women's lives.

A successful campaign is not someone standing at a podium lecturing a message. It is a conversation that speaks both to change that has come before and change that is yet to come. It is also a conversation with our communities, our allies and yes, even our opponents. It is through and within these conversations that change happens and where action is generated from others. In recognising misogyny as a hate crime, Nottinghamshire restarted a conversation about women's experiences and the continuum of violence against women and girls, of which the policy is only the beginning. We invite you to continue this conversation, critique it, improve it, support it, challenge it – but don't end it, not until misogyny is a thing of the past.

Notes

1 Testimony at the launch of the No Place For Hate Commission (Anon 2014)
2 From the surveys, as included in the No Place For Hate Report (Nottingham Citizens 2014)
3 Citizens recommendation relating to misogyny
4 Misogyny Hate Crime Evaluation Report (Mullany and Trickett 2018)
5 Law Commission visit July 2019

References

Anon, 2014. *Testimony at the Launch of Nottingham Citizens No Place for Hate Commission*. Nottingham: Anon.

Anon, 2019. *Testimony at the Law Commission's Visit to Nottingham*. Nottingham: Anon.

Bacchi, C., 2009. The issue of intentionality in frame theory. In: Lombardo, E., Meier, P. and Verloo, M., eds. *The Discursive Politics of Gender Equality*. New York: Routledge, pp. 19–35.

Benford, R.D. and Snow, D., 2000. Framing processes and social movements: an overview and assessment. *Annual Review of Sociology*, 26, pp. 611–639.

Brown, B., 2016. Wolf-whistling a hate crime? What an insult to real victims of abuse. *The Daily Mail* [online]. Available at: https://www.dailymail.co.uk/news/article-3691284/Wolf-whistling-hate-crime-insult-real-victims-abuse.html [Accessed 1 December 2020].

Chakraborti, N., 2012. Introduction: hate crime victimization. *International Review of Victimology*, 18(1), pp. 3–6. DOI: 10.1177/0269758011422162.

Chakraborti, N. and Zempi, I., 2012. The veil under attack: gendered dimensions of Islamophobic victimisation. *International Review of Victimology*, 18(3), pp. 269–284. DOI: 10.1177/0269758012446983.

Centre for Women's Justice, End Violence against Women Coalition, Imkaan, and Rape Crisis England and Wales, 2020. The Decriminalisation of Rape: why the justice system is failing rape survivors and what needs to change. [online]. Available at: https://www.endviolenceagainstwomen.org.uk/wp-content/uploads/C-Decriminalisation-of-Rape-Report-CWJ-EVAW-IMKAAN-RCEW-NOV-2020.pdf [Accessed 23 May 2021].

Collins, D., 2016. Wolf whistling now a hate crime. *The Sun* [online]. 13 July. Available at: https://www.thesun.co.uk/news/1437301/police-to-start-recording-

unwanted-sexual-advances-in-same-crime-category-as-racist-abuse/ [Accessed 1 December 2020].
Gill, A.K. and Mason-Bish, H., 2013. Addressing violence against women as a form of hate crime: limitations and possibilities. *Feminist Review*, 105(1), pp. 1–20.
Hardy, S. and Chakraborti, N., 2017. *Hate Crime: Identifying and Dismantling Barriers to Justice*. Leicester: University of Leicester.
Hollaback! 2020. *About* [online]. About | Hollaback! we have the power to end harassment. ihollaback.org. [Accessed 30 November 2020].
Hollaback!; DLA Piper; Thomas Reuters Foundation, 2014. Street harassment: know your rights [online]. Available at: http://www.ihollaback.org/wp-content/uploads/2014/10/Street-Harassment-Know-Your-Rights.pdf [Accessed 1 December 2020].
hooks, b., 1984. *Feminist Theory from Margin to Centre*. Boston, MA: South End Press.
Kelly, L., 1987. The continuum of sexual violence. In: Hanmer, J. and Maynard, M., eds. *Women, Violence and Social Control*. London: MacMillan Press Limited, pp. 46–74.
Kelly, L., 1988. *Surviving Sexual Violence*. Cambridge: Polity Press.
Langelan, M.J., 1993. *Back Off! How to Confront and Stop Sexual Harassment and Harassers*. New York: Simon & Schuster.
Logan, L.S., 2015. Street harassment: current and promising avenues for researchers and activists. *Sociology Compass*, 9(3), pp. 196–211. DOI: 10.1111/soc4.12248.
Lombardo, E., Meier, P. and Verloo, M., 2009. *The Discursive Politics of Gender Equality: Stretching, Bending and Policy Making*. New York: Routledge.
Mason-Bish, H. and Zempi, I., 2019. Misogyny, racism and Islamophobia: street harassment at the intersections. *Feminist Criminology*, 14(5), pp. 540–559. DOI: 10.1177/1557085118772088.
McAdam, D., McArthy, J.D. and Zald, M.N., 1996. Introduction: opportunities, mobilizing structures and framing processes - towards a synthetic, comparative perspective on social movements. In: McAdam, D., McArthy, J.D. and Zald, M.N., eds. *Comparative Perspectives on Social Movements: Political Opportunities, Mobilizing Structures and Framing Processes*. Cambridge: Cambridge University Press, pp. 1–20.
Mullany, L. and Trickett, L., 2018. *Misogyny Hate Crime Evaluation Report*. Nottingham: Nottingham Women's Centre.
Nottingham Citizens, 2014. No place for Hate Commission for hate [online]. Available at: https://d3n8a8pro7vhmx.cloudfront.net/newcitizens/pages/1065/attachments/original/1469204592/A-CITIZENS-COMMISSION-NO-PLACE-FOR-HATE.pdf?1469204592 [Accessed 17 January 2021].
Nottingham Insight, 2020. Office for National Statistics [online]. Available at: https://www.nottinghaminsight.org.uk/population/ [Accessed 30 November 2020].
Nottinghamshire Police, 2016. *Hate Crime Policy*. Nottingham: Nottinghamshire Police.
Nottinghamshire Police, 2018. Written submission from Nottingham Police (SPP0049): misogyny as a hate crime to Women and Equalities Committee: inquiry into sexual harassment of women and girls [online]. Accessible at: Written evidence - Nottinghamshire police (parliament.uk) [Accessed 17 January 2021].
Office for National Statistics, 2020. *Crime Survey for England and Wales, Year Ending 31st March 2019*. London: Office for National Statistics.

Retter E., 2016. Joanna Lumley defends wolf-whistling and insists women are offended by 'everything'. *The Mirror* [online]. Available at: https://www.mirror.co.uk/3am/celebrity-news/joanna-lumley-defends-wolf-whistling-8980221 [Accessed 30 November 2020].

Ridley L., 2016. Women who helped make wolf whistling a hate crime have now been bombarded with sexist abuse. *Huffington Post* [online]. Available at: https://www.huffingtonpost.co.uk/entry/wolf-whistling-misogyny-hate-crime-nottingham_uk_579756cce4b06d7c426da55d?guccounter=1&guce_referrer=aHR0cHM6Ly93d3cuZ29vZ2xlLmNvbS8&guce_referrer_sig=AQAAADNEuY-jqZe470zQlzo1LiJb0FlQVoqslHJ067px1-fKFLMRaX4F9VBR1ZG05q4kmTVPT9XgfixhFxGSBPVFFNY5yP-BdRGx--KvfM7y1GKzx6jir8Xce9s4Yz-1FPXgh4hinX5u1wwxg6O0UVcJB0k4s7YdZeH-7NS9AidB22kR [Accessed 30 November 2020].

Stop Street Harassment, 2020. About. Available at: http://www.stopstreetharassment.org/about/ [Accessed 30 November 2020].

The Everyday Sexism Project, 2020. About [online]. Available at: http://everydaysexism.com/about [Accessed 30 November 2020].

Vera-Gray, F., 2014. *The great problems are in the street: a phenomenology of men's stranger intrusions on women in public space*. PhD thesis, London Metropolitan University, London.

13 Policing misogyny as a hate crime – the Nottinghamshire Police experience

Sue Fish

Introduction

In April 2016, Nottinghamshire Police were the first police force in the country to recognise, record and investigate misogyny as a hate crime (Khomami 2016). This policy arose out of a hate crime inquiry carried out in 2014 by the local branch of the social justice campaign group Citizens UK, and in my role as the then Chief Constable of Nottinghamshire Police. I was pivotal in the decision-making processes undertaken by Nottinghamshire Police in terms of adopting this policy, and its subsequent implementation. In this chapter, I will reflect on the considerations which influenced the policy development (such as the inclusion, or not, of domestic violence) and the reactions to this policy, including how policing both understands and treats women's lived experiences. I will also examine the constitutional and legal position of the tripartite structure between the Chief Constable, Police and Crime Commissioner, and the Home Secretary at local and national levels, as well as look at the legitimacy of such decision making, and the impact of the policy on other police forces. I will also consider some of the evidence gathered which demonstrates the efficacy of this hate crime policy, and evaluation of the approach adopted in Nottinghamshire. Meaningful evaluation is increasingly important in policing, so that the impact of policy changes – whether positive or otherwise – is evident and transparent. The rigorous evaluation of our policy undertaken by academics (Mullany and Trickett 2018), is another essential element of the approach of Nottinghamshire Police. The evidenced narrative of this chapter demonstrates the national innovation of the policy, and suggests international good practice.

Local and national evidence for adopting the policy

Nottingham Citizens (the local branch of Citizens UK) carried out an investigation in 2014 into the reporting of hate crimes in Nottingham; this was known as the Citizens Hate Crime Commission 2014 (Nottingham Citizens 2014). The study was overseen by Associate Professor Loretta Trickett from Nottingham Trent University in order to ensure that its methodology and

DOI: 10.4324/9781003023722-13

analysis were rigorous, and its findings credible. The recording of hate crime based on the nationally-recognised five protected characteristics (race, religion, transgender, sexual orientation, and disability) was considered as part of the research (Nottingham Citizens 2014). Gender was not initially included in the survey, but as the researchers began analysing the results, they found one very clear trend emerging: female respondents reported being victimised simply because they were women (Nottingham Citizens 2014). No similar claims about gender were made by male participants. The investigation highlighted a need for further work to identify and catalogue crimes and incidents perpetrated towards women solely because of their gender. Specifically, the Citizens Hate Crime Commission (Nottingham Citizens 2014) found that:

- 38% of women reported hate crime explicitly linked this to gender, a category currently not recognised in hate crime legislation, enforcement, sentencing, and data collection.
- Women were even less likely to report incidents motivated by misogyny to the police than other types of hate crimes.
- Only 28% of women surveyed would report any crimes to the police.
- The greatest number of hate crimes and incidents took place in the street, and also occurred on public transport, work, home, and school/college/university.
- The impact of hate crimes and hate incidents on victims was significant, with "psychological wellbeing acutely undermined" (Nottingham Citizens 2014, p. 7).

The Citizens Hate Crime Commission (Nottingham Citizens 2014) also identified how experiencing multiple oppressions, also known as intersectionality, disproportionately increased the chances of women being subject to hate crime; experiencing hate based on other aspects of their identity in addition to gender. This was especially pronounced in cases of Islamophobia, antisemitism, homophobic, and transphobic hate crimes. This was echoed by one of the respondents who reported being subject to intersectional hate crime as being a "triple whammy", namely being a woman, a Muslim, and having brown skin (Citizens UK 2019).

The findings of the Citizens Hate Crime Commission (Nottingham Citizens 2014) drew out significant aspects of women's victimisation, such as the "normalisation" of incidents, under-reporting, and a lack of confidence in the response of agencies. This was consistent across their experiences of victimisation and reporting patterns to authorities, including the police. These were exacerbated in hate crime cases where race, religion, sexuality, and/or disability were motivating factors. The systematic nature of patriarchy, apparent within the Criminal Justice System, has not only an exclusionary and also a debilitating effect on women, preventing women from being seen being heard, and having their lived experiences as well as the consequences of their victimisation being recognised. Together these make achieving justice for all women difficult, and near impossible for those from more marginalised groups. One might recognise that some women may manage to get justice, but they are usually from particularly privileged backgrounds.

The Citizens Hate Crime Commission (Nottingham Citizens 2014) also found that many women did not know how or where to report the misogyny experienced, and that being on the receiving end of such behaviour was perceived to be 'normal'. The assumption of those within policing is that "everyone" knows how to report crimes and that there are no real barriers to reporting if an incident really occurred. However, there is a considerable body of research on reporting rates of crime, which suggests that when women are victimised because of their gender – particularly by domestic violence and sexual offences, – reporting rates are low. The assumption also speaks to the white male norm that reporting mechanisms are known, understood, and that there is confidence in being taken seriously and believed. Even when women do report to the police or third parties, they are being told to accept unlawful behaviour as normal – the inference being that unless very serious, such behaviour is not "really" criminal, and women should put up with comments or assault, and accept that they will be heckled, harassed, and threatened. It should not be a case that women are told that harassment is just a 'part of life' and not worth being investigated. The Citizens Hate Crime Commission (Nottingham Citizens 2014, p. 30) specifically recommended that:

> Nottinghamshire Police should work with Nottingham Women's Centre and other groups specialising in gender equality to monitor crimes and incidents motivated by misogynistic intent. Nottinghamshire Police can break new ground by moving to categorise and monitor the substantial volumes of incidents, particularly public harassment, perceived to be motivated by hatred of their gender. Nottinghamshire Police should clarify their current recording systems and ensure there are processes in place to pick up the wider spectrum of misogynistic offences that women experience.

For Nottinghamshire Police to make a positive decision to adopt misogyny as a hate crime, the Citizens Hate Crime Commission (Nottingham Citizens 2014) was considered as local evidence. In addition, national evidence was also examined. A number of studies were also relevant to Nottinghamshire Police's decision making to adopt misogyny as a hate crime when recording crime. A study by Demos (2014, p. 4) found that, between 26 December 2013 and 9 February 2014, there were around 100,000 instances of the word 'rape' used in English from UK-based Twitter accounts. They estimated that around 12% of those were threatening (Demos 2014, p. 4). They also found that, between 9 January and 4 February 2014, there were around 131,000 cases of 'slut' or 'whore' used in English from UK-based Twitter accounts, 18% of which appeared to be misogynistic (Demos 2014, p. 5). Furthermore, the Pew Research Centre's study of online harassment (Duggan 2014) found that approximately 50% of young people aged between 18 and 24 had been called offensive names online, 26% of young women had been stalked, 25% of young women had been sexually harassed, and around 23% of young people had been physically threatened.

However, this is not an issue for which the evidence solely exists online. Founder of the Everyday Sexism Project, Laura Bates, wrote in *The Guardian* (Bates 2016):

> I have spoken to hundreds of women and girls whose lives are affected on a daily basis by verbal and physical harassment in public spaces...A woman being followed home by a man aggressively sexually propositioning her and refusing to take no for an answer; a 14-year-old girl being shouted at by men making lewd gestures as she walks to school in her uniform; a pregnant woman being groped on the bus; a runner being made to feel so unsafe by repeated verbal harassment that she simply gives up exercising outside.

A poll run by the group End Violence Against Women found that 85% of women aged 18–24 had experienced unwanted sexual attention and nearly half of this group had experienced unwanted sexual touching. The survey further found that 63% of women generally feel unsafe in public spaces and almost half undertake deliberate 'safety planning' when they go out in the evenings (Sandhu 2016). Similarly, Hollaback! also found that most women experience catcalling for the first time between the ages of 11–17, with 90% of British women having experienced street harassment by the age of 17 (Fenton 2015) (see also Chapter 6 in this book). Overall, this substantial evidence base has continued to grow and simply endorses that misogyny is widespread, women do not report to police, intersectionality is significant, and the impact on women is cumulative and devastating. These studies were relevant to Nottinghamshire Police's decision to adopt misogyny as a hate crime.

As well as the evidence from Citizens UK and the wider studies discussed above, we considered evidence from Nottingham Women's Centre. In response to the Citizens Hate Crime Commission (Nottingham Citizens 2014), Nottingham Women's Centre put forward the case that misogyny was a missing category under current hate crime definitions and that, given the scale of harassment and abuse that women face daily, policies should be revised to include misogyny as a hate crime. An inaugural *Safer for Women* Summit (Equation 2015) was held in September 2015, coordinated by Nottingham Women's Centre, Nottinghamshire's Police and Crime Commissioner, and Nottingham Trent University. I chaired as the then Deputy Chief Constable. The conference heard powerful testimony from victims of street harassment, as well as about the ground-breaking *Project Guardian* from British Transport Police. The event culminated in a call for individuals, agencies, and businesses to make a pledge towards a new Women's Safety Charter for Nottinghamshire, which Nottinghamshire Police signed up to.

Furthermore, it is important to bear in mind the socio-cultural backdrop within which this work took place. Specifically, this work took place in 2014 and 2015, several years ahead of the popularisation of the #MeToo movement (which gained international prominence in 2017) and the highly influential Time's Up campaign (in 2018) (Lagone 2018). Both the #MeToo movement and the Time's Up campaign have encouraged women to speak up about sexual harassment, assault, inequalities, with the combination of these two movements having arguably transformed the mainstream media narrative and reporting of sexual harassment (Lagone 2018).

Internal debates and processes for adopting the policy

Turning a policy pledge into practice meant significant internal debate in Nottinghamshire Police, and engagement with Paddy Tipping, the Police and Crime Commissioner (PCC) for Nottinghamshire. To understand the path to introducing misogyny as hate crime in Nottinghamshire, it is helpful to describe the constitutional position of the PCC.

Until 2012 governance of policing was a tripartite arrangement between a local Chief Constable, a local Police Authority, and the Home Secretary (Home Affairs Committee 2008). In the 2010 British General Election campaign, the Conservative and Liberal Democrat manifestos outlined plans, to, respectively, replace or reform the existing system; both political parties raising concerns about the perceived lack of accountability of police authorities to the communities they serve (Conservative Party 2010; Liberal Democrats 2010). Following the 2010 General Election, the Coalition Government agreement pledged the following (HM Government, 2010):

> We will introduce measures to make the police more accountable through oversight by a directly elected individual, who will be subject to strict checks and balances by locally elected representatives.

The introduction of elected PCC's occurred following the enactment of the Police Reform and Social Responsibility Act 2011. The first elections for PCC posts were held in November 2012 (UK Parliament 2012). The core functions of PCCs are to secure the maintenance of an efficient and effective police force within their area, and to hold the Chief Constable to account for the delivery of the police and crime plan. Police and Crime Commissioners set the budget for their policing area and have responsibility for raising the local policing precept from council tax payments from residents. Police and Crime Commissioners are also responsible for the appointment, suspension, and dismissal of the Chief Constable (APCCS 2020). In short, the PCC sets the strategic direction for their police force, and the Chief Constable has responsibility for the operational matters. The Policing Protocol Order 2011 sets out the relationship between PCC and Chief Constable and is explicit in relation to operational independence. It states:

> The Chief Constable is accountable to the law for the exercise of police powers, and to the PCC for the delivery of efficient and effective policing, management of resources and expenditure by the police force. At all times the chief constable, their constables and staff, remain operationally independent in the service of the communities that they serve.
> (Policing Protocol order 2011, paragraph 2)

I outline these distinct responsibilities because it is necessary to understand where the decision-making power sits within those police forces who decide to record misogyny as a hate crime. It is an operational decision and therefore one for the Chief Constable and, on paper, the Chief Constable alone. Though PCCs do not have operational control of policing, the priorities of a PCC may exert significant influence and pressure on the Chief Constable. For example, if the PCC made implementing misogyny as a hate crime a priority the Chief Constable would have to have regard to it.

However, in practice whilst the roles of PCC and Chief Constable are separate and distinct, the most effective working model is that of partnership between the two. This was certainly the case in Nottinghamshire, where the strategic leadership of the PCC, Paddy Tipping, and the operational leadership of myself, the Chief Constable, were in harmony. The PCC pledged to tackle street harassment and misogynistic hate crime, prioritising it in his Police and Crime plan for 2016/2017. This complemented the operational decision undertaken by me. PCC Tipping reinforced this by reiterating this priority in his 2017/2018, and subsequent, police and crime plans (Nottinghamshire PCC 2018). The motivation guiding Nottinghamshire Police and the PCC has been a need to increase women's willingness to report misogynistic hate crime. It was felt that the subsequent increase in the number of hate crimes reported would encourage women to be more confident to report misogynistic hate crime: both in allowing them to recognise that reporting such behaviour is legitimate, and that it will be taken seriously.

As Nottinghamshire's Police Chief Constable at the time, I worked with colleagues, stakeholders, universities and media locally and nationally. Following Nottinghamshire's Police decision to record misogyny as a hate crime, there was concern on a number of fronts expressed by police colleagues, especially outside of Nottinghamshire. Indeed, very little concern was expressed locally – I would like to think that this was due to the levels of engagement with colleagues and partners in formulation of the policy and the comprehensive training about hate crime given to all our front-line officers and staff. However, many senior police colleagues across the country appeared unconvinced by our innovative approach. It was apparent to me that 'double standards' were at play as every objection was raised. Firstly, there was the concern that the police could be perceived as "making up new legislation" and acting unconstitutionally. The view was, quite properly, that the legislature makes our laws and the police then implement and enforce (criminal) laws. However, Nottinghamshire Police *were not* making any new legislation, we were simply identifying, recording, and investigating a new category of hate crime. The substantive offences, for example criminal damage or assault, remained as per existing statute; we simply added a provision that where such offences were perceived to be motivated by misogyny, they would be recorded on the police database as such, in the same way that other hate motivators were recorded. Rather this view of 'creating new legislation' was expressed by those wanting to find a reason to deny misogyny as a hate crime. This felt extremely subjective, because many forces in England and Wales had already successfully adopted the recording of other forms of hate crime, such as alternative sub-cultures (goths, emos, punks, metallers) without any similar concerns being raised. Rather, such initiatives were praised for being innovative and responsive to vulnerable groups in the local community (BBC 2013; Owen 2014). A second concern expressed was that it was felt that the Nottinghamshire police were taking the "moral high ground" or that we were engaging in active campaigning, and it was not for the police to act in this way. Again, I would reference the adoption of additional types of other hate crimes with no similar concerns being expressed, and I believe it is institutional sexism, if not misogyny, which has driven such differences in response.

Some colleagues across England and Wales recognised the issue and its importance. They were, however, concerned that our limited police resources would be used doing nothing but deal with these "new" offences: there was concern that we would be faced by a tsunami of new demand, especially at a time when financial resources were still shrinking and other crimes such as modern slavery and child sexual exploitation were growing. Nevertheless, in understanding the nature, scale and significance of the problem, many colleagues failed to understand the well-evidenced barriers to women reporting and the de-normalisation of these behaviours. This fundamental failing must be addressed. By adopting and implementing misogyny as a hate crime police leaders have a real opportunity to improve policing.

Given the failure of policing to understand and address women's experiences of victimisation together with police responses, the following section outlines certain challenges that need to be considered when formulating approaches to improving women's lived experiences and the subsequent response of policing. I have considered it helpful to briefly share three very different analyses of women's victimisation. The analyses have recurring themes of women's under-reporting, lack of confidence in the criminal justice system and poor experiences of policing.

Domestic abuse and sexual offending

In examining domestic abuse, whilst knowing it is very common, it is often difficult to accurately quantify this type of crime due to lack of reporting. Indeed, domestic abuse is a largely 'hidden' crime. Victims often do not report or disclose domestic abuse to the police or authorities more generally, and often under-report domestic abuse in surveys and particularly during face-to-face interviews. There are no reliable prevalence data on domestic abuse, but the Crime Survey of England and Wales (CSEW) offers the best data available. This survey relies on the self-reporting of victimisation. According to these data, for the year ending March 2019, an estimated 1.6 million women aged 16–74 years experienced domestic abuse in the last year (ONS 2019). Other data suggests that the police in England and Wales receive over 100 calls relating to domestic abuse every hour (HMIC 2014).

In terms of reporting to the police, the data presents an equally grim picture. According to CSEW, data for the year ending March 2018, only 18% of women who had experienced partner abuse in the last 12 months reported the abuse to the police (ONS 2018). Research into drug facilitated sexual assault found that 19% of survivors had reported their victimisation to the police. Amongst those who did report to the police, 54% had a negative or very negative experience, 23% said their experience was neutral, and only 8% had a very positive experience (Harvey et al. 2014). The influential online parenting website Mumsnet published a survey in 2012 which concluded that many women felt unable to report rape or sexual assault (Rape Crisis 2020):

- Over four-fifths (83%) of respondents who had been raped or sexually assaulted did not make a report to the police.
- Over one-quarter (29%) did not tell anyone at all (including friends or family) about the assault/rape.
- Over two-thirds (68%) said that low conviction rates would make them hesitant in reporting to the police.
- And over half (53%) would not report because of shame or embarrassment.

On the basis of the evidence that women are reluctant to report domestic abuse and sexual violence, it was difficult to reconcile why there would be an expectation that women's reporting patterns of misogyny as a hate crime would be any different; and why adopting misogyny as a hate crime would run the risk of overwhelming forces. Nonetheless, this argument was peddled as a self-evident truth, with the retort that the police had 'real crime' to deal with instead. Importantly this argument was persistently articulated by two of the most senior police officers in the country at the time – who ironically were both women. The then National Police Chiefs Council (NPCC) Chair Sara Thornton, in a speech to a joint conference of the NPCC and the Association of Police and Crime Commissioners (APCC), stated that while treating misogyny as a hate crime is a "concern for some well organised campaigning groups" the police should focus their resources elsewhere, namely "solving more burglaries and bearing down on violent crime" (Kang 2018). The Commissioner of the Metropolitan Police endorsed this view (Quinn 2018).

Initially as Deputy Chief Constable and latterly as Chief Constable at Nottinghamshire Police, I worked in partnership with the Nottingham Women's Centre and other partners, such as Nottingham City Council, Nottingham Trent University, and the Office of the Police and Crime Commissioner from Nottinghamshire, to embed misogyny as a hate crime across the City and County. This included establishing a multi-agency steering group and establishing policy, procedures, and a clear training package for police officers and staff. There was considerable support in the Force for this policy, ranging from the Chief Officer Team, the Black Police Association and Women's Support Network (NEWS), to the Police Federation who gave it cautious welcome with a worry of increased workload for their members. There were two particularly powerful factors for me in growing active support for the policy. The first was the persuasive and powerful endorsement by Superintendent Ted Antill (ITV 2018), who was the hate crime lead for the Force and the first "alpha male" to advocate in favour of the policy: reinforcing the importance of allyship and of men being involved in such campaigns. Secondly, that as training was first delivered to Control Room staff – predominantly female – they gave personal testimony of their own experiences and its impact on them, which in turn resonated around the force.

Since its adoption by Nottinghamshire in 2016, misogyny hate crime has the same procedural approach as any other hate crimes; it therefore benefits from well-established good practice, amended to include misogyny as a recorded strand of hate crime. All relevant operational and control room officers and staff received training in recognising and responding to misogyny hate crime, which was carried out by a staff member from Nottingham Women's Centre and the Nottinghamshire Police training team. The external trainer was funded by the Police and Crime Commissioner. It was important to the Force to demonstrate a clear commitment and ensure understanding not only of this new approach but also why it was necessary and how it complemented our approach to hate crime and vulnerability more broadly. Therefore, a comprehensive training intervention was developed and delivered on divisional training days. The particular session covered the inclusion of misogyny and alternative sub-cultures within the Force's hate crime policy. This initial training has now been mainstreamed, forming part of the mandatory training for all new recruits and transferees to Nottinghamshire Police. Importantly, my experience of delivering training to the police indicates that, even though domestic abuse was not included within the hate crime policy, officers were often able to recognise that misogyny was likely to be at its root. Similarly, officers identified that misogyny hate crime can act as a bridge to women talking about (and recognising) other forms of violence against them. Where women may feel that domestic abuse is something that happens to 'other women' and is not linked to inequality, it is possible that they are more readily able to recognise this with misogyny hate crime.

In formulating the policy for Nottinghamshire Police, there was considerable discussion with Violence Against Women and Girls (VAWG) stakeholders. There were mixed views about the proposed policy – some were concerned about the potential of a diversion of funding and focus away from domestic abuse, including increased demand. Some partners working in the Domestic Abuse (DA) area were particularly concerned about the interpretation of hate crime applied to all DA, both in risk assessment terms but also for victims in this complex area. There is a detailed bespoke risk assessment for all DA victims and there is a different one for hate crime victims – so there was a practical issue of how this would work in practice, as well as the complexity of how victims can sometimes view both their supposed culpability together with their belief in motivations of perpetrators who they may well be or have been in an intimate relationship. In other words, many victims of domestic violence are made to believe that it is their own fault that they are victims and they may also believe that they are in a loving not an abusive relationship – layering in misogyny with the complexities of being a victim/survivor of domestic violence may be a step too far for some women.

I would argue that VAWG is misogynistic in some respect. I do not think that you can make a distinction between a 'stranger' rape and rape in marriage. Rape is about entitlement and power, regardless of whether that is with a stranger or someone with whom a victim is already in a relationship. In fact, it shows the deep lack of understanding of rape. For example, many people still see rape being predominantly motivated by sexual attraction and unstoppable sexual desire, not power and domination. The underlying message here is also that a 'date rape' or rape in marriage must somehow be a 'mistake' i.e., 'he did not mean it, she gave him mixed messages' etc... rather than he thought that, as a man, he was entitled to take what he wanted from her. I think it is easy to get tied up in knots with all of these differing views. From my perspective, I think that the only sensible way to deal with it is to either park it completely and only apply misogyny as a hate crime to crimes other than domestic abuse or sexual violence. On reflection, it now seems to me that it was a process issue which won the day in Nottinghamshire – i.e., the risk assessment and services that are available for victims and survivors of domestic abuse could conflict for those for hate crime. Therefore, we chose to keep it simple for those delivering services rather than focussing solely on the needs of victims and survivors, as well as perpetrator motivation. The alternative position is that all crime is able to be the subject of misogynistic behaviour and should be recorded as such with dual risk assessments and potentially competing interventions.

Furthermore, I do not believe that we should start creating different 'tiers' of domestic abuse or sexual offending because of a misogynistic element through enhanced sentencing, and this still requires further consideration. As a result, when this initially came up with our local Violence Against Women and Girls (VAWG) partners, we debated it thoroughly and arrived at the same conclusion. Logically, if there is a socio-cultural shift and we begin to accept that misogyny is an actual identifiable entity in and of itself, then eventually that would help to increase our understanding of the main driver of VAWG, which in turn, will help all stakeholders. However, this does mean that we have to keep the two things quite separate in terms of sentencing, to ensure the avoidance of any confusion or any unwanted impact. Nationally this is being considered as part of the Law Commission's recommendations from its review into hate crime.

Media responses to the policy

The introduction of misogyny as a form of hate crime by Nottinghamshire Police in 2016 became a very high-profile event (BBC 2016). Inevitably, there was criticism within the media, which broadly speaking, was characterised as trivialising the behaviours experienced by women (e.g. referring to "wolf whistling", see for example Brown 2016), that this is discriminating against men, and that the police are trying to regulate social interaction (such as flirting). For example, when contacted by a researcher from the BBC Radio 4 programme Today his first question was "why I had outlawed wolf whistling" followed up with "hadn't the police force got anything better to do." There was also some misunderstanding that Nottinghamshire Police had amended the law – which of course it had not as it is only Parliament that can do this. Interestingly, most of the positive media coverage when we went public in July 2016 was from overseas – ranging from magazines in Canada carrying articles to an English language newspaper in China.

Using the evidence base for the decision to address misogyny – including that the behaviours experienced routinely by women are seriously sexually aggressive, obscene, and violent – Nottinghamshire Police was well placed to refute the trivialisation of these behaviours by the media as well as the assertion that this was "normal" male/female interaction. Indeed, much of the criticism of misogyny as hate crime mirrors very closely the 'excuses' made for other forms of hate crime, both in the past and currently, namely that it is "banter", that victims lack a sense of humour/perspective, unnecessary over-reaction on the part of the victim, and "political correctness" by a "liberal elite". Much of the online criticism of our policy was misogynistic in nature.

Notwithstanding some criticism, particularly from more right-wing publications, the media coverage overall was assessed by Nottinghamshire Police as being supportive and positive; it was notable that in almost every piece containing some degree of question there was a voice (generally a woman's) being given the space in high-profile public domains to express very clear and direct support as a means to provide counterbalance.

Reporting and evaluation of the policy

There was some suggestion and concern expressed by colleagues within Nottinghamshire Police and subsequently by those in the wider police family that the introduction of our policy would open a floodgate of reports that the police would not be able to cope with. This too mirrors the concerns that were present when other forms of hate crime were introduced. As with other forms of hate crime and indeed with many other crime types when women are victimised, the real issue is still under-reporting. Nottinghamshire Police therefore did not expect to be inundated with reports and at the time of writing this chapter this has not happened. In 2018/2019 there was a publicity campaign (Citizens UK 2018) alongside national debate in Parliament (HC Deb 7 March 2018), which resulted in raising the profile of the misogyny as a hate crime policy and in this time period, we can see a link between reporting levels and a swell in national publicity. The number of incidents reported to Nottinghamshire Police since 2016/2017 is as follows (Nottinghamshire Police 2020) (Table 13.1).

All police forces survey victims of hate crime to assess satisfaction levels with the service offered. In line with this national policy, victims of misogyny as hate crime were included in the surveys from the inception of adopting misogyny as a hate crime. The evidence from the survey shows that when victims report to the police, in the main, they do appreciate the service that they receive. Surveying of victims of misogyny hate crime showed in 2017/2018 and 2018/2019 that 83% and 85% respectively were satisfied with the service they received. Since 2019 Nottinghamshire Police has not separated satisfaction of misogyny hate crime victims in satisfaction data.

Understanding the evidence base is a key element of policing practice; however, it is the one area that is frequently overlooked. Historically, policy initiatives or changes have been "doomed to succeed" as vanity projects of leaders or those seeking advancement within the sector. For example, if everyone who took part in a promotion process had reduced crime as much as they said then we would have virtually no crime! In addition, evaluation is historically poor. With misogyny as hate crime, the rationale for introducing the policy was clear, well evidenced, and transparent. To continue this evidenced and transparent approach, it was viewed as essential by the leadership of the Force, the PCC and our key partner, Nottingham Women's Centre, that an academic evaluation should be carried out after

Table 13.1 Number of incidents reported to Nottinghamshire Police 2016–2020

Year	Number reported
2016/2017	97
2017/2018	70
2018/2019	131
2019/2020	93

two years of the policy being in place. This was commissioned and carried out by Professor Louise Mullany, University of Nottingham, and Associate Professor Loretta Trickett, Nottingham Trent University. It was published in July 2018 (Mullany and Trickett 2018). Chapter 15 provides an in-depth discussion of the evaluation of the policy; however, it is useful to provide a brief outline of the key findings of the evaluation here (Mullany and Trickett 2018):

- Misogyny Hate Crime in Nottinghamshire is very widespread and under-reported. The initial work of Citizens UK (Nottingham Citizens 2014) made it clear how widespread and significant an issue misogyny hate crime is, as well as highlighting women's lack of understanding about and confidence in reporting to the Police. Wider national evidence confirmed the scale of misogynistic behaviours, both online and face to face, as well as the issues with reporting due to "normalisation" and the reluctance of women to report sexual offences. The evaluation found that 94% of survey respondents had experienced or witnessed street harassment in Nottinghamshire though only 6% reported the incident to the police – an even lower level of reporting than the research previously quoted. However, in contrast with studies quoted above, of those individuals that did report, 75% had positive experiences, and 100% of those who did report said that they would report again. This is fairly consistent with the satisfaction data found by Nottinghamshire Police. The academic evaluation found that victim satisfaction centred around the police taking women seriously and the ability to demonstrate empathy. Satisfaction was clearly not limited to whether a perpetrator was caught and/or action was taken against them – many participants expressed the view that they appreciated how difficult it was for an unknown perpetrator to be caught, especially as incidents happened quickly, and often with little opportunity for a good description of the perpetrator. Instead, what was important was the opportunity to report and to be taken seriously. This evidence demonstrates that the levels of positive prosecution outcomes for the police do not have to be the only measure for victim satisfaction.
- Misogyny has a serious and significant impact on victims. Again, this is consistent with and reflects the previous evidence. The evaluation found that high percentages of women have experienced harassment at the higher end of the crime continuum: unwanted sexual advances (40%), groping (46%), sexually explicit language (54%), and indecent exposure (26%). A quarter of respondents had experienced sexual assault (25%). A fifth of all respondents had also experienced online abuse (22%). Women from BAME groups often experienced misogyny hate crime and racial hate crime simultaneously and felt doubly vulnerable to attack – reflecting the evidence base of Citizens UK (Nottingham Citizens 2014). The evaluation also found that 75% of respondents said that the incident had a long-term impact on them; 63.1% of respondents

changed their behaviour as a consequence of the harassment; they reported feelings of intimidation and living in fear of what may happen to them in public spaces.
- Overwhelmingly the public who took part in the research supported the policy developed by Nottinghamshire Police. This was endorsed by both men and women. Interestingly, virtually all the male respondents found these behaviours to be completely unacceptable. They also articulated a strong willingness to be involved and engaged as part of the solution, rather than be seen as solely the problem.
- Misogyny Hate Crime should be rolled out nationally. The policy was evidenced by the evaluation as a forward-thinking policy that Nottinghamshire should be proud of, and that it was needed to be implemented consistently across the UK.

Subsequent to the publication of the evaluation there has been a flurry of further evidence gathering, publication of research, and reports which lend further weight to the adoption of a national policy, and a change in legislation to properly protect women from unwanted behaviour. All the following explicitly draw on and/or reference Nottinghamshire's ground-breaking work.

The Women and Equalities Select Committee (2018) published the findings of their inquiry into sexual harassment in public spaces in 2018. Their report found that "The Government has a responsibility to show leadership in eradicating sexual harassment and making public places safe" and that "the damage done by sexual harassment needs to be better reflected in policy and law" (Women and Equalities Select Committee 2018). Stella Creasy MP, an advocate for the adoption of misogyny as a hate crime, proposed an amendment to what was known as the "Upskirting" Bill which would require misogyny to be adopted as a hate crime category across England and Wales (HC Deb 5 September 2018). Although the amendment did not succeed, as a direct result the Government commissioned the Law Commission to review Hate crime across England and Wales with specific consideration of misogyny hate crime in its terms of reference (Law Commission 2018). Because of the COVID-19 pandemic, the Law Commission did not publish its report until September 2020. It concluded that there is a "strong in principle case that can be made for the inclusion given the wealth of evidence of targeting women and the additional harm that this causes. We therefore provisionally propose inclusion of the characteristic of sex or gender" (Law Commission 2020).

Scotland has been ahead of England and Wales, with the Scottish Government Review into hate crime published in April 2018, led by Lord Bracadale (Scottish Government 2018). It recommended adoption of gender as a hate crime, and all recommendations have been accepted by the Scottish Government and are now being drafted into legislation (Hate Crime and Public Order Bill (Scotland) 2020). Following suit, the Marrinan review into hate crime was commissioned in 2019 in Northern Ireland: its report is also awaited (Department of Justice 2020).

A group of MPs, including Stella Creasy and Christine Jardine, tabled amendments to the Domestic Abuse Bill 2020, requiring the recording misogyny as a hate crime by the police – the same approach as adopted in Nottinghamshire. The amendments were not successful, but the effect of this amendment would have been to ensure all police forces in England and Wales record any crimes where the victim, or any other person, perceived the crime to be motivated by gender hostility or perceived the perpetrator to have demonstrated hostility towards the gender in committing the crime. The police would then also have been required to assess how this interacts with domestic abuse by making an assessment of how many of these crimes meet the definition as set out in this legislation. Proposals to recognise misogyny as a category of hate crime – much like in Nottinghamshire – would not therefore make anything illegal if it was not already. Instead, this amendment would have helped to bring together the understanding of the forms of violence and abuse that women and girls experience by ensuring all were recorded (Creasy 2020). Most recently, in June 2020, Sadiq Khan, the mayor of London, Andy Burnham, the mayor of Greater Manchester, Steve Rotheram, the mayor of the Liverpool city region, and Dan Jarvis, the mayor of the Sheffield city region, have made explicit commitments to making misogyny a hate crime (Sparrow 2020).

Finally, research by Samanani and Pope (2020) argues that hate crime law should focus on protecting oppressed groups and highlights the disproportionality in terms of gender-based hate. The research identified that:

> on average, men were more likely to be victims of existing forms of hate crime than women, gender-motivated criminal targeting was disproportionately experienced by women. 31.1% of all women sampled reported experiencing gendered-motivated criminal targeting, compared to 9.9% of all men. For men reporting gender-motivated criminal targeting, this was almost always as an additional factor, alongside targeting on the basis of other protected characteristics.
> (Samanani and Pope 2020, p. 40)

In addition, they found that 2.1% (equates to 3 individuals) of the men in the sample reported being targeted because of their gender in comparison to 24.8% of the women in the sample and 23.6% of women who reported crime based solely on their gender (Samanani and Pope 2020, p. 40).

Samanani and Pope (2020) recommend that misogyny should be recognised as a hate crime. This was supported by 83% of their survey participants. They also found disproportionate rates of under-reporting by women (compared to men) for both hate crime and when no hate element was present, and evidence of intersectionality. They recommended pathways for criminal prosecution based on multiple protected characteristics in addition to misogyny hate crime being recognised; the provision of both criminal law and guidance for judges, juries, and prosecutors being joined up with non-criminal approaches; and that there should be a statutory duty for designated public bodies, such as schools and public transport providers, to take on responsibility for preventing, monitoring, and reporting hate crime.

With this clear momentum for change I do hope that it not be long before all women and girls enjoy the protection of the law, and we see a significant shift in some of the misogynistic behavioural norms that so many women and girls face on a daily basis.

Conclusion

The approach of Nottinghamshire Police in adopting misogyny hate crime is regarded as national, as well as international, best practice. The following points provide an overall summary of the crucial steps in making this process a success:

- A local partnership approach and commitment from the PCC were important determinants of successful implementation.
- Misogyny is the foundation in which violence against women and girls grows. I argue that it is misogyny that is a hate crime not gender as a hate crime.
- Joint training with the women's sector and testimony of women were critically important for the policy's credibility and acceptance by a male-dominated policing organisation.
- Police officers in Nottinghamshire have an improved understanding of the link between sexual harassment of women and girls, and violence and sexual offending against women and girls.
- The prevalence of sexual harassment is not reflected in the volume of instances reported to police, consistent with under-reporting of other types of the crime where women are victims.
- The impact of sexual harassment of women and girls in public places is significant and must not be underestimated.
- The intersectional nature of misogyny hate crime is a significant factor e.g. Islamophobia disproportionally directed towards Muslim women.
- Victim satisfaction levels are high for women who have reported their experience of misogyny to Nottinghamshire Police.
- Impact of implementing misogyny as a hate crime, particularly on women in terms of confidence in policing and their own confidence should not be underestimated.
- Independent academic evaluation by Nottingham Trent University and University of Nottingham strongly endorsed the policy.
- Other police forces have adopted the policy with others committed awaiting outcome of the Law Commission's current review of hate crime.

- The National Independent Advisory Group on hate crime which advises Government and the Police Service has unanimously backed misogyny as hate crime.
- Significant amount of campaigning and engagement with stakeholders across the country working towards national adoption and rollout resulting in real momentum for change.
- Legislation and sentencing require amending to reflect the inclusion of misogyny as a hate crime.

I believe that the leadership of the Police Service owe it to the communities that we serve, not only the women, girls, mothers, daughters, wives, aunties, nieces, and grandmothers but to the men and boys, whether they are victims or perpetrators, to take this issue seriously. Adopting misogyny hate crime as a sixth recognised hate crime strand will send the message that the criminal justice system does precisely that and will encourage more women and girls to engage with the police.

References

APPCS, 2020. Role of the PCC [online]. Available at: https://www.apccs.police.uk/role-of-the-pcc [Accessed 18 January 2021].

Bates, L., 2016. Wolf-whistling is no crime – but it is part of our misogynistic culture. *The Guardian* [online]. 14 July. Available at: https://www.theguardian.com/commentisfree/2016/jul/14/wolf-whistling-hate-crime-misogyny-nottinghamshire-police [Accessed 17 January 2021].

BBC, 2013. Hate crime: police record attacks on punks, emos and goths [online]. *BBC*. 4 April. Available at: https://www.bbc.co.uk/news/uk-england-lancashire-22018888 [Accessed 18 January 2021].

BBC, 2016. Nottinghamshire Police records misogyny as a hate crime [online]. 13 July. Available at: https://www.bbc.co.uk/news/uk-england-nottinghamshire-36775398 [Accessed 25 January 2021].

Brown, B., 2016. Wolf-whistling a hate crime? What an insult to real victims of abuse [online]. 15 July. Available at: https://www.dailymail.co.uk/news/article-3691284/Wolf-whistling-hate-crime-insult-real-victims-abuse.html [Accessed 25 January 2021].

Citizens UK, 2018. Media reaction: misogyny hate crime campaign. 12 July. Available at: https://www.citizensuk.org/misogyny_media [Accessed 25 January 2021].

Citizens UK, 2019. *Citizens UK Conference*. 25 March 2019. Nottingham.

Conservative Party, 2010. Invitation to join the government of Great Britain [online]. Available at: https://general-election-2010.co.uk/2010-general-election-manifestos/Conservative-Party-Manifesto-2010.pdf [Accessed 18 January 2021].

Creasy, S., 2020. Why we're fighting to change the law and make misogyny a hate crime [online]. *Daily Telegraph*. 11 June. Available at https://www.telegraph.co.uk/women/politics/fighting-change-law-make-misogyny-hate-crime/ [Accessed 25 January 2021].

Demos, 2014. Misogyny on Twitter [online]. Available at: https://www.demos.co.uk/files/MISOGYNY_ON_TWITTER.pdf [Accessed 17 January 2021].

Department of Justice 2020. Hate crime legislation in Northern Ireland [online]. Available at: https://www.justice-ni.gov.uk/sites/default/files/publications/justice/hate-crime-review.pdf [Accessed 25 January 2021].

Domestic Abuse Bill (2019–2021) HL Bill 124. *Parliament: House of Commons*. London: UK Parliament.

Duggan, 2014. Online misogyny [online]. Available at: https://www.pewinternet.org/2014/10/22/online-harassment [Accessed 17 January 2021].

Equation, 2015. Safer for Women Summit: 24 September 2015 [online]. Available at: https://equation.org.uk/safer-for-women-summit-24-sept-2015/ [Accessed 18 January 2021].

Fenton, S., 2015 Most British women first experience street harassment between age 11 and 17. *The Independent* [online]. 29 May. https://www.independent.co.uk/news/uk/most-british-women-first-experience-street-harrassment-between-age-11-and-17-10284574.html [Accessed 17 January 2021].

Harvey, S. et al., 2014. *Not Worth Reporting: Women's Experiences of Drug-Facilitated Sexual Assault* [online]. London: AVA. Available at: https://avaproject.org.uk/wp-content/uploads/2016/03/Not-worth-reporting-Full-report.pdf [Accessed 19 January 2021].

Hate Crime and Public Order Bill (Scotland) 2020. Available at: https://beta.parliament.scot/bills-and-laws/bills/hate-crime-and-public-order-scotland-bill [Accessed 25 January 2021].

HC Deb 7 March 2018 vol 637 cWH131–149.

HC Deb 5 September 2018 vol 646 c253–254.

HM Government, 2010. The coalition: our programme for government [online]. Available at: https://assets.publishing.service.gov.uk/government/uploads/system/uploads/attachment_data/file/78977/coalition_programme_for_government.pdf [Accessed 18 January 2021].

HMIC, 2014. Increasingly everyone's business: a progress report on the police response to domestic abuse [online]. Available at: https://www.justiceinspectorates.gov.uk/hmicfrs/wp-content/uploads/2014/04/improving-the-police-response-to-domestic-abuse.pdf [Accessed 19 January 2021].

Home Affairs Committee, 2008. Home affairs – seventh report [online]. Available at: https://publications.parliament.uk/pa/cm200708/cmselect/cmhaff/364/36402.htm [Accessed 18 January 2021].

ITV, 2018. Police force gets 150 reports of inappropriate behaviour towards women since making misogyny a hate crime [online]. 17 January. Available at: https://www.itv.com/news/central/2018-01-18/police-force-dealt-with-150-reports-of-men-behaving-inappropriately-towards-women [Accessed 20 January 2021].

Kang, B., 2018. Chief Constable Sara Thornton wants us to 'focus on crime, not misogyny' – why doesn't see misogynistic abuse as criminal? *The Independent* [online]. 1 November. Available at: https://www.independent.co.uk/voices/chief-constable-sara-thornton-misogyny-crime-police-cuts-a8613166.html [Accessed 20 January 2021].

Khomami, N., 2016. Nottinghamshire police to count wolf-whistling in street as a hate crime. *The Guardian* [online]. 13 July. Available at: https://www.theguardian.com/lifeandstyle/2016/jul/13/nottinghamshire-police-count-wolf-whistling-hate-crime [Accessed 17 January 2021].

Lagone, A., 2018. #MeToo and Time's Up founders explain the difference between the 2 movements – and how they're alike [online]. *Time*. 22 March. Available at:

https://time.com/5189945/whats-the-difference-between-the-metoo-and-times-up-movements/ [Accessed 18 January 2021].

Law Commission, 2018. Law Commission review into hate crime announced [online]. Available at: https://www.lawcom.gov.uk/law-commission-review-into-hate-crime-announced/ [Accessed 25 January 2021].

Law Commission, 2020. Hate crime laws. A consultation paper [online]. Available at: https://s3-eu-west-2.amazonaws.com/lawcom-prod-storage-11jsxou24uy7q/uploads/2020/10/Hate-crime-final-report.pdf [Accessed 25 January 2021].

Liberal Democrats, 2010. Liberal Democrat manifesto 2010 [online]. Available at: https://www.markpack.org.uk/files/2015/01/Liberal-Democrat-manifesto-2010.pdf [Accessed 18 January 2021].

Mullany, L. and Trickett L., 2018. Misogyny hate crime evaluation report [online]. Nottingham Woman's Centre. Available at: http://www.nottinghamwomenscentre.com/wp-content/uploads/2018/07/Misogyny-HateCrime-Evaluation-Report-June-2018.pdf [Accessed 17 January 2021].

Nottingham Citizens, 2014. No place for hate commission for hate [online]. Available at: https://d3n8a8pro7vhmx.cloudfront.net/newcitizens/pages/1065/attachments/original/1469204592/A-CITIZENS-COMMISSION-NO-PLACE-FOR-HATE.pdf?1469204592 [Accessed 17 January 2021].

Nottinghamshire PCC, 2018. The police and crime plan [online]. Available at: https://www.nottinghamshire.pcc.police.uk/Document-Library/Public-Information/Police-and-Crime-Plan/New-Plan-2018-2021/Police-and-Crime-Plan-2018-2021.pdf [Accessed 18 January 2021].

Nottinghamshire Police, 2020. Personal communication. Management Information Team. July 2020.

ONS, 2018. Domestic abuse: findings from the Crime Survey for England and Wales: year ending March 2018 [online]. Available at: https://www.ons.gov.uk/peoplepopulationandcommunity/crimeandjustice/articles/domesticabusefindingsfromthecrimesurveyforenglandandwales/yearendingmarch2018 [Accessed 20 January 2021].

ONS, 2019. Domestic abuse victim characteristics, England and Wales: year ending March 2019 [online]. Available at: https://www.ons.gov.uk/peoplepopulationandcommunity/crimeandjustice/articles/domesticabusevictimcharacteristicsenglandandwales/yearendingmarch2019 [Accessed 19 January 2021].

Owen, J., 2014. Police told to beef up reports of hate crime. *The Independent* [online]. Available at: https://www.independent.co.uk/news/uk/crime/police-told-to-beef-up-reports-of-hate-crime-9537725.html [Accessed 18 January 2021].

Police Reform and Social Responsibility Act 2011 (c. 13).

Policing Protocol Order 2011 S.I. 2011/2744.

Quinn, B., 2018. Met police chief backs call to focus on violent crime not misogyny. *The Guardian* [online]. 2 November. Available at: https://www.theguardian.com/uk-news/2018/nov/02/metropolitan-police-chief-cressida-dick-backs-call-focus-violent-crime-misogyny [Accessed 20 January 2021].

Rape Crisis, 2020. Mumsnet launches 'We Believe You' campaign [online]. Available at: https://rapecrisis.org.uk/news/mumsnet-launches-we-believe-you-campaign/ [Accessed 20 January 2021].

Samanani, F. and Pope, S., 2020. *Overcoming Everyday Hate in the UK: Hate Crime, Oppression and the Law.* London: Citizens UK.

Sandhu, S., 2016. International Women's Day: 85% of younger women have been sexually harassed in public. *The Independent* [online]. 8 March. Available at: https://

www.independent.co.uk/news/uk/home-news/international-women-s-day-85-younger-women-uk-have-been-sexually-harassed-public-a6918566.html [Accessed 17 January 2021].

Scottish Government, 2018. Independent review of hate crime legislation in Scotland. Final report [Online]. Available at: https://www.gov.scot/binaries/content/documents/govscot/publications/progress-report/2018/05/independent-review-hate-crime-legislation-scotland-final-report/documents/00535892-pdf/00535892-pdf/govscot%3Adocument/00535892.pdf [Accessed 20 January 2021].

Sparrow, A., 2020. Labour mayors back plan to make police record misogyny as hate crime [online]. *The Guardian*. 5 July. Available at: https://www.theguardian.com/uk-news/2020/jul/05/labour-mayors-back-plan-to-make-police-record-misogyny-as-hate [Accessed 25 January 2021].

UK Parliament, 2012. Police and Crime Commissioner elections 2012 [online]. Available at: https://commonslibrary.parliament.uk/research-briefings/rp12-73/ [Accessed 18 January 2021].

Women and Equalities Select Committee, 2018. Sexual harassment of women and girls in public places [online]. Available at: https://publications.parliament.uk/pa/cm201719/cmselect/cmwomeq/701/70104.htm#_idTextAnchor001 [Accessed 25 January 2021].

14 Informing legal change

The language of misogyny hate crime, gender and enhancing protection through criminal law

Louise Mullany, Loretta Trickett and Victoria Howard

Introduction

In this chapter, we explore the challenges and benefits of including 'misogyny' as a hate crime category, initially at the level of policy change enacted by individual police forces, and then as a change in the law at a national level in England and Wales. Being the first police force in the UK to include misogyny as a hate crime (see also Chapters 12 and 13 in this book), Nottinghamshire Police extended its definition of hate crime to include 'misogyny' in April 2016. This policy change has led to an increase in women reporting hate crimes and hate incidents, with 174 cases reported in the first two years, despite there being no change in the law. In 2017–2018, Mullany and Trickett undertook a research evaluation of the policy change (see Mullany and Trickett 2018a, 2018b, 2020; Trickett and Mullany 2018). Other police forces in England have now followed suit and in 2018, the Law Commission was tasked by the UK government to carry out a review of hate crime including to consider whether 'misogyny' should be incorporated as a new hate crime category.

Taking an interdisciplinary approach in our collaborative research, we integrate criminology with the study of language and linguistics in order to analyse the impact of misogyny hate crime from multiple stakeholder perspectives. One of the key principles behind our research has been to evaluate, assess and learn from the experiences of the police, victims and members of the general public so that implications for a wider national roll-out can be assessed and recommendations made. We have worked with Nottinghamshire Police, The Office for the Nottinghamshire Police and Crime Commissioner, Nottingham Women's Centre, Citizens UK, The Fawcett Society, Stella Creasy MP's office and the Law Commission at various points on this research journey.

In this chapter, we focus upon the following key issues in terms of moving from regional to national legal change, drawing on our substantial bank of research evidence (Mullany and Trickett 2018a, 2018b, 2020; Trickett and Mullany 2018). We consider the full impact of misogyny hate crime on

DOI: 10.4324/9781003023722-14

everyday lives of women and girls, language policies and terminological decisions about 'misogyny' hate crime from a language policy and linguistic perspective, how the research base we have acquired has fed directly into the Law Commission review and next steps. We outline the future importance of practical tools for engaging with multiple stakeholders, including members of the public, members of the criminal justice system, educators and the wider voluntary sector within communities in order to successfully implement a national legislative change.

Background and methods

The aims and objectives of our research evaluation of Nottinghamshire Police's misogyny hate crime policy change included the following areas, which will be focused upon in this chapter:

- To understand who experiences harassment in Nottinghamshire, and what behavioural changes and restrictions are made as a consequence
- To understand who perpetrators are and what they say/do
- To measure how the public and police evaluate the language of the policy
- To discover whether the policy change has influenced the decision of women in Nottinghamshire to report such incidents to the police
- To interview men to find their views about this initiative, and whether it has influenced their behaviour
- To find out about the experiences of women who have reported to Nottinghamshire Police: what happened to them, why they chose to report, whether they were happy with the police response and whether they would choose to report in the future

Chapters 12 and 13 in this book set out the detailed background and rationale to Nottinghamshire Police's decision to record misogyny hate crime in 2016 and have identified gaps in existing hate crime laws. In order to investigate the aims and objectives of the research evaluation, we conducted a quantitative survey and held a series of focus groups and interviews, which included 691 participants in total who lived in the Nottinghamshire area (591 survey respondents and 88 focus group and interview participants, see Mullany and Trickett 2018a, 2020). Despite our attempts, we were unable to gain access to perpetrators as they were unwilling to participate in the research (see Mullany and Trickett 2018a), though from a linguistic perspective we did have victims' accounts of what was said and what happened to them (see Mullany and Trickett 2020).

After we had completed our independent analysis of the impact that the misogyny hate crime policy was having on Nottinghamshire and assessed the consequences of our findings for the everyday lives of women and girls, we then decided that we had an obligation to our research informants to use the evidence gathered to contribute to the agenda of ending violence against women and girls in the UK and internationally through influencing policy-makers and government (see Mullany and Trickett 2020 for further discussion). First and foremost, as one of the key findings of the data was significant support for the policy change and an emphasis on the positive difference that it had made to the everyday lives of women and girls in Nottinghamshire who were aware of the policy's existence, we decided to advocate that the human rights of women and girls are respected and upheld in our society by introducing a national policy roll-out, to contribute to the global agenda of bringing about 'Gender Equality', Goal 5 of the United Nation's Sustainable Development Goals 2030 (United Nations 2015), as part of what we have termed a form of research 'activism' (Mullany 2020).

In this chapter, we next focus on what we found to be of most value when considering a national roll-out of the policy. We will begin by examining the extent, nature and overall impact of the harm that misogynistic hate incidents cause to women and girls, by considering the prevalence of misogyny hate crime, police reporting and what this means in relation to the law and legal change.

Impact on the everyday lives of women and girls

Prevalence, police reporting and the law

93.7% of all respondents to our survey had experienced or witnessed misogyny hate crime. The following table shows the percentage of survey participants who had experienced behaviours towards the most serious end of the crime continuum of misogynistic incidents against women in public spaces (Table 14.1).

Table 14.1 Survey participants who reported experiencing misogynistic behaviours (adapted from Mullany and Trickett 2018, p. 9)

Behaviour type	Percentage
Groping	46.2
Indecent exposure	25.9
Being followed home	25.2
Sexual assault	24.7

A further 54.3% of participants had experienced sexually explicit language in public spaces, 51.8% had experienced threatening, aggressive or intimidating behaviour and 48.9% had experienced unwanted sexual advances. These figures illustrate the prevalence of misogynistic behaviour towards women and girls from our survey participants.

However, in terms of police reporting, it is notable that only 6.6% of survey respondents had reported these experiences to the police, indicating the presence of barriers inhibiting women from approaching the police and the normalisation of such incidents, to the extent that women did not consider them even to be reportable offences.

The focus group and interview data gave more detailed, qualitative understandings of specific crimes and incidents experienced by women and girls in Nottinghamshire. Again, unsurprisingly, in this data sample, police reporting was low. Out of 88 participants, only five reported going to the police. Interestingly, four out of these five women had reported their crime in full knowledge that the misogyny hate crime policy existed and cited it as a reason as to why they reported. The other participant reported after she had been the victim of a serious assault on a busy city centre street (see Mullany and Trickett 2020). Many of the behaviours reported in focus group and interview data constituted criminal offences, including psychic assaults, battery, sexual assault or offences under either the Public Order Act 1986 or the Protection From Harassment Act 1997:

1. I have been followed, in the middle of the night, might I add, by a guy who was like "You're really pretty," and I'm like "thank you", and he was like, "No I wanna talk to you," and then I'm like, "No thank you". I ran in heels and he was following me and I ran into a club and I was like to a bouncer, "I don't know what he's going to do". [...] I thought that he was going to kill me.
2. I've had girlfriends before who've been felt up being outside, just in the street as well, outside Broadway Cinema y'know she's having a cigarette and a drink with friends and a guy put his hand right up her skirt.
3. Jogging on the road, man's driving along, winds the window down, calls me an F-ing fat slag.

Comment 1 constitutes an assault under section 39 Criminal Justice Act 1988 if the 'guy' intentionally or recklessly caused the woman to fear that he was going to commit immediate unlawful violence. Comment 2 constitutes a sexual assault, assuming that the woman was touched sexually without consent, as reported in this short vignette of vicarious experience told by this woman's male partner. Comment 3 constitutes a public order offence under section 4A Public Order Act 1986 if the man intended to cause harassment, alarm or distress by using abusive and insulting language.

Some behaviours were less clearly captured by existing offences. Examples elicited include:

4. Somebody walked past and took a picture of my chest.
5. I worked at [company name] and he [a customer] kneeled over the [counter] and took a picture of my chest.

Comments 4 and 5 are unlikely to fall within any specific existing sexual offence; even the recently enacted Voyeurism (Offences) Act 2019 creates an offence of taking images of buttocks or genitals without consent, but not chests. Changes to hate crime law, as proposed by the Law Commission (2020) to include the category of 'misogyny' or 'sex/gender', would allow this motivation to be considered as an aggravating factor to baseline offences, leading to the availability of higher penalties and enhanced sentencing. Importantly, Nottinghamshire Police's misogyny hate crime policy did not create new offences or change the law, but instead the policy change allowed the police to additionally *record* offences and incidents carried out with this motivation. Although comments 4 and 5 would probably still not fall within a specific offence, under Nottinghamshire Police's misogyny hate crime policy, or with the changes to law proposed by the Law Commission (2020), each would still be recorded as a 'hate crime incident'. For some women, the impact of misogynistic street harassment is intersectional and its impact may be compounded, as regular abuse is also linked to other aspects of identity including ethnicity, race and religion (Bowman 1993; Citizens UK 2020). Our research documented a series of vignettes from women who regularly received intersectional misogynistic and racist abuse:

6   I was with a friend when these two men by the shops, they were sitting outside the shop, and they said, "Oh Chinese Chinese mmm" or something. If you battle it every time it's exhausting.
7   A few months ago I was sitting in the bus stop with my friend, and she's covering her face, and somebody on the bicycle, he was going in the street and then, while he was going on his way, he just said the F-word and few words and, then continued his [journey] [...] and now I didn't see her for the last two months.

Indeed, Citizens UK (2020) found that Muslim women were most likely to be subject to street harassment, violence and abuse.

Visibility and knowledge of the policy

One of the key reasons behind bringing in the misogyny hate crime policy was to raise awareness of misogyny hate crime in order to encourage women to report such incidents and to give them confidence that they would be taken seriously by the police (see also Chapter 13 in this book). Overarchingly, the policy was also intended to 'contribute to a societal shift in how such behaviours are viewed' (Mullany and Trickett 2020, p. 252), reassuring women that they do not have to tolerate being targeted in this way on the basis of their gender.

Many members of the public who participated in our focus groups and interviews did not know that Nottinghamshire's misogyny hate crime policy existed, which draws attention to the significance of education and visibility, particularly through publicity around the policy change (see 'Next steps: changing public' perceptions below). Importantly, when asked whether they would call the police before they knew about the existence of the misogyny hate crime policy, the majority of women said that they would not report. They reported feeling that they would not be taken seriously enough, or, even though they knew it was wrong, the behaviour they had experienced was seen as 'normal' and something that women just had to put up with:

8   It's a fine line between compliments and abuse, and I think that's where the whole, "Oh do the police take it seriously?" when those issues arise. Because a lot of the time, I mean I hadn't realized how I've actually probably been in loads of situations that weren't consensual or entirely legal and you just don't think. But equally, I just wouldn't go to the police.
9   I just thought it was something that I had to deal with… and I always thought the police was for serious crimes, so if I called the police I would feel like I was gonna be arrested for wasting police time or something, you know?
10 I wish I had reported some of the abuse I had whilst waitressing. I wasn't tempted because I thought this is how the world is sadly.

Once the policy had been defined and explained to those members of the public participating in focus groups and interviews who had been unaware of it, there was a common view that the policy change would encourage women to report these incidents to the police. The existence of such a policy was perceived to help challenge current societal perceptions, thus demonstrating genuine support for the policy change. For example:

11 I think it's a great idea personally. I think of how much if angers me personally, and I know it angers a lot of other women, I was asking people how they felt about it, and how they feel about being grabbed or being shouted at, and putting the policy in place means that a lot of other places around the country have started to look at it as well. So I think it's very important.
12 I feel like when other women know that if you call the police, something will happen, a lot of women will. Because I would have run to the bouncer and called the police then, rather than standing there for 30 minutes waiting, because there's always police officers around the town […] and I probably would have reached home a whole lot quicker, if I'd have just called someone or done something else rather than just be, you know, the scared girl.
13 I think it will [make a difference to reporting], because I think it will make people realise that it's not just a normal thing to happen. I think it'll make women realise that you don't have to put up with it, and I think it'll make people that are more emotional or vulnerable than I am, it'll probably make them report it so they feel safer.
14 I saw all the media stuff about this policy a couple of years ago, saw it all over Twitter and thought, yeah that's fantastic, what a great development, but I've not done anything about, I've received plenty of abuse.

I suppose part of it is particularly the sort of stuff I face [harassment from male drivers whilst running], it's over so fast because they're gone in their car.

Notably, in comment 14, although this participant positively evaluates the policy change using the evaluative adjectives 'fantastic' and 'great' to express support, she then uses the conjunction 'but' to explain that it has not caused her to report, even though she had received 'plenty of abuse'. This draws attention to the major difficulties in reporting, as well as the fact that most street harassment is from strangers and is over very quickly.

On a more positive note, police officers made the following observations which indicates a potential shift in catcalling women from building sites, which was directly attributed to the misogyny policy change:

15   What has changed – I spoke to a builder, apparently a lot of building companies are putting it in a policy now that if they shout stuff they get sacked.
16   Rather than… going to the police they might be going to the building company rather than us… that's what we found with a few people – report it to the company they're working for and sort it with them, which is why they've got these policies in place… and get them sacked which is more of a problem for them than getting spoken to by the local cop.

Changing behaviours: restrictions on freedom and fear

63% of survey respondents (Mullany and Trickett 2018a) who had experienced misogynistic street harassment reported actively and consciously changing their behaviour as a result, particularly by self-restricting their movements, demonstrating the negative impact on the freedom and human rights of girls and women in UK society. The following narrative experiences from focus group and interview participants demonstrate the range of fears, alongside how such fears result in conscious changes and decisions which restrict their behaviour:

17   I organise running groups, these kind of couch to 5k programmes for women… I've only been able to do it of an evening and I've said to them, "Gosh, I'm so impressed that you've turned out here in a winter's evening, seven o'clock and it's pitch black" and they say, "No, this is why we've done it, because nobody can see us" and clearly fear is a bigger thing.
18   I run extra fast down the alleyway… I do change my behaviour and I have my phone with me on 999.
19   I don't like going from place to place, I'd rather stay in one place that I feel safe in and take a taxi home. I wouldn't walk home after dark now, but I think that's just a safety thing that I have always adhered to.

Additionally, participants reported avoiding certain areas of the city and public transport, only travelling in groups, choosing not to exercise outside or go to the gym, pretending to be on the phone, wearing headphones, altering what they wore and restricting use of the internet due to online abuse. Such precautionary measures taken by women and girls have also been thoroughly documented by researchers in earlier studies (Stanko 1987; Pain 1997), demonstrating that very little has changed in recent years. Women still describe being constantly vigilant and altering their behaviour during the day and night.

Indeed, young women quickly come to realise that there is a cultural expectation that they will police their own bodies and movements in order to avoid sexual assaults by men (Walklate 1997; Cops and Pleysier 2011). This has been utilised in previous government attempts to assuage women's fear of crime by encouraging women to change their behaviour and adopt precautionary measures to minimise encounters with male strangers (Walklate 1997; Cops and Pleysier 2011) – thus placing the emphasis on women to take on all the responsibility, as opposed to addressing the issue of changing men's behaviours. The normalisation of sexual harassment in public places is fuelled by the argument that it is a 'compliment' (see Brown 2016; Oppenheim 2016) or an acceptable and harmless form of male behaviour (Salmon 2021). Such conceptualisations of sexualised street harassment as harmless serve to greatly underplay the effect of such behaviour upon women and girls, both in terms of immediate and longer-term impact on their lives.

Women respondents in our research recounted feeling intimidated, anxious, scared, belittled, humiliated, embarrassed and sometimes angry both during and after experiences of street harassment by unknown men. As Bates (2014) notes, such accounts testify to women's subjective experiences of street encounters as assertions of male power that objectify them as sexual objects who are potentially available to any man (see also Kissling 1991; Laniya 2005). Indeed, women participants in our dataset explained the following:

20 It is assertion of power…in an inappropriate setting for a particular purpose, to intimidate.
21 It's a power thing. To me, unconsciously perhaps, but men seem to own public space more than women.

In relation to street harassment in particular, encounters with unknown men have been identified as unnerving for women because they are unsure whether the situation will escalate into physical or sexual assault (Bates 2014). An all too common experience from our research was men often turning aggressive if women they approached did not respond to what was said or done. Previous researchers have argued that it is this fear of escalation posed by sexualised street harassment that greatly fuels women's fear of crime. Women's fear of rape is formed against the background of their lives including experiences in public and private spaces (Kelly 1987; Stanko 1987, 1990; Goodey 1994; Pain 1995). This was also reflected in our data:

22. I'm just like 'Er rapist'. And it's so bad that you just put the two and two together, but it's also like, is sexualised street harassment a gateway? If you're that type of person where you're gonna say that, what would you do to me in a dark alley?

This helps explain why street harassment of women and girls affects their feelings of safety and security, their freedom of movement and use of social space. Both Kelly (1988) and Stanko (1987) in their research on fear of sexual assault show how women develop routine practices to manage their lives under the threat of male harassment and sexual violence. Women's fear of crime therefore needs to be contextualised within a gendered stratified society including socialisation processes as well as experiences of crime and victimisation such as street harassment (Stanko 1987; Kelly 1988; Sacco 1990; Pain 1991, 2000; Goodey 1994; Walklate 1997). In this way, the normative discourses that excuse street harassment against women and girls as harmless continue to deny and downplay its pernicious impact on women's fear of crime, their quality of life and their freedom of movement. One of the key positives of making misogyny a hate crime is to directly challenge these normative discourses and instead make street harassment socially and culturally unacceptable, a practice that is viewed as harmful and prejudicial, something that police officers take seriously and something that is worth reporting to police.

Evaluating language choices: 'misogyny'

By making the decision to name the police policy change *misogyny* hate crime (see Chapter 13 in this book), Nottinghamshire Police intended to reinforce the social unacceptability and, in many cases, the illegality of such incidents committed by *men* towards *women*. Part of the rationale behind this decision was to encourage reporting in order to challenge deeply embedded societal misogyny (see Chapter 13 in this book). A key area of linguistic focus for our research was to evaluate both the police and the general public's perceptions of Nottinghamshire Police's lexical choice of 'misogyny' as a pre-modifier for the category 'hate crime' and to consider the merits of alternative pre-modifiers, such as 'gender'. This involved investigating participants' knowledge and understanding first of the term 'misogyny' to obtain assessments by both members of the general public and the police of the socio-political advantages and disadvantages of using the term misogyny. Whilst a consideration of 'hate crime' is beyond the scope of this chapter, see Mullany and Trickett (2020, pp. 256–261) for a detailed discussion of this category.

Mullany and Trickett (2018a, 2020) highlight that members of the public, women and men, and the police had doubts about the appropriacy of the term 'misogyny'. Many participants in our focus groups explained that they were unclear on the meaning of 'misogyny' and/or had concerns about its accessibility and its comprehensibility to the wider population:

23 I had to Google it, I didn't know what it was and I have a degree.
24 It sounds like a term academics would use.
25 Hard to remember, it's a long word.
26 It's a hard term. I think it scares people.
27 Misogyny is not a word that people are massively familiar with, it's not common.
28 It is not familiar enough for a thing that you want to be talking about as often as you want to be talking about it.
29 I don't think there is an understanding of what it is.
30 If you haven't come across that word, does that relate to women? There's no stem part to it where you, as a layperson, you might think how does that refer to females, or women, or feminine? So I think laypeople wouldn't know what it... I asked my nieces, and none of them knew what it meant.
31 If people aren't familiar with it and they look it up and it just says hatred of women or something they might not think... well that's not right. There might be some sexism within their family but they might think "well that uncle doesn't hate me".

Comment 23 suggests that 'misogyny' was not a familiar term to the participant prior to them agreeing to participate in the focus group. They admitted having to 'Google it' and implied through the declarative second clause 'and I have a degree', that if even an educated person like them had to look it up, the general public would really struggle. Comment 24 illustrates the participant's concern that the term belongs to an 'academic' register not in common usage in the general population. The elitism and classism associated with 'misogyny' is similarly implied in comments 25 and 26 which evaluate it as an intimidating term because it is a 'long word' and a 'hard term' that 'scares people'. Comments 27 to 29 indicate that 'misogyny' is not a sufficiently frequently-used word to seem familiar or understandable to the public. Comment 30 explains concerns that the lack of discernible link in 'misogyny' to 'women' hinders its intelligibility and 31 adopts a narrow interpretation of the term through a hypothetical narrative where people unfamiliar with the term look it up and find 'hatred or women or something' confusing. This also highlights views of some participants that these incidents are not caused by 'hate'. Overall, these comments point to 'misogyny' presenting a barrier to the public's understanding of the new hate crime category, therefore reducing the likelihood that uptake would be effective.

A further issue addressed by participants was the appropriacy of adopting a hate crime category which linguistically excluded men and protected only women. Views about this were mixed, with some feeling that the

Informing legal change 279

pre-modifier 'misogyny' effectively reflected the power dynamic and experiences of those targeted by such behaviour. For example, a male respondent commented:

32 If policy adjustments are made to include men and misandry it misses the point. It doesn't need to include all genders. It's women who are in the majority of the firing line and if you take that away and make it about men as well it sort of waters it down... that's not very helpful.

Through the shooting metaphor 'in the majority of the firing line' this participant recognised the disproportionate targeting of, and harm inflicted on women, which is borne out by the reporting statistics (Nottinghamshire Police 2016). On the other hand, there were concerns from another male respondent about the fairness of protecting women but not men:

33 I think it should include misandry as well. 100%. Absolutely... If we want women to report, we've got another 30 million people in the country called men who might help women to report things to the police and then maybe men report as well... I don't think it could ever succeed unless it was inclusive. It will absolutely fail if it only gives women protection and men not because that's not equality before the law... I think it's a bit divisive, in a lot of ways potentially damaging to say there is no misandry or it's not being reported but there is misogyny. Just bring it all together.

This respondent used emphatic intensifiers '100%' and 'absolutely' to underscore his support for the inclusion of men within a wide, gender-based category, instead of restricting the definition to women through adoption of the term 'misogyny'. He equated success of the policy with being 'inclusive' of men and failure with excluding men because 'that's not equality before the law' and as a consequence, it could be 'divisive' and 'potentially damaging'. It is notable that comment 33 was directly referenced by the Law Commission's (2020, p. 275) hate crime consultation, to illustrate their concern that, if 'misogyny' was selected as the hate crime term, then the campaign could fail due to accusations that the policy was not inclusive of all genders, thus demonstrating a breach of equality before the law.

These concerns were also echoed by the police participants, including the following officer, who felt that protection under the law should be fairly balanced:

34 If you've having a box targeted because 'I'm a woman' and 'I'm being targeted because I'm a man'.

These comments indeed raise points about the importance of a commitment to equality when enshrining new provisions and principles in law. Mullany and

Trickett's (2018a) evidence has been directly cited as one reason why the Law Commission have put forward the view of 'gender or sex' being used as an alternative to the term 'misogyny'. The Law Commission (2020, pp. 275–276) state that: 'The Nottingham Misogyny Hate Crime Evaluation Report expressed some concern that the term "misogyny" might be too academic and inaccessible to gain broad acceptance'. The Law Commission (2020, p. 273) therefore made the following recommendation: 'We provisionally propose that gender or sex should be a protected characteristic for the purposes of hate crime law.'

The Law Commission (2020, p. 194) also made the following observation about the work in Nottinghamshire Police more generally:

> There is significant practical benefit that recognition of hate crime brings to policing and social policy. As many stakeholders have told us, recognition of the nature of the problem, and the particular harms caused by hate, has led to police taking these incidents more seriously. This in turn often leads to better experiences for victims. The experiences of police recognising hate crime against sex workers in Merseyside, and more recently misogyny in Nottingham, were cited as particularly good examples of this.

In terms of the other police forces who have followed Nottinghamshire's lead of bringing in a policy change, it is notable that, whilst six other police forces have introduced the policy, three of these six have opted for 'gender' and not 'misogyny' (Northamptonshire, Leicestershire, Surrey) and Avon and Somerset have opted for 'gender-based'.

Next steps: changing public perceptions

It is clear that there remain a number of issues with misogyny hate crime that require a major re-think within society. The first issue is to acknowledge the scale of the problem and its impact on women and girls by getting their accounts and stories not just heard but actually acknowledged in terms of a social and legal commitment to change. If the Law Commission's recommendation is accepted this will very soon be the case, with a legal change to gender/sex as a category of hate crime.

Recognising the wider impact of gender/sex hate crime upon all women and girls in terms of the restrictions it places on their freedom of movement and full participation in public life through fear of sexual violence is essential. Hate crime laws have long noted the greater impact on individuals given the targeting of their identity by the offender (Iganski 2001) and the wider impact on others that share that identity, both of which contribute to the overall seriousness and provision of enhanced sentences which largely informed the introduction of the misogyny policy in the first place.

Importantly, in hate crime recording, including racially aggravated offences, the perception of the victim is absolutely paramount, in line with recommendations from the Stephen Lawrence Inquiry (Macpherson 1999, Recommendation 12). Such approaches are in line with other criminal offences that place a strong emphasis on the perspective of the victim, including psychic assault, where a key component of the actus reus is that the victim feared imminent violence due to the language and or/actions of the offender, even if, in reality, such was not the case (*R v Ireland; R v Burstow* [1998] AC 147). Therefore it is the perception of the victim in terms of how they perceive the interaction and the impact upon their lives, both in the immediate moment and in the longer term that is crucial to recognise here.

This can help us to challenge and dismantle the suggestions that some men and women in society have that some forms of street harassment are 'a compliment' and 'a normal and acceptable part of male behaviour' (Sullivan et al. 2010; Brown 2016; Oppenheim 2016). It is not enough to just challenge such arguments; rather they must be exposed as linguistic devices that perpetuate the abuse and devalue the fundamental rights of women and girls in daily life, serving to hide what is, in reality, a considerable range and amount of criminal offences and anti-social behaviour which society has a duty to tackle. It must be recognised that street harassment and other forms of public harassment of women and girls are a global issue and form the cornerstone of the global problem of violence against women. Global movements such as the UN's #heforshe campaign (Heforshe 2020) and the advent of global political movements such as #metoo, are critical here in enabling different geographical regions to learn from the experiences of each other and share best practices.

If women can be routinely objectified as sexual objects, disrespected, dehumanised, humiliated and intimidated when simply going about their daily lives with societal and legal immunity for perpetrators then equality can never be achieved. The continued failure to recognise this contributes to the view that women are worthy of disrespect and abuse by men, which fuels much of the violence against women and girls which involves expression of male power, violence and control including both intimate partner violence and sexual abuse by non-intimate partners.

Of course, men are not simply the problem but part of the solution. We must learn from the majority of men and boys that do not engage in street harassment of women and girls who are important allies to the overall cause. Indeed, many of our male research participants, whilst they had an awareness that women were on the receiving end of street harassment and misogyny hate crime, were often unaware of the scale and impact of the problem and were often alerted to this through the experiences of their female partners and associates or sometimes through the research itself:

35 My wife has also had people try and grope her in the street or in public transport you feel someone grope you or something like that.
36 I was talking about this with my partner sort of the last week or so and she told me a horrific story about how a guy who'd approached her when

she was out with her mates, she'd turned him down kind of thing, he was being quite lecherous and she left the club and he followed her out and punched her in the face.

If the Law Commission implements the category of 'gender/sex as a hate crime', as expected at the time of writing, then the next challenge is to implement legislative change effectively. A key part of its success lies in changing attitudes and cultural expectations through education, as well as government and a number of groups, including police forces and other areas of the criminal justice system including the CPS and courts, working together with community groups and organisations. Many of our research informants shared their ideas and views on how this could be achieved; the most dominant theme was through educational initiatives.

On the basis of our research and as a first step towards this goal of improving education about street harassment, we have produced a short graphic comic titled *Changing Minds: The Real Impact of Street Harassment* (Nottingham University 2020), targeted at 14–25 year olds, to be used as an educational/training resource in schools, colleges, universities and other public institutions. It is based on the narrative experiences of our research participants in Mullany and Trickett (2018a). There are other emergent examples that can be used as educational tools and templates to engender debate and bring about long-term change, including video resources where the scale and impact of street harassment has been brought home to men through the filming of social experiments, including '10 Hours of Walking in NYC as a Woman' (Rob Bliss Creative 2014) where a woman is continually catcalled by a variety of men and followed for a significant time period by another. Other social experiments have included 'Dads React to Their Daughters Getting Catcalled' (Iris 2015a) and 'Sons React to Their Moms Getting Catcalled' (Iris 2015b). In both videos men were shocked at the amount and type of harassment women in their lives experienced. Another YouTube social experiment details a male actor's shock at the scale and impact of the harassment he experiences when walking the streets dressed as a woman (Courtesy Belail Productions 2013). Other examples include men calling out the behaviour of men that engage in this practice, questioning their motives and indicating its impact and undesirability.

Other recent attempts to challenge the behaviour of men who publicly harass women can also be seen in genres such as advertising, with innovative campaigns such as Gillette's re-writing of its long-standing '*The Best a Man Can Get*' campaign re-framed and re-worded as '*The Best Men Can Be*' (see for example, Hassan 2019), indicating that men are part of the solution and need to hold other men to account. With this change in slogan, from a linguistic perspective it is notable that the shift is from the indefinite article and singular noun 'a man' to losing the indefinite article to using a collective noun 'men', the choice of which carries with it a direct connotation of collective responsibility of men. Additionally, this is not about what men can 'get', as a sense of entitlement but instead, 'can be' as a verb phrase brings with it instead connotations of collective achievement and improvement. Despite the rather predictable backlash in some areas of the popular and social media to this campaign, such a shift in socio-cultural messaging in media discourse should be accelerated and become part of a changing tide of attitudes towards gender-based violence and public harassment of women and girls. We all have a role to play in ensuring that the attitudes of those men that fuel harassment and abuse of women in public places are tackled and those that continue in the practice are properly held to account.

Towards the future

When bringing together all of the complex legal, linguistic and policy issues that have been raised in this chapter from the interdisciplinary perspectives of criminology and linguistics, it is important to acknowledge how far the campaign for misogyny hate crime has come. With its initial origins with Nottinghamshire Police's policy change, we are now at the point where, if the Law Commission's recommendation goes ahead, we are on the verge of seeing 'gender/sex as a hate crime' enter into law for England and Wales, which will enable either aggravated[1] sentencing as already exists for religious or racially aggravated offending and for race of religious hate crime (see Owusu-Bempah and Walters 2016) or enhanced sentencing[2] as already exists for hate crimes expressing hostility towards disability, sexuality or transgender (s146 Criminal Justice Act 2003) to be brought in by courts. The next stage of this work is to raise awareness and understanding of the new hate crime law and use this as part of the long-standing global campaign to end violence against women and girls, as well as violence against men in society. Despite having a change in law in place, we know from rape statistics that victims of these crimes are not coming forward and under-reporting is still a fundamental barrier – the Ministry of Justice (2018) estimated that of 97,000 victims of rape or sexual assault (aged between 16 and 59) only 15% report reported to police.

Additionally, we would argue that the Law Commission's decision to recommend adding the category of gender/sex hate crime is increasingly timely as there is growing evidence that higher numbers of women and girls have experienced street harassment during periods of Covid-19 pandemic lockdown (Plan International UK 2020). In a poll of over 1,000 girls at the end of the sixth week of the first national lockdown, Plan International UK (2020) reported that one in five girls aged 14–21 had experienced street harassment, with their experiences getting worse during the pandemic. Unsurprisingly, in accordance with the long-established reporting patterns already seen in this chapter, Plan International UK reported that 26% of girls did not tell anyone at all about the incident, let alone think about reporting it to the police. Furthermore, 33% of girls reported that they stopped going outside as a consequence of being harassed, again giving further evidence that fear of street harassment results in restrictions of movement and freedom. Reported experiences included unwanted sexual attention, unwanted sexual or physical contact and indecent exposure. In a recent interview with activist Laura Bates (Aspinall 2020), Bates observes:

> There are several factors about lockdown that exacerbate the problem... streets are unusually quiet and a lack of witnesses emboldens perpetrators. Women are being encouraged to take less travelled routes they might usually avoid in order to observe social distancing and there are fewer places to turn for refuge as many shops and other businesses are closed.

The impact of this harassment has left many of these girls and women reluctant to leave the house at all during lockdown. Thus arguably, the need for a change in the law has become even more acute during the Covid-19 pandemic, as the dynamics of public space have changed and become more unsafe due to fewer bystanders being present. Caldwell (2020), CEO of Plan International UK, recently made the following observations:

> Even a national lockdown is not enough to prevent perpetrators carrying out this abuse. Girls are still getting catcalled and harassed when they venture outside for their daily exercise, for essentials or even to work – so much so that some do not feel safe walking alone outside at all. And it's making them feel ashamed, angry and frightened...girls' voices must be heard so we can meet their needs in this lockdown and beyond, but many currently don't feel able to tell anyone that they feel unsafe and unable to walk the streets they live in. We cannot allow the lockdown to turn back the clock on girls' rights: we need to send a clear message that street harassment is not okay, make sure girls can access the support they need and work with bystanders, including men and boys, to ensure they feel able to call out street harassment.

In summary, we would argue that there is an urgent and acute need for a national roll-out of 'gender' as a hate crime category and this needs to happen imminently. Once this takes place, interventionist work must accelerate in order to bring in educational initiatives that promote awareness of the existence of the policy and what it means for all genders, the illegality and unacceptability of hate crime and hate incidents. Multiple stakeholders including educators, community groups, charities, NGOs and police must be engaged to implement community-based, grassroots initiatives involving all genders that will play a part in the longer-term goal of eradicating gender-based violence in future.

Notes

1 As under Crime and Disorder Act s. 29–42 where a crime motivated by hostility towards race or religion is an aggravated offence attracting higher penalties. S145 of the Criminal Justice Act 2003 where hostility on the basis of race or religion requires an aggravated penalty at the sentencing stage.
2 As is currently the case for hate crimes motivated by hostility towards disability, sexuality or transgender – under S146 Criminal Justice Act 2003.

References

Aspinall, G., 2020. Women are being chased and stalked: the terrifying rise of street harassment in lockdown. *Grazia* [online]. Available at: https://graziadaily.co.uk/life/in-the-news/sexual-harassment-lockdown/ [Accessed 13 January 2021].

Bates, L., 2014. Women should not accept street harassment as "just a compliment". *Guardian*[online].Availableat:https://www.theguardian.com/lifeandstyle/womens-blog/2014/feb/28/women-street-harassment-power-control-violence [Accessed 14 January 2021].

Bowman, C.G., 1993. Street harassment and the informal ghettoization of women. *Harvard Law Review*, 106(3) pp. 517–580.

Brown, B., 2016. Wolf-whistling a hate crime? What an insult to real victims of abuse. *Mail Online* [online]. Available at: https://www.dailymail.co.uk/news/article-3691284/Wolf-whistling-hate-crime-insult-real-victims-abuse.html [Accessed 10 January 2021].

Caldwell, R., 2020. 1 in 5 girls have experienced street harassment during lockdown. *Plan International UK* [online]. Available at: https://plan-uk.org/media-centre/1-in-5-girls-have-experienced-street-harassment-during-lockdown [Accessed 14 January 2021].

Citizens UK, 2020. 'Overcoming everyday hate in the UK: Hate crime, oppression and the law'. [Online] Available at: https://d3n8a8pro7vhmx.cloudfront.net/newcitizens/pages/3760/attachments/original/1599728331/Academic_Report_V.6_-_web_compress_3.pdf?1599728331 [Accessed 15 January 2021]

Cops, D. and Pleysier, S., 2011. 'Doing gender' in fear of crime: the impact of gender identity on reported levels of fear of crime in adolescents and young adults. *The British Journal of Criminology*, 51(1), pp. 58–74.

Courtesy Belail Productions, 2013. Male actor dresses as woman to experience sexual harassment [online]. Available at: https://www.youtube.com/watch?v=LvNZt1T5rAQ [Accessed 4 January 2021].

Crime and Disorder Act 1988 c. 37.

Criminal Justice Act 1988 c. 33.

Criminal Justice Act 2003 c. 44.

Goodey, J., 1994. Fear of crime: what can children tell us? *International Review of Victimology*, 3(3), pp. 195–210.

Hassan, A., 2019. The exec behind *that* Gillette ad says brands have a responsibility to challenge toxic masculinity. *Quartz* [online]. Available at: https://qz.com/quartzy/1626698/pg-exec-behind-viral-gillette-ad-talks-toxic-masculinity/ [Accessed 12 January 2021].

Heforshe, 2020. #*Heforshe* [online]. https://www.heforshe.org/en [Accessed 12 January 2021].

Iganski, P., 2001. Hate crimes hurt more. *American Behavioral Scientist*, 45(4), pp. 626–638.

Iris, 2015a. Dads react to their daughters getting catcalled [online]. Available at: https://www.youtube.com/watch?v=ud3DLjREV34 [Accessed 4 January 2021].

Iris, 2015b. Sons react to their moms getting catcalled [online]. Available at: https://www.youtube.com/watch?v=KNfE_Det2Fo [Accessed 4 January 2021].

Kelly, L., 1987. The continuum of sexual violence. In: Hanmer, J. and Maynard, M., eds. *Women, Violence and Social Control*. London: Palgrave Macmillan, pp. 46–60.

Kelly, L., 1988. How women define their experiences of violence. In: Yllö, K. and Bograd, M., eds. *Feminist Perspectives on Wife Abuse*. Newbury Park, CA: Sage Publications, Inc., pp. 114–132.

Kissling, E.A., 1991. Street harassment: the language of sexual terrorism. *Discourse & Society*, 2(4), pp. 451–460.

Laniya, O.O., 2005. Street smut: gender, media, and the legal power dynamics of street harassment, or hey sexy and other verbal ejaculations. *Columbia Journal of Gender and Law*, 14(1), pp. 91–130. DOI: 10.7916/cjgl.v14i1.2503.

Law Commission, 2020. hate crime laws: a consultation paper [online]. Available at: https://s3-eu-west-2.amazonaws.com/lawcom-prod-storage-11jsxou24uy7q/uploads/2020/10/Hate-crime-final-report.pdf [Accessed 15 January 2021].

Macpherson, W., 1999. The Stephen Lawrence inquiry [online]. Available at: https://assets.publishing.service.gov.uk/government/uploads/system/uploads/attachment_data/file/277111/4262.pdf [Accessed 15 November 2020].

Ministry of Justice, 2013. An overview of sexual offending in England and Wales [online]. Available at: https://assets.publishing.service.gov.uk/government/uploads/system/uploads/attachment_data/file/214970/sexual-offending-overview-jan-2013.pdf [Accessed 15 November 2020].

Mullany, L., 2020. Rethinking professional communication: new departures for global workplace research. In: Mullany, L., ed. *Professional Communication: Consultancy, Advocacy, Activism*. London: Palgrave, pp. 1–26.

Mullany, L. and Trickett, L., 2018a. Misogyny hate crime evaluation report [online]. Available at: https://www.nottingham.ac.uk/lipp/documents/misogyny-evaluation-report.pdf [Accessed 19 January 2021].

Mullany, L. and Trickett, L., 2018b. Misogyny hate crime: new research reveals true scale of issue – and how the public are united against it. *The Conversation* [online]. Available at: https://theconversation.com/misogyny-hate-crime-new-research-reveals-true-scale-of-issue-and-how-the-public-are-united-against-it-100265 [Accessed 19 January 2021].

Mullany, L. and Trickett, L., 2020. The language of "misogyny hate crime": politics, policy and policing. In: Mullany, L., ed. *Professional Communication: Consultancy, Advocacy, Activism*. London: Palgrave, pp. 249–272.

Nottingham University, 2020. Changing minds: the real impact of street harassment 2020 [online]. Available at: https://www.nottingham.ac.uk/lipp/documents/300620-changing-minds-comic.pdf [Accessed 2 January 2021].

Nottinghamshire Police, 2016. *Hate Crime Report: Misogyny 2016*. Nottingham: Nottinghamshire Police.

Oppenheim, M., 2016. Joanna Lumley: "wolf whistling isn't sexist, it's a compliment. We're offended by everything. *The Independent* [online]. Available at: https://www.independent.co.uk/news/people/joanna-lumley-wolf-whistling-sexist-compliment-comment-a7345826.html [Accessed 19 January 2021].

Owusu-Bempah, A. and Walters, M.A., 2016. Racially aggravated offences: when does section 145 of the Criminal Justice Act 2003 apply? *Criminal Law Review*, 2, pp. 116–123.

Pain, R., 1991. Space, sexual violence and social control: integrating geographical and feminist analyses of women's fear of crime. *Progress in Human Geography*, 15(4), pp. 415–431.

Pain, R.H., 1995. Elderly women and fear of violent crime: The least likely victims? A reconsideration of the extent and nature of risk. *The British Journal of Criminology*, 35(4), pp. 584–598.

Pain, R.H., 1997. 'Old age' and ageism in urban research: the case of fear of crime. *International Journal of Urban and Regional Research*, 21(1), pp. 117–128.

Pain, R., 2000. Place, social relations and the fear of crime: a review. *Progress in Human Geography*, 24(3), pp. 365–387.

Plan International UK, 2020. 1 in 5 girls have experienced street harassment during lockdown. *Plan International UK* [online]. Available at: https://plan-uk.org/media-centre/1-in-5-girls-have-experienced-street-harassment-during-lockdown [Accessed 14 January 2021].

Public Order Act 1986 c. 64.

Protection From Harassment Act 1997 c. 40.

R v Ireland; R v Burstow [1998] AC 147.

Rob Bliss Creative, 2014. 10 hours of walking in NYC as a woman [online]. Available at: https://www.youtube.com/watch?v=b1XGPvbWn0A [Accessed 4 January 2021].

Salmon, K., 2021. Well where's the harm? An in-depth exploration of intergenerational women's perspectives of stranger harassment in public space. *Westminster* [online]. Available at: https://graziadaily.co.uk/life/in-the-news/sexual-harassment-lockdown/ [Accessed 4 January 2021].

Sacco, V.F., 1990. Gender, fear, and victimization: a preliminary application of power-control theory. *Sociological Spectrum*, 10(4), pp. 485–506.

Stanko, E.A., 1987. Typical violence, normal precaution: men, women and interpersonal violence in England, Wales, Scotland and the USA. In: Hanmer, J. and Maynard, M., eds. *Women, Violence and Social Control*. London: Palgrave Macmillan, pp. 122–134.

Stanko, E.A., 1990. *Everyday Violence: How Women and Men Experience Sexual and Physical Danger*. London: HarperCollins.

Sullivan, H., Lord, T. and McHugh, M., 2010. Creeps and Casanovas: experiences, explanations and effects of street harassment. *Victims of Sexual Assault and Abuse: Resources and Responses for Individuals and Families*, 1, pp. 237–258.

Trickett, L. and Mullany, L., 2018. Misogyny hate crime. *The Law Society Gazette* [online]. Available at: https://www.lawgazette.co.uk/commentary-and-opinion/misogyny-as-hate-crime/5067192.article [Accessed 19 January 2021].

United Nations, 2015. Transforming our world: the 2030 agenda for sustainable development [online]. Available at: https://sustainabledevelopment.un.org/content/documents/21252030%20Agenda%20for%20Sustainable%20Development%20web.pdf [Accessed 14 January 2021].

Walklate, S., 1997. Risk and criminal victimization: a modernist dilemma? *The British Journal of Criminology*, 37(1), pp. 35–45. DOI: 10.1093/oxfordjournals.bjc.a014148.

15 Our Streets Now
Demanding an end to public sexual harassment

Maya Tutton

Introduction

'Sexual harassment affects the lives of nearly every woman in the UK' (Women and Equalities Committee 2018). For most, the harassment starts while underage: two-thirds of schoolgirls in the UK have experienced unwanted sexual attention in public space (Plan UK 2016). This form of gender-based violence impacts the lives of women and girls profoundly, from affecting their mental health to changing their everyday decisions about clothing and transport routes (Vera-Gray 2017). Our Streets Now started as a direct response to this lived reality. We are a campaign which aims to end this violence, through cultural and legislative change. I co-founded the campaign alongside my younger sister Gemma in April 2019. Our focus is on gender-based harassment, centring the experiences of women and girls suffering from misogyny in public space. By women and girls, we refer to anyone who identifies as such, and stress the high rates of violence that transgender women face. Furthermore, we platform the experiences of anyone who suffers from misogyny, including femme-presenting non-binary people but also incidents when non-binary people or transgender men are misgendered. We use a gendered lens alongside an intersectional one (Crenshaw 1991), recognising that all forms of harassment are interlinked and often occur on multiple intersecting grounds. No matter the grounds, these intrusions are about power and control.

Unlike most academic chapters, I have chosen to write this in the first person. I have done so because my work at Our Streets Now has been a deeply personal project. As well as giving a broader outline of the campaign, I have tried to zoom into moments and memories that have stuck out to me throughout this process, in the hope of giving the reader an insight into my lived experience not only as a young woman, but as the co-founder of this campaign. As such, I feel it is only right to write in a register and tone which is more reflective of our work.

The first part of the chapter will introduce the term public sexual harassment and our campaign against it. In recounting the reasons behind starting the campaign, I will go into some depth about the prevalence and impact of

DOI: 10.4324/9781003023722-15

sexual harassment on my own life and on that of the majority of women and girls in the UK. Exploring the two key aspects to the campaign, awareness and education on the one hand and legislative solutions on the other, I hope to give an insight into how Our Streets Now is trying to tackle this violence. The second part of the chapter will include a reflection on two crucial aspects of our work: the implications of digital feminist campaigning, and the importance of young people, particularly young women, in social justice movements. In examining the work of this grassroots campaign to tackle public sexual harassment, I hope to give an insight into a global wave of women and girls standing up and speaking out for a misogyny free world.

Introducing Our Streets Now

The power in naming

Fiona Vera-Gray refers to the disagreements around the naming of harassment in public space as the 'problem of naming' (Vera-Gray 2017). What I want to do here is reflect on how Our Streets Now has confronted this problem, and through it attempted to find power in naming.

Throughout this chapter, I will be referring to these unwanted intrusions in public space using the term public sexual harassment (PSH). By PSH, I refer to unwelcomed and unwanted attention, sexual advances and intimidating behaviour that occurs in public spaces, both in person and online. Our discussions around wording began after a conversation with Chilean anti-PSH activist, María José Guerrero González. Guerrero reached out to our Facebook account offering her support and experience from their campaign in Chile (Observatorio Contra el Acoso Chile 2014). We had a lengthy Skype conversation in which Guerrero explained how activists in Argentina worked to change the language around PSH. Previously, the term 'piropo' was used to refer to verbal harassment, a word which implies flattery or a compliment. These activists worked to shift the wording towards 'acoso callejero' (street assault), a phrase which reflects the violence of PSH. After this conversation, I read about the academic debate around the terminology used to describe this concept. These interactions have come under many different names, from the colloquial terms 'wolf-whistling' and 'catcalling', to the more phenomenological term "men's stranger intrusions" (Vera-Gray 2016) and the more legalistic 'public sexual harassment'. As a campaign, we had previously used the most commonly employed term 'street harassment'. Following the conversation with Guerrero, discussions with our legal advisors Charlotte Proudman and Dexter Dias and after reading through the academic literature, Gemma and I decided on our preferred wording and then put it to a vote on our Instagram, @OurStreetsNow.

Our campaign put forward the term 'public sexual harassment' as a suggested replacement, for three key reasons. Firstly, we felt the term linked these intrusions to other forms of sexual harassment, which was crucial for us in stressing the interlinked nature of violence against women and girls and the continuum along which it exists (Kelly 1988). Secondly, we felt that the word 'public' helped expand people's understandings beyond just street-based incidents to include all public spaces, from gyms and parks to shops and nightclubs. Finally, inspired by Guerrero's point about using wording that carries a normative weight, we felt that moving away from pre-existing phrases like 'catcalling' might allow people's preconceived notions of intrusions as compliments to fall away. We felt the new terminology should carry a different weight, one which emphasises the gravity of this issue. We were influenced by Catherine MacKinnon's statement that the legal concept of sexual harassment has re-entered our society and shaped 'the social definitions of what may be resisted or complained about, said aloud, or even felt' (MacKinnon 1979, p. 57). We wanted to encourage women and girls to feel justified in speaking out about PSH, and we felt that including it within the broader umbrella of sexual harassment might help them do just that. Once we chose the wording 'public sexual harassment', we put it to our Instagram community. Over 90% voted for using the term 'public sexual harassment' instead of 'street harassment', citing all the reasons we have mentioned above and many more. Since renaming this violence 'public sexual harassment', we have seen a notable rise in its use, particularly in the form of 'PSH'. The widespread use of the acronym PSH is very important. It is clearly memorable and impactful, and we hope that it will become as recognisable as the acronym of female genital mutilation, FGM.

We have therefore attempted to overcome the 'problem of naming' by finding power within it. Rebecca Solnit argued that the feminist movement is overcoming what Betty Friedan called 'the problem that has no name' (Friedan 1986) by naming it 'bit by bit: with old words like patriarchy and gaslighting put back to work, with new words like marginalisation, mansplaining' (Solnit 2020). For us, refusing to use the commonly used phrases of 'catcalling' and 'wolf-whistling' has been about reclaiming agency and narrative over the myths and misunderstandings with which victims are confronted.

Growing up a girl in the UK

I don't remember my first experience of being sexually harassed. It must have happened when I was around 12 or 13, and it has blended into a stock memory of being verbally abused in public. The only times that stick out for me, the incidents I remember, are the scariest ones. One incident I remember clearly was when I was 14 years old and subjected to vitriolic abuse and threats of sexual violence on my walk to a friend's house. I was overwhelmed with fear. These incidents profoundly changed the way I viewed public space, as well as kickstarting the continual process of decision making I go through every day in order to keep myself safe. Since then, I have regularly been subjected to sexual harassment. I have had misogynistic abuse shouted at me on the street, been groped at festivals and suffered regularly from workplace harassment.

My relationship with sexual harassment is as depressing as it is commonplace. Facing harassment as an underage girl is more likely to happen than not, with two out of three girls in the UK having experienced sexual attention in a public place, and over one in three (38%) experiencing it at least once a month (Plan UK 2016). Not remembering your first incident of harassment is also not unusual. One of Gemma and I's first digital projects was the #MyFirstTime campaign, when we collected videos of women and girls discussing the first time that they were sexually harassed. Many could not recollect their first incident, citing reasons such as the fact that they have experienced PSH too many times to distinguish between them, or that they have blocked from it from their own memories. The fear I experienced is also customary, as reflected in the majority of testimonies we have received. Fears of escalation are justified. In November 2019, a Chicago University student named Ruth George was killed after ignoring verbal harassment by a man in a parking garage. Prosecutors stated that the man was 'angry that he was being ignored' after she didn't respond to his persistent catcalls (Bosman 2017). George's killing reminds us of the potential threat of physical violence that underpins incidents of public sexual harassment.

My changed relationship to public space and consequent behavioural change is also a documented consequence of public sexual harassment, labelled 'safety work' (Kelly 2012). Women and girls are 'routinely making strategic decisions to avoid sexual harassment and other forms of sexual violence', be it by taking different routes home or putting in headphones (Vera-Gray and Kelly 2020). With violence an ordinary part of a woman's life, it becomes managed and embedded into safety rituals which women take to enhance their personal safety (Stanko 1990). Suffering from workplace harassment is also unremarkable. In February 2020, we spoke on a campaigning call hosted by the Trade Union Congress to highlight the results of their #ThisIsNotWorking campaign, which found that one in two women have been sexually harassed at work, as well as two in three LGBTQ+ people (TUC 2019). Even being sexually assaulted at festivals is not unusual, with two in five young female festival goers being subjected to sexual assault or harassment (YouGov 2018). These findings are mirrored by research which found that festival attendees report high levels of concern about sexual harassment and assault, with a third of women having experienced harassment at a festival (Bows 2019).

What prompted our campaign against public sexual harassment was not, however, my own experiences, but rather my sister's. An 11-year-old when the abuse started, Gemma has been the victim of repeated harassment which has significantly impacted her life. As an older sister having to witness this abuse, and indeed explain it to her, the horrendous truth about public sexual harassment became clear. It was in explaining to her that although awful, her experience was in many ways unremarkable, a 'normal' part of being a girl, that the normalisation of this behaviour hit home. In explaining that this first incident of harassment would likely be neither the last, nor the scariest, I understood how trivialised it had become, even for me.

In 2018, Gemma and I watched the viral video of Marie Laguerre, a French woman, being punched in the face in a Paris cafe after shouting back at a harasser (Laguerre 2018). We watched the French government pass a law shortly after, specifically addressing the issue of PSH (Outrage sexiste ou sexuel 2018). We then saw a successful campaign by Plan UK (Assad 2019) convince the UK Government to recognise street harassment as a form of gender-based violence in their refreshed Violence against Women and Girls strategy (HM Government 2019). We realised that governments could and should take action against this everyday violence, and that ours, beyond recognising that the problem existed, was not taking action against it in education, policy or law. In the meantime, Gemma and I continued to be harassed, as did our friends, and their friends. The sad truth is that for every year that PSH continues to be normalised and trivialised, we see another generation of young girls being raised to view their bodies as public property. Eventually, we decided enough was enough, and founded Our Streets Now on 18 April 2019. It was originally going to be named Our Streets: we added the Now in order to stress the urgency of tackling this problem. We are demanding equal access to public space and an end to PSH, now.

Our campaign

Our Streets Now was born out of our anger and frustration. We began by launching a petition calling on the UK to 'Make Street Harassment Illegal'. Within 100 days, it had gained 100,000 signatures, been covered across national media and encouraged hundreds of women and girls to come forward with their experiences. The combined impact of these acts was to force the spotlight onto PSH, its impact and its prevalence. The campaign has 25,000 followers on Instagram as of January 2021, a large online community which has been used to create space for victims to come forward with their experiences, to feel 'heard'. Gemma and I have spoken about our campaign at events in Parliament, at conferences and in universities. Most importantly, we have reached thousands of women and girls who have experienced PSH and want an avenue to take action. In April 2020, Our Streets Now expanded from being a campaign predominantly run by Gemma and I to become a larger team with over 25 members. These individuals have brought their own perspective and focus within the broader umbrella of public sexual harassment: from those whose focus has been around defending our right to exercise in peace, to those working to spotlight how transgender women suffer from transmisogyny. Our aims have widened beyond campaigning for legal change to tackling PSH through cultural change too. As such, we have split the campaign into two parts: awareness and education on the one hand, legislation and politics on the other. We recognise that groundwork cultural change is crucial in tackling the roots of PSH, which is why it is the bedrock of our campaign.

Awareness and education

We believe that the first step to tackling a problem is recognising it. That is why the majority of our work is focused on raising awareness about the problem of PSH. We want to communicate three key things: what PSH is, what its impacts are and how prevalent it is in the lives of women and girls. A particularly important part of this work is using intersectionality as a prism through which to see and understand how inhabiting various oppressed identities can affect individual experiences of PSH (Crenshaw 1991). At Our Streets Now we have focused from the outset on PSH as a form of gender-based violence, on understanding these intrusions as a product of misogyny and patriarchy. However, our intersectional approach means that we do not focus solely on gender. Gender-based harassment interlocks with other forms of oppression in these experiences, and so taking an intersectional approach is essential to our campaign and to understanding the experiences of all those who experience misogyny.

Getting our messages into public consciousness has taken many forms so far, and we hope will take many more over the coming months and years. Our social media is our most important form of communication. Having complete control over what we put out gives us the freedom to raise awareness in the exact manner we wish to do so. It gives us the space to add nuance to these experiences and explore different facets of PSH in conversation with our followers. The use of Instagram as our primary platform, a space which is shaped by images and art, has allowed us to centre visual representations of this violence, with each illustrated testimony foregrounding a particular story. Instagram has also been an important platform to us because of the younger audience it reaches (Perrin and Anderson 2019). The age of our followers, 82% of them under 34, is in keeping with the age at which women and girls experience the highest rates of harassment (Women and Equalities Committee 2018).

In traditional media, what we lose in narrative control, we gain in numbers. Having coverage by media sources like the Guardian, the BBC and The Times has allowed us to reach an audience previously unimaginable. Furthermore, it has allowed us to access groups which our social media does not reach. An interesting difference came to light between the reactions of listeners to two different radio shows. In the case of our BBC 5 Live interview, where our message reached a majority male audience, the response was shock; this contrasted starkly to the unsurprised resignation of many listeners to BBC Woman's Hour. In our interviews, podcast appearances, op-eds and more, we have tried to use our campaign story to spotlight the problem of PSH. The irony is of course that many women and girls already know the reality of PSH because it is their lived experience. What we are doing is merely speaking about this problem in public. In a similar way, the current movement to destigmatise periods and period poverty, spearheaded by campaigners like Free Period's founder Amika George (George 2017) and anti-tampon tax campaigner Laura Coryton (Hearing 2016) has been about unveiling the taboos around discussing the subject in the public sphere.

Beyond the media, our aim is to raise awareness in a more thorough way through educational resources and programmes. With Gemma being a secondary school pupil and myself a university student, educational change has been a key priority. The fact that PSH is experienced by underage girls also makes early educational programmes all the more important. These aims have been developed in a new, separate part of the campaign: in September 2020, 'Our Schools Now' was launched, a project to include public sexual harassment as part of PSHE/RSE lessons in schools across the UK (Our Streets Now 2020). In doing so, 'Our Schools Now' hopes to raise a new generation of girls and femme-presenting people who never blame themselves for the misogynistic harassment they will likely face, and a generation of boys who never become perpetrators of this violence. The report (Sefton et al. 2020) released alongside the project, based on the findings of a survey run by the campaign of over 150 secondary school pupils and recent school leavers, found that 64% of the students had never been taught about PSH, despite the majority of respondents being victims of harassment. Furthermore, nearly half (47%) of students said that they would not report any incidents of PSH to staff for fear of not being taken seriously, or not even knowing how to report. Of those who did report PSH, 72% of pupils described a negative response by staff, or no action taken at all. This report therefore paints a (limited) yet important picture of how public sexual harassment is ignored and belittled in many school contexts. When we asked pupils what changes they wanted introduced, the vast majority communicated a desire for lessons and teaching about PSH, as well as better reporting procedures within the school. 'Our Schools Now' was launched as a direct response to these findings, with the creation of a whole host of freely available student and teacher resources to engage with the issue.

As well as secondary school pupils, we surveyed higher education students about their experiences. We found that nearly 90% of students had experienced public sexual harassment themselves, and an even greater number felt that this was an issue for university students. Once again, most of the answers suggested pushing for greater education and awareness, with ideas like consent workshops and well-funded awareness campaigns being the most common responses. In October 2020, we launched 'Our Schools Now: Higher Education', a network of students across higher education facilities who run their own institution-specific campaigns. Both our educational campaigns, in secondary and higher education, have come directly from voices of students affected by this issue and driven by their priorities for change.

Another key part of our societal work, which is underdeveloped as of yet, is how to educate and bring awareness to perpetrators. Research has found that 'nearly one in three of the young men surveyed in the UK had made sexually harassing comments to a woman or girl they didn't know in a public place (...) in the previous month' (Heilman 2018). The sheer scale of this problem can therefore feel daunting, but we are determined to confront it. Without working with perpetrators, we have little chance of ending public sexual harassment, and we are therefore committed to doing our best to enter predominantly male spaces in order to make the message heard.

Legislation & politics

As well as our work on education and awareness, Our Streets Now supports finding legislative solutions to tackling PSH. We do so with a recognition that the current criminal justice system discriminates against people of colour (particularly BME people), women (especially when reporting gender-based violence), disabled people, transgender people and other marginalised groups like homeless people. We also recognise that, like all crimes, legislation alone can never end public sexual harassment. It must be seen as one tool amongst others in tackling this violence. Nonetheless, we believe that our government could and should be doing more to make public spaces safer for women. In this belief, we are joined by our 200,000 petition signers, our legal advisors Dexter Dias and Charlotte Proudman, as well as a number of women and children's organisations such as Plan International and UN Women UK.

One of our legislative aims is for a specific criminal offence to be introduced criminalising in-person public sexual harassment. This legislation would fill the gaps in current legislation in order to give all victims of PSH a legal avenue to pursue. Our aim is to end the patchwork of laws which cover this behaviour inadequately to create legislation which would catch all cases, rather than just those which include either a course of conduct (repeated harassment by the same individual) or specific forms of PSH which are legislated against already, such as indecent exposure (Sexual Offences Act 2003) or upskirting (Voyeurism (Offences) Act 2019).

The lack of legislation surrounding public sexual harassment is notable. Our laws reflect our society, and the normalisation of this form of gender-based violence is entrenched by the lack of legislation against it. The over 200,000 people who have signed our petition signal to us the strong desire for legislative solutions to PSH. As one member told us during a legal consultation 'We have no way to enforce our human right to partake in public life'. In March 2019, the UK government recognised street harassment as a form of gender-based violence in its refreshed Violence against Women and Girls strategy (HM Government 2019). We believe that it should now tackle it and fulfil the requirements of the Istanbul Convention – which it has signed but not yet ratified (Atkins 2019) – to criminalise all forms of violence against women and girls. Article 40 in particular demands that sexual harassment in all its forms be met with punishment (Council of Europe 2011). Many countries have introduced specific legislation addressing PSH, including France (Parlement Francais 2018), Portugal (Assembleia de Republica 2015) and Costa Rica (Asamblea Legislativa de Costa Rica 2020).

In conjunction with this aim, Our Streets Now campaigns for misogyny to be made a hate crime. We supported Stella Creasy's proposed amendment 35 to the Domestic Abuse Bill, which would have required all police forces to record misogyny as a hate crime and assess how it influences the experience of domestic abuse (Creasy 2020). We also spoke in support of misogyny being made a hate crime on the panel at the Parliamentary meeting on the 'Campaign to Make Misogyny History'. We believe making misogyny a hate crime is essential to tackling public sexual harassment for two key reasons. The first is that doing so allows us to recognise the role misogyny plays in the disproportionate violence suffered by women and girls in society. The other reason is that gathering evidence and data about the prevalence of VAWG in society, which the police would be required to do were misogyny made a hate crime, is an essential first step in tackling it.

Making misogyny a hate crime would not, however, criminalise any new behaviour. This is why we believe that a dual approach of both creating a specific criminal offence and making misogyny a hate crime is needed in order to most effectively tackle PSH. We are also arguing for the data collected about misogyny hate crime to record other identity features in order to allow it to capture the disproportionate violence faced by those with multiple intersecting identities. We are open to further legislative provisions and strongly believe that gains will have to be made bit by bit and in a variety of ways in order to find the best route. Cynthia Bowman asserts that "the law has developed thus far largely without the participation of women, but that women's input can force the legal system to take account of our experiences now" (Bowman 1993). It is this belief, that we can use the legal system in order to change it, which drives our work on legislative change.

It is crucial however that we recognise that the criminal justice system itself is deeply flawed. The police and criminal justice system in the UK discriminate against BME communities. To take the example of our prisons, Black people make up 12% of the inmates despite only being 3% of the population (Lammy 2017). This over-representation can also be found in the handing down of fines by police: during lockdown, BAME people were 54% more likely to be fined under coronavirus rules than white people (Busby and Gidda 2020). The legislative system is also stacked against individuals reporting violence against women and girls. The proportion of reported rapes prosecuted in England and Wales currently stands at just 1.4%, with a 37.7% drop in the number of rape case being charged by the Crown Prosecution Service in 2018/2019 (CPS 2018). This has led to a whole coalition of women's groups warning that rape has effectively been 'decriminalised' in the UK (Centre for Women's Justice 2019). Within the treatment of violence against women and girls we see a division between those give routes to safety and those who are not: the denial of vital routes to safety for abused migrant women in the Domestic Abuse Bill passing through Parliament in 2020 shows how even when legislating against violence against women and girls, certain groups of women, in this case migrant women, are left behind (Southall Black Sisters 2019). As Imkaan (a women's organisation dedicated to addressing violence against Black and minoritised women and girls) stated: the 'VAWG pandemic is gendered and intersectional' (Imkaan 2020).

Furthermore, it is important to acknowledge that legislative change alone can do little without the societal change that must accompany it. The work we do on the political side of the campaign is therefore done with a strong awareness that legislative solutions can only work if the cultural change is simultaneous. Research on why men harass has found a direct link between the perpetration of sexual harassment and attitudes about what it is to be a man (Heilman 2018). A framework created by the European Commission found that among others, key factors contributing to sexual harassment include the devaluing of women and girls in society and the lack of sanctions for this behaviour (Hagemmann-White et al. 2010). Our campaign aims to end public sexual harassment by tackling both those problems, as well as endeavouring to help support victims of PSH along the way.

Reflecting on Our Streets Now

Reclaiming space online

In just over 18 months, Our Streets Now has formed an online community of over 28,000 people across our 4 social media platforms (listed in order of following): Instagram, Twitter, Facebook and TikTok. In this section, I will reflect on how our campaign has used digital activism in order to reclaim the space denied to us in the offline world by PSH. Mendes et al.'s writing on the use of digital feminist activism in the wake of #MeToo provides us with a useful framework to consider how online space has provided anti-harassment campaigning with both opportunities and challenges (Mendes et al. 2018). I will use their writing and some broader literature around online campaigning and abuse in order to consider our work as digital campaigners here at Our Streets Now.

Our Streets Now uses online space to speak out about PSH. We are far from being the first organisation to do so. There is an important and notable history of online space and, particularly social media, being used by anti-harassment campaigners. Chalk Back (Sandberg n.d.), Hollaback! (Hollaback! 2005), Everyday Sexism (Bates 2016) and Cheer Up Luv (Hatch n.d.) are all examples of projects using online space in order to challenge the normalisation of PSH. Chalk Back is an international movement 'committed to ending gender-based street harassment with public chalk art, digital media and education' (Sandberg n.d.). With hundreds of Instagram accounts across the world, Chalk Back has used a decentralised and youth-led mode of campaigning to spread awareness about PSH. Similarly, the Cheer Up Luv photo campaign founded by Eliza Hatch aims to raise awareness about sexual harassment through portraits of women and non-binary people. Through her Instagram account (Hatch n.d.), the photographer has been able to help marginalised genders reclaim space and agency by giving them a platform to speak out about their experiences. The use of online space by these campaigns is similar to ours; they respond to an event which happens in the offline public sphere by raising awareness about it through the online public realm. Indeed, Vera-Gray proposed that the extensive use of online spaces to record and respond to offline PSH 'may stem in part from contextual factors inherent in the encounter itself' (Vera-Gray 2017, p. 3). One of these factors, she suggests, is that online space, like offline public sexual harassment, bears a public nature. Another is that of accessibility, online space provides 'an avenue for immediate active response to intrusion' without the threat of escalation (Vera-Gray 2017, p. 3). For individuals submitting their stories for public chalk art, being photographed by Hatch or having their testimony converted into art by Our Streets Now, the online space gives individuals a way to respond. This form of agency is direct and tangible, allowing victims to "answer back" without the risks normally incurred when challenging the perpetrator themselves.

Mendes et al. (2018, p. 240) argue that digital platforms are important in 'providing spaces to develop both individual and collective feminist consciousness'. At Our Streets Now, our social media and, in particular our Instagram, aims to do just that. An educational platform, our Instagram hopes to increase public consciousness around public sexual harassment and its impacts. It also hopes to reach wider audiences through 'takeovers' (when one account temporarily puts its own content on another account) of larger Instagram profiles. Gemma and I have spoken about PSH on a number of influential accounts like UN Women and I Weigh, both platforms with over 1 million followers. What this allows us to do is reach a wider collective feminist consciousness with our message about PSH.

We also try and help individuals with their own relationship to, and fears of, PSH. Our number one aim is for victims to know that they are not alone, and that it is never their fault. We aim to reduce the feelings of powerlessness and shame which often mark these encounters with harassers by explicitly linking personal experiences to misogyny and the patriarchy. Sharing hundreds of experiences of PSH allows us to show how widespread the problem of harassment is, and also that it can happen in any and all circumstances. Furthermore, we endeavour to give our community a way to process their own experiences through the submission of testimony. People can submit stories either through the message function of our social media platforms or through our website. This is central to our work in trying to support victims of PSH.

Our aim in collecting testimonies is threefold. Firstly, we hope that the process of giving a testimony can make people feel listened to and heard.

Many of the testimonies we receive include a sentence or two explicitly thanking us for taking the time to answer. Many of our followers are girls, women or non-binary people who may not feel comfortable telling anyone else about their experiences. During the first national lockdown in response to the Covid-19 pandemic, one in five girls experienced public sexual harassment, but a quarter (26%) told no one about their experience (Plan UK 2020). Followers who send us their testimonies want someone to acknowledge what has happened to them. Our second reason for stressing the process of giving testimonies is best explained in Sara Ahmed's (2020) work on complaint: she writes that when submitting a complaint, one must first 'to admit *to* something, to recognise something as being wrong, as something you need to complain *about*'. The process of giving a testimony is similar since it requires an individual to reflect on what has happened to them. In this way, submitting a testimony allows one to admit and to recognise without necessarily bearing the consequences of a complaint. Submitting an anonymous story of harassment is a low-risk way of responding to one's own experience. This bring us to the third reason we centre the submission of testimonies. A report by Hollaback! and Cornell University found that targets of PSH who chose to take action during or after being harassed 'appeared to experience less negative emotional impact than those who did not' (Livingston et al. 2012). In sharing their testimony, we aim to give victims of PSH an avenue for action, a way to reclaim agency over their own experience. We use testimonies, with explicit consent, in order to make and inspire art, create resources and lobby for legislative change. By giving us their stories, women and girls can change their own relationship to PSH, and, we hope, create change.

At the heart of our work in both individual and collective consciousness-raising has been an attempt to use intersectionality as praxis. Using an intersectional lens is a key aspect to 'fourth wave' digital feminism (Munro 2013), a wave we form part of. In terms of PSH, using intersectionality to inform our awareness work has been essential. As the anonymous essayist 'yrfatfriend' put it so powerfully 'We so often hear the harassment stories of such a narrow slice of people – usually young, usually women, usually able-bodied, usually thin' (Friend 2016). The fact that Our Streets Now was started by a girl and a woman who identify as all those things means that our campaign could have easily centred this privileged experience. That is why we have tried from the outset to work conscientiously against such a limited representation of PSH. The main way to do this has been using our platforms to share others' experiences, both through printed testimonies but also artwork. In sharing hundreds of stories, we hope to diversify the collective consciousness around PSH to include experiences beyond the media-friendly one. Nonetheless, Gemma and I recognise the power we hold as gatekeepers of our Instagram, particularly during the first year of the campaign. Having a team since April 2020 who helps run our digital media has allowed us to widen the scope of those who choose our content, but in its nature running a platform gives us a position of power over our followers.

It is important that we acknowledge this, and when called out for overlooking a certain experience rather than responding defensively, acknowledge our own errors and areas for improvement. Individual and collective feminist consciousness raising will only succeed if we do the work in going beyond our own experiences and use intersectionality to include stories everyone can relate to.

This process of consciousness raising is undermined by the misogynistic abuse which can happen as a consequence of speaking out. A growing body of scholarship has documented the rise of online anti-feminist abuse, from considering its impact to examining the different ways in which women and girls have responded (Jane 2017, 2014; Smith 2019). Across our social media platforms, individuals who have shared their experiences of public sexual harassment on our platform have faced abusive backlash, from comments about their body hair ("okay I get this but her armpits…") to targeted fatphobic language ("Sorry, I didn't follow you to get lectured by some fat girl"). Gemma and I have also faced misogynistic abuse, particularly on platforms like Twitter and YouTube where video content about the campaign has been posted by larger media sources. Crucially, 'the impact of online gendered hate goes beyond those immediately targeted' (Smith 2019, p. 289). All those who see the misogynistic, racist, fatphobic or transphobic comments on our posts are being affected. The threat of violence becomes present for all users, as they can see the abuse they might potentially face for speaking out. It can also be triggering for individuals who are reminded of offline experiences of abuse (Lewis et al. 2015), as is the case for many of our social media followers. We are reminded once again of the continuum of violence, how all forms of violence against women and girls are inextricably linked (Kelly 1988). It is unsurprising therefore that scholarship on online abuse has found it to be 'an extension of offline gendered realities, where violence and abuse is the 'wallpaper' (Lewis et al. 2015) of everyday life for women and girls' (Lewis et al. 2016, p. 1479).

The goal of this abuse is clear: to silence women (Jane 2014). In the case of Our Streets Now and so many other digital feminist campaigns, this aim has clearly failed. Although the abuse has continued, so has the reach of our message. For every misogynistic or mocking comment, there are hundreds of supportive ones. For every perpetrator of this abuse, there are dozens of individuals who challenge their behaviour. Many of those who choose to fight back against abuse do so as allies, supporting either targeted individuals, or the campaign itself. Smith's article on women's responses to online abuse shows us how individuals can take different routes to tackle this violence, from reporting to social media companies to one-on-one engagements (Smith 2019). Members of our community choose all these routes, with some reporting comments and others engaging in debates with those undermining our work. Smith argues that fighting back can be important in "making a visible stand and saying 'this is unacceptable' to wider Internet society" (Smith 2019, p. 299). Individuals tackling online abuse on our platform do seem to reclaim a sense of power over the intrusion of an individual into our online community.

Mendes et al. (2018, p. 244) found in their study of feminists tackling rape culture on Twitter that despite the high prevalence of abuse online, 'digital feminism can simultaneously be experienced as extremely positive in generating community, connection and support for feminist views'. Online abuse certainly marks the landscape of our online campaigning, but it does not succeed in its aim to neutralise the positive work which we, and so many others, are doing. The tactics that allies have used to fight back have been effective in maintaining our space as a safe one. Our attempt to raise feminist and individual consciousness of PSH, in an intersectional way, has continued, in spite of and sometimes in response to, online abuse. Reclaiming our space online can be difficult, but it is essential to our work to end PSH.

Centring young women's voices

Gemma and I were recently asked to take part in research by Harvard University on behalf of National Geographic about youth activism. They interviewed us about why it was important to have young people lead social justice movements, and what barriers we have come across because of it. In this section, I want to explore both these points, arguing for the importance of including young people and particularly young women and non-binary voices in politics whilst also being honest about the real emotional and financial toll youth campaigning can take.

At Our Streets Now we are firm advocates of young people being included and listened to in politics. Gemma was 14 and I was 20 when we started Our Streets Now. As young women activists, we have felt belittled and patronised throughout our campaigning. In meetings with parliamentarians, radio presenters, lawyers and adults in our lives, we have felt the ageist stereotypes of young people being oversensitive 'snowflakes' or ignorant children. This has been particularly stark for Gemma who is now only 15. Ageism and sexism combine to devalue the importance of young women's voices.

Yet our voices are essential to social justice movements, particularly to those campaigns tackling issues young women disproportionately face. Young women aged 18–24 are one of the categories which report the highest rates of harassment (Women and Equalities Committee 2018). The vast majority of girls will also face public sexual harassment before their 18th birthday. Despite this over-representation in the figures however, younger women and girls are often under-represented in decision-making bodies. Girls are excluded from formal representation because of their age. Eighteen to 24 year olds have the vote but still struggle to have their opinions and views heard. This is in part because, as a demographic group, they are the one of the least likely to vote, making them easier to overlook in favour of those with higher electoral turnout (Electoral Reform Society 2017). Young people are criticised for their low turnout at elections, but what is labelled as disengagement is, I believe, disillusionment. In 2019, 72% of 18–24 year olds said that their confidence in politicians had plummeted, while the number who identified as feminists and attended political demonstrations rose (Young Women's Trust 2019). What this demonstrates is that young women are aware of the inequality they face, and that they want to create change.

Our Streets Now is an example of this phenomenon. Since the beginning, we have been supported by the activism of incredible young women. Lawyer Deeba Syed (Syed 2020), secondary school student Anya Chung and VAWG frontline worker Ammaarah Zayna (Zayna 2020) are just three of the many women, girls and non-binary people who joined our ranks early on to demand an end to public sexual harassment. For the first year, we mostly worked informally with activists, academics, lawyers and influencers, who helped us enormously in getting the campaign off the ground. Since April 2020, we have created a formal team of volunteers. These are young people, predominantly young women, who volunteer their time because of their commitment to creating change. This means that unlike most formal organisations or institutions, Our Streets Now can connect and campaign on the premise of a shared struggle and commitment to change. Our work to highlight intersectional experiences of PSH has become more prominent as members of the team have shared and centred their own experiences and brought in voices from their respective communities. Friendships too have been formed through our activism, creating a whole network of feminists across the country standing up against harassment. Our Streets Now would not exist without the power and voices of young women.

Alongside hope and enthusiasm, I also feel concerned about the current media focus on young people in activism. Over the past few years, with the rise of activists like Greta Thunberg, Malala Yousafzai and Emma González, we have seen a growing focus on young women speaking out about social and climate injustice. As I mentioned before, the work of these young women is crucial; their impact should be measured not only in terms of their causes but also their influence as symbols of powerful young women for girls to aspire to. It was in this context that Gemma and I's campaign emerged, and without these voices demanding to be heard, ours might never have been.

The role of privilege and financial security in being able to do this unpaid work is, however, rarely questioned or even acknowledged. When expanding Our Streets Now into a team of 25 people, we faced this dilemma. Asking more young women to do unpaid work is not an easy decision to make. The intersection of gender and age is crucial here; encouraging the unpaid labour of young women is problematic. It is important to recognise that financial security often curtails who can be a recognised activist. Well-funded grant schemes and mentoring to support young BME activists and individuals from lower socio-economic groups are just two potential solutions to this problem. As well as noting who has the time and financial resources to do unpaid work, we must also acknowledge which voices are listened to and which are ignored. Our Streets Now's message would be far less palatable were the campaign not co-founded by two white, southern English, middle-class sisters. Facing up to the role of privilege in campaigning is crucial to changing it for the better.

The difficult and hidden emotional labour (Hochschild 2012) behind digital feminist activism is also something that is very little understood or discussed. Mendes et al. rightly raise questions around this form of activism's sustainability 'in light of online abuse, burn-out and other issues around work–life balance in the digital age' (Mendes et al. 2018, p. 239). In our case, Gemma has had to run Our Streets Now on top of studying for her GCSEs, and for me it's been alongside studying full-time for my undergraduate degree. Putting pressure on young people to change the world and get an education can be a heavy burden. It should not be my 15-year old sister's job to create a campaign because of the relentless harassment she has faced as a girl. The online and offline abuse I discussed in the previous section is another worrying aspect of being an activist that is not often highlighted.

On 4 February 2020, Our Streets Now hosted an event in conjunction with UN Women UK and I Weigh to launch the 'Safe Spaces Now' project, which aims to bring together policymakers and grassroots campaigners to create safer, more inclusive public spaces. During the panel discussion, all of the activists onstage, Amika George, Gina Martin, Gemma and I, shared our struggles with the labour of youth activism. From the negative impact on our mental health and social lives to the unpaid nature of this work, our discussion about how digital and offline feminist campaigning had influenced our lives did not obscure the more difficult consequences of this work. We must look beyond the simplistic figure of the 'empowered woman activist' to acknowledge the emotional, financial and physical toll of this work. There are negative consequences to placing the responsibility of saving the world on the shoulders of young people.

Conclusion

Our Streets Now was born out of our anger and frustration. Since then it has become so much more than that. I see hope in our work, and a determination in our team and our supporters to confront misogyny in public space and declare 'no more'. Our work on education and awareness hopes to challenge the underlying roots of this problem. Our legislative proposals aim to give legal recourse to those who choose to go down that road, by challenging the normalisation of this violence in society. Through our online presence we have reclaimed a space which, although intruded upon by perpetrators of online abuse, remains a strong community that women and girls can find solace and solidarity in. We have used the theory of intersectionality (Crenshaw 1991) as praxis, informing our work in order to build an inclusive movement. Founded and led by young women and girls, the campaign has allowed us and our followers to create a sense of agency over the sexual harassment we have faced. This shared energy is inspiring, particularly when I remember that Our Streets Now is just one campaign, in one country. Worldwide movements like Everyday Sexism (Bates 2016) and Chalk Back (Sandberg n.d.) have shown us the global nature of this problem, and the way it can be tackled transnationally. Localised projects like Bristol Zero Tolerance and Draw the Line Sheffield have highlighted the power generated when communities stand up to violence against women and girls. Across all of this work, what stands out is the resourcefulness, drive and passion with which women and girls are tackling sexual harassment. We should respect, honour and support their work; I certainly do.

References

Ahmed, S., 2020. In the thick of it [online]. Available at: https://feministkilljoys.com [Accessed 1 December 2020].

Asamblea Legislativa de Costa Rica, 2020. Ley Contra el Acoso Sexual Callejero.

Assad, P., 2019. #ISayItsNotOK: street harassment gets recognised as gender-based violence. Available at: https://plan-uk.org/blogs/street-harassment-gets-recognised-as-gender-based-violence [Accessed 1 December 2020].

Assembleia de Republica, 2015. Codigo Penal.

Atkins, V., 2019. Istanbul Convention ratification: 2019 report on progress [online]. Available at: https://www.theyworkforyou.com/wms/?id=2019-10-31.HCWS58.h [Accessed 1 December 2020].

Bates, L., 2016. *Everyday Sexism*. New York: Thomas Dunne Books, St. Martin's Griffin.

Bosman, J., 2017. A college student was killed by a man whose catcalls she tried to ignore, prosecutors say [online]. Available at: https://www.nytimes.com/2019/11/27/us/chicago-college-student-killed-catcall.html [Accessed 1 December 2020].

Bowman, C.G., 1993. Street harassment and the informal ghettoization of women. *Harvard Law Review*, 106(3), pp. 106–517. DOI: 10.2307/1341656.

Bows, H., 2019. Researching sexual violence at UK music festivals [online]. Available at: https://www.thebritishacademy.ac.uk/blog/researching-sexual-violence-uk-music-festivals/ [Accessed 1 December 2020].

Busby, M. and Gidda, M., n.d. BAME people fined more than white population under coronavirus laws [online]. Available at: https://www.theguardian.com/world/2020/may/26/bame-people-fined-more-than-white-population-under-coronavirus-laws [Accessed 1 December 2020].

Centre for Women's Justice, 2019. Collapse in number of rape cases charged by CPS despite huge rise in reports - response [online]. Available at: https://www.centreforwomensjustice.org.uk/news/2019/9/12/collapse-in-number-of-rape-cases-charged-by-cps-despite-huge-rise-in-reports-response [Accessed 1 December 2020].

Council of Europe, 2011. Convention on preventing and combating violence against women and domestic violence [online]. Available at: https://www.coe.int/en/web/gender-matters/council-of-europe-convention-on-preventing-and-combating-violence-against-women-and-domestic-violence [Accessed 1 December 2020].

CPS, 2018. *Violence against Women and Girls Report*. London: Crown Prosecution Service.

Creasy, S., 2020. Why we're fighting to change the law and make misogyny a hate crime. *The Telegraph* [online]. Available at: https://www.telegraph.co.uk/women/politics/fighting-change-law-make-misogyny-hate-crime/ [Accessed 1 December 2020].

Crenshaw, K., 1991. Mapping the margins: intersectionality, identity politics, and violence against women of color. *Stanford Law Review*, 43, p. 1241. DOI: 10.2307/1229039.

Electoral Reform Society, 2017. Closing the registration generation gap [online]. https://www.electoral-reform.org.uk/closing-the-registration-generation-gap/ [Accessed 1 December 2020].

Friedan, B., 1986. *The Feminine Mystique*. London: Penguin Books.

Friend, Y.F., 2016. When catcalling is fatcalling [online]. Available at: https://medium.com/@thefatshadow/when-catcalling-is-fatcalling-1b601eb98fd0 [Accessed 14 July 2020].

George, A., 2017. Free periods [online]. Available at: https://www.freeperiods.org [Accessed 14 July 2020].

Hagemmann-White, C., Kavemann, B., Kindler, H., Meyson, T. and Puchert, R., 2010. Factors at play in the perpetration of violence against women, violence against children and sexual orientation violence [online]. Available at: https://www.humanconsultancy.com/assets/understanding-perpetration/understanding-perpetration.html [Accessed 14 July 2020].

Hatch, E., n.d. Cheer up luv [online]. Available at: http://www.cheerupluv.com/ [Accessed 10 May 2021].

Hearing, A., 2016. Tampon tax: how Laura Coryton started the 'Stop Taxing Periods' campaign while still a student. *The Independent* [online]. Available at: https://www.independent.co.uk/student/student-life/tampon-tax-how-laura-coryton-started-stop-taxing-periods-campaign-while-still-student-a6891336.html [Accessed 14 July 2020].

Heilman, B., 2018. *Unmasking Sexual Harassment – How Toxic Masculinities Drive Men's Abuse in the US, UK, and Mexico and What We Can Do to End It*. Washington, DC: Promundo.

HM Government, 2019. *Ending Violence against Women and Girls: Strategy Refresh*. London: HM Government.

Hochschild, A.R., 2012. *The Managed Heart: Commercialization of Human Feeling, Updated with a New Preface*. Berkeley: University of California Press.

Hollaback!, 2005. Hollaback! [online]. Available at: https://www.ihollaback.org [Accessed 14 July 2020].

Imkaan, 2020. The impact of the dual pandemics: violence against women & girls and covid-19 on black and minoritised women and girls [online]. Available at: https://829ef90d-0745-49b2-b404-cbea85f15fda.filesusr.com/ugd/2f475d_2c6797da42c6454f933837a7290ffe21.pdf [Accessed 14 July 2020].

Jane, E.A., 2014. 'Back to the kitchen, cunt': speaking the unspeakable about online misogyny. *Continuum*, 28, pp. 558–570. DOI: 10.1080/10304312.2014.924479.

Jane, E.A., 2017. Misogyny online: a short (and brutish) history. *European Journal of Communication*, 32, pp. 504–504. DOI: 10.1177/0267323117730203d.

Kelly, L., 1988. *Surviving Sexual Violence, Feminist Perspectives*. Cambridge: Polity Press.

Kelly, L., 2012. Standing the test of time? Reflections on the concept of the continuum of sexual violence. In: Brown, J.M. and Walklate, S.L., eds. *Handbook on Sexual Violence*. London: Routledge, pp. xvii–xxvi.

Laguerre, M., 2018. Woman harassed and hit by a man in the streets of Paris [online]. Available at: https://www.nytimes.com/2018/08/01/world/europe/france-assault-video.html [Accessed 1 December 2020].

Lammy, D., 2017. *The Lammy Review: An Independent Review into the Treatment of, and Outcomes for, Black, Asian and Minority Ethnic Individuals in the Criminal Justice System*. London: Lammy Review.

Lewis, R., Rowe, M. and Wiper, C., 2016. Online abuse of feminists as an emerging form of violence against women and girls. *British Journal of Criminology*, 57(6), pp. 1462–1481. DOI: 10.1093/bjc/azw073.

Lewis, R., Sharp, E., Remnant, J. and Redpath, R., 2015. 'Safe spaces': experiences of feminist women-only space. *Sociological Research Online*, 20, pp. 105–118. DOI: 10.5153/sro.3781.

Livingston, B.A., Wagner, K., Diaz, S.T. and Angela, L., 2012. *The Experience of Being Targets of Street Harassment in NYC: Preliminary Findings from a Qualitative Study of a Sample of 223 Voices Who Hollaback! Cornell University and Hollaback!*. Ithaca, NY: The Worker Institute.

MacKinnon, C.A., 1979. *Sexual Harassment of Working Women: A Case of Sex Discrimination*. New Haven, CT: Yale University Press.

Mendes, K., Ringrose, J. and Keller, J., 2018. #MeToo and the promise and pitfalls of challenging rape culture through digital feminist activism. *European Journal of Women's Studies*, 25(2), pp. 236–246. DOI: 10.1177/1350506818765318.

Munro, E., 2013. Feminism: a fourth wave? *Political insight*, 4(2), pp. 22–25. DOI: 10.1111/2041-9066.12021.

Observatorio Contra el Acoso Chile, 2014. 1era encuesta de Acoso Callejero [WWW Document] [online]. Available at: https://www.ocac.cl/1era-encuesta-de-acoso-callejero/ [Accessed 1 December 2020].

Our Streets Now, 2020. Our Schools Now [online]. Available at: https://www.ourstreetsnow.org/our-schools [Accessed 1 December 2020].

Outrage sexiste ou sexuel, 2018.

Parlement Francais, 2018. Outrage sexiste ou sexuel, 621-1.

Parliament, H. of C., 2003. Sexual Offences Act.

Parliament, H. of C., 2019. Voyeurism (Offences) Act, 67A.

Perrin, A. and Anderson, M., 2019. *Share of U.S. Adults Using Social Media, Including Facebook, Is Mostly Unchanged Since 2018*. Washington, DC: Pew Research Centre.

Plan UK, 2016. Street harassment - it's not okay [online]. Available at: https://plan-uk.org/street-harassment/its-not-ok [Accessed 1 December 2020].

Plan UK, 2020. 1 in 5 girls have experienced street harassment during lockdown [online]. Available at: https://plan-uk.org/media-centre/1-in-5-girls-have-experienced-street-harassment-during-lockdown [Accessed 1 December 2020].

Sandberg, S., n.d. Chalkback [online]. Available at: https://www.chalkback.org [Accessed 13 July 2020].

Sefton, K., Warren, I., Wacko, H. and Leigh, J., 2020. *They Saw My Fear and Laughed: Tackling Public Sexual Harassment in Education*. London: Our Streets Now.

Smith, J., 2019. 'When i saw women being attacked ... it made me want to stand up and fight': reporting, responding to, and resisting online misogyny. In: Lumsden, K. and Harmer, E., eds. *Online Othering*. Cham: Springer International Publishing, pp. 287–308.

Solnit, R., 2020. Younger feminists have shifted my understanding. *The Guardian* [online]. Available at: https://www.theguardian.com/world/2020/feb/29/rebecca-solnit-younger-feminists-shift-understanding-give-new-tools [Accessed 1 December 2020].

Southall Black Sisters, 2019. The domestic abuse bill and migrant women [online]. Available at: https://southallblacksisters.org.uk/news/the-domestic-abuse-bill-migrant-women-briefing-paper-2/ [Accessed 1 December 2020].

Stanko, E.A., 1990. *Everyday Violence: How Women and Men Experience Sexual and Physical Danger.* London: Pandora.

Syed, D., 2020. Deeba Syed: political activist, women's rights advocate and campaigner, sexual harassment lawyer [online]. Available at: https://www.deebasyed.com [Accessed 1 December 2020].

TUC, 2019. 1 in 2 women have been sexually harassed at work – Isn't it time the Government did something about it? [online]. Available at: https://www.tuc.org.uk/news/1-2-women-have-been-sexually-harassed-work-isnt-it-time-government-did-something-about-it [Accessed 1 December 2020].

Vera-Gray, F., 2016. Men's stranger intrusions: rethinking street harassment. *Women's Studies International Forum*, 58, pp. 9–17. DOI: 10.1016/j.wsif.2016.04.001.

Vera-Gray, F., 2017. *Men's Intrusion, Women's Embodiment: A Critical Analysis of Street Harassment, Routledge Research in Gender and Society.* London: Routledge.

Vera-Gray, F. and Kelly, L., 2020. Contested gendered space: public sexual harassment and women's safety work. *International Journal of Comparative and Applied Criminal Justice*, 44(4), pp. 1–11. DOI: 10.1080/01924036.2020.1732435.

Women and Equalities Committee, 2018. Sexual harassment of women and girls in public places [online]. Available at: https://committees.parliament.uk/committee/328/women-and-equalities-committee/news/102169/sexual-harassment-in-public-places/ [Accessed 1 December 2020].

YouGov, 2018. Two in five young female festival goers have been subjected to unwanted sexual behaviour [online]. Available at: https://yougov.co.uk/topics/lifestyle/articles-reports/2018/06/21/two-five-young-female-festival-goers-have-been-sub [Accessed 1 December 2020].

Young Women's Trust, 2019. Young women's feminism and activism 2019 [online]. Available at: https://www.youngwomenstrust.org/research/young-womens-feminism-and-activism-2019/ [Accessed 1 December 2020].

Zayna, A., 2020. Ammaarah Zayna: political activist. Writer. Gender-based violence educator [online]. Available at: https://www.ammaarahzayna.com [Accessed 1 December 2020].

Conclusion

Irene Zempi and Jo Smith

Throughout the chapters of this edited collection, authors have given accounts of how misogyny/gender hate crime might be theorised and understood, and of some of the ways in which gender intersects with other identity characteristics. Activists have described their work and the grassroots efforts made to compel change. Policy makers and practitioners have described their role in designing, applying and evaluating how their work has pushed forward societal acknowledgement of misogyny as hate crime. Together this presents a broad range of ideas and experiences to help us better understand the potential benefits and the possible pitfalls associated with misogyny as hate crime. With the ongoing Law Commission (2020) review of the hate crime legislation in England and Wales comes the opportunity to reform the law of hate crime. There is keen academic, practitioner, activist and public interest in whether there should be changes to the hate crime legislation, and more specifically whether such reform should include adding misogyny or gender to the protected characteristics. The eventual outcome of the Law Commission's review is likely to be presented later in 2021, whereupon the question of whether to reform the law on hate crime in England and Wales will rest with Parliament.

The legal recognition of misogyny as hate crime has the potential to be beneficial to women, although there are risks and challenges associated with this, as discussed throughout the chapters of this edited collection. We suggest, in line with many others working in this area, that tackling misogyny is not something which requires a single approach, but rather multiple tactics that span academia, education, legislation, activism, local and national policy and beyond. Whilst legislating to prohibit hatred fuelled by misogyny or motivated by gender is a significant part of challenging gender-based hate, it is equally important not to underestimate the other ways in which misogyny can be challenged. However, the work of grassroots activists and campaigners, of local groups and organisations and of individual police forces should not be used to minimise the need for formal policy and practice. It is also necessary that this is work undertaken by everyone – not just women – such that women do not become burdened with the responsibility of policing their own safety. Misogyny has persisted for centuries, propping

DOI: 10.4324/9781003023722

up a patriarchal system that benefits from the oppression of women and girls. As such, responding to misogyny hate crime:

> requires us to look to the societies in which we live, to the ways in which we as women are Othered, oppressed, and disempowered. It demands that we look at the intersections of power structures and the oppressions that result from these. It calls for change on a structural level.
> (Smith 2019, p. 255)

References

Law Commission, 2020. *Hate Crime Laws: A Consultation Paper.* London: Law Commission. Available at: https://s3-eu-west-2.amazonaws.com/lawcom-prod-storage-11jsxou24uy7q/uploads/2020/10/Hate-crime-final-report.pdf Accessed [25 January 2021].

Smith, J., 2019. *Feminist women's experiences of online gendered hate.* PhD thesis, University of Surrey.

Index

Note: **Bold** page numbers refer to tables and page numbers followed by "n" denote endnotes.

adolescent girls, SH of: category and gender, reports by crime **130**; changed behaviour 122–123; compliments 128–129; confusion and fear 131–134; coping strategies 129–130; details of sexualised dialogue 127–128; distress of SH 132–133; emotional reactions 122–123, 126–127, 134–135; 'Eve teasing' 123; experiences 121–135; focus groups 131–134; free-text descriptions 125, 127, 129, 130; language of managing SH incidents 126–131; learning, negative impact on 131–134; legal and educational contexts 123–125; methodology 125–126; multiple-choice questions 125, 129; narrative responses 127; negative thinking and harmful behaviour 133–134; non-criminal behaviour 130; perceived safety 122–123; police investigation 131; Positive and Negative Affect Schedule for Children 126; and public safety 123–125; reporting incidents 132; reports of crime by gender **130**; traumatic experiences, naming of 132; trust right people 133; unpredictable public disorder incidents 131–132; verbal harassment 128; written description 127
Adorno, T.W. 158
affaires 144
aggravated offences 4–7, 14n3, 76, 85–86, 280, 283, 284
Agius, C. 99, 102
Ahmed, A. 196

Ahmed, S. 299
aims of hate crime law 67–68
Aizura, A. 198
Akiwowo, S. 165
Albert, M. 126
Aldridge, J. 181
Aldridge, M.L. 21
Ali, N. 148
Alkiviadou, N. 91
All-Party Parliamentary Group Against Antisemitism 171n1
Allport, G. 111
"all women are like that" (AWALT) 107, 110
Alvi, S. 24
Anderson, M. 293
Andersson, J. 1
Angiolini, E. 187
Ansara, Y.G. 195, 198–200
Anthias, F. 196
Anti-Defamation League 102, 110
anti-discrimination legislation 48
Antjoule, N. 28, 205–207, 214
antisemitism: anti-Zionism 157–158; COVID-19 conspiracy theories 160; definition 156–160; description of 158; gendered (*see* gendered antisemitism); IHRA Definition of Antisemitism 156–158; "International Definition" 156; and misogyny, intersection of 11, 155–156; nature of 158; "white genocide" 159
Antisemitism Policy Trust (AST) 155, 161–165, 171n1
Arayasirikul, S. 200
Archibald, M. 100

Arjomand, S. 126
asexuality 7, 31
Ashcroft, E. 82
Aspinall, G. 284
Assad, P. 292
Association of Police and Crime Commissioners (APCC) 256
Atkins, V. 295
Ault, A. 27, 32
Austin, Z. 126
Awan, I. 80, 142
awareness raising, need for 55–56
Azad, Z. 12, 231–246

Bacchi, C. 235, 236
Bachmann, C.L. 197
Baele, S.J. 106, 111
Bailey, B. 128
Bailey, J.M. 219
Bailey, M. 150
Bakalis, C. 9, 65–77
#BalanceTonPorc 55
Balderston, S. 179–182, 186
Bandura, A. 124, 133
Banet-Weiser, S. 100
Barbaret, R. 25, 33
Barclay, H. 180, 183, 184, 186, 187
Barker, K. 10, 79–93, 109
Barkhuizen, G. 127
Barlow, C. 80
Bartle, E. 28
Bastomski, S. 122
Bates, L. 252, 276, 284, 297, 304
Bates, S. 24
Bauberot, J. 144
Bauer, G.R. 216
Beazley, S. 181
Becker, M.J. 166
Bender-Baird, K. 221
Benford, R.D. 235
Bergmann, W. 157
Berkowitz, D. 220
Berners-Lee, R. 80
Berners-Lee, T. 80
'*The Best Men Can Be*' campaign 282
Betcher, T.M. 198
Betts, L.R. 11, 121–135
Biblarz, T.J. 205
Biderman, A.D. 51
Bindel, J. 203
Blais, M. 101
Blumer, M.L.C. 198
Boeckmann, R.J. 9

Bornstein, K. 47
Bosman, J. 291
Bowman, C.G. 122, 123, 131, 273, 296
Bows, H. 291
Boyd, J. 158
Boyle, K. 188n2
Boys Don't Cry (film) 202
Braun, V. 217
Briere, J. 24
Bristol Zero Tolerance 304
British General Election campaign, 2010 253
British Society of Criminology Hate Crime Network 2
Britton, D. 24, 25
Brogaard, B. 169
Brown, A. 111
Brown, B. 241, 259, 276, 281
Browne, K.D. 21, 205, 222
Browning, K. 92
Brownmiller, S. 22, 23
Brown, R. 178, 207
Brownridge, D.A. 180, 183, 186
Bruder, C. 180
Bucchianeri, M.M. 121
Buckley, N. 131
Buila, S. 180
Burgess, A. 216
Burr, V. 126
Burt, M. 21, 22
Busby, M. 296

Caldwell, R. 284
Cameron, L. 181
campaigns, misogyny 10; absence of online misogyny 79, 84; coalition of campaign groups 42; and law, definitional conundrum 83–84; *No Place for Hate* report 84; Nottinghamshire Police in 2016 82; recording misogyny as hate crime 82, 83
Campbell, R. 13n2, 31
Casey, M. 218
Cavanagh, S. 221, 223
Cecco, L. 106
Cerise, S. 33
Chakraborti, N. 3, 29, 46, 48, 68, 72, 179, 180, 183, 185, 186, 200, 204–205, 214, 215, 224, 234, 238
Chalk Back 297–298, 304
Changing Minds: The Real Impact of Street Harassment (comic) 282

Index   313

Charlottesville 'Unite The Right' rally 102
Cheer Up Luv 297, 298
Chen, K. 52, 58
Chenoweth, L. 31
child abuse 49
Children's Commissioner, establishment of 123
cisgenderism 12; binary thinking about gender 197–198; Fundamental Rights Agency (FRA) 201; 'gender non-conformists' 199; 'gender terrorism' 199; hate-motivated crime or incidents 199–200; "hyper-vigilance" in public space 202; meso (community or organisational) level 198, 200; microaggressions 200–201; notions of belonging or non-belonging 198; oppositional sexism 199; racism and sexism 198; scholarship on 198–199; traditional sexism 199; trans and non-binary young people's lives 202; 'trans-erasure' 199; Trans Murder Monitoring Project (TMM) 202; transphobia 198–202; trans-related homicides 202
Citizens Hate Crime Commission 249; crimes and incidents 250, 251; domestic violence and sexual offences 43, 50, 251; End Violence Against Women 52, 239, 252; intersectionality 250; local evidence 251–252; Nottingham Women's Centre 252; women's victimisation 24, 250–251, 255
Citizens UK 1, 2, 6, 42, 231, 244, 249–250, 252, 260–261, 269, 273
Citron, D.K. 24, 91, 100
Clapp, J. 131
Clarke, V. 217
Clement, S. 178, 186
Cohen, C. 82
Cohen, L. 24
Coleman, N. 180, 184, 186
Collins, D. 241
Collins, P.H. 26
Colliver, B. 12, 213–225
Comerford, R. 167
Committee of Ministers of the Council of Europe 109
Communications Act 2003 7, 88–91
communications regulatory framework 86–87

Community Security Trust 159, 160, 164, 165, 167–171, 172n14
Conaghan, J. 56, 57
Connell, R.W. 56, 217
Convention on the Elimination of All Forms of Discrimination against Women (CEDAW) 93
Copeland, L. 47
Cops, D. 276
Corner, P. 44
Corteen, K. 21, 28
Counter Islamophobia Collective in Belgium (CCIB) 140, 146, 151n3
Counter Islamophobia Collective in France (CCIF) 140, 146, 151n2, 151n3
Covid-19 50, 160, 168, 262, 283–284
Coyle, A. 213, 224
CPS's Public Sector Equality Duty (EHRC 2020) 50
Creasy, S. 42, 52, 79, 84, 87, 88, 244, 262, 263, 269, 296
Crenshaw, K. 26, 145, 156, 182, 183, 288, 293, 303
Crime and Disorder Act 1998 4, 41, 85, 284n1
Crime Survey for England and Wales (CSEW) 6, 14n4, 124, 256
Criminal Justice Act 2003 4, 5, 41, 57, 85, 214, 215, 233, 283, 284n1, 284n2
Criminal Justice and Courts Act 2015 58n3
criminal justice service 53, 57
critical feminist race theory 34
Crown Prosecution Service (CPS) 3, 4, 28, 31, 47, 49–50, 109, 171n4, 282, 296
Crowther-Dowey, C. 24
Cunningham, S. 179
Cyber Lads 103–104
cybersexism 24

'The Daily Stormer' 102
Dargie, E. 197
Davidson, M. 122, 131
Davies, P. 141
Day, A.S. 22
Dayter, D. 104
Deakin, J. 121, 126, 130
decision-making process 13, 249
DeKeseredy, W.S. 24
Dempsey, B. 53
DiAngelo, R. 200
Digital Services Act 91, 94n13
Dignam, P. 107

'dirty Arabs' 146, 150
disability hate crime 5, 12; conviction of 31; factors affecting 178–179; female participant interview details 181, **182**; identity or dimensions of social life 183; intersectionality as research framework 182–183; interview participants, sexual abuse and assaults 183–185; lack of disability awareness 179; 'master category' or element of identity 182; methodology 181; misogyny, and hatred, intersections of 185–188; perfect storm 188; protectionism 179; risk of victimisation 180; scarcity of research 181; self-categorisation 182–183; Sexual Assault Referral Centres (SARC) 187; sexual offences investigation techniques (SOIT) 187; as stranger-crime 180; victim and offender, relationship between 180; victims' physical and mental health 179; Violence Against Women and Girls 31, 179–181, 187; women's experiences of 183–185
Dittman, R.J. 28, 29
Doan, P.L. 196, 200, 214, 222
Dobash, R. 20
Doe, T. 180
domestic abuse (DA) 7–9, 31, 49, 50–54, 244, 256–259, 263, 296, 297
Domestic Abuse Bill 52–53, 263, 296–297
Domestic and Sexual Violence and Abuse (DSVA) 237, 245
domestic violence: as 'everyday terrorism' 23–24; women engage in 22
Donath, J. 91
Donovan, C. 22
Drury, S. 179
Duff, R.A. 53, 74
Duggan, M. 9, 19–34, 65, 206, 252
Dunbar, E. 56
Dupont, I. 181
Dupuis-Deri, F. 101
Duriesmith, D. 80
Dustin, H. 33
Dutton, E. 103
Dvorak, P. 202
Dyck, D.R. 200, 202, 207

Easat-Daas, A. 11, 140–151
Ebesutani, C. 126

Edwards, C. 187
Eichhorn, K. 111
El Bachiri, M. 147
Elgot, J. 30, 162
Ellis, S.J. 223
Emerson, E. 181
enhanced sentencing 4, 6, 14n3, 85, 86, 236, 259, 273, 283
Equality Act 2010 213
The European Convention on Human Rights 47
European Union Monitoring Centre on Racism and Xenophobia (EUMC) 157
Evans, K.M. 48
Everard, Sarah 1
Everyday Sexism 233, 252, 297, 304
'Eve teasing' 123
Eyler, A.E. 199

Fairchild, K. 122, 130
Faktor, A. 223
'fallen women' 32
The Fappening 100
Fayard, N. 144
Felson, M. 24
female genital mutilation (FGM) 8–9, 20, 49, 290
female infanticide 20
femicide 20, 233
feminism: 'agents of terror' 29; "an entirely Jewish invention" 165; ethnic minority women 30, 33; hate crime paradigm 10, 19, 20, 25–32, 52, 77; is Zionist conspiracy 165; on misogyny 20–25
feminist activism 33, 80, 297, 303
feminist disability studies, emergence of 26
feminist praxis 12–13, 231; concept of 'continuum of sexual violence' 233; context of "men's power and women's resistance" 233; evaluation of policy, back to community 242–245; Everyday Sexism project in 2012 233, 252; evolving language and activism on street harassment 232–234; into future 245–246; International Street Harassment Week 233; language of 'harassment' 233; Nottingham Citizens 231, 235, 237–239; Nottinghamshire Police 232, 234–235, 238–241; from Nottingham to nation 241–242; Nottingham

Women's Centre 231, 237–244; policy into practice 239–240; reflexive framing 236; strategic framing 235–236; violence against women 232–234, 239, 245, 246; Women and Equalities Committee's Inquiry into Sexual Harassment of Women and Girls 234; women's experiences of hate crime 238

feminist theoretical exploration: academic scholarship and research 29; cisgender heterosexual ('cishet') white women 32, 34; 'compound oppression' 31; within existing hate crime paradigm 25–32; fear, safety and space 21–23; feminist campaigning 25–27; identity politics and violence 25, 145; intersectional experiences of women 26–27; intersectional margins 31–32; 'marred by sexism' 27; on misogyny 19–25; policy makers 19; 'sex' or 'gender' 20; violence against lesbians 27–28; 'vulnerability' of groups of women 32; women as weapons 29–32; Yazidi women in ISIS 29

femmephobia 46, 53, 218, 220, 224

"femoids" or "foids" 106

Fenton, S. 252

Ferguson, K. 167

Fileborn, B. 121, 122

Filipovic, J. 1

Fine, R. 158, 160

Finkelstein, N. 160

Fish, S. 13, 239, 244, 249–265

Flood, A. 103

forced marriage 8, 9, 20, 49

Fraser, J. 171n7

Fraser, N. 26

Freitas, I. 103

Friedan, B. 290

Friend, Y.F. 299

Gadd, D. 222

Gaffney, P. 47

Gallagher, B. 124, 130, 131

Gallagher, C. 171n6

Gamergate 100, 101, 103

Gardner, C. 121, 122, 128

Garland, J. 3, 13n1, 46, 48, 68, 72, 180, 186, 200, 205, 215

gay liberation movement 56

Gearon, A. 123

Gekoski, A. 121

gender: based hate crime category 9; based hate incidents 6; as bias crime 48; conceptualising 46; definition 46; femmephobia 46; inclusion/exclusion of 47–48; as protected characteristic (*see* protected characteristics); theorising 196–197

gender bias 49; bias category 47, 51, 53–54; Domestic Abuse Bill 52, 53; in domestic abuse cases 51–54; femmephobia 53; 'hate crime' characteristic 45, 52; male-on-female violence 53; prevalence of abuse against women 51, 81; protected characteristics 52; 'proving gender animus' 54

'gender defender' concept 47

gendered antisemitism: abuse targeting Jewish women (*see* Jewish women); British Jewish female entertainers 165; "feminism is a Zionist conspiracy" 165; "gender trolling phenomenon" 164; goals 167; House of Commons 160–162, 166–167; language of politics 162–163; mainstream social media sites 165–166; and online abuse 164–167; online violence against women 163; reputation for racism and antisemitism 165; Sara Conference 160–161; sexual abuse 161–162; use of violent language 162; victims of online 164, 166–167; violent threats 163–164; ways of thinking 162

gendered Islamophobia: case of Muslim women 145, 149; 'dirty Arabs,' Muslim women 146; experiences of Black women in USA 145, 150; French Muslim politician 149; gendered Muslimness in France 145; institutional 148; *Les Cannelles* (formerly *Bruxelloise et voilée*) groups 151; likelihood of experiencing 149; *Mamans toutes égales* (Mothers are all equal) campaign 150–151; Muslim women's political participation in Belgium 147; Orientalism and Intersectionality 141, 143; Oriental or Muslim woman 150; political discourse and legislation 148–149; prejudice against women 150, 161; rise of Islamophobic hate crimes 147, 148; terror attacks 146, 147; theoretical frameworks 143–145; in UK, France

and Belgium 11; verbal to physical attacks 146, 147
gender identity 12, 45, 48, 52, 112, 196, 197, 198, 200, 201, 203, 204, 206–208, 213, 214, 217, 219, 223, 232, 235
Gender Recognition Act 2004 (GRA) 213
"gender trolling phenomenon" 164
George, A. 231, 294, 303
Gidda, M. 296
Gill, A.K. 22, 25, 27, 65, 185, 237
Gill, B. 125
Ging, D. 81, 101, 102, 107
Gomberg, H.L. 170
Gooch, B. 197
Goodey, J. 52, 277
Goodman, L.A. 48
Gordon, D. 202
Gotell, L. 103
Gottschalk, L.H. 204
Graham, D. 158
Grant, J.M. 197
Grattet, R. 29, 41, 47
Greed, C. 222
Grewal, K. 30
Grunwald-Spier, A. 155
The Guardian 42, 252, 293
Guasp, A. 205

Hagemmann-White, C. 297
Hague, G. 180, 186
Hale, S. 218
Hall, M. 179
Hall, N. 215
Hamilton, P. 132
Harding, R. 11, 121–135
Hardy, S. 239
Hargreaves, A.G. 144, 148
Harpin, L. 30, 156, 160
Harpin, P. 167
Harrison, B. 157, 158
Harvey, S. 256
Hassan, A. 282
Hatch, E. 297, 298
hate crime: aggravated offences 4; data from Office of National Statistics 5–6; definition of 3–4, 215; disability 5; emergence of 148; enhanced sentencing 4; incidents of 215–216; Law Commission consultation 6–9; legal provisions 4–5; legislation 9, 10, 27, 40, 42, 43, 47, 49, 52, 53, 57, 65–68, 70–77, 79, 85, 88, 250, 308;

policy development, benefits of 31; protected characteristics 4, 5; race 5, 243; racialist chanting offence 5, 6; religious 5; sexual orientation 5, 28; statistics 3, 5–6, 51, 140, 141, 142, 215; "stirring up" hatred offences 4–7; transgender identity 5
"Hate Crime Act" 7, 13n1
Hate Crime and Public Order (Scotland) Bill 2020 65–66, 76, 79, 262
Hate Crime (Misogyny) Bill 2019–2021 42, 43, 82, 141
hateful violence and abuse, disabled women 31
hate-motivated violence 49, 199, 208
"hate speech" offences 4; *see also* online hate speech
Haynes, A. 65, 74
Healy, J.C. 12, 178–188
Hearing, A. 294
Hegarty, P. 195, 198, 199, 200
Heilman, B. 295, 297
Heise, L.L. 48
Henry, N. 24, 30, 113
Henwood, K. 126
Heritage, F. 106
Hester, M. 22
'hierarchies of hate' 10, 69, 71–74
Hill, D.B. 199
Hines, S. 203, 204
Hirsh, D. 155, 171
Hlavka, H.R. 129
Hobhouse, W. 42, 79
Hochschild, A.R. 303
Hodge, J.P. 53, 54, 161
Hodkinson, P. 13n2
Hoffman, B. 105, 106
Hogan, B. 103
Hohl, K. 187
Hollaback! 233, 240, 252, 297, 299
homophobia 7, 8, 21, 27–28, 44, 48, 86, 165, 238
honour-based violence 49, 244
'honour' killings 20
hooks, b. 24, 236
'Hope Not Hate' 102, 109
Horder, J. 66, 74
Horkheimer, Max 158
Horvath, M.A.H. 182
Hoskin, R.A. 46, 218
Howard, V. 13, 269–284
Hoyle, C. 186
Hudson-Sharp, N. 205, 206

Hughes, K. 180
Human Rights Campaign (HRC) 28
Human Rights Council 110–111
human trafficking 49
hybristophilia 107–108, 110, 112
Hymas, C. 82
hypergamy 107, 110

identification: gender identity (internal identification) 196; identity by others (external ascription) 196, 197; notion of positionality 196; similarity and difference function 196
Iganski, P. 183, 215, 280
image-based sexual abuse 24, 100, 113
Inagaki, K. 1
in-built prejudice 40, 43
incels 10, 102, 103, 105–109, 111–113, 114n2
individual police force policy changes 13, 269
'institutional gendered Islamophobia,' emergence of 148
institutional misogyny 33
institutional violence 21, 31
International Network of Hate Studies (INHS) 2
internet 1, 80, 81, 166, 167, 276
'in terrorem' effect 24
intersectionality 11, 141, 182–183, 250; importance of 2, 12; intersectional discourse 170
intimate partner violence 20, 48, 103, 281
Islamophobia: *affaires* 144; definition of 142; dominant narratives of 144; French secularism, or *laïcité* 144, 148; gendered (*see* gendered Islamophobia); Islam and Muslimness 144; 9/11 attacks 142; Tell Mama 140, 146, 147, 148, 149, 151n1; UK political parties 142
Istanbul Convention 50, 54, 295

Jacobs, J.B. 141, 215
Jaime, K. 202
Jaki, S. 106
Jamel, J. 214
James, D. 131
Jane, E.A. 80, 102, 300
Jauk, D. 201, 206, 216
Jeffreys, S. 203, 204
Jenkins, R. 196

Jenness, V. 29, 41, 47–49, 54
"Jewish Princess" or "Jewish American Princess" ("JAP") 155
Jewish women: Community Security Trust in 2018, incidents 169; consequence of COVID-19 outbreak 168–169; "Dirty Jew" 171; gendered antisemitism 168–171; offline antisemitic abuse 168; politicians 160–164; in public spaces 167–171; verbal abuse 167–168; victims of antisemitic abuse 168, 169–170
Jewkes, R. 48
Jones, C. 105
Jones, L. 131
Jordan, J. 24
Julius, A. 158, 159
Jurasz, O. 10, 79–93, 109

Kang, B. 257
Kavanagh, A. 31
Kazyak, E. 103
Kearl, H. 127
Kelly, A. 101
Kelly, L. 22, 52, 182, 233, 234, 277, 290, 291, 300
Kentish, B. 30, 163
Kessler, S.J. 46
Khan, F.A. 125
Khomami, N. 2, 249
Kimmel, M. 101, 106, 113
Kissling, E.A. 128, 276
Kitzinger, C. 196
Klaff, L. 11, 155–171
Knowles, M.S. 124
Koch, D.E. 199, 204
Koller, V. 106
Koulouris, T. 81
Krendel, A. 10, 99–114
Kroese, B. 180

Laachir, K. 148
Lagone, A. 253
Laguerre, M. 55, 292
Lammy, D. 296
Landman, R.A. 180
Langelan, M.J. 233
Laniya, O.O. 122, 276
LaViolette, J. 103
Law Commission: 'adding sex or gender to the protected characteristics' 1; aims of hate crime law 67–68; characteristics 7–8; "communications

offences" 7; criminalising hate crime in England and Wales 2; equalise protection 7; gender-neutral approach 8; key provisional proposals for reform 6–7; racist "football chanting" offences 7; review 308; review on hate crime legislation 67; "stirring up hatred" offences 7; women, sex or gender 8–9
Law Commission's (2020) Hate Crime Consultation 13, 279
Law, I. 144
law reform proposals 9, 65
Lawrence, F.M. 74
Lawrence, J. 187
legal change: aims and objectives 270–271; changing behaviours 275–277; changing public perceptions 280–283; evaluating language choices 277–280; impact on everyday lives of women and girls 270–277; Law Commission (2020) 6, 7, 9, 68, 69, 273, 280, 308; misogynistic behaviours 271, **271**; prevalence, police reporting and law 271–273; Protection From Harassment Act 1997 57n3, 87, 233, 272; Public Order Act 1986 4, 58n3, 85, 87, 233, 272; restrictions on freedom and fear 275–277; towards future 283–284; visibility and knowledge of policy 273–275; Voyeurism (Offences) Act 2019 272, 295
letterbox, Muslim women 148
Levitt, H. 46, 53
Lewis, L. 1
Lewis, R. 24, 80, 91, 102, 163, 300
LGBTQ+ spaces 12; 'acceptable femininity' 220; femmephobia 218, 220, 224; gay men's relationship with femininity 218–219; 'gender binary' 220; gender identity 219; participants narratives 219, 220, 222, 225; performative femininity 220, 221; racialised masculinity 220
Liasidou, A. 182
Lilly, M. 102, 133
Lin, J. 105
Livingston, B.A. 299
Livingstone, J. 169
Loach, K. 166
Logan, L.S. 121, 233
Logue, P. 171n6

Lombardi, E. 201
Lombardo, E. 236
Long, J. 22, 49
'Loose Women,' TV programme 45, 55
Lorenzo-Dus, N. 127, 128
Lorenz, T. 92
Lovett, J. 52, 187
Low, H. 31
Lubitow, A. 197, 199, 201
Lumsden, K. 104
Luther, M. 163

Macdonald, S. 178
MacEoin, D. 156
MacKinnon, C.A. 23, 290
Macpherson, W. 281
Magley, V.J. 130
Magowan, P. 180
Maij, M. 91
male violence 19; fatal violence 20; towards lesbian, bisexual and queer women 21; violence against women 49–51, 56
Malin, H. 132
Manne, K. 10, 99, 103, 105, 109, 112
manosphere 99; 'aggrieved entitlement,' experiences of 101, 103, 106, 113; and alt-right movement 102–103; incels 10, 102, 105–109, 111–113; men and women, gender relations between 11; Men-Going-Their-Own-Way 10, 101–102, 103, 105, 108; men's rights activists 10, 101, 102, 103–104; pick-up artists 10, 102, 104, 107, 108, 109; 'sub-cultural trolls' 102; TRP 10, 107–108, 110
Mantilla, K. 100, 164
Marche, S. 107, 108
Marinucci, M. 203
Marley, J.A. 180
Marshall, S.E. 53, 74
Martinson, J. 166
Marwick, A. 102
masculinity 12, 21, 34, 46, 56, 101, 106, 199; racialised 220; theories 34
Maskell, S. 12, 231–246
Mason-Bish, H. 5, 9, 19–34, 47, 52, 65, 140, 146, 150, 178, 185, 186, 237, 238
Mason, G. 73, 180
Mason, J. 126
Massanari, A. 101, 112
Masters, J. 1
Matsuzaka, S. 199, 204

Mays, J. 26
May, V. 197
McAdam, D. 235
McCall, L. 183
McCarthy, K.J. 48
McCarthy, M. 180, 186
McCollum, H. 48, 55, 56
McCurry, J. 1
McGlynn, C. 24
McGuire, K. 9, 40–57
McKeown, E. 220
McPhail, B.A. 25, 47, 51, 52, 65
Meaker, M. 165, 166
Megarry, J. 100, 112
Mellgren, C. 132
Mendes, K. 297, 298, 301, 303
Men-Going-Their-Own-Way (MGTOW) 10, 101–102, 103, 105, 108, 111
men's rights activists (MRA) 10, 101–105
Metcalf, H. 205, 206
'message crimes' 47, 216, 234
Metcalf, H. 205
#MeToo movement 1, 2, 55, 233, 253, 281, 297
Miller, G. 80, 88–89
Miller, P. 188n1
Miltner, K. 99, 100
Mishcon de Reya 100, 112
misogyny: base offence 44; challenges and benefits 269; definition of 141, 232; evaluating language choices 277–280; in-built prejudice 40, 43; legal recognition 308–309; Misogyny Hate Crime Review 42–43; multiple stakeholder perspectives 13, 269; naming the problem 234–235; reconceptualisation of current 'hate crime' concept 43–44; as systemic oppression 23–25; unleashed, backlash to the policy 241
Monro, S. 196, 203
Mora, K. 1
Moran, L. 26, 32
Morgan, D. 80
Morris, J. 31
Mountford, J. 107
Mullany, L. 1, 13, 42, 43, 75, 82, 84, 127, 141, 240, 242, 244, 249, 261, 269–273, 275, 277, 282
Mulligan, D. 180, 183, 184, 186, 187
Munro, E. 299
Murphy, J. 181
Murray, S. 186, 187

Muslim women: to gendered Islamophobia, misogyny and hate crime 11; in today's society reflect orientalist discourses 11
#MyFirstTime campaign 291

Nadal, K.L. 200
Nash, C. 218
Nasty Black Or Brown Man™ 32
National Institute of Economic and Social Research (NIESR) 205
National Police Chiefs Council (NPCC) 1, 256
"negging" (negative complimenting) 104
networked misogyny 100; The Fappening 100; Gamergate 100, 101, 103
New Zealand's Summary Offences Act 1981 54
Nice White Lady™ 32
Nicholas, L. 99, 102
Nind, M. 181
Nixon, J. 31
non-binary identities: 'cisgender,' or 'cis' 197; man/woman binary 197; theorising 196–197
Nottingham City Council 257
Nottinghamshire police 1, 2, 4, 12, 13, 42, 75, 82, 84, 215, 232, 234, 235, 238, 239, 240, 241, 249–265, 269, 270, 273, 277, 279, 280, 283; *see also* policing misogyny, Nottinghamshire police experience
Nottingham Women's Centre 1, 2, 12, 231, 237, 238, 239, 240, 241, 242, 243, 244, 251, 252, 257, 260, 269
Nowell, L. 126

Oberhauser, C. 171n5
Oberman, T. 166, 167, 172n9
obscenity 49, 162, 163
Oda, S. 1
Office for National Statistics (ONS) 6, 31, 50–51, 88, 123–124, 236, 240, 256
offline hateful speech 111–112
offline violence 24, 105, 106
Ojeda, T. 218
Online Harms programme of work 91–92
Online Harms White Paper 92, 112
online hate speech: concept of incitement 110; danger of 'manosphere' language 110–111; definition 108–111, 113; Hope

Not Hate 102, 109; issues 112; 'manosphere' subreddits 101, 112–113; participation in online groups 80, 111; 'physical attack' 111, 113, 146, 147, 171; Reddit platform 108, 109–110; stalking and gendered harassment 109; types of hateful expression 111; UK Government's Online Harms White Paper 92, 112; and website regulations 108–113
online misogyny 24; avenues for reform 82, 89–92; as communications challenge 86–89; EU Fundamental Rights Agency Reporting 81; existence of misogynistic hostility 10; gender aggravator 90–91; gender problem 79–80, 92–93; within hate crime framework 85–86; Internet's rapid evolution 80; legacy of patriarchy 79–80; legal status quo 82, 84–89; misogyny campaigns 82–84; online abuse of women 80–82, 84; prevalence of violence 80–81; rise in 80; *R v Nimmo and Sorley* 88, 89, 90; *R v Viscount St Davids* 88–89, 91; sexist language 10, 99, 109, 110, 113; social media content offences 82, 91–92; socio-cultural phenomena 81
Online Safety Bill 91–92
online sexism: analysis of #mencallmethings hashtag 100; cyber-stalking 100; expressing sexist opinions 100; harassing women 99–100; 'networked misogyny' 100; Reddit, ethnographic study of 101
Online Violence Against Women (OVAW) 82, 163
Oppenheim, M. 276, 281
Organisation for Security and Co-operation in Europe (OSCE) 68, 70, 171n4
Orientalism 11, 141, 143
Oriental or Muslim woman 150
othering 32, 196
'Our Schools Now' 294
'Our Streets Now' campaign 13; awareness and education 289, 292–295; centring young women's voices 301–303; description of 292–293; growing up girl in UK 290–292; legislation & politics 295–297; power in naming 289–290; reclaiming space online 297–301
Owen, J. 255
Owusu-Bempah, A. 283

Pain, R.H. 37, 197, 227, 276, 277
Palmer, L. 30
partner violence 20, 40, 48, 51, 103, 281
Pavlenko, A. 127
Pearce, R. 223
Peart, S. 11, 121–135
Peláez, M.W. 55
Perrin, A. 293
Perry, B. 3, 24, 46, 183, 200, 202, 207, 215, 216, 220
Perry, J. 179
Petersilia, J. 178–180
Pettitt, B. 179, 180
Philpot, R. 172n8
Phipps, A. 23, 80, 204
Phua, V.C. 219
physical violence 6, 55, 163, 172n8, 179, 217, 291
pick-up artists 10, 102, 104, 107, 108, 109, 114n1
Piggott, L. 183
Pleysier, S. 276
Poland, B. 24, 91
Polce-Lynch, M. 127
Police and Crime Commissioner (PCC) 13, 42, 239, 242, 249, 252–254, 256, 257, 260, 264, 269
Police and Crown Prosecution Services 28
Police Reform and Social Responsibility Act 2011 253
policing misogyny, Nottinghamshire police experience: comprehensive training intervention 257; domestic abuse and sexual offending 256–259; 'hate incident' 3–4; internal debates and processes 253–255; local and national evidence 249–253; media responses 259; reporting and evaluation **260,** 260–264; roles of PCC and Chief Constable 253–254; success, steps 264–265
Policing Protocol Order 2011 254
Pollard, A. 159
Pope, S. 6, 263
Porat, D. 156
pornography 49
Potter, K. 141, 215
Powell, A. 24, 113, 186, 187
Pritchard, A. 221
prejudice 2, 3, 8, 9, 13n2, 14n3, 19, 30, 32, 40, 42, 43, 47, 48, 57, 82, 83, 85, 86, 111, 141–143, 145, 150, 157, 161, 185, 215, 232, 235, 236, 238
principle of minimal criminalisation 70, 74, 75

prosecution, rates for 31, 41, 43, 44, 45, 48, 51
prostitution 49
protected characteristics 4, 9; Bracadale's independent review 66–67; criteria for deciding 69–70; issues relating to adding gender (stage 2) 70–77; Law Commission's review 67, 308; legal analysis 66; Marrinan's review 67; Northern Irish approach 70; principled case for including gender (stage 1) 67–70; purpose of hate crime law 67–69; Scottish approach 69–70; themes, analysis of (*see* themes, protected characteristics); *see also* gender
Protection from Harassment Act 1997 57n3, 87, 233, 272
Public Order Act 1986 4, 58n3, 85, 87, 233, 272
public sexual harassment (PSH) 13, 288–304

queer theory 34, 203–204
queer theory and feminism 203–204
Quinn, B. 84, 257
Quinn, Z. 100
Quiroz, N. 1

Racial and Religious Hatred Act 110
racist "football chanting" offences 5–7
Radford, J. 22
Rafail, P. 103
rape: corrective rape 238; ethnic cleansing strategy 29; false rape accusations 105; as gendered hate crime 185; gendertrolling 100; hate crime policy 31; legal definitions of 22; married women 22, 258; men's rights activist websites 103; Mumsnet survey 2012 256; Muslim women 29, 238; online misogynistic abuse 88; rape apology 103; rape culture 23, 103, 301; rape myths 22; rape threats 100, 102, 163; and sexual violence 184; 'stranger' rape 258; Teena's rape/murder case 202
Raymond, J. 203
recording misogyny 4, 82, 83, 240, 263
reflexive framing process 236
Reid, K. 47
Reiser, C. 56
religious hate crimes 5, 45, 283
Retter, E. 241
'revenge porn' 24, 57–58n3

Ribeiro, M. 102, 108, 110, 111
Richardson, K. 179, 218
Richardson, N. 218
Richardson-Self, L. 109
Ridley, L. 241
Ristock, J. 52
Roberts, C. 183
Robinson, A. 166, 187
Rocheron, Y. 144
Rodger, E. 106, 107
Roebuck, E. 181
Rogers, C. 135
Rogers de Waal, J. 159
Rogers, M. 12, 195–208
Rohlinger, D. 107
Roulstone, A. 31, 179, 181
Rudiger, S. 104
Rudman, L. 122, 130
Russell, D. 22
Russell, L. 123
Russo, A. 25

Sacco, V.F. 277
Sadique, K. 31, 179
Said, E. 143
Salmon, K. 276
Samanani, F. 6, 263
Sanchez, F.J. 219
Sanday, P.R. 23
Sandberg, S. 297, 304
Sandhu, S. 252
Sara Conference Against Misogyny and Antisemitism, 2018 155, 160–161
Saunders, B.A. 130
Savci, E. 205
Schiek, D. 48
Schilt, K. 197, 198, 201
Schmitz, R. 103
Schwartz, M.D. 24
Schweppe, J. 65, 73, 74, 86
Scotland: distinct legal systems 65; 'hate crime' concept 44–45, 67; Hate Crime and Public Order Bill 76, 79; Lord Bracadale 44, 65, 262; misogyny and sexism 44–45, 169; motivated by hostility or demonstrated hostility 44; Scottish Government Review 262–263
Sefton, K. 294
Serano, J. 195, 197–199, 204, 216, 217, 224
sexism: antisemitism 161, 165; cisgender privilege 195; cybersexism 24; definition of 99, 109; Everyday Sexism project in 2012 233, 252, 297; feminist disability 31; gender normativity 198;

hate crime legislation 27; manosphere 99, 101–108; and misogyny 10, 19, 44, 99; online 99–101 (see also online sexism); online hate speech and website regulations 108–113; oppositional sexism 199; traditional sexism 199
sex-segregated spaces 12, 218; element of 'hyper-vigilance' 221; experiences of participants 221–223; transgender women experiences 223; 'women-only' spaces 221, 224
sexual assault 12, 28, 31, 42, 54, 57n3, 130, 150, 180, 184, 185, 188, 238, 256, 261, 272, 276, 277, 283, 291
sexual harassment/violence 20, 43, 54–55; adolescents' emotional responses 11; on adolescents' learning 11; of lesbian women 48; and rape, threats of 29; 'sexist outrage' law 54; 'sexual or sexist' behaviour 55
sexual offences 7–9, 76, 77, 124, 187, 233, 251, 261, 272
Sexual Offences Act 2003 57n3, 233
sexual orientation 4, 5, 7, 8, 10, 19, 28, 41, 44, 45, 48, 49, 85, 86, 112, 183, 201, 203, 204, 232, 235, 250
sexual terrorism 23, 29
sexual violence 6, 12, 155, 171, 179, 184–187, 204, 223, 240, 256, 258, 277, 280, 290, 291; hate crime women's experiences 12, 22; false rape accusations 103; men's 22–23; men's experiences 103; manosphere attitudes113; online activities 24; sexual harassment 54
sex workers 8, 31–32, 280
Shah, S. 26
Shapland, J. 179
Sharpe, A.N. 26
Sheffield, C. 23
Sherry, M. 31, 179, 181, 184–186
Siapera, E. 81, 101, 102
Silberzahn, R. 126
Silvestri, M. 24
Simplican, S.C. 31
Sin, C.H. 178, 179, 181, 183, 187
Sjolin, C. 11, 121–135
Sloan, J. 26
Smart, C. 25
Smith, G. 87
Smith, J. 1–13, 42, 300, 308–309
Smith, P. 122
Snow, D. 235
Sobieraj, S. 80, 100

Sobsey, D. 180
Solnit, R. 290
Sorial, S. 110, 112
Southgate, J. 123
Southern Poverty Law Center 102
Sparrow, A. 1, 263
Spencer, P. 158, 160
Spivak, G.C. 145
Stanko, E.A. 21, 23, 24, 33, 53, 180, 184, 187, 276, 277, 291
Stavri, Z. 32
Stein, M. 79
Stephens-Davidowitz, S. 30
"stirring up" hatred offences 4–5, 6, 41
Stoegner, K. 156, 162
Stone, A. 214
Stotzer, R.L. 204
strategic framing 235–236
street harassment (SH) 11, 31, 32, 54, 55, 113, 121, 123, 134, 232, 233, 235, 241, 245, 273; adolescents' experiences (see adolescent girls, SH of); definition 121; evolving language and activism 232–234; illegal 1; range of behaviours 121
Stryker, S. 198
subreddits 100, 101, 103, 112, 113
Sue, D.W. 200
Sullivan, H.B. 128, 281
Sutton, J. 126
Swartz, S. 132
Syed, D. 302
systemic genderism 28
systemic violence 23, 25, 216

Talboys, S.L. 123
Tapsfield, J. 167
Taylor, Y. 203
technology-facilitated sexual violence 24
text-based abuses 81, 86
textual and image-based violence 80
themes, protected characteristics: issues specifically relating to gender 71, 75–77; opened or closed protected characteristics/hierarchies of hate 71, 72–74; symbolic and practical aspects of hate crime legislation 71–72; use of evidence for deciding protected characteristics 71, 74–75
Thiara, R.K. 31, 180
#ThisIsNotWorking campaign 291
Thoennes, N. 24
Thomas, P. 180
Thomas, R. 217

threats 5, 6, 29, 30, 49, 87–89, 100, 102, 162–164, 205
Thunberg, G. 80
Thurber, A. 200
Tidley, A. 54
#TimesUp 1, 93, 253; *see also* online misogyny
Tjaden, P. 24
'Together we can End Violence Against Women and Girls: a strategy' 52
Tominey, C. 159
Topping, A. 42
trafficking 20, 49, 123
'trans-erasure' 199
Trans-Exclusionary Radical Feminists (TERFs) 195, 204
trans-gender identity 10; 'gender-neutral' spaces 213; and hate crime 5, 199–202; 'The Hierarchical Nature of Hate Crime Victimisation' 218; methodology 217–218; 'Normalcy and the Everyday' 218; qualitative data 217–218; research project 218; semi-structured interviews 217; 'Space, Place and Belonging' 218; theorising 196–197; transphobic hate crime 214–217; women experience 12; *see also* transphobic hate crime; cisgenderism
trans-misogyny 12, 214–216, 219, 221, 222, 224; and gender policing in 'sex-segregated spaces' 12, 221–224; in LGBTQ spaces 12, 218–221; sex-segregated spaces 12; 'women-only' space 224–225
transphobic hate crime 12; and cisgenderism 199–202; feminist scholarship 203–204; queer theory and feminism 203–204; theorising 203–204; Trans-Exclusionary Radical Feminist (TERF) 204
Tregidga, J. 179, 180, 183, 207
Trickett, L. 1, 13, 42, 43, 75, 82, 84, 127, 141, 240, 242, 244, 249, 261, 269–273, 275, 277, 282
TRP 10, 107–108
Tumath, J. 65, 76
Turnbull, M. 131
Turner, L. 200
Turpin-Petrosino, C. 178
Tutton, M. 13, 288–304
Tyson, J. 181

UK, transphobic hate crime: and categories 204–205; Criminal Justice Act 214, 215; experiences of violence or harassment 206; factors in non-reporting 206–207; Government Equalities Office (GEO) 205–206; 'hate crime' categories 40; issues of hate crime 215; Legal Aid, Sentencing and Punishment of Offenders Act 214; LGBT people, experiences of 205; mechanism of 'intimidation and control exercised' 216; media representations 216–217; 'message crimes' 47, 216; the 'Other' 216; perception of threat 207; positionality and processes of identification 208; problems with under-reporting 207; process of 'gender policing' 216; qualitative data 217–218; research and literature 214; scope and nature 205; semi-structured interviews 217; transgender identity 215; 2011–2020 **207**
Ungoed-Thomas, J. 165, 166
United Nations Convention on the Rights of the Child 123, 125
United Nations Conventions on Violence Against Women 50
UN's #heforshe campaign 281
"Upskirting" Bill 244, 262, 295
US comparison 48–49
Urbanska, K. 126

Vahapassi, V. 202
Valfort, M.-A. 149
Van Reybrouck, D. 147
Van Staden, L. 187
Van Valkenburgh, S. 107, 108, 110
Vaughan, H. 84
Vera-Gray, F. 19, 121, 128, 131–133, 233, 288, 289, 291, 298
victim-focused framework 33
victimisation: of individual 3; interpersonal 32; of lesbians 28; male 21; of Muslim women 146; outside home 124; proportional rates 146; sexual 22; targeted 32; terror attacks 146; virtual 24; of women 23; women's experiences of targeted 20
Vilain, E. 219
Vincent, F. 178, 179
Violence Against Women and Girls (VAWG) 33; crimes 8; Crown Prosecution Service 49–50; definition 46, 47; domestic violence 50–51; examples of 49–51; feminist praxis 232–234; gender bias 49–51; 'honour-based' violence 49; partner violence 51; policy for Nottinghamshire Police 258;

sexual harassment 50; statistics 50–51; Strategy for 2017–2020 49–50
Virtual Victims 24, 103, 104
Vivenzi, L. 105
voyeurism 57n3
Voyeurism Bill 244
Voyeurism (Offences) Act 2019 272
vulnerability or sexual orientation 3, 21, 31, 32, 47, 49, 72, 73, 112, 179, 186, 205, 257

Wajcman, J. 81
Walby, S. 20
Waldron, J. 110, 112
Walker, P. 162
Walklate, S. 276, 277
Wallace, S. 124
Walters, M.A. 13n1, 28, 65, 76, 178, 186, 197, 200, 205–207, 283
Wanggren, L. 121
watershed moment 1
Waxman, B.F. 186
Westbrook, L. 24, 197
Wetzel, J. 157
"white genocide" 159
White Ribbon Organisation (2020) 50
Whitham, B. 148
whorephobia 32

Wilkinson, S. 196
Williams, M.L. 24, 100, 112, 180, 207
Willoughby, B.L.B. 199
Wilson, E.C. 200
Winter, B. 144, 150
Wistrich, R. 158
Witten, T.M. 199
Wojcieszak, M. 111
Wolfe, L. 47
Women and Equalities Select Committee 262
Woollacott, E. 100
World Health Organization (WHO) 179, 188n1
Wright, D. 11, 104, 105, 121–135
Wright, S. 105
Wu, B. 100

Yazidi women in ISIS, "weapons" of war 29
Young, I. 23, 25

Zayna, A. 302
Zempi, I. 1–13, 29, 140, 142, 146, 150, 238
Zimmerman, S. 106, 111
Zonshine, I. 159
Zuckerberg, D. 108